Course   Taking Sides:
         Clashing Views in
         Childhood and Society, 10e
Course Number   **by Kourtney Vaillancourt**

http://create.mheducation.com

ISBN-10: 1308008848   ISBN-13: 9781308008844

Contents

Credits

Preface

When I was in college, I took many classes related to child development. I learned the most important theories, talked about the latest strategies for dealing with problems children face, and generally feel like I gained a solid understanding of childhood and society. I was well informed and opinionated and was sure that I knew what children need. Then, I had children of my own. My boys have challenged me from the beginning, even before they were born! Becoming a parent made me consider issues from different perspectives. The things I had previously discussed only as abstract notions now became personal. Should I return to work or stay home with them? If I do put them in daycare, how do I evaluate the choices? Should they be allowed to play video games? All of these questions that I previously could answer with "facts" became much muddier when I was thinking about them in terms of my own children.

This book is intended to encourage the reader to consider differing perspectives on issues that children and families face today. For each of the issues addressed, a pro and a con perspective based on research is provided. I encourage you, whether you are a parent or not, to carefully consider the cases that each author makes. Personalize the material, ask yourself what you would tell a parent or caregiver about these issues. Or, ask yourself what you would do if it were your child or what you would have wanted your parents to do. You may find yourself agreeing with one side or the other, or you may find that your opinions fall somewhere in between the two sides. The outcome is not important, there is generally merit to each side of the argument. What is really important is that you allow yourself to consider differing perspectives and are able to apply it to your future professional work and family life. Practice thinking about "why" you agree or disagree with a particular author.

Plan of the book *Taking Sides: Clashing Views in Childhood and Society,* tenth edition, is designed to be used for courses in child development, human development, or parenting. The issues can be studied consecutively or in any order, as each is designed to be independent of the other. I have included 19 issues encompassing 38 selections from a wide variety of sources and authors. Each unit of the book deals with one of four developmental phases of childhood: infancy, early childhood, middle childhood, and adolescence. Within each unit are issues related to aspects of child development at that stage. Each issue has an *introduction,* which provides some background about the controversy, briefly describes the authors, and gives a brief summary of the positions reflected in the issue. Each issue concludes with critical thinking and reflection questions and some points to consider about whether there is a common ground to the debates, and offers a additional related readings, should you want to explore the topic further.

A listing of all the *contributors* to this volume is included at the back of the book to give you additional information on the scholars, practitioners, educators, policymakers, and social critics whose views are debated here.

Changes to this edition The tenth edition of *Taking Sides: Clashing Views in Childhood and Society* includes some important changes from the ninth edition. Three new issues have been added, and six previous issues have new selections. As a result, there are fifteen new readings. In addition, editorial notes with updated statistics and new developments have been added to the existing selections.

The issue, "Is Institutional Child Care Beneficial to Children?" has one new selection. The issue, "Does Maternal Employment Have Negative Effects on Children's Development?" has two new selections. The issue, "Is Spanking Detrimental to Children?" has two new selections. The issue, "Is Viewing Television Violence Harmful for Children?" has two new selections. The issue, "Are Male Teens More Aggressive than Female Teens?" has two new selections. And, new issues, "Do Video Games Increase Aggression in Teenagers?" and "Is Cyberbullying Really a Problem?" and "Should Parents Be Able to Genetically Engineer Their Children?" have been included.

A word to the instructor An *Instructor's Resource Guide with Test Questions* (both multiple-choice and essay) is available through the publisher for the instructor using this volume of Taking Sides. A general guidebook, *Using Taking Sides in the Classroom,* which discusses methods and techniques for integrating the pro–con approach into any classroom setting, is also available. An online version of *Using Taking Sides in the Classroom* and a correspondence service for Taking Sides adopters can be found at www.mhcls.com/usingts.

Taking Sides: Clashing Views in Childhood and Society is only one title in the Taking Sides series. If you are interested in seeing the table of contents for any of the other titles, please visit the Taking Sides website at www.mhcls.com/takingsides/.

Acknowledgments

I would like to thank Amelia Trujillo for assisting with the tenth edition of this book.

I would also like to thank Bob & Diana Del Campo for entrusting me with the newest edition of the book that they so excellently began.

I also want to extend a warm thanks to Jade Benedict, Senior Developmental Editor, McGraw Hill Contemporary Learning Series.

Kourtney Vaillancourt
New Mexico State University

I look forward to receiving feedback and comments on this tenth edition of *Taking Sides: Clashing Views in Childhood and Society* from both faculty and students who experience the book. I can be reached via the Internet (kvaillan@nmsu.edu), or you can write to me in care of the Taking Sides series at McGraw-Hill Contemporary Learning Series.

Academic Advisory Board Members

Members of the Academic Advisory Board are instrumental in the final selection of articles for each edition of TAKING SIDES. Their review of articles for content, level, and appropriateness provides critical direction to the editors and staff. We think that you will find their careful consideration well reflected in this volume.

Correlation Guide

The Taking Sides series presents current issues in a debate-style format designed to stimulate student interest and develop critical thinking skills. Each issue is thoughtfully framed with an issue summary, an issue introduction, learning outcomes, critical-thinking questions, and an exploring the issue. The pro and con essays—selected for their liveliness and substance—represent the arguments of leading scholars and commentators in their fields.

Taking Sides: Clashing Views in Childhood and Society, 10/e is an easy-to-use reader that presents issues on important topics such as *homeschooling, bilingual education programs, transracial adoptions,* and *male aggression.* For more information on Taking Sides and other *McGraw-Hill Create*™ titles, visit www.mcgrawhillcreate.com

This convenient guide matches the issues in Taking Sides: Childhood and Society, 10/e with the corresponding chapters in two of our best-selling McGraw-Hill psychology textbooks by Papalia/Feldman and Santrock.

Taking Sides: Childhood and Society, 10/e	A Child's World: Infancy Through Adolescence, 13/e by Papalia/Feldman	Children, 12/e by Santrock
Is Institutional Child Care Beneficial to Children?	**Chapter 6:** Physical Development and Health During the First Three Years **Chapter 7:** Cognitive Development During the First Three Years **Chapter 8:** Psychosocial Development During the First Three Years	**Chapter 5:** Physical Development in Infancy **Chapter 7:** Socioemotional Development in Infancy
Does Maternal Employment Have Negative Effects on Children's Development?	**Chapter 6:** Physical Development and Health During the First Three Years **Chapter 7:** Cognitive Development During the First Three Years **Chapter 8:** Psychosocial Development During the First Three Years	**Chapter 7:** Socioemotional Development in Infancy
Should Parents Be Able to Genetically Engineer Their Children?	**Chapter 1:** Studying a Child's World **Chapter 2:** A Child's World: How We Discover It	**Chapter 2:** Biological Beginnings
Do Federal Laws Make Transracial Adoptions More Commonplace?		
Is Spanking Detrimental to Children?	**Chapter 10:** Cognitive Development in Early Childhood **Chapter 11:** Psychosocial Development in Early Childhood	**Chapter 9:** Cognitive Development in Early Childhood
Are Fathers Really Necessary?	**Chapter 5:** Birth and the Newborn Baby **Chapter 8:** Psychosocial Development During the First Three Years **Chapter 11:** Psychosocial Development in Early Childhood **Chapter 14:** Psychosocial Development in Middle Childhood **Chapter 17:** Psychosocial Development in Adolescence	**Chapter 10:** Socioemotional Development in Early Childhood
Does Divorce Create Long-Term Negative Effects for Children?	**Chapter 7:** Cognitive Development During the First Three Years **Chapter 8:** Psychosocial Development During the First Three Years **Chapter 10:** Cognitive Development in Early Childhood **Chapter 11:** Psychosocial Development in Early Childhood **Chapter 13:** Cognitive Development in Middle Childhood **Chapter 14:** Psychosocial Development in Middle Childhood **Chapter 16:** Cognitive Development in Adolescence **Chapter 17:** Psychosocial Development in Adolescence	**Chapter 6:** Cognitive Development in Infancy **Chapter 8:** Physical Development in Early Childhood **Chapter 10:** Socioemotional Development in Early Childhood **Chapter 11:** Physical Development in Middle and Late Childhood **Chapter 13:** Socioemotional Development in Middle and Late Childhood

(Continued)

Taking Sides: Childhood and Society, 10/e	*A Child's World: Infancy Through Adolescence,* 13/e by Papalia/Feldman	*Children,* 12/e by Santrock
Is Viewing Television Violence Harmful for Children?	**Chapter 8:** Psychosocial Development During the First Three Years **Chapter 11:** Psychosocial Development in Early Childhood **Chapter 14:** Psychosocial Development in Middle Childhood **Chapter 17:** Psychosocial Development in Adolescence	**Chapter 8:** Physical Development in Early Childhood **Chapter 10:** Socioemotional Development in Early Childhood **Chapter 16:** Socioemotional Development in Adolescence
Does Marriage Improve Living Standards for Children?	**Chapter 8:** Psychosocial Development During the First Three Years **Chapter 11:** Psychosocial Development in Early Childhood **Chapter 14:** Psychosocial Development in Middle Childhood **Chapter 17:** Psychosocial Development in Adolescence	**Chapter 10:** Socioemotional Development in Early Childhood **Chapter 13:** Socioemotional Development in Middle and Late Childhood **Chapter 16:** Socioemotional Development in Adolescence
Do Children Who Are Homeschooled Have a Limited View of Society?	**Chapter 8:** Psychosocial Development During the First Three Years **Chapter 11:** Psychosocial Development in Early Childhood **Chapter 14:** Psychosocial Development in Middle Childhood **Chapter 17:** Psychosocial Development in Adolescence	**Chapter 7:** Socioemotional Development in Infancy **Chapter 13:** Socioemotional Development in Middle and Late Childhood **Chapter 16:** Socioemotional Development in Adolescence
Is the Media Responsible for the Rise in Child-hood Obesity?	**Chapter 6:** Physical Development and Health During the First Three Years **Chapter 9:** Physical Development and Health in Early Childhood **Chapter 12:** Physical Development and Health in Middle Childhood **Chapter 15:** Physical Development and Health in Adolescence	**Chapter 8:** Physical Development in Early Childhood **Chapter 11:** Physical Development in Middle and Late Childhood **Chapter 14:** Physical Development in Adolescence
Do Bilingual Education Programs Help Non-English-Speaking Children Succeed?	**Chapter 7:** Cognitive Development During the First Three Years **Chapter 10:** Cognitive Development in Early Childhood **Chapter 13:** Cognitive Development in Middle Childhood **Chapter 16:** Cognitive Development in Adolescence	**Chapter 9:** Cognitive Development in Early Childhood **Chapter 12:** Cognitive Development in Middle and Late Childhood **Chapter 15:** Cognitive Development in Adolescence
Is Gay Adoption and Foster Parenting Healthy for Children?	**Chapter 8:** Psychosocial Development During the First Three Years **Chapter 11:** Psychosocial Development in Early Childhood **Chapter 14:** Psychosocial Development in Middle Childhood **Chapter 17:** Psychosocial Development in Adolescence	**Chapter 7:** Socioemotional Development in Infancy **Chapter 10:** Socioemotional Development in Early Childhood **Chapter 13:** Socioemotional Development in Middle and Late Childhood **Chapter 16:** Socioemotional Development in Adolescence
Should the HPV Vaccination Be Mandatory for Girls in Later Childhood?	**Chapter 12:** Physical Development and Health in Middle Childhood **Chapter 15:** Physical Development and Health in Adolescence	**Chapter 11:** Physical Development in Middle and Late Childhood
Are Male Teens More Aggressive Than Female Teens?	**Chapter 17:** Psychosocial Development in Adolescence	**Chapter 16:** Socioemotional Development in Adolescence

Taking Sides: Childhood and Society, 10/e	A Child's World: Infancy Through Adolescence, 13/e by Papalia/Feldman	Children, 12/e by Santrock
Is Abstinence-Only Sex Education the Best Way to Teach About Sex?	**Chapter 15:** Physical Development and Health in Adolescence **Chapter 16:** Cognitive Development in Adolescence **Chapter 17:** Psychosocial Development in Adolescence	**Chapter 14:** Physical Development in Adolescence **Chapter 15:** Cognitive Development in Adolescence **Chapter 16:** Socioemotional Development in Adolescence
Is the Internet a Safe Place for Teens to Explore?	**Chapter 17:** Psychosocial Development in Adolescence	**Chapter 16:** Socioemotional Development in Adolescence
Do Video Games Increase Aggression in Teenagers?	**Chapter 14:** Psychosocial Development in Middle Childhood **Chapter 17:** Psychosocial Development in Adolescence	**Chapter 11:** Physical Development in Middle and Late Childhood **Chapter 14:** Physical Development in Adolescence
Is Cyberbullying Really a Problem?	**Chapter 14:** Psychosocial Development in Middle Childhood **Chapter 17:** Psychosocial Development in Adolescence	**Chapter 11:** Physical Development in Middle and Late Childhood **Chapter 14:** Physical Development in Adolescence

Topic Guide

This topic guide suggests how the selections in this book relate to the subjects covered in your course. You may want to use the topics listed on these pages to search the Web more easily.

All issues and their articles that relate to each topic are listed below the bold-faced term.

Abuse

Is Spanking Detrimental to Children?

Adolescents

Are Male Teens More Aggressive Than Female Teens?
Do Video Games Increase Aggression in Teenagers?
Is Abstinence-Only Sex Education the Best Way to Teach About Sex?
Is Cyberbullying Really a Problem?
Is the Internet a Safe Place for Teens to Explore?

Adoption

Do Federal Laws Make Transracial Adoptions More Commonplace?
Is Gay Adoption and Foster Parenting Healthy for Children?

Aggression

Are Male Teens More Aggressive Than Female Teens?
Do Video Games Increase Aggression in Teenagers?
Is Viewing Television Violence Harmful for Children?

Behavior

Are Male Teens More Aggressive Than Female Teens?
Is Cyberbullying Really a Problem?
Is Spanking Detrimental to Children?

Child Care

Does Maternal Employment Have Negative Effects on Children's Development?
Is Institutional Child Care Beneficial to Children?

Child Development

Does Maternal Employment Have Negative Effects on Children's Development?
Is Institutional Child Care Beneficial to Children?

Communication

Do Bilingual Education Programs Help Non-English-Speaking Children Succeed?

Computers

Is Cyberbullying Really a Problem?
Is the Internet a Safe Place for Teens to Explore?

Culture

Do Bilingual Education Programs Help Non-English-Speaking Children Succeed?

Cyberbullying

Is Cyberbullying Really a Problem?
Is the Internet a Safe Place for Teens to Explore?

Development, Social

Are Fathers Really Necessary?
Do Children Who Are Homeschooled Have a Limited View of Society?
Does Maternal Employment Have Negative Effects on Children's Development?
Is Institutional Child Care Beneficial to Children?

Discipline

Is Spanking Detrimental to Children?

Divorce

Does Divorce Create Long-Term Negative Effects for Children?

Early Childhood

Are Fathers Really Necessary?
Does Divorce Create Long-Term Negative Effects for Children?
Is Spanking Detrimental to Children?
Is Viewing Television Violence Harmful for Children?

Education

Do Bilingual Education Programs Help Non-English-Speaking Children Succeed?
Do Children Who Are Homeschooled Have a Limited View of Society?
Is Institutional Child Care Beneficial to Children?

Employment

Does Maternal Employment Have Negative Effects on Children's Development?

Ethnicity

Do Bilingual Education Programs Help Non-English-Speaking Children Succeed?

Family

Are Fathers Really Necessary?
Does Divorce Create Long-Term Negative Effects for Children?

Family Structure

Are Fathers Really Necessary?
Does Divorce Create Long-Term Negative Effects for Children?

Family Values

Is Gay Adoption and Foster Parenting Healthy for Children?

Fatherhood

Are Fathers Really Necessary?

(Continued)

Gender

Are Male Teens More Aggressive Than Female Teens?

Genetic Engineering

Should Parents Be Able to Genetically Engineer Their Children?

Health

Is the Media Responsible for the Rise in Childhood Obesity?
Should the HPV Vaccination Be Mandatory for Girls in Later Childhood?

Infancy

Do Federal Laws Make Transracial Adoptions More Commonplace?
Is Institutional Child Care Beneficial to Children?
Does Maternal Employment Have Negative Effects on Children's Development?
Should Parents Be Able to Genetically Engineer Their Children?

Internet

Is Cyberbullying Really a Problem?
Is the Internet a Safe Place for Teens to Explore?

Homosexuality

Is Gay Adoption and Foster Parenting Healthy for Children?

Juvenile Delinquency

Are Male Teens More Aggressive Than Female Teens?
Do Video Games Increase Aggression in Teenagers?
Does Divorce Create Long-Term Negative Effects for Children?
Is Cyberbullying Really a Problem?

Language

Do Bilingual Education Programs Help Non-English-Speaking Children Succeed?

Learning

Do Bilingual Education Programs Help Non-English-Speaking Children Succeed?
Do Children Who Are Homeschooled Have a Limited View of Society?
Is Abstinence-Only Sex Education the Best Way to Teach About Sex?
Is Institutional Child Care Beneficial to Children?
Is the Media Responsible for the Rise in Childhood Obesity?
Is Viewing Television Violence Harmful for Children?

Marriage

Does Marriage Improve Living Standards for Children?

Media

Is the Internet a Safe Place for Teens to Explore?
Is the Media Responsible for the Rise in Childhood Obesity?
Is Viewing Television Violence Harmful for Children?

Middle Childhood

Do Bilingual Education Programs Help Non-English-Speaking Children Succeed?
Do Children Who Are Homeschooled Have a Limited View of Society?
Does Marriage Improve Living Standards for Children?
Is Gay Adoption and Foster Parenting Healthy for Children?
Is the Media Responsible for the Rise in Childhood Obesity?
Should the HPV Vaccination Be Mandatory for Girls in Later Childhood?

Motherhood

Does Maternal Employment Have Negative Effects on Children's Development?

Parenting

Are Fathers Really Necessary?
Do Children Who Are Homeschooled Have a Limited View of Society?
Do Video Games Increase Aggression in Teenagers?
Does Divorce Create Long-Term Negative Effects for Children?
Does Maternal Employment Have Negative Effects on Children's Development?
Is Abstinence-Only Sex Education the Best Way to Teach About Sex?
Is Cyberbullying Really a Problem?
Is Gay Adoption and Foster Parenting Healthy for Children?
Is Institutional Child Care Beneficial to Children?
Is Spanking Detrimental to Children?
Is the Media Responsible for the Rise in Childhood Obesity?
Is the Internet a Safe Place for Teens to Explore?

Punishment

Is Spanking Detrimental to Children?

Relationships

Does Marriage Improve Living Standards for Children?
Does Maternal Employment Have Negative Effects on Children's Development?

School Curriculum

Do Bilingual Education Programs Help Non-English-Speaking Children Succeed?
Do Children Who Are Homeschooled Have a Limited View of Society?
Is Abstinence-Only Sex Education the Best Way to Teach About Sex?

School Reform

Do Bilingual Education Programs Help Non-English-Speaking Children Succeed?
Is Abstinence-Only Sex Education the Best Way to Teach About Sex?

Schools

Do Children Who Are Homeschooled Have a Limited View of Society?
Is Institutional Child Care Beneficial to Children?

Sex Education

Is Abstinence-Only Sex Education the Best Way to Teach About Sex?

Social Change

Do Federal Laws Make Transracial Adoptions More Commonplace?
Does Marriage Improve Living Standards for Children?
Is Abstinence-Only Sex Education the Best Way to Teach About Sex?
Is Gay Adoption and Foster Parenting Healthy for Children?
Should Parents Be Able to Genetically Engineer Their Children?

Social Media

Is Cyberbullying Really a Problem?
Is the Internet a Safe Place for Teens to Explore?

Teaching

Do Children Who Are Homeschooled Have a Limited View of Society?

Television

Is the Media Responsible for the Rise in Childhood Obesity?
Is Viewing Television Violence Harmful for Children?

Vaccination

Should the HPV Vaccination Be Mandatory for Girls in Later Childhood?

Values

Do Children Who Are Homeschooled Have a Limited View of Society?
Does Marriage Improve Living Standards for Children?

Is Gay Adoption and Foster Parenting Healthy for Children?
Should Parents Be Able to Genetically Engineer Their Children?

Violence

Is Viewing Television Violence Harmful for Children?

Introduction

Children in Society

Childhood can be a wondrous time when days are filled with play and new discoveries, nights provide rest and security, and dedicated, loving parents nurture their children and meet their needs. Some children do indeed experience the full joy of childhood; however, regretfully, there are other, more sobering scenarios: There are children who do not have nurturing adults to guide them, who go to bed hungry, and some who do not even have homes. Most typically, childhood experiences fall between these two extremes. So there is a wide variety of experiences that can impact the developing child, and larger social forces are at work as well. Ask yourself as you debate the issues in this book the extent to which society must collectively address and resolve them. This is a vital function of society because children are society's future.

To understand and appreciate children in contemporary society, it may be useful to briefly review how society's views of children have changed over time. Most child development texts review the history of adult perceptions of children in western European society. Would it surprise you to know that in ancient times children were sometimes killed as religious sacrifices and buried in the walls of buildings? People believed that this practice would strengthen a building's structure. Up until the fourth century, parents were legally allowed to kill their newborns if the children were not in good health at birth. They were also permitted to do away with a child if they already had too many children, if the child was female, or if the child was illegitimate. In A.D. 374, the Romans outlawed infanticide, hoping that this would end the killing. Since parents could no longer legally kill their children, unwanted infants began to be abandoned. This practice endured for more than 1000 years. It was not until the 1600s that child abandonment was outlawed throughout most of Europe.

During the seventeenth century, foundling homes were established to provide for the needs of unwanted children. During this period, children were considered to be miniature adults. They were dressed like adults and were expected to act as adults would act. By contemporary standards, parents took a rather casual attitude toward their children. This was probably due to the high child mortality rate at the time. Since parents thought it likely that their children would die in infancy or childhood, they did not get as emotionally close to their young children as parents typically do today. It was not until the end of the century that society began to look upon children as different from adults.

Early in the 1700s European societal attitudes about children underwent further change. Children were no longer considered to be miniature adults, and literature written specifically for children began to emerge. By the end of the century, children who went to school were grouped by age, reflecting an awareness of stages of growth. The eighteenth century also marked the rise of the systematic study of children, which centered around the moral development of children and child-rearing problems.

It was not until the beginning of the twentieth century that three distinct age groupings emerged in the study of human development: infancy through age four or five; childhood to late puberty or early adulthood; and adulthood. This time period also marked the beginnings of the distinct field of child study. Early child study emphasized descriptive accounts of individual children and was mainly concerned with aspects of physical growth. As the century progressed, the term *child study* was changed to *research in child development*. Mothering became an important concept in the study of early child development, and the psychological aspects of development began to be examined more rigorously. Today, in the twenty-first century, research in child development focuses on issues related to family systems and the larger social issues that affect child development.

Nature-Nurture Controversy

There are many things that impact individuals as they progress through the human life cycle. People, places, events, illnesses, education, success, failure—have you ever thought about the number of experiences each of us encounters in our lives? If one were to place all of the variables that influence human development into two general categories, those categories would be heredity and environment. As you may know, your genetic blueprint was determined at the moment of conception with chromosomes contributed by your father and mother. In a sense, for many of us, environment is also determined at the moment of conception. A good portion of the major elements of what makes up one's environment is often determined before a person is born. The society in which one will live, one's cultural and ethnic heritage, and one's family and subsequent socioeconomic status, for example, are usually predetermined for a child.

For this edition of *Taking Sides: Clashing Views in Childhood and Society,* I have selected articles that look at children in general and how they affect or are affected by the issues raised, rather than give you, the reader, clinical case examples of issues related to a certain child or children. For the purposes of this book, I make three assumptions: (1) When I discuss a child's environment, I am usually describing elements of the society in which a child is growing, developing, and otherwise being socialized; (2) all child development occurs within this social context; and (3) children cannot help but affect and be affected by the societal forces that surround them. In most university classes, students derive a certain sense of security in receiving definitions of terms that are used frequently in a given class. I offer the following one for *society*, which I have adapted from Richard J. Gelles's 1995 textbook *Contemporary Families*:

> Society is a collection of people who interact within socially structured relationships. The only way that societies can survive their original members is by replacing them. These "replacements" are the children about whom the issues in this book are concerned.

Determining an appropriate group of societal issues and fitting them into the confines of only one work on children and society is a challenging task. Consider, for example, the diversity of contemporary society. We live in a sea of divergent and unique subcultures and ethnicities. Categorizing and describing the myriad values, customs, and belief systems of these groups could fill many volumes. In America and Canada, for example, there are many ethnic subgroups of citizens who are considered to be of Anglo descent, such as English, Irish, Italian, Polish, German, Greek, Russian, and Scottish. There are people of native descent, who are affiliated with scores of different tribes and subtribes. Some Canadian and American citizens trace their heritages to a variety of Asian countries, including China, Japan, Vietnam, Cambodia, Thailand, and the Philippines. Among blacks, there are those who trace their roots to the Caribbean region and those who identify with different regions of Africa.

In light of the foregoing, it may be reasoned that there are really no "typical" children in society! Although there are strong arguments supporting similarities within each of these general groups, there is a wide array of subgroupings and differences in customs and beliefs. As a consequence, when reading a book such as this one, it is important to be mindful of the extent to which differences might exist for those who may be of another race, ethnicity, religion, or socioeconomic status than the target group of children about which a selection focuses. It would also be prudent to consider geographic locale—rural, urban, northeastern, southwestern—when considering the relevance of a given argument to a specific subgroup of children.

Children in Contemporary Society

It is worth understanding children's points of view as they are molded by society. It can be astonishing to take a step back and observe children as they undergo the socialization process in contemporary society. They come into the world totally helpless, unable to feed, care for, or protect themselves. As they grow and develop, children undertake the process of acquiring a sense of identity and learning the rules of the society in which they live. This process of socialization is fostered by many of the subsystems of society that provide prescriptions for behavior in particular areas of life. These subsystems include the family, the peer group, the school system, religion, and the media.

One important consideration is that up to about age five, children are oblivious to most racial, ethnic, religious, or socioeconomic differences. Typically, children can only realize differences in external appearance. One implication of this fact is that children can be much more amenable to learning and embracing a variety of cultural behaviors, attitudes, and even languages when they are young. Only as children move into middle childhood do they begin to recognize and understand other, more subtle differences. It is important to note that although young children may be oblivious to these differences, they are nonetheless impacted by them in the way they are socialized by their parents, families, and the significant others in their lives. This is done through family rituals, traditions, and outings; religious ceremonies; types of food prepared in the home; location where children live; and things that are found in the home, such as books, magazines, music, and so on.

Societal influences on children do not stop within the family system. As children grow, other institutions in society, such as schools, the economy, politics, and religion, expand their life experiences. Controversy arises as to how children react to these experiences. Consider, for example, what happens to children when both parents are employed outside the home. There are factions in our society who adamantly ascribe many of the problems associated with children to the fact that many parents are overly involved with work at the expense of time with their children. They contend that one parent (usually the mother) should stay home with the children, especially when they are young. Children who care for themselves after school and the quality of after-school child care are also hotly contested, related issues.

Few readers of this book will be unfamiliar with the attacks on the mass media for its portrayal of violence in movies, television programming, and video games targeted at children. Again, researchers, clinicians, teachers, policymakers, and others fall on both sides of what should be done to address this.

As children move toward adolescence and become more independent, concerns regarding identity, values, morals, and sexual behavior become issues of controversy. Homosexuality, for example, which often is first evidenced by a person in adolescence, is considered by many to be a learned and abhorrent form of sexual expression. Others believe that there are people who are predisposed to homosexuality for reasons that are as yet unclear.

Events in contemporary society have a direct or indirect impact on children, despite attempts to protect them. Violence, inflation, war, poverty, AIDS, racism, and new technology are just a few of the phenomena that shape the society in which our children are socialized.

Researching Children

In finding answers to controversial topics, policymakers and the public alike often look to research literature for clues. The typical college student might think of researching a topic as going to the library or logging onto the Internet and looking up information on a subject, reading that information, formulating a conclusion or opinion about the topic, and writing a paper that conveys the student's findings. This is not the type of research about which we are referring! The type of research that we refer to here is called empirical research. This means that there is some question or group of interrelated questions to be answered about a topic. Data are then collected relative to the topic, and these typically shed light on how one goes about answering the question.

Data collection in research on children is undertaken from a variety of approaches. It could entail things like observing children at play in preschool or interacting with their parents at home. This is called observing children in a natural setting. With this method, observers must code behavior in the same way each and every time it is seen. Most of the information we have today on physical growth and developmental stages was acquired through observation by child development pioneers such as Arnold Gessell and Louise Bates Ames. You can imagine how time consuming this form of study must be.

Another type of data collection is called an experiment. Experimental researchers systematically control how certain things happen in a situation and then observe the results. In this type of research, an experimental group and a control group are chosen. Both groups are examined to determine that they are the same before the experiment begins. The experimental group then receives some kind of treatment, while the control group receives no treatment. Then tests are conducted to see what kind of change, if any, has occurred between the two groups.

Interviewing children with a structured set of questions or giving children a structured questionnaire on a given research topic are other ways of collecting data. Projective techniques, where children might reveal their first thoughts about a picture or word, is also a form of the interview method.

The study of children can be organized in a variety of ways. One is by stages. The parts of this book (infancy, early childhood, middle childhood, and adolescence) are one type of stage organization. Another way to organize research endeavors is by topics. Topics are usually organized within the context of social, emotional, intellectual, physical, creative, and even spiritual aspects of development.

The time frames used to gather data on children also vary. In longitudinal data collection, information is collected from the same subjects over a long period of time. For example, one could examine the effects of preschool education on performance in elementary school by following and testing the same children during the preschool years and all the way through the elementary years. Because this type of research can take years to complete, a shorter method, cross-sectional research, could be used. In the previous example, one group of preschoolers would be compared with a similar group of elementary school children in order to answer the research question.

There are ethical considerations in studying children that some other disciplines may not face. Children should never be manipulated or put in danger in designing an experiment to answer research questions. Similarly, experiments that would not be in a child's best interests should not be conducted. Studies of abuse and neglect, for example, rely on retrospective techniques in which children who have already been abused report what has previously happened to them. No ethical researcher would ever put children at risk in order to observe the effects of abuse on children. Because of these ethical constraints, it can be frustrating for a researcher to fully answer questions raised in a research project. Additionally, it may take years to demonstrate the effectiveness of intervention for a particular social problem. Consequently, research on children and resultant intervention initiatives rarely offer "quick fixes" to the problems of children and society.

Future Directions

The study of children in society can begin to offer solutions to many of the more pressing societal problems. Quality child care, parenting skills, education, stress reduction, affordable housing, job training, and humane political policies are a few ideas for solutions to some of the controversies that will be raised in this book.

The imbalance between work and family in the United States has created problems in the economy as well as in the family system. Workers are expected to produce quality goods and services, but they receive little social support in raising their families. Employers must acknowledge the strain that workers feel as they are pulled between work and family responsibilities. Health insurance, family-friendly work policies, flexible work schedules, parental and dependent care leave, exercise facilities, quality child care and sick child care, on-site or nearby one-stop service centers with post offices, grocery stores, and dry cleaners would be ways of providing support for families in the workplace.

Schools contribute to the problems of child-care arrangements by keeping to an antiquated schedule that was first developed to meet the needs of the farm family. Years ago, schools were let out in the early afternoon and all summer so that children could help with the crops, livestock, and other farm-related chores before sunset. However, ours has been a predominantly industrial society for a large part of the twentieth century and into the twenty-first century. As a result, a different type of schedule is required. Many concerned families advocate activities for children after school and schools that are open all year long to match the schedules of workers. The economy has changed and families have changed; why have educational institutions remained static?

The majority of children somehow manage to grow and develop successfully in a variety of family forms, but the stressors on all families are constantly increasing, which may, in turn, decrease the likelihood of continued success. Parents worry that the cost of a college education will be more than they can afford; parents worry about their children and AIDS, violence, and drugs; they worry about if their child is being bullied, or is bullying someone else, and how that might impact their long-term development; parents are concerned that in adulthood their children will not be able to live as well as they have lived. Families need emotional support, and parents need opportunities to learn stress management and parenting skills.

Society can promote the optimal growth and development of its children by taking responsibility for them. There is an old saying, "It takes a village to raise a child." Our society can raise its children by establishing policies in schools, workplaces, and other institutions that reflect the importance of nurturing children.

Kourtney Vaillancourt
New Mexico State University

Unit 1

Infancy

*I*nfancy and toddlerhood encompass the time period from birth to age two or three. During this time, the most dramatic growth of a child's life takes place. Traditionally, much of the literature on infancy has dealt with the physical aspects of development; more recently, however, researchers, practitioners, and policymakers have begun to be concerned with the interaction of brain development on later learning and the social and emotional aspects of the infant's development. The issues examined in this section focus on how the family and social institutions influence children's development from the time they are born.

Selected, Edited, and with Issue Framing Material by:
Kourtney Vaillancourt, *New Mexico State University*

ISSUE

Is Institutional Child Care Beneficial to Children?

YES: Greg Parks, from "The High/Scope Perry Preschool Project," *Juvenile Justice Bulletin* (October 2000)

NO: U.S. Department of Health & Human Services, NIH, from "The NICHD Study of Early Child Care and Youth Development: Findings for Children up to Age 4½ Years" (2006)

Learning Outcomes

After reading this issue, you should be able to:

- Summarize the dilemmas faced by families when deciding who will care for their children.
- Explain the impact that institutional child care can have on children.
- Discuss risk factors for delinquency and some of the prevention models that have been developed.
- Discuss recommendations for providing quality child care in institutional settings.

ISSUE SUMMARY

YES: Greg Parks, an intern program specialist at the Office of Juvenile Justice and Delinquency Prevention, details the results of the Perry Preschool Project. Parks contends that evaluations of the program show significant benefits in adulthood for the children who attended the preschool.

NO: The NICHD Study that the National Institutes of Health conducted was a multiyear study that describes some of the possible outcomes associated with the quality and quantity of institutional child care. The findings indicate that the quantity and quality of institutional child care do have a slightly negative impact on children's development.

Increasingly, parents are placing their children in some kind of child care during the day so that they are able to work to support the family economically. This is true not only for single parents but also for parents in a two-parent household who must work in order to live even modestly. In the past, the majority of children in child care were cared for in a family setting by a relative or a home day care with a few children. Today, many families have no relatives who stay at home during the day and are close by to whom they can turn for help. In addition, mothers used to take as much time as possible after the birth of a baby and stay at home during a large part of the child's infancy. Things have changed; due in large part to limited leave policies by employers, many women return to work within six weeks of giving birth and, when faced with choices for child care, find that they must place their infant in an institutional or chain-type day-care facility.

These day-care centers usually serve children of varying ages, from infancy to four or five years of age, and often have after-school programs for elementary school children. These centers often have many rooms and are housed in a large building with as many as 20 caregivers. Child-caregivers must meet minimum, state-imposed licensing standards, but because of the low pay and no benefits, the child-care industry is plagued with a high turnover rate. Thus, caregivers might change many times during a child's stay, depending upon the center's pay structure and the administration's philosophy of quality care. These types of centers look somewhat institutional because of their large building size, numerous rooms, and large number of personnel. Many object to the institutional-type child-care centers because they do not have the home-type atmosphere that one usually associates with the quality of care expected for very young children.

An April 2001 release of the results from a longitudinal study by the National Institute of Child Health and Human Development, a federal agency that has been studying children in child-care settings for 10 years, made headlines and caused a furor in the child-care industry. Some conclusions of the study, many say, were taken out of context and sensationalized by the press. It was reported that children who attended day care were found to be more aggressive than their stay-at-home counterparts. In actuality, the level of aggression for day-care children was still within the normal range of behavior. These kinds of misinterpretations and partial facts create confusion for parents who are just trying to do the best they can for their children. American society asks parents to work to support their families but then asks them to stay home to take care of their children. This dichotomy of thinking and expectations makes it difficult to feel good about any choice made related to child care.

The quality of child care appears to be one of the most important issues in the debate over whether or not to send young children to child-care centers. Low adult-child ratios, competent and caring caregivers, and clean and nurturing environments are what contribute to quality child care. Is this type of setting preferable over being at home with a parent who does not want to be there and who does nothing to stimulate a child intellectually or emotionally? Consider another alternative—poor-quality child care, with multiple caregivers who have no training and no desire to work with young children in a dirty, nonstimulating environment. Contrast this scenario with a child's being at home with a parent who loves the child and provides educational materials and one-on-one interaction most of the day. These are the extremes that are presented when the question of how and where to best care for young children arises.

Another factor that confounds this argument is how much time and what quality of time parents who use day care spend with their children when they are at home. Mediocre out-of-home care can be mitigated by a stimulating home environment when children and parents are together. On the other hand, a poor, nonnurturing home environment, which could be devastating for a child's development, can be supplemented positively by a quality child-care experience.

What is a parent to do? Parents must work to support their families, and they must find a safe place to leave their children. Is a large institutional-like setting appropriate for infants and toddlers who need the security of a close, warm environment? Will these young children be harmed by having several caregivers within a week, or is institutional child care the best environment for children? This is the dilemma discussed in the following two selections. The NICHD study presented by the NIH identifies some of the challenges that are more likely as quantity of child care outside of the home increases, with consideration given to the quality of the care as well. In contrast, the Perry Preschool Project results, which are detailed by Greg Parks, indicate that child care is beneficial for children. Longitudinal data from the Perry Preschool Project span over 40 years and show the program to have been beneficial for the children who attended the center.

YES ↵

Greg Parks

The High/Scope Perry Preschool Project

The Office of Juvenile Justice and Delinquency Prevention (OJJDP) recently published *Costs and Benefits of Early Childhood Intervention* (Greenwood, 1999), a Fact Sheet reviewing the benefits of early childhood intervention in the prevention of later delinquency. Among the most notable and longstanding secondary prevention programs considered was the High/Scope Perry Preschool Project of Ypsilanti, MI.[1] This [selection] examines this successful program model, which demonstrates a potential link between early childhood intervention and delinquency prevention.

The High/Scope Perry Preschool Project is a well-established early childhood intervention that has been in operation for almost 40 years. A review of the program's findings is useful at this time in light of the field's growing knowledge of risk factors associated with juvenile delinquency, including early childhood risk factors that may be diminished by secondary prevention programs targeted at high-risk populations. Juvenile justice research has made great strides in identifying risk factors that may be precursors to delinquency. Although the problem of delinquency increases with the number of risk factors, specific risk factors appear to vary according to a child's stage of development and may be reduced with appropriate preventive measures. These developmental differences for risk factors indicate the need for targeted interventions that address specific age-related factors (Wasserman and Miller, 1998). Given this link between early risk factors and later delinquency, it is important for practitioners to plan intervention programs for high-risk youth early in a youth's life so that he or she can develop a strong foundation for later development.

Background

The High/Scope Perry Preschool Project, which began in 1962, is the focus of an ongoing longitudinal study—conducted by the High/Scope Educational Research Foundation—of 123 high-risk African American children.[2] Participants were of low socioeconomic status, had low IQ scores (between 70 and 85, the range for borderline mental impairment) with no organic deficiencies (i.e., biologically based mental impairment), and were at high risk of failing school. Fifty-eight of these 3- and 4-year-old children were assigned to the program group, and 65 of these children were assigned to a control group that did not go through the program. The groups were matched according to age, IQ, socioeconomic status, and gender. There were no differences between the groups with regard to father absence, parent education level, family size, household density, or birth order. Researchers collected followup data annually when the children were between ages 4 and 11 and at ages 14, 15, and 19 and collected age 27 data from 1986 to 1991 (Schweinhart, Barnes, and Weikart, 1993; Schweinhart and Weikart, 1995).[3]

The High/Scope Perry Preschool Project's high-quality educational approach is based on an active learning model that emphasizes participants' intellectual and social development. Children attended the preschool Monday through Friday for 2.5 hours per day over a 2-year period. During that same period, a staff-to-child ratio of one adult for every five or six children enabled teachers to visit each child's family in their home for 1.5 hours each week. In addition, parents participated in monthly small group meetings with other parents, facilitated by program staff.

Although it was initiated as an educational intervention, the High/Scope Perry Preschool Project has demonstrated a number of other positive outcomes, including a significantly lower rate of crime and delinquency and lower incidence of teenage pregnancy and welfare dependency. Overall, the program group has demonstrated significantly higher rates of prosocial behavior, academic achievement, employment, income, and family stability as compared with the control group. The success of this and similar programs demonstrates intervention and delinquency prevention in terms of both social outcome and cost-effectiveness and has a number of useful implications for policy, practice, and ongoing research. This Bulletin reviews the program outcomes, describes the early childhood risk factors that can be targeted with intervention, and explores the relationship between program components and risk factors.

Program Outcomes

Outcomes of the High/Scope Perry Preschool longitudinal study can be divided into three major categories: social responsibility, scholastic success, and socioeconomic success (Schweinhart et al., 1985). Social responsibility variables include delinquency, marital status, and pregnancy. Scholastic success is determined by a number of factors including graduation rate, grade point average, and postsecondary education, whereas socioeconomic success is measured in terms of employment, earnings, and welfare

Parks, Greg. From *Juvenile Justice Bulletin*, a publication of the Office of Juvenile Justice and Delinquency Prevention/National Institute of Justice, (October 2000) pp. 1–6. References omitted.

assistance. Cost-benefit is included as an additional outcome because of the long-term savings to society as a result of program success.

Social Responsibility

Delinquency Data collected from police and court records show that juvenile delinquency was significantly lower for the High/Scope Perry Preschool program group as compared with the control group, including fewer arrests and fewer juvenile court petitions (Schweinhart, Barnes, and Weikart, 1993; Schweinhart and Weikart, 1995). Only 31 percent of the program group had ever been arrested, compared with 51 percent of the control group. In addition to police and court records, data collected from respondents at age 19 were used as an overall indicator of delinquency. When study participants were 19 years old, researchers found significant differences between the program and control groups. The program group had fewer arrests overall than the control group (averages of 1.3 versus 2.3 arrests per person), fewer felony arrests (averages of 0.7 versus 2.0 arrests per person), and fewer juvenile court petitions filed (averages of 0.2 versus 0.4 petitions per person).

Like the criminal record data, a misconduct scale based on teacher-report data and self-report data from the 19-year-old respondents demonstrates a significant difference between the program and control groups, as reflected by the following results for the program group:

- Lower overall scores for total misconduct and serious misconduct at ages 15 and 19.
- Lower incidence of fighting and other violent behavior.
- Lower incidence of property damage.
- Fewer police contacts.

Data collected from respondents at age 27 indicate significant differences between the program group and control group for adult arrests: the control group underwent more than twice as many arrests as the program group (averages of 4.0 versus 1.8 arrests per person). Thirty-six percent of the control group accounted for 98 felony arrests between ages 19 and 27, while 27 percent of the program group accounted for 40 felony arrests during the same period. Thirty-five percent of the control group were considered frequent offenders (defined as five or more arrests), compared with only 7 percent of the program group. In addition, 25 percent of the control group had been arrested for drug-related offenses, versus 7 percent of the program group. The control group also averaged more months on probation (6.6 versus 3.2 months) and had more than twice as many of its members placed on probation or parole for longer than 18 months (20 percent versus 9 percent).

Marital status and pregnancy Marital status among the males was the same for both groups, with 26 percent married at age 27, although program group males, on average,

had been married for a longer period (6.2 versus 3.3 years). Marital status among the females differed significantly, with 40 percent of program group females married, compared with 8 percent of the control group females. Although fewer females in the program group were parents (64 percent versus 75 percent), significantly more of them were married, cohabiting parents (28 percent versus 8 percent). Fifty-seven percent of mothers in the program group gave birth out of wedlock, compared with 83 percent of mothers in the control group. In measures related to family stability, the program group scored significantly higher on a measure of closeness to family and friends (66 percent versus 48 percent) and the ability to maintain persistence at tasks (i.e., work or study hard all day) (47 percent versus 33 percent).

Scholastic Success

Participants in the High/Scope Perry Preschool study were characterized by better academic performance than those in the control group, as measured by higher graduation rates, better grades, higher standardized test scores, and fewer instances of placement in special education classes. In addition, the program group spent more time on homework and demonstrated more positive attitudes toward school at ages 15 and 19. More parents of program group members had positive attitudes regarding their children's educational experiences and were hopeful that their children would obtain college degrees. The program group demonstrated significant academic differences in the following areas:

- **Special education for mental impairment.** Only 15 percent of the program group had been placed in special education programs for mental impairment, compared with 34 percent of the control group.
- **Test scores.** Each year from ages 7 to 14, the mean achievement test scores of the program group were noticeably higher than those of the control group (an average difference of 16 percent). The difference in the final achievement test scores of the two groups at age 14 was particularly significant: the program group's scores were 29 percent higher than those of the control group.
- **Grade point average.** The mean high school grade point average of the program group was higher than that of the control group (2.09 versus 1.68).
- **Graduation from high school.** Seventy-one percent of the program group graduated from high school, compared with 54 percent of the control group. The difference was largely accounted for by graduation rates among females (84 percent and 35 percent, respectively).

Socioeconomic Success

Data collected at ages 19 and 27 indicate that the program group has been more successful socioeconomically than the control group. The data for age 19 reveal that significantly more program group members were employed (50 percent versus 32 percent) and self-reporting

(45 percent versus 25 percent). These data also reflect that fewer program group members received welfare assistance (18 percent versus 32 percent). The data for age 27 reveal a continuation of significant economic differences characterized by more economic stability among the program group members, as measured by the following indicators:

- **Public assistance.** Fifteen percent of the program group were receiving public assistance, versus 32 percent of the control group.
- **Monthly earnings.** Twenty-nine percent of the program group had monthly earnings of $2,000 or more, versus 7 percent of the control group (36 percent versus 11 percent, respectively, when comparing only employed members in each group).
- **Household earnings.** When the income of the spouses of the study participants was taken into account, 47 percent of the program group had household income earnings of $3,000 or more per month, versus 17 percent of the control group.
- **Home ownership.** Thirty-six percent of the program group owned a home, versus 13 percent of the control group.
- **Automobile ownership.** Thirty percent of the program group owned a second car, versus 13 percent of the control group.

Cost-Benefit Analysis

A cost-benefit analysis of the High/Scope Perry Preschool study indicates a savings to the public of more than seven times the initial investment per child, with a return of $7.16 for every dollar spent (Barnett, 1983). When adjusted for inflation and a 3-percent discount rate, the investment in early childhood prevention resulted in a taxpayer return of $88,433 per child from the following sources:

- Savings in welfare assistance (prior to welfare reform).
- Savings in special education.
- Savings to the criminal justice system.
- Savings to crime victims.
- Increased tax revenue from higher earnings.

An independent reanalysis is provided in a recent RAND Corporation report (Karoly et al., 1998). This report found that eliminating the largest and least reliable savings category (savings to crime victims) still left a return of more than twice the initial investment. Savings to crime victims make up 65 percent of the total investment return in the earlier analysis (Barnett, 1993). Although victim savings should be considered a significant outcome and societal benefit of early childhood intervention, this factor is also distinct from the other factors that can be estimated based on direct governmental costs and savings. With victim savings factored out of the analysis, the largest savings category is in criminal justice costs

(40 percent), followed by increased taxable revenue (26 percent), reduced educational services (25 percent), and reduced welfare costs (9 percent).

Early Childhood Risk Factors for Delinquency

An understanding of early childhood risk factors for delinquency is helpful to interpreting the success of the High/Scope Perry Preschool Project. One factor identified with risk for delinquency is poor language skills. (Stattin and Klackenberg-Larsson, 1993). As a component of overall mental development, language functions as an indicator of later intelligence and is a critical factor in the relationship between intelligence and delinquency. Additional early risk factors include poor attachment to caregivers (Egeland and Farber, 1984; Shaw and Bell, 1993), poor parenting skills (Hawkins et al., 1998; Loeber and Stouthamer-Loeber, 1986), and multiple family stressors (Fergusson and Lynskey, 1996; Shaw et al., 1998). These risk factors may not only directly affect delinquency but may also indirectly influence other factors that interact with delinquency, such as school- and community-related risk factors.

As demonstrated in the Prenatal and Early Childhood Nurse Home Visitation Program supported by OJJDP (Olds, Hill, and Rumsey, 1998), prenatal and early postnatal prevention are shown to reduce risk factors that contribute to the development of antisocial behavior in childhood. Early childhood intervention during the preschool years also offers an opportunity to halt the developmental trajectory toward delinquency and related behavioral disorders. Family support services help develop parenting skills, attachment, and coping mechanisms that have a positive effect on family stressors. A multicomponent approach to enhancing child development promotes protective factors and reduces risk factors by addressing the many systems and influences that affect a child's development.

Program Components and Related Risk Factors for Delinquency

The components of the High/Scope Perry Preschool Project affect a number of the early childhood risk factors associated with later delinquency and other behavioral problems. In addition to directly reinforcing early developmental processes in the educational setting, the program strengthens positive parenting skills.

The High/Scope Educational Research Foundation explains the effectiveness of the High/Scope Perry Preschool model in terms of empowerment, which includes developing skills for success by enabling children to be active and independent learners, helping parents to support the development of their children, and providing teachers with effective training and support (Schweinhart and Weikart, 1995).

Because an ongoing home-school relationship enhances socialization, involving parents early in the educational process is critical to the later success of participants in an early childhood intervention such as High/Scope Perry Preschool (Seitz, 1990). Weekly home visits by teachers and regular parent group meetings promote the strengthening of parent-child relationships and increase parent involvement in the educational process. A more recent OJJDP longitudinal study, the Rochester Youth Development Study (Thornberry et al., 1998), confirmed a significant relationship between parents' involvement in their children's lives and reduced delinquency.

In addition to enhancing parent attachment, parent involvement, and parenting skills, early childhood intervention aimed at both parents and children influences a child's attachment to school and later commitment to school success (Thornberry et al., 1998). Findings from the Rochester study confirm earlier research linking poor school attachment, commitment, and achievement to delinquent behavior and drug use (Krohn et al., 1995; Smith et al., 1995). Another OJJDP study, the Seattle Social Development Project (Hill et al., 1999), found that a lack of success in elementary school was linked to later gang membership. Even in the midst of multiple other factors placing youth at high risk for delinquency, school success (as indicated by higher standardized test scores, school commitment, attachment to teachers, college aspirations, and parent expectations) appears to be a protective factor against delinquency (Smith et al., 1995). Academic achievement outcomes of the High/Scope Perry Preschool study indicate that the program group was more successful than the control group in school-related factors that appear to protect against delinquency.

The positive outcomes of the High/Scope Perry Preschool study are the result of a cumulative effect that begins with increased school readiness (Berrueta-Clement et al., 1987; Zigler, Taussig, and Black, 1992). School readiness results in positive reinforcement from teachers in the early grades followed by enhanced academic performance in subsequent grades and an overall stronger commitment to school. A correlational analysis of the High/Scope Perry Preschool data reveals a strong association between school motivation in the early years and literacy scores at age 19 (Schweinhart, Barnes, and Weikart, 1993). School motivation is also higher correlated with the highest year of schooling completed, which is associated with higher monthly earnings in adulthood and fewer lifetime arrests.

Program and Policy Implications

The outcomes of the High/Scope Perry Preschool study demonstrate the value of prevention and early intervention efforts in promoting protective factors that reduce delinquency. The program was developed for high-risk children who stood to benefit the most from such an intervention. The intervention also affected multiple risk factors and was carried out in multiple domains (i.e.,

home and school). In an extensive review of early childhood interventions, Yoshikawa (1995) concluded that the combination of an early educational component with family support, as exemplified by the High/Scope Perry Preschool Project, is a determining factor in long-term effects on antisocial behavior. Other combination programs that have demonstrated long-term effects on delinquency include the Yale Child Welfare Project (Seitz and Apfel, 1994), Houston Parent Child Development Center (Johnson and Walker, 1987), and Syracuse Family Development Research Program (Lally, Mangione, and Honig, 1988). Single-component models, such as those that address only educational factors, have not been shown to demonstrate significant results.

In addition to the need to target appropriate populations and address multiple risk factors in multiple domains, program quality is essential to success. The High/Scope Perry Preschool model is based on a high-quality educational approach that assumes a low staff-to-child ratio, an active learning curriculum, and a home visitation component that engages parents in the educational process. Furthermore, teachers are well educated, adequately compensated, and well supported in their tasks.

Head Start, perhaps the largest and best-known early childhood intervention program, has recently made efforts to expand and improve its effectiveness by emphasizing family support, staff training, and performance standards (U.S. Department of Health and Human Services, 1999). The 1994 legislation reauthorizing Head Start incorporated a number of recommendations from the Advisory Committee on Head Start Quality and Expansion (1993), including increased parent involvement, a lower staff-to-child ratio, and increased mental health services.[4] Head Start has increased the emphasis on curriculum and child outcomes as a result of this reauthorization and has formed Head Start Quality Research Centers to respond to the need for additional research in the area of early childhood intervention. Further research is clearly needed to build on the limited existing knowledge base and assess the effectiveness of programs across various demographic groups, risk factors, and co-occurring factors that are related to delinquency, such as mental health issues and substance abuse (Yoshikawa, 1995).

Although the High/Scope Perry Preschool study's sample size was small in proportion to its eventual influence, its strong experimental design has contributed to its prominence in the field of early childhood education. Subsequent early childhood research that is carefully controlled and longitudinal in design remains limited. The limited research involving similar models that combine educational and family support components, however, supports the positive outcomes of the High/Scope Perry Preschool model. Subsequent independent evaluations of the programs that have implemented the High/Scope model have rated those programs significantly higher than comparison programs, with 58 percent of High/Scope programs versus 40 percent of comparison programs being rated as high quality (Epstein, 1993). In addition, 72 percent of children in High/Scope programs versus 57 percent of children in comparison programs scored high on measures of emotional, social, cognitive, and motor development.

Some targeted, multicomponent early childhood interventions have been demonstrated to exceed their costs in eventual savings and benefit to the public. However, implementing an effective prevention strategy requires a commitment to provide empirically based quality programming and to invest the up-front resources that will result in long-term savings and positive social change in the lives of children and families. The High/Scope Perry Preschool Project provides one such model for early childhood intervention that has proven successful when executed with quality and commitment to long-term results. The complexity of juvenile delinquency requires multiple strategies that address the problem at various stages of development; early childhood intervention is one promising component in the context of a more comprehensive approach, as recommended in OJJDP's *Comprehensive Strategy for Serious, Violent, and Chronic Juvenile Offenders* (Wilson and Howell, 1993). The High/Scope Perry Preschool model is worthy of consideration as an effective early childhood intervention as communities attempt to implement a comprehensive strategy that includes prevention, intervention, and graduated sanctions (Howell, 1995; Wilson and Howell, 1993).

Notes

1. Unlike primary prevention programs, which are directed at the general population, secondary prevention programs target children at risk for school failure or delinquency.

2. The original Perry Preschool no longer exists, but the High/Scope Educational Research Foundation—founded in 1970 by Perry Preschool researcher David Weikart—continues to collect followup data from the participants of the 1962 study. The foundation is an independent organization dedicated to nonprofit research, development, training, and public advocacy. Its principal goals are to promote the learning and development of children worldwide from infancy through adolescence and to support and train educators and parents as they help children learn. In a High/Scope program, students should learn through active involvement with materials, events, and ideas. The Foundation disseminates the High/Scope Preschool model worldwide.

3. Researchers are currently collecting followup data from the original program participants. Called the High/Scope Perry Preschool Midlife Study, researchers have already interviewed 30 of the 39- to 41-year-old participants. The interview emphasized health and the performance of the program participants' children. The researchers expect to complete the data collection by the end of 2001. This study is funded by the McCormick Tribune Foundation in Chicago, IL. [97% of the study participants still living were interviewed at age 40. Additional data were gathered from the subjects' school, social services, and arrest records. The study found that adults at age 40 who had the preschool program had higher earnings, were more likely to hold a job, had committed fewer crimes, and were more likely to have graduated from high school than adults who did not have preschool. The major conclusion of the mid-life phase is that high-quality preschool programs for young children living in poverty contribute to their intellectual and social development in childhood and their school success, economic performance, and reduced commission of crime in adulthood. This study confirms that these findings extend not only to young adults, but also to adults in midlife. It confirms that the long-term effects are lifetime effects. (Reference-www.highscope.org)]

4. Head Start Act Amendments of 1994. Pub. L. No. 103–252, tit. 1 § 108, Stat. 624 (1994).

GREG PARKS is an Intern Program Specialist, Research and Program Development Division, Office of Juvenile Justice and Delinquency Prevention.

**U.S. Department of Health &
Human Services, NIH**

The NICHD Study of Early Child Care and Youth Development: Findings for Children up to Age 4½ Years

In the early 1990s, the majority of children began some non-maternal care by 6 months of age. Results from the NICHD Study of Early Child Care and Youth Development show that, in its demographically and ethnically diverse sample of more than 1,000 children, the average child spent 27 hours a week in non-maternal care over the first 4½ years of life. During the children's first 2 years of life, most child care took place in family homes with relatives or in child care homes; as children got older, more were in center-based care.

When it come to understanding how these experiences might influence children, knowing simply whether a child was or was not ever in non-maternal care provided little insight into a child's development. Children who were cared for exclusively by their mothers did not develop differently than those who were also cared for by others.

Quality, quantity, and type of non-maternal care were modestly, but not strongly, linked to the children's development regardless of family features.

Children Who Were Cared for Exclusively by Their Mothers Did Not Develop Differently Than Those Who Were Also Cared for by Others

- Children in higher quality non-maternal child care had somewhat better language and cognitive development during the first 4½ years of life. They were also somewhat more cooperative than those who experienced lower quality care during the first 3 year of life.
- Children with higher quantity (total combined number of hours) of experience in non-maternal child care showed somewhat more behavior problems in child care and in kindergarten classrooms than those who had experienced fewer hours.
- Children who attended child care centers had somewhat better cognitive and language development, but also showed somewhat more behavior problems in child care and in kindergarten classrooms than children who experienced other non-maternal child care arrangements.

Parent and family characteristics were more strongly linked to child development than were child care features. And, parent and family characteristics predicted some developmental outcomes that were not predicted by child care. For instance, children showed more cognitive, language, and social competence and more harmonious relationships with parents when parents were more educated, had higher incomes, and provided home environments that were emotionally supportive and cognitively enriched, and when mothers experienced little psychological distress.

Family and parenting experiences were as important to the well-being of children who had extensive child care experience as family and parenting experiences were for children with little or no child care experience.

During the past 30 years, increasing numbers of families in the United States have used non-parental child care. Such arrangements include care by relatives or in-home nannies, family child care homes, and center-based care.

The decision to use child care is rarely an easy one. How will non-maternal child care affect the child's development? How do parents know that their children are getting good care? What type of child care setting is best? Will being separated from the mother on a regular basis affect the child's relationship with her or with other family members?

With so many books, articles, talk shows, and other resources available to offer advice and recommendations, it's hard to find reliable, research-based information about child care. It's even more difficult when the advice of one "expert" disagrees with the recommendations of another.

The National Institute of Child Health and Human Development (NICHD), part of the National Institutes of Health (NIH) within the U.S. Department of Health and Human Services, began a study in 1991 to collect information about different non-maternal child care arrangements, and about children and families who use child care as well as those who do not. The result, the NICHD Study of Early Child Care and Youth Development (SECCYD), is the most comprehensive study to date of children and the many environments in which they develop. It provides reliable, accurate, research-based information about non-maternal child care and its links to children's development.

National Institute of Child Health and Human Development, NIH, HHS. (2006). *The NICHD Study of Early Child Care and Youth Development (SECCYD): Findings for Children up to Age 4½ Years* (05-4318). Washington, DC: U.S. Government Printing Office.

The findings will not answer all of your child care questions, but they will help you make more informed choices to meet the needs of your child and your family. They will also help you understand how you home environment and your parenting behaviors are related to your child's development. . . .

How Is Quality of Child Care Related to Children's Development?

Researchers examined process quality (child care quality in terms of process features) and various outcomes, while taking into account children's family features (such as ethnic background and parents' education) and other child care features (such as child care setting). These analyses allowed researchers to identify links between child care quality and child development outcomes.

Child Care Quality and Cognitive and Language Development Outcomes

- Results showed that children who experienced higher quality child care consistently showed somewhat better cognitive function and language development across the first 3 years of life.
- The most important feature of quality for predicting cognitive and language development up to age 3 was the language used by the caregiver. More stimulation from the caregiver—asking question, responding to vocalizations, and other forms of talking—was linked to somewhat better cognitive and language development.
- Higher quality child care also predicted greater school readiness at 4½ years of age, as reflected in standardized tests of literacy and number skills.

Even though child care quality was associated with cognitive and language development, the link was not a strong one. Family and parent features were more important predictors of this development than child care quality. So, the differences between outcomes for children in higher and lower quality care were small relative to the differences associated with family characteristics (the mean score for the pre-academic skills test was 100, with a standard deviation of 15).

Child Care Quality and Social Development Outcomes

- Children who experienced higher quality child care had mothers who were more likely to show slightly higher (rather than slightly lower) levels of sensitivity when interacting with their children at age 6 months, 1½ years, 2 years, and 3 years.

- Children who experienced higher quality child care were somewhat more cooperative and compliant and slightly less aggressive and disobedient at 2 years and 3 years of age.
- Children were somewhat more likely to be insecurely attached to their mothers if they were in lower quality care, but only if their mothers were also lower in sensitivity during interactions with their children.
- Higher quality child care predicted more positive interactions with other children at age 3 years.

The links between child care quality and social outcomes were weak and were more slight than links between family features and the same aspects of social development.

Child Care Quality and Health Outcomes

Child care quality did not predict children's health. However, it is important to note that the study did not address issues related to hygiene. The few measures of hygiene that were included were not statistically significant predictors of health outcomes. It is possible, though, that hygiene was similar in the different settings because of state or local standards.

What Is Quantity of Child Care?

Quantity of child care is the average amount of time a child spent in child care each week.

On average, children in the NICHD Study spent 27 hours each week in child care between the ages of 6 months and 4½ years.

In addition, older children were more likely to spend more time in care than younger children were. For example, the number of children in care for an average of 30 hours or more per week increased from 37 percent when children were between the ages of 3 months and 1½ years, to 50 percent when they were between 3 and 4½ years old. At the same time, many children who were not in regular care (less than 10 hours a week) as infants increased their time in care by the time they were preschool age. As a result, the percentage of children in care between 10 and 30 hours each week stayed relatively the same over time.

Note the following about the chart:

- Between the ages of 3 months and 1½ years, 27 percent of the children were in child care for at least 10 hours each week, and 37 percent were in child care for more than 30 hours each week.
- Between the ages of 1½ and 3 years, 44 percent of the children were in child care for more than 30 hours each week.
- Between the ages of 3 and 4½ years, 50 percent were in child care for 30 or more hours each week.

How Is Quantity of Child Care Related to Children's Development?

To understood how quantity of child care may influence child development, researchers considered the amount of time a child spent in child care since birth, while taking into account children's family features (such as ethnic background and parents' education) and other child care features (such as child care quality). They examined development of the children at ages 1½, 2, 3 and 4½ years and compared children's development to standards or milestones for those ages. These analyses allowed researchers to identify relationships between child care quantity and some child development outcomes.

Chid Care Quantity and Cognitive and Language Development Outcomes

The amount of time spent in child care was not related to children's cognitive or language skills or to their school readiness at any age prior to school entry.

Child Care Quantity and Social Development Outcomes

- For young children whose mothers showed low levels of sensitivity during mother-child interactions, more than 10 hours of care each week increased the risk of insecure attachment to their mothers.
- Children who spent more time in child care were somewhat less cooperative, more disobedient, and more aggressive at age 2 and age 4½, and in kindergarten, but not at age 3. These findings were based on reports from caregivers, mothers, and/or teachers about children's behavior.
- Children who averaged 30 hours of child care or more each week during their first 4½ years of life were somewhat more likely to show problem behaviors at age 4 and in kindergarten, based on caregiver reports. But child care quantity did not predict problem behaviors in the home environment as reported by the mothers.
- Time spent in child care did not predict clinical levels (behaviors that may require special attention) of behavior problems or psychopathology.
- Once again, family features were stronger predictors of children's social behavior and development than was quantity of child care.

When children spent more (rather than less) time in child care, their mothers showed lower levels of sensitivity when interacting with them across their first 3 years of life. The same pattern occurred when mother-child interaction was studied at age 4½ years and again in first grade, but only for white children. For African American and Hispanic children, the opposite was true: More (rather than less) time spent in child care across the first 4 years of life predicted higher levels of sensitivity when children were age 4½ and in first grade. In other words, after age 3, linkages between time spent in child care and mothering style were different for white and for African American children.

Child Care Quantity and Health Outcomes

Even though children in child care may be exposed to communicable illnesses (that is, sicknesses you can catch from someone else, such as a cold), the quantity of child care each week had little to do with the likelihood of catching such illnesses, except for two specific situations:

- Children in more hours of child care each week during their first year of life were 8 percent more likely to have on ear infection.
- Children in more hours of care each week during theri first year of life were 4 percent more likely to have stomach illness (such as an upset stomach or brief stomach "flu").

What Is the Bottom Line?

The amount of time that children spend in child care from infancy through age 4½ is not related in their cognitive outcomes prior to school entry. Children who spend many hours in child care, however, show somewhat more behavior problems and more episodes of minor illness than those in fewer hours of child care. The amount of time a child spent in child care is also associated with mother-child relationships to some degree.

U.S. Department of Health & Human Services, NIH is the United States government's principal agency for protecting the health of all Americans and providing essential human services, especially for those who are least able to help themselves.

EXPLORING THE ISSUE

Is Institutional Child Care Beneficial to Children?

Critical Thinking and Reflection

1. Parks asserts that single-component models are not successful in early childhood intervention and delinquency prevention. He contends that a multifaceted approach must be used in order to be successful. Do you agree or disagree? Support your answer with specific concepts discussed in the reading.
2. What would you suggest to parents who do not want their children to be placed in a full-time day-care setting, but would still like some time each day where their child is out of the home and interacting with other children and adults?
3. What are some strategies that you might suggest to parents who want to ensure that they spend quality time with their child even though they must rely on full-time child care in an institutional setting while they work?
4. What do you consider to be the most important aspect of child care: the setting it is provided in, or the quality of the care? Why?

Is There Common Ground?

The issue of child care is a touchy subject for debate. Is it an issue that should be debated in public or in a more private family setting? In most instances, choosing what kind of care a child will receive is a decision made by parents for financial or personal reasons. Does institutional child care hinder children from getting all the nurturing they need during their younger years? Or, does institutional child care provide the needed nurturing for children to grow to become productive adults? Researchers may agree that the issue of child care is a complicated one, but they definitely disagree on how to confront this issue.

Perhaps if there were greater resources (e.g., more money to be able to hire more staff) available to child-care institutions, they could guarantee a high level of nurturing to children. Or, perhaps if the workplace could offer families greater flexibility in scheduling and leave policies, the families could afford to provide child care at home for a longer period of time. If both of these were in place, families would have the luxury of choosing either option and feeling more comfortable that they are doing the right thing for their children.

Additional Resources

American Academy of Child & Adolescent Psychiatry. (2002, November). Making Daycare a Good Experience. Retrieved on March 2, 2011, from www.aacap.org/cs/root/facts_for_families/making_day_care_a_good_experience

An article posted on the Internet that provides tips and suggestions for helping parents select a day care that is optimal for their child(ren).

Pendley, J. (2010, November). Choosing Child Care. Retrieved on March 2, 2011, from http://kidshealth.org/parent/positive/family/child_care.html

An article posted on the Internet that discusses the types of day care available and offers advice to parents on how to select the right care for their child(ren).

Zolten, K. & Long, N. (1997). How to Select Daycares. Retrieved on March 2, 2011, from www.parenting-ed.org/handout3/General%20Parenting%20Information/daycare.htm

An article posted on the Internet that discusses the types of day care available, benefits and challenges of the different types, and advice for how to select the day care that is right for a child.

Create Central

www.mhhe.com/createcentral

Internet Reference . . .

Day Care Issues (2001, February). Retrieved on March 2, 2011

An article posted on the Internet that discusses the types of day care available, tips on how to select the

right day care, and advice for transitioning a child to a day-care setting.

www.keepkidshealthy.com/welcome/daycare.html

Selected, Edited, and with Issue Framing Material by:
Kourtney Vaillancourt, *New Mexico State University*

ISSUE

Does Maternal Employment Have Negative Effects on Children's Development?

YES: Patricia M. Anderson, Kristin F. Butcher, and Phillip B. Levine, from "Maternal Employment and Overweight Children," *National Bureau of Economic Research,* 2002

NO: Daniel de Vise, from "Study: Working Mothers Not Necessarily Harmful to Child Development," *The Washington Post* (July 2010)

Learning Outcomes

After reading this issue, you should be able to:

- Summarize the effects that maternal employment can have on children.
- Discuss differences in outcomes based on when mothers return to work.
- Explain why some researchers believe there is a link between maternal employment and delinquency.

ISSUE SUMMARY

YES: Researchers Patricia Anderson, Kristin Butcher, and Phillip Levine from the National Bureau of Economic Research conclude that there is a connection between maternal employment and the risk of children being overweight.

NO: Daniel de Vise describes the results of a study conducted at Columbia University, which indicate that the negative and positive effects of maternal employment balance each other out to yield a neutral effect.

The number of women who combine work and motherhood has risen steadily in the past 35 years or so. Fifty-six percent of married mothers with a child under age 1 are employed, and 59 percent of unmarried mothers with a child under 1 are employed. The percentages of women entering the labor force increases as their children get older. Sixty-two percent of married mothers with a child aged 2 are working, and 75 percent of unmarried moms with a child aged 2 are working. Attitudes toward maternal employment have changed somewhat because of societal changes. It has become more socially acceptable today for moms to work. As more women obtain high-profile jobs in politics and corporations, more workplace assistance programs have been developed. These include on-site child care, flexible work hours, and allowing moms to work from home via computer technology. The realization that it is an economic necessity for single moms as well as both parents in a dual-parent household to work has created more of an acceptance for working mothers. Many families need two incomes to make ends meet.

Time-saving appliances such as self-cleaning ovens, dishwashers, and microwave ovens have given working moms more time to spend with their children. Obtaining food for dinner from the growing number of restaurants offering drive-through or pick-up service has also relieved working moms from the hassle of running home from work to make dinner.

Of course, these time-saving means are only available to those who can afford them. Women with lower wages still struggle to balance work and family time. Welfare reform created a predicament for those who believed mothers should stay at home with their infants. With no governmental monetary support, how does a single mom stay at home with her children and still make a living for her family?

As more women moved into the workforce in the 1960s, research on maternal employment's effects on children became a popular topic of study. For the past 20 years, maternal employment has evolved from being studied as a single factor affecting children's development to being studied as a more complex issue. It was once thought that maternal employment had a direct single influence on children. Now researchers agree that maternal employment is more than a question of whether or not the mother works. The issue needs to be studied within the context of the family, the society, and cultural norms. Researchers do agree that maternal employment's effects on children need to be examined through the interaction of multiple variables, such as child-care quality, control over work situation, and family and societal support systems. They do not, however, agree on which sets of variables combine to give an accurate picture of how a mother's employment affects children's development. Study on maternal employment's effects must face the complicated task of simultaneously answering these questions. What quality of child care does the child receive? How does the mother feel about working? What societal and family support do the mother and child receive?

Researchers are not only divided on what variables to study, there is also a lack of agreement about what methods to use in studying maternal employment effects. For example, some researchers combine several social classes to study the interactive effects of working mothers with child-care arrangements, whereas others examine only one social class and how it intersects with the mother's personality traits and type of work and family environment. It is difficult to control for all characteristics that may affect the outcome of studies on maternal employment. Researchers suggest that more studies be conducted on a larger population so that they might generalize the results for the population as a whole. It is also suggested that the research methods include a larger diversity of ethnic groups and social classes to gain a better understanding of how maternal employment affects a child's development and behavioral outcomes.

The effects of maternal employment on children are determined by many factors such as mother's work satisfaction and morale, amount of and control over work, and mother's perception of quality versus quantity time with her children. Depending on which studies one reads, how the data were collected, and which combination of variables was studied, different conclusions are reported. For example, some studies show that working moms spend more quality time with their children than nonworking moms, while other studies show exactly the opposite results.

Research on maternal employment continues to become more refined, yet the question still remains: Should moms stay home with their babies? Often women who have the opportunity to do so will drop out of the workforce for at least the first few years to stay home and care for their children in order to make a connection. The concept that mother-child attachment in the first few years is critical to the child's later development has been established from years of significant research. Conversely, other research suggests that quality child-care providers may be able to meet the same attachment needs that mothers previously met. In addition, research shows that being exposed to a variety of quality caregivers, including other family members, fosters positive personality characteristics and independence in the child later on.

Young children want to be with their parents and need their parents to care for them. In an ideal world, most people want babies to be cared for by someone who loves them. In all but extreme abuse cases, this is generally the mom or dad. In our society, those who want to stay at home and care for their children should have the opportunity to do so. Yet, the economic environment prevents this from happening. Perhaps another way to look at the issue of maternal employment's effects on children's development is to develop ways to allow moms who want to stay home to raise their children to do so and to give social support to those moms who want to work outside the home.

In the YES selection, Patricia Anderson, Kristin Butcher, and Phillip Leving argue that maternal employment has negative effects on children, in that it increases the likelihood for overweight children. They describe how these effects are probably caused by time constraints that working mothers have, which limit their ability to supervise a child's nutritional intake and energy expenditure. In the NO selection, Daniel de Vise describes a study that indicates that maternal employment does not affect children's development negatively or positively. He found that maternal employment during the child's first year of life has negative and positive effects that balance each other out.

YES

Patricia M. Anderson, Kristin F. Butcher, and Phillip B. Levine

Maternal Employment and Overweight Children

The increase in maternal employment and the rise in overweight children represent two of the most notable trends in the American family over the past several decades. From 1970 to 1999, the fraction of married women with children under six who participate in the labor force doubled, rising from 30 percent to 62 percent. Married women with children ages 6 to 17 dramatically increased their labor force participation as well, rising from 49 percent to 77 percent over this period (U.S. Bureau of the Census, 2000). The prevalence of overweight children has also soared. Over the 1963–1970 period 4 percent of children between the ages of 6 and 11 were defined to be overweight; that level had more than tripled by 1999, reaching 13 percent (Centers for Disease Control, 2001). Childhood overweight may be one of the most significant health issue facing children today. Thus, a better understanding of its determinants is of critical importance.

The existence of upward trends in both maternal employment and overweight among children could simply be a coincidence. In fact, the prevalence of overweight and obesity in adults has increased as well. However, the incidence of overweight in children relative to adults has increased. In the 1960's the ratio of overweight among children to adults was about 0.3, but had risen to almost 0.5 by 1999 (Centers for Disease Control, 2001). The purpose of this paper is to explore whether the relationship between maternal employment and childhood overweight is causal.

Using the National Longitudinal Survey of Youth (NLSY), supplemented with additional information from the 1988–1994 National Health and Nutrition Examination Survey (NHANES III) and the 1994–1996, 1998 Continuing Survey of Food Intakes by Individuals (CSFII), we first document the extent to which a raw correlation exists between maternal employment and overweight. The remainder of the paper attempts to identify whether these simple relationships are causal, or whether they reflect a spurious correlation in which children whose mothers work fulltime would still be overweight even if their mothers did not work. Our results indicate that those mothers who worked more intensively, in the form of greater hours per week, since their child's birth are indeed significantly more likely to have an overweight child. A mother who worked an additional 10 hours per week is estimated to increase the likelihood of her child being overweight by

roughly one-half to one full percentage point. This effect is too small to explain a large fraction of the time series trend in childhood obesity, however, indicating that other factors must have played a larger role. . . .

Discussion

Overall, the results of this analysis indicate that a positive relationship exists between maternal employment and childhood overweight. In particular, we have found that a measure of the intensity of mother's work over the child's lifetime is consistently shown to be positively related to the child's likelihood of being overweight. A 10-hour increase in the average hours worked per week while working over the child's entire life is estimated to increase the likelihood that the child is overweight by about one half to one full percentage point. Thus, a mother moving from part-time (20 hours per week) work to full-time (40 hours) work is expected to increase the probability that her child is overweight by 1 to 2 percentage points. On the other hand, we found no evidence that the number of weeks a mother works over her child's life has any impact on the likelihood that her child will be overweight. These findings suggest that the link between maternal employment and a child's weight status may be the time constraints faced by mothers who work intensively. This result makes sense if it is the day-to-day routines that matter for a mother's ability to supervise her child's nutritional intake and energy expenditure. Working fewer hours per week allows more time for shopping, cooking, and energy expending play dates or organized sports. . . .

One of the other potentially important factors is the growth of adult overweight and obesity. Estimates indicate that obesity (BMI greater than 30) among women between the ages of 30 and 39 rose from 15 to 26 percent between 1976–80 and 1988–94 and overweight (BMI greater than 25) rose from 35 to 47 percent over this period. To the extent that adult behavior changes nutritional patterns in households in a way that affects children increased overweight among adults should correlate with increased overweight among children. Based on the estimates (and with all appropriate precautions against a causal interpretation of those findings), these increases in adult BMI would be predicted to increase childhood overweight by 0.9 percentage points. Therefore the increase in adult weight problems can "explain" about 11 percent in the trend in overweight among children. This effect is only slightly bigger than the effect of increases in the intensity of mothers' work habits. Nevertheless, even combining these two potential contributors leaves most of the trend in childhood overweight unexplained.

This project lays the groundwork for future research into the causes of childhood overweight. The contribution of this work is several-fold. First, much of the research on childhood overweight reports simple correlations between overweight and various characteristics of the child or the family. This project is among the first to grapple with issues of causality. It presents robust evidence of a positive and significant impact of maternal work on the probability that a child is overweight. Further, it presents prima facie evidence that the mechanism through which this takes place is constraints on mother's time; it is hours per week, not the number of weeks worked, that affects children's probability of overweight.

There is much more to learn about causal factors related to the epidemic of overweight among children in the United States. These include understanding direct contributors to childhood overweight and the mechanisms through which mothers' working translates into overweight children. For example, how does child care quality affect children's nutrition and energy expenditure? Additionally, we need to know more about children's opportunities for vigorous exercise, including physical education in school, after-school programs, and access to parks or other recreational facilities. This deeper understanding is important if society is going to develop appropriate policy responses to this important public health issue.

PATRICIA M. ANDERSON is Professor of Economics at Dartmouth and a Research Associate at the National Bureau of Economic Research in Cambridge, MA. She received her BA Economics and Mathematics from William and Mary in 1985, and her PhD in Economics from Princeton in 1991. Prof. Anderson's research interests fall broadly in the field of applied microeconomics, with specific interests in child health & nutrition and in social insurance programs. She is a Co-editor for the Journal of Human Resources and is on the Editorial Board for B.E. Journals in Economic Analysis and Policy.

KRISTIN F. BUTCHER is Assistant Professor of Economics, Boston College (on leave), and a Program Officer at the MacArthur Foundation.

PHILLIP B. LEVINE is Katharine Coman and A. Barton Hepburn Professor of Economics and the Economics Department Chair at Wellesley College.

LEVINE'S RESEARCH has examined such issues as the impact of abortion policy changes on pregnancy, abortion, and birth; the impact of the business cycle on retirement behavior; and the ability of alternative public policies to raise the adult incomes of children who grow up in poverty.

Daniel de Vise

Study: Working Mothers Not Necessarily Harmful to Child Development

A new study finds that babies raised by working mothers don't necessarily suffer cognitive setbacks, an encouraging finding that follows a raft of previous reports suggesting that women with infants were wiser to stay home.

Researchers at Columbia University say they are among the first to measure the full effect of maternal employment on child development—not just the potential harm caused by a mother's absence from the home, but the prospective benefits that come with her job, including higher family income and better child care.

In a 113-page monograph, released this week, the authors conclude "that the overall effect of 1st-year maternal employment on child development is neutral."

The report is based on data from the most comprehensive child-care study to date, the National Institute of Child Health and Human Development Study of Early Child Care. It followed more than 1,000 children from 10 geographic areas through first grade, tracking their development and family characteristics.

Infants raised by mothers with full-time jobs scored somewhat lower on cognitive tests, deficits that persisted into first grade. But that negative effect was offset by several positives. Working mothers had higher income. They were more likely to seek high-quality child care. And they displayed greater "maternal sensitivity," or responsiveness toward their children, than stay-at-home mothers. Those positives canceled out the negatives.

The study may bring hope to working mothers, who have labored under a collective societal guilt since the 2002 publication of landmark research showing that early maternal employment hampered child development. The same research team behind that report produced this one.

"We can say now, from this study, what we couldn't say before: There's a slight risk, and here's the three things that you, Mom, can do to make a difference," said Jeanne Brooks-Gunn, the lead author. "This particular research has a positive message for mothers that the earlier research didn't."

The study, "First-Year Maternal Employment and Child Development in the First 7 Years," reaffirms the now-established point that women who work full time in the first year of motherhood risk mild developmental harm to their children. Part-time employment has no negative effect, nor does it matter whether a mother works full time after the first year.

The reason may be that a mother with a full-time job cannot provide an infant "the kinds of intensive interaction that babies require," needs that diminish in the toddler years, Brooks-Gunn said. High-quality child care, too, is hard to find for an infant.

The new study is "every bit as important as you might think," because it suggests mothers can decide, without guilt, "whether they want to stay home with their children," said Greg Duncan, a scholar at the University of California at Irvine, who is president of the Society for Research in Child Development.

DANIEL DE VISE is higher education reporter at *The Washington Post* and author of the College Inc. blog. He has worked as a journalist for 20 years, including stints at the Boca Raton News, Long Beach Press-Telegram, San Diego Union Tribune, and Miami Herald.

EXPLORING THE ISSUE

Does Maternal Employment Have Negative Effects on Children's Development?

Critical Thinking and Reflection

1. de Vise talks about how the study he describes identifies the guilt that working mothers may face. In your opinion, what is society's role in that guilt?
2. What are some creative ways that you can identify that would allow moms who want to stay home to raise their children to do so, as well as to give social support to those moms who want to work outside the home?
3. What do you consider to be the biggest influence on mothers' decision making about whether or not they should work outside of the home?

Is There Common Ground?

Each reading in this issue centers around a research group at Columbia University. Some of the information is hopeful, and some of it is bothersome. Yet, the researchers all recognize that many mothers must work and therefore must work to mitigate any potential negative effects that their working may have on their children.

Families must have discussions about the type of care that they want for their children, and how they can accommodate their lifestyles to obtain that care. And, society must take action to support mothers in whatever choice they make by providing quality child care for those who work and supportive leave policies and social support systems for those who do not.

Additional Resources

Columbia University School of Social Work. (2010). New Evidence on First-Year Maternal Employment and Child Outcomes. Retrieved on March 8, 2011, from www.columbia.edu/cu/ssw/news/jul10/maternity.html

An article posted on the Internet that provides a more nuanced understanding of how maternal employment might impact children.

Parenthood in America. (1998). The Effects of the Mother's Employment on the Family and the Child. Retrieved on March 8, 2011, from http://parenthood.library.wisc.edu/Hoffman/Hoffman.html#top

An article posted on the Internet that provides information on maternal employment trends throughout the years and discusses multiple factors that impact the effects of maternal employment on children.

Create Central

www.mhhe.com/createcentral

Internet References . . .

Selected, Edited, and with Issue Framing Material by:
Kourtney Vaillancourt, *New Mexico State University*

ISSUE

Should Parents Be Able to Genetically Engineer Their Children?

YES: **Richard Alleyne**, from "Genetically Engineering 'Ethical' Babies Is a Moral Obligation, Says Oxford Professor," *The Telegraph* (August 2012)

NO: **Bill McKibben**, from "Designer Genes," *Orion Magazine* (May/June 2003)

Learning Outcomes

After reading this issue, you should be able to:

- Describe the reasons for genetically engineering children.
- Discuss some of the ethical issues associated with genetic engineering.
- Summarize the vision of genetic engineers.

ISSUE SUMMARY

YES: Richard Alleyne reports on an expert in practical ethics and his argument that it is a moral obligation for parents to pursue genetically engineering children who are superior by identifying and removing genes associated with problem behaviors. The argument indicates that doing so will benefit society by producing more intelligent and less violent children.

NO: Bill McKibben discusses the vision of genetic engineers and some of the ways that genes can be modified to "improve" a human. He argues that the technology is not perfected, thus it may contain flaws. Additionally, he argues that much of the humanity within people stands to be lost if scientists begin to interfere with human nature.

With advances in genetic research, including being able to identify which genes contribute to characteristics such as aggression and intelligence, society's debate over the possiblity of replicating more favorable attributes in unborn children is becoming even more heated.

On the one hand, if we were able to identify genes that might cause someone to develop an incurable disease and shut them off, the potential to save lives is pretty appealing. And, if we are able to determine the personality and attributes of children when they are being created, we might be able to realize a more perfect society. On the other hand, the potential for the science to still have kinks that have not been worked out is pretty big. And, there are those that argue that "creating" babies in a lab goes against nature.

So, is genetically engineering children morally and ethically wrong? Is the potential benefit to families and society worth the risks that come along? Could our society ever truly get to a point of utopia where there is peace because everyone's "violent" genes have been turned off?

As you read the following selections, try to suspend the personal attitudes about this issue that you may have developed. Try to learn about the process, what it truly is intended to do, and what it could possibly accomplish. In addition, consider what could be the consequences of allowing this. Some questions to consider include the following: Would we be better off if the federal government decided to fund genetic engineering research to help regulate it? Would we be better off if this was banned completely and totally?

In the following selections, Richard Alleyne discusses the argument that there is a moral obligation for us to pursue this technology, in order to form a more intelligent and less violent society. He describes practical ethics professor Julain Savulescu's argument in favor of this issue. Bill McKibben contends that the technology is not perfected and may never come to a point where a "new version" isn't going to come along. He also discusses the potential loss of the human process that can occur when babies are created rather than conceived.

YES

Richard Alleyne

Genetically Engineering 'Ethical' Babies Is a Moral Obligation, Says Oxford Professor

Genetically screening our offspring to make them better people is just 'responsible parenting,' claims an eminent Oxford academic.

Professor Julian Savulescu said that creating so-called designer babies could be considered a "moral obligation" as it makes them grow up into "ethically better children."

The expert in practical ethics said that we should actively give parents the choice to screen out personality flaws in their children as it meant they were then less likely to "harm themselves and others."

The academic, who is also editor-in-chief of the *Journal of Medical Ethics,* made his comments in an article in the latest edition of *Reader's Digest.*

He explained that we are now in the middle of a genetic revolution and that although screening, for all but a few conditions, remained illegal it should be welcomed.

He said that science is increasingly discovering that genes have a significant influence on personality—with certain genetic markers in embryo suggesting future characteristics.

By screening in and screening out certain genes in the embryos, it should be possible to influence how a child turns out.

In the end, he said that "rational design" would help lead to a better, more intelligent and less violent society in the future.

"Surely trying to ensure that your children have the best, or a good enough, opportunity for a great life is responsible parenting?" wrote Prof Savulescu, the Uehiro Professor in practical ethics.

"So where genetic selection aims to bring out a trait that clearly benefits an individual and society, we should allow parents the choice.

"To do otherwise is to consign those who come after us to the ball and chain of our squeamishness and irrationality.

"Indeed, when it comes to screening out personality flaws, such as potential alcoholism, psychopathy and disposition to violence, you could argue that people have a moral obligation to select ethically better children.

"They are, after all, less likely to harm themselves and others."

"If we have the power to intervene in the nature of our offspring—rather than consigning them to the natural lottery—then we should."

He said that we already routinely screen embryos and foetuses for conditions such as cystic fibrosis and Down's syndrome and couples can test embryos for inherited bowel and breast cancer genes.

Rational design is just a natural extension of this, he said.

He said that unlike the eugenics movements, which fell out of favour when it was adopted by the Nazis, the system would be voluntary and allow parents to choose the characteristics of their children.

"We're routinely screening embryos and foetuses for conditions such as cystic fibrosis and Down's syndrome, and there's little public outcry," he said.

"What's more, few people protested at the decisions in the mid-2000s to allow couples to test embryos for inherited bowel and breast cancer genes, and this pushes us a lot closer to creating designer humans."

"Whether we like it or not, the future of humanity is in our hands now. Rather than fearing genetics, we should embrace it. We can do better than chance."

RICHARD ALLEYNE is a senior general news reporter for *The Daily Telegraph* in London.

Bill McKibben

 **NO**

Designer Genes

Lured by the prospect of making better babies, we stand on the threshold of changing forever what it means to be human.

I grew up in a household where we were very suspicious of dented cans. Dented cans were, according to my mother, a well-established gateway to botulism, and botulism was a bad thing, worse than swimming immediately after lunch. It was one of those bad things measured in extinctions, as in "three tablespoons of botulism toxin could theoretically kill every human on Earth." Or something like that. . . .

The vision of genetic engineers is to do to humans what we have already done to salmon and wheat, pine trees and tomatoes. That is, to make them better in some way; to delete, modify, or add genes in developing embryos so that the cells of the resulting person will produce proteins that make them taller and more muscular, or smarter and less aggressive, maybe handsome and possibly straight. Even happy. As early as 1993, a March of Dimes poll found that forty-three percent of Americans would engage in genetic engineering "simply to enhance their children's looks or intelligence."

Ethical guidelines promulgated by the scientific oversight boards so far prohibit actual attempts at human genetic engineering, but researchers have walked right to the line, maybe even stuck their toes a trifle over. In the spring of 2001, for instance, a fertility clinic in New Jersey impregnated fifteen women with embryos fashioned from their own eggs, their partner's sperm, and a small portion of an egg donated by a second woman. The procedure was designed to work around defects in the would-be mother's egg—but in at least two of the cases, tests showed the resulting babies carried genetic material from all three "parents."

And so the genetic modification of humans is not only possible, it's coming fast; a mix of technical progress and shifting mood means it could easily happen in the next few years. Consider what happened with plants. A decade ago, university research farms were growing small plots of genetically modified grain and vegetables. Sometimes activists who didn't like what they were doing would come and rip the plants up, one by one. Then, all of a sudden in the mid-1990s, before anyone had paid any real attention, farmers had planted half the corn and soybean fields in America with transgenic seed.

Every time you turn your back this technology creeps a little closer. Gallops, actually, growing and spreading as fast as the internet. One moment you've sort of heard of it; the next moment it's everywhere. But we haven't done it yet. For the moment we remain, if barely, a fully human species. And so we have time yet to consider, to decide, to act. This is arguably the biggest decision humans will ever make.

Right up until this decade, the genes that humans carried in their bodies were exclusively the result of chance—of how the genes of the sperm and the egg, the father and the mother, combined. The only way you could intervene in the process was by choosing who you would mate with—and that was as much wishful thinking as anything else, as generation upon generation of surprised parents have discovered.

But that is changing. We now know two different methods to change human genes. The first, and less controversial, is called somatic gene therapy. Somatic gene therapy begins with an existing individual—someone with, say, cystic fibrosis. Researchers try to deliver new, modified genes to some of her cells, usually by putting the genes aboard viruses they inject into the patient, hoping that the viruses will infect the cells and thereby transmit the genes. Somatic gene therapy is, in other words, much like medicine. You take an existing patient with an existing condition, and you in essence try and convince her cells to manufacture the medicine she needs. . . .

But all this work will require one large change in our current way of doing business. Instead of making babies by making love, we will have to move conception to the laboratory. You need to have the embryo out there where you can work on it—to make the necessary copies, try to add or delete genes, and then implant the one that seems likely to turn out best. Gregory Stock, a researcher at the University of California and an apostle of the new genetic technologies, says that "the union of egg and sperm from two individual . . . would be too unpredictable with intercourse." And once you've got the embryo out on the lab bench, gravity disappears altogether. "Ultimately," says Michael West, CEO of Advanced Cell Technology, the firm furthest out on the cutting edge of these technologies, "the dream of biologists is to have the sequence of DNA, the programming code of life, and to be able to edit it the way you can a document on a word processor." . . .

Here's one small example. In the 1980s, two drug companies were awarded patents to market human growth hormone to the few thousand American children

McKibben, Bill. From *Orion Magazine*, May/June 2003, pp. 1–8 (Edited). Copyright © 2003 by Bill McKibben. Reprinted by permission of the author.

suffering from dwarfism. The FDA thought the market would be very small, so HGH was given "orphan drug status," a series of special market advantages designed to reward the manufacturers for taking on such an unattractive business. But within a few years, HGH had become one of the largest-selling drugs in the country, with half a billion dollars in sales. This was not because there'd been a sharp increase in the number of dwarves, but because there'd been a sharp increase in the number of parents who wanted to make their slightly short children taller. Before long the drug companies were arguing that the children in the bottom five percent of their normal height range were in fact in need of three to five shots a week of HGH. Take eleven-year-old Marco Oriti. At four foot one, he was about four inches shorter than average, and projected to eventually top out at five foot four. This was enough to convince his parents to start on a six-day-a-week HGH regimen, which will cost them $150,000 over the next four years. "You want to give your child the edge no matter what," said his mother.

A few of the would-be parents out on the current cutting edge of the reproduction revolution—those who need to obtain sperm or eggs for in vitro fertilization—exhibit similar zeal. Ads started appearing in Ivy League college newspapers a few years ago: couples were willing to pay $50,000 for an egg, provided the donor was at least five feet, ten inches tall, white, and had scored 1400 on her SATs. There is, in other words, a market just waiting for the first clinic with a catalogue of germline modifications, a market that two California artists proved when they opened a small boutique. Gene Genies Worldwide, in a trendy part of Pasadena. Tran Kim-Trang and Karl Mihail wanted to get people thinking more deeply about these emerging technologies, so they outfitted their store with petri dishes and models of the double helix, and printed up brochures highlighting traits with genetic links: creativity, extroversion, thrill-seeking criminality. When they opened the doors, they found people ready to shell out for designer families (one man insisted he wanted the survival ability of a cockroach). The "store" was meant to be ironic, but the irony was lost on a culture so deeply consumer that this kind of manipulation seems like the obvious next step. "Generally, people refused to believe this store was an art project," says Tran. And why not? The next store in the mall could easily have been a Botox salon. . . .

"For all his billions, Bill Gates could not have purchased a single genetic enhancement for his son Rory John," writes Gregory Stock, at the University of California. "And you can bet that any enhancements a billion dollars can buy Rory's child in 2030 will seem crude alongside those available for modest sums in 2060." It's not, he adds, "so different from upgraded software. You'll want the new release."

The vision of one's child as a nearly useless copy of Windows 95 should make parents fight like hell to make sure we never get started down this path. But the vision gets lost easily in the gushing excitement about "improving" the opportunities for our kids. . . .

We try and shape the lives of our kids—to "improve" their lives, as we would measure improvement—but our gravity is usually weak enough that kids can break out of it if and when they need to. (When it isn't, when parents manage to bend their children to the point of breaking, we think of them as monstrous.) "Many of the most creative and valuable human lives are the result of particularly difficult struggles" against expectation and influence, writes the legal scholar Martha Nussbaum.

That's not how a genetic engineer thinks of his product. He works to ensure absolute success. Last spring an Israeli researcher announced that he had managed to produce a featherless chicken. This constituted an improvement, to his mind, because "it will be cheaper to produce since its lack of feathers means there is no need to pluck it before it hits the shelves." Also, poultry farmers would no longer have to ventilate their vast barns to keep their birds from overheating. "Feathers are a waste," the scientist explained. "The chickens are using feed to produce something that has to be dumped, and the farmers have to waste electricity to overcome that fact." Now, that engineer was not trying to influence his chickens to shed their feathers because they'd be happier and the farmer would be happier and everyone would be happier. He was inserting a gene that created a protein that made good and certain they would not be producing feathers. Just substitute, say, an even temperament for feathers, and you'll know what the human engineers envision. . . .

Say the gene work went a little awry and left you with a kid who had some serious problems; what kind of guilt would that leave you with? Remember, this is not a child created by the random interaction of your genes with those of your partner, this is a child created with specific intent. Does Consumer Reports start rating the various biotech offerings?. . .

These new technologies show us that human meaning dangles by a far thinner thread than we had thought. If germline genetic engineering ever starts, it will accelerate endlessly and unstoppably into the future, as individuals make the calculation that they have no choice but to equip their kids for the world that's being made. The first child whose genes come in part from some corporate lab, the first child who has been "enhanced" from what came before—that's the first child who will glance back over his shoulder and see a gap between himself and human history. . . .

These new technologies, however, are not yet inevitable. Unlike global warming, this genie is not yet out of the bottle. But if germline genetic engineering is going to be stopped, it will have to happen now, before it's quite begun. It will have to be a political choice, that is—one we make not as parents but as citizens, not as individuals but as a whole, thinking not only about our own offspring but about everyone.

So far the discussion has been confined to a few scientists, a few philosophers, a few ideologues. It needs to spread widely, and quickly, and loudly. The stakes are absurdly high, nothing less than the meaning of being human. And given the seductions that we've seen—the intuitively and culturally delicious prospect of a better child—the arguments against must be not only powerful but also deep. They'll need to resonate on the same intuitive and cultural level. We'll need to feel in our gut the reasons why, this time, we should tell Prometheus thanks, but no thanks.

BILL MCKIBBEN's first book, *The End of Nature*, has now appeared in twenty foreign editions. His essay in this issue is excerpted from his 2003 book, *Enough: Staying Human in an Engineered Age*, published this spring by Times Books, an imprint of Henry Holt and Company, and reprinted by permission. He lives with his wife, writer Sue Halpern, and daughter in Vermont. His *Orion* column, "Small Change," appears three times a year.

EXPLORING THE ISSUE

Should Parents Be Able to Genetically Engineer Their Children?

Critical Thinking and Reflection

1. One factor that people argue about related to genetic engineering is who determines who has the right to select what is "favorable" and not. What do you think would be necessary to regulate the technology so that someone didn't, for example, genetically engineer an army of super-humans who could dominate a society?
2. Many people have previous ideas about genetic engineering from what they have heard on television or read in magazine articles. Think about the previous notions that you had about the issue and what you learned from these articles that you did not previously know. Did either of these articles change your position?

Is There Common Ground?

The future will ultimately tell us whether we will make a mistake by either allowing genetic engineering and tampering with the natural order of things or by dismissing it as science fiction and consequently watching many people die whose lives could have been saved.

Create Central

www.mhhe.com/createcentral

Additional Resources

Nature Education. Human Genetic Engineering. Retrieved on May 21, 2013, from www.nature .com/scitable/topicpage/genetic-inequality-human-genetic-engineering-768

Association for Reproductive Health Professionals. Human Cloning and Genetic Modification. Retrieved on May 21, 2013, from www.arhp .org/publications-and-resources/patient-resources/ printed-materials/cloning

Bright Hub. Pros and Cons of Genetic Engineering in Humans. Retrieved on May 21, 2013 from www .brighthub.com/science/genetics/articles/22210.aspx

Internet Reference . . .

Intelligence Squared Podcast

http://www.npr.org/2013/02/15/172137776/should-we -prohibit-genetically-engineered-babies

Selected, Edited, and with Issue Framing Material by:
Kourtney Vaillancourt, *New Mexico State University*

ISSUE

Do Federal Laws Make Transracial Adoptions More Commonplace?

YES: Ezra E. H. Griffith and Rachel L. Bergeron, from "Cultural Stereotypes Die Hard: The Case of Transracial Adoption," *The Journal of the American Academy of Psychiatry and the Law* (2006)

NO: Elizabeth Bartholet and Diane H. Schetky, from "Commentary: Cultural Stereotypes Can and Do Die: It's Time to Move on with Transracial Adoption," *The Journal of the American Academy of Psychiatry and the Law* (November 3, 2006)

Learning Outcomes

After reading this issue, you should be able to:

- Describe some of the reasons that adoptions are necessary in America.
- Discuss the reasons that transracial adoptions might be preferable to institutional care.
- Discuss the arguments against transracial adoption, specifically what researchers argue the challenges might be.

ISSUE SUMMARY

YES: Ezra Griffith and Rachel Bergeron, formerly professors at Harvard Law School, suggest that there is a cultural preference for race matching in adoptions. As a result, federal statutory attempts to omit race as a factor in child placement decisions have not been effective.

NO: Elizabeth Bartholet, the Morris Wasserstein Professor of Law and faculty director of the Child Advocacy Program at the Harvard Law School, and Diane Schetky, clinical professor of psychiatry at the Maine Medical Center, state that the current law is clear and effective in prohibiting adoptions based on race. They suggest that in the future, the need for legislation in this area will diminish even further.

Our society has always preferred finding loving and caring adoptive parents for children rather than placing them in institutions. A family unit not only socializes a child but provides a child with nurturance, a sense of security, and unconditional love. Unfortunately, there are hundreds of thousands of children in America who, for various reasons, are not with their biological families. These children are mostly nonwhite, minority children. Although the research literature suggests that, regardless of the race of the parents or children, all children do better in adoptive families than in institutions, there still seems to be a "concern" about placing children transracially.

Transracial adoption typically refers to a family in which a minority child (e.g., Asian American, Native American, African American, or Latino) or a child with a mixed racial background is adopted by an Anglo-American couple. These adoptions account for about 15 percent of all adoptions in the United States annually. Due to world events, transracial adoption became more commonplace in the United States in the late 1940s. Children with mixed backgrounds came from Europe and Asia after World War II. After the Korean War, Korean American children and refugee Chinese children were adopted by Anglo-American couples in the United States. Finding adoptive homes for Native American children followed. The movement to place African American children with Anglo-American families is the most recent evolution of transracial adoption.

The Multi-Ethnic Placement Act of 1994 and the 1996 amendments to that act forbade using race as a sole factor when determining if a family can adopt a child. The National Association of Black Social Workers (NABSW) strongly opposes transracial adoption because they believe the adopted child will have many problems dealing with his or her ethnic identity or ethnic community. Other organizations disagree and base their support of transracial adoptions on the principle of adoption being in the best interest of the child. The only time a transracial adoption process can be delayed because of race is if mental health professionals determine the prospective adoptee is a special case and an intra-racial adoption is in that child's best interest. It should be noted that there is virtually no information related to the issue of minority families adopting white children. This has occurred, but only in rare instances over the generations. Although it is likely that the research literature would come to similar conclusions about the welfare of these adopted children, there is a need for research on this type of transracial adoption as well. At this time it is not possible to say if society could embrace such adoptions without any "concern."

The following two sections describe the debate between restricting transracial adoptions and making transracial adoptions more commonplace via federal law. Despite the law, should race be a factor that is considered in adoption? Do you agree that attitudes and trends *have* changed and the controversy over transracial adoptions is no longer as large an issue as it was a decade or two ago?

**Ezra E. H. Griffith and
Rachel L. Bergeron**

Cultural Stereotypes Die Hard:
The Case of Transracial Adoption

The adoption of black children by white families, commonly referred to as transracial adoption in the lay and professional literature, is the subject of a debate that has persisted in American society for a long time. On one side of the divide are those who believe that black children are best raised by black families. On the other are the supporters of the idea that race-matching in adoption does not necessarily serve the best interests of the child and that it promotes racial discrimination.

Coming as it does in the midst of myriad other discussions in this country about black-white interactions, transracial adoption has occupied an important place in any debate about adoption policy. But in addition, as can be seen in language utilized by the Fifth Circuit Court in a 1977 case, there is a long-held belief that since family members resemble one another, it follows that members of constructed families should also look like each other so as to facilitate successful adoption outcomes. . . .

In utilizing this language, the court acknowledged that transracial adoption ran counter to the cultural beliefs that many people held about the construction of families. Still, the court concluded that while the difficulties attending transracial adoption justified the consideration of race as a relevant factor in adoption proceedings, race could not be the sole factor considered. With a bow to both sides in the transracial adoption debate, the argument could only continue.

As the debate marches on, mental health professionals are being asked to provide expert opinions about whether it would be preferable for a particular black child to be raised by a black family or by a family or adult of a different ethnic or racial group. There are, of course, different scenarios that may lead to the unfolding of these adoption disputes. For example, the question may arise when a black child is put up for adoption after having spent a number of months or years in an out-of-home placement. The lengthy wait of black children for an adoptive black family may understandably increase the likelihood of a transracial adoption. In another situation, the death of a biracial child's parents, one of whom was white and the other black, may lead to competition between the white and black grandparents for the right to raise the child. In a third possible context, the divorce of an interracial couple may result in a legal struggle for custody of the biracial child, with race trumpeted at least as an important factor if not the crucial factor to be considered in the decision about who should raise the child. . . .

We have already alluded to two significant factors that have played a role in the evolution of adoption policy concerning black children, particularly with respect to the question of whether race-neutral approaches make sense and whether transracial adoption is good practice. One factor has been judicial decision-making. In a relatively recent review, Hollinger reminded us that, in general, racial classifications are invalidated unless they can survive the "strict scrutiny" test, which requires meeting a compelling governmental interest. Hollinger suggested that the "best-interest-of-the-child" standard commonly used in adoption practice would serve a substantial governmental interest. Such argumentation would allow the consideration of race as one element in an adoption evaluation. Following this reasoning, while race-neutral adoption may be a lofty objective, the specific needs of a particular child could legally allow the consideration of race.

The second factor to influence the evolution of adoption policy in this arena has been the academic research on transracial adoption. This work has cumulatively demonstrated that black children can thrive and develop strong racial identities when nurtured in families with white parents. Transracially adopted children also do well on standard measures of self-esteem, cognitive development, and educational achievement. However, neither judicial decision-making nor scholarly research has settled the debate on transracial adoption policy.

In this article, we focus on a third factor that emerged as another mechanism meant to deal with transracial adoptions and the influential race-matching principle. These statutory efforts started with the Multiethnic Placement Act, which Hollinger stated "was enacted in 1994 amid spirited and sometimes contentious debate about transracial adoption and same-race placement policies." We will point out that even though the statutory attempts were meant to eliminate race as a controlling factor in the adoption process, their implementation has left room for ambiguity regarding the role that race should play in adoption proceedings. Consequently, even though the statutes were intended to eliminate adoption delays and denials because of race-matching, they may have allowed the continued existence of a cultural stereotype—that black children

Griffith, Ezra E.H.; Bergeron, Rachel L. From *The Journal of the American Academy of Psychiatry and the Law*, vol. 34, no. 3, 2006, pp. 303–314 (edited). Copyright © 2006 by American Academy of Psychiatry and the Law. Reprinted by permission via S&S Management Services, Inc.

belong with black families—and may have facilitated its continued existence. This article is therefore principally about statutory attempts in the past decade to influence public policy concerning transracial adoption. Secondarily, we shall comment on potential implications of these developments for the practice of adoption evaluations. . . .

Brief Review of Race-Matching in Adoption

Feelings about who should raise a black child have run high in the United States for a long time. These feelings come from different groups for different reasons. Kennedy presented a number of historical cases to illustrate this. Among the cases he described, Kennedy told the early 1900s story of a white girl who was found residing with a black family. The authorities concluded that the child had been kidnapped and rescued her. They then placed her with a white family. When it was learned later that the child was black, she was returned to the black family because it was not proper for the black child to be living with a white family. This case, along with others described by Kennedy, is part of the fabric of American racism and racial separatist practices. Kennedy also pointed to the practice during slavery of considering "the human products of interracial sexual unions" as unambiguously black and the mandate that they be reared within the black slave community as an attempt to undermine any possibility of interracial parenting.

Whites have not been the only ones to support the stance of race-matching—the belief that black or white children belong with their own group. In 1972, the National Association of Black Social Workers (NABSW) stated unambiguously that white families should never be allowed to adopt black children. The NABSW opposed transracial adoption for two main reasons: the Association claimed that transracial adoption prevents black children from forming a strong racial identity, and it prevents them from developing survival skills necessary to deal with a racist society.

Since its 1972 statement, the NABSW has remained steadfast in its opposition to transracial adoption. In testimony before the Senate Committee on Labor and Human Resources in 1985, the President of the NABSW reiterated the Association's position and stated that the NABSW viewed the placement of black children in white homes as a hostile act against the black community, considering it a blatant form of race and cultural genocide.

In 1991, the NABSW reaffirmed its position that black children should not be placed with white parents under any circumstances, stating that even the most loving and skilled white parent could not avoid doing irreparable harm to an African-American child. In its 1994 position paper on the preservation of African-American families, the NABSW indicated that, in placement decisions regarding a black child, priority should be given to adoption by biological relatives and then to black families. Transracial adoption "should only be considered after documented evidence of unsuccessful same race placements has been reviewed and supported by appropriate representatives of the African American community." . . .

Race-matching has been and remains an influential and controversial concept regarding how best to construct adoptive families. Matching, in general, has been a classic principle of adoption practice, governing non-relative adoptions for much of the 20th century. Its goal was to create families in which the adoptive parents looked as though they could be the adopted child's biological parents. Matching potential adoptive parents and children on as many physical, emotional, and cultural characteristics as possible was seen as a way of insuring against adoptive failure. It was not uncommon for potential adoptive parents to be denied the possibility of adoption if their hair and eye color did not match those of a child in need of adoption. Differences among family members in constructed families were seen as threats to the integration of an adopted child and the child's identification with the adoptive parents. Race, along with religion, was considered the most important characteristic to be matched, and it continued to be important even as the matching concept regarding other characteristics began to shift. . . .

Matching, of course, continued to influence child placement decisions outside of adoption agencies, as evidenced by the comments of the Drummond court. Following that court's decision, the general rule has been that trial courts may consider race as a factor in adoption proceedings as long as race is not the sole determinant.

Statutory Attempts at Remedies

. . . The Black Social Workers had a quick and striking effect on transracial adoption policy. Following the appearance of the paper, adoption agencies, both public and private, either implemented race-matching approaches or used the NABSW position to justify already existing race-matching policies. As a result, the number of transracial adoptions were estimated to drop significantly—39 percent within one year of the publication of the NABSW statement. Although robust data were lacking, it was thought that the number and length of stay of black children in out-of-home placements increased as social workers and other foster care and adoption professionals, believing that same-race placements were in the best interest of the child, searched for same-race foster and adoptive parents. Agencies and their workers had considerable discretion in deciding the role race played in placement decisions. States, while generally requiring that foster care and adoption decisions be made in the best interest of the child, varied in their directions regarding the extent to which race, culture, and ethnicity should be taken into account in making the best-interest determination.

While race-matching policies were not the sole determinant of increasing numbers of black children in institutions and out-of-home placements, there was growing concern that such policies, with their focus on same-race placement and their exclusion of consideration of loving, permanent interracial homes, kept black children from being adopted. Because he was concerned that race had become the determining factor in adoption placements and that children were languishing in foster care homes and institutions, Senator Howard Metzenbaum introduced legislation to prohibit the use of race as the sole determinant of placement. Senator Metzenbaum believed that same-race adoption was the preferable option for a child, but he also believed that transracial placement was far preferable to a child's remaining in foster care when an appropriate same-race placement was not available.

Multiethnic Placement Act

Congress passed the Howard Metzenbaum Multiethnic Placement Act (MEPA) and President Clinton signed it into law on October 20, 1994. MEPA's main goals were to decrease the length of time children had to wait to be adopted; to prevent discrimination based on race in the placement of children into adoptive or foster homes; and to recruit culturally diverse and minority adoptive and foster families who could meet the needs of children needing placement. In passing MEPA, Congress was concerned that many children, especially those from minority groups, were spending lengthy periods in foster care awaiting adoption placements. Congress found, within the parameters of available data, that nearly 500,000 children were in foster care in the United States; tens of thousands of these children were waiting for adoption; two years and eight months was the median length of time children waited to be adopted; and minority children often waited twice as long as other children to be adopted.

Under MEPA, an agency or entity receiving federal funds could not use race as the sole factor in denying any person the opportunity to become an adoptive or foster parent. Furthermore, an agency could not use race as a single factor to delay or deny the placement of a child in an adoptive or foster care family or to otherwise discriminate in making a placement decision. However, an agency could consider a child's racial, cultural, and ethnic background as one of several factors—not the sole factor—used to determine the best interests of the child. . . .

So, under MEPA, agencies could consider a child's race, ethnicity, or culture as one of a number of factors used to determine the best interests of the child, as long as it was not the sole factor considered, and they could consider the ability of prospective parents to meet the needs of a child of a given race, ethnicity, or culture.

Following the passage of MEPA, the Department of Health and Human Services (DHHS), Office of Civil Rights, provided policy guidance to assist agencies receiving federal financial assistance in complying with MEPA. The guidance permitted agencies receiving federal assistance to consider race, culture, or ethnicity as factors in making placement decisions to the extent allowed by MEPA, the

U.S. Constitution and Title VI of the Civil Rights Act of 1964.

Under the Equal Protection Clause of the Fourteenth Amendment, laws or practices drawing distinctions on the basis of race are inherently suspect and subject to strict scrutiny analysis. To pass such analysis, classifications or practices based on race have to be narrowly tailored to meet a compelling state interest. The Supreme Court has not specifically addressed the question of transracial adoption. It has considered race as a factor in a child placement decision in the context of a custody dispute between two white biological parents when the mother, who had custody of the child, began living with a black man, whom she later married. The Court found the goal of granting custody on the basis of the best interests of the child to be "indisputably a substantial government interest for purposes of the Equal Protection Clause." The DHHS guidance on the use of race, color or national origin as factors in adoption and foster care placements addressed the relevant constitutional issues and indicated that the only compelling state interest in the context of child placement decisions is protecting the best interests of the child who is to be placed. So, under MEPA, consideration of race or ethnicity was permitted as long as it was narrowly tailored to advance a specific child's best interests. Agencies receiving federal funds could consider race and ethnicity when making placement decisions only if the agency made a narrowly tailored, individualized determination that the facts and circumstances of a particular case required the contemplation of race or ethnicity to advance the best interests of the child in need of placement. Agencies could not assume that race, ethnicity, or culture was at issue in every case and make general policies that applied to all children. The guidance also specifically prohibited policies that established periods during which same-race searches were conducted, created placement preference hierarchies based on race, ethnicity, or culture, required social workers to justify transracial placement decisions or resulted in delayed placements to find a family of a particular race, ethnicity, or culture.

The DHHS policy guidance did address MEPA's permissible consideration of the racial, cultural, or ethnic background of a child and the capacity of the prospective foster or adoptive parents to meet the needs of a child of this background as one of a number of factors in the best-interest-of-the-child determination. The guidance allowed agencies to assess the ability of a specific potential adoptive family to meet a specific child's needs related to his or her racial, ethnic, or cultural background, as long as the assessment was done in the context of an individualized assessment. . . .

However, agencies were not allowed to make decisions based on general assumptions regarding the needs of children of a specific race, ethnicity, or culture or about the ability of prospective parents of a specific race, ethnicity, or culture to care or nurture the identity of a child of a different race, ethnicity, or culture.

To increase the pool of potential foster or adoptive parents, MEPA also required states to develop plans for the recruitment of potential foster and adoptive families that reflected the ethnic and racial diversity of the children needing placement. The recruitment efforts had to be focused on providing all eligible children with the opportunity for placement and on providing all qualified members of the community with an opportunity to become an adoptive or foster parent. As a result, while MEPA sought in a reasonable way to recruit a broad racial and cultural spectrum of adoptive families, the law was at the same time underlining the idea that there was something special about a black child's being raised by a black family.

Those who objected to the permissive consideration of race in MEPA asserted that it allowed agencies to continue to delay adoptions of minority children based on race concerns. They also argued that race-matching policies could and did continue under MEPA. Social workers could, for example, use race as a factor to support a finding that a transracial adoption was not in a given child's best interest. Supporters of MEPA reached their own conclusion that it did not accomplish its goal of speeding up the adoption process and moving greater numbers of minority children into foster care or adoption placements and that the permissive consideration of race allowed agencies legitimately to continue race-matching to deny or delay the placement of minority children with white adoptive parents. Senator Metzenbaum himself agreed with this conclusion about MEPA and worked for its repeal. As we shall see later, the arguments and counterarguments about the effectiveness of MEPA were being made in the absence of robust data.

The Interethnic Adoption Provisions

MEPA was repealed when on August 20, 1996, President Clinton signed the Small Business Job Protection Act of 1996. Section 1808 of the Act was entitled "Removal of Barriers to Interethnic Adoption" (The Interethnic Adoption Provisions; IEP). MEPA's permissible consideration provision was removed and its language changed. . . .

Under the IEP, states were still required to "provide for the diligent recruitment of potential foster and adoptive families that reflect the ethnic and racial diversity of children in the State for whom foster and adoptive homes are needed."

Failure to comply with MEPA was a violation of Title VI of the Civil Rights Act of 1964; failure to comply with the IEP is also a violation of Title VI. Under MEPA, an agency receiving federal assistance that discriminated in its child placement decisions on the basis of race and failed to comply with the Act could forfeit its federal assistance and an aggrieved individual had the right to bring an action seeking equitable relief in federal court or could file a complaint with the Office of Civil Rights. The IEP added enforcement provisions that specified graduated fiscal sanctions to be imposed by DHHS against states found to be in violation of the law and gave any individual aggrieved by a violation the right to bring an action against the state or other entity in federal court.

The Department of Health and Human Services issued two documents to provide practical guidance for complying with the IEP: a memorandum and a document in question-and-answer format. According to the guidance, Congress, in passing the IEP, clarified its intent to eliminate delays in adoption or foster care placements when they were in any way avoidable. Race and ethnicity could not be used as the basis for any denial of placement nor used as a reason to delay a foster care or adoptive placement. The repeal of MEPA's "permissible consideration" provision was seen as confirming that strict scrutiny was the appropriate standard for consideration of race or ethnicity in adoption and foster care placements. DHHS argued that it had never taken the position that MEPA's permissible consideration language allowed agencies to take race into account routinely in making placement decisions because such a view would be inconsistent with a strict scrutiny standard. It reaffirmed that any decision to consider race as a necessary element in a placement decision has to be based on concerns arising out of the circumstances of the particular situation. . . .

The guidance again made clear that the best interest of the child is the standard to be used in making placement decisions. So, according to the guidance, the IEP prohibits the routine practice of taking race and ethnicity into consideration ("Public agencies may not routinely consider race, national origin, and ethnicity in making placement decisions"), but it allows for the consideration of race, national origin, and ethnicity in certain specific situations ("Any consideration of these factors must be done on an individualized basis where special circumstances indicate that their consideration is warranted"). Once again, such language seems to suggest that, in certain contexts, the adoptive child may well benefit from placement in a same-race family.

The DHHS guidance seemed to frame the possibility for adoption agencies to continue the practice of race-matching. For example, while warning that assessment of a prospective parent's ability to serve as a foster or adoptive parent must not act as a racial or ethnic screen and indicating that considerations of race must not be routine in the assessment function, the guidance conceded that an important aspect of good social work is an individualized assessment of a prospective parent's ability to be an adoptive or foster parent. Thus, it allows for discussions with prospective adoptive or foster care parents about their feelings, preferences, and capacities regarding caring for a child of a particular race or ethnicity. . . .

Discussion

In considering the best interests of a child who is being placed for adoption, DHHS is suggesting that there could be special circumstances uniquely individualized to the child that require consideration of ethnicity and race of the potential adoptive parents. Presumably this should not be done routinely and should not be seen as serving as a proxy for a consistent and mundane contemplation of ethnicity or race in the adoption context. Undoubtedly, what constitutes special circumstances in the practices of any given adoption agency is likely to be a matter of interpretation. While agencies can readily assert what their routine practices are, much may turn on how vigorously supervised are the claims that special circumstances exist with respect to a particular black child that dictate consideration of ethnicity and race in that child's case. As a practical result, while it appears no one is now allowed to claim that every black child needs a black family, it may still be reasonable and practicable to claim that a black child requires adoption by a black family, as dictated by consideration of the best interests of that child. For example, Kennedy has raised the possibility that an older child might say he or she wanted to be adopted only by a black family. Such a context could indeed make it difficult for the child's wish to be refused outright, without any consideration whatsoever.

Such reasoning is articulated starting from the point of view of the child. Giving consideration to the interests of the potential adoptive parent is another matter. In other words, what should we consider about the adoptive parent's interest in raising black children and the parent's ability to do so? The opinions about this matter remain divided. Kennedy and Bartholet have proposed that prospective adoptive parents be allowed to state a preference for adopting a child from a particular ethnic group. This is, in their view, permissible race-matching that ultimately serves the best interests of the child. After all, what would be the use of forcing a family to adopt a child they really did not want? In addition, both authors also have argued that state intervention in such racial selectivity in the formation of families would be akin to imposing race-based rules on the creation of married couples. However, Banks has opposed this accommodationist stance, where in practice adoption agencies would simply show prospective adoptive parents only the class of ethnic children the adoptive parent was interested in adopting. Banks thought this merely perpetuated the status quo, as white adoptive parents had little interest in black children. This would result in black children's continuing to languish in out-of-home placements, and their time spent awaiting adoption would remain prolonged.

Kennedy and Bartholet were permissive in their attitude toward the racial selectivity of prospective adoptive parents, respecting parents' choice to construct families as they wish.

There has been and continues to be strong support for the belief that black children belong with black adoptive parents. It is not only the NABSW, which has called for the repeal of the IEP, that has taken this position. For example, in a 1998 letter to the Secretary of the Depart-

ment of Health and Human Services, a former executive director of the Child Welfare League of America strongly disagreed with the DHHS's interpretation of MEPA/IEP, stating that prohibiting any consideration of race in adoptive and foster care placement decisions contradicts best-practice standards in child welfare. . . .

The CWLA, in its most recent *Standards of Excellence for Adoption Services* (2000), reiterated its belief that race is to be considered in all adoptions and that placement with parents of the same race is the first choice for any child. Other placements should be considered only after a vigorous search for parents of the same race has failed. . . .

In its most recent policy statement on foster care and adoption (2003), the National Association of Social Workers also reiterated its position that consideration of race should play a central role in placement decisions. . . .

Others have espoused the view that inracial adoption is the preferred option for a black child because black families inherently possess the competence to raise children with strong black identities and the ability to cope with racism. While questions of cultural competence to raise a black child often arise about prospective white adoptive parents, no such questions are posed about prospective black adoptive parents. The competence of black families to raise black children is regularly referred to as though black families are culturally identical or homogeneous and all are equally competent to raise black children and equip them to live in our society. We may all think about black cultural competence as though it is a one-dimensional concept. Indeed, we may all be referring simply to stereotypical indicators of what we think it means to be black. We may be referring to our own personal preferences for the stereotypic activities of black people: involvement in a black church; participation in a community center where black-focused programs are operating; viewing movies with a clearly black theme; reading literature authored by blacks. What is rarely considered is that some black families are drawn to rap music, others to jazz greats, and still others to traditional classical music. Indeed, some families obviously manage to exhibit an interest in all these genres of music. With respect, therefore, to even these stereotyped indicators of what it means to be black, black families vary in the degree of their attachment to the indicators. This is to say that blacks differ in their level of commitment to the salience of black-oriented culture in their individual and family lives. As a result, there is considerable cultural heterogeneity among black families. Such variability may well lead to differences in black families' ways of coping with racism.

To date, the statutory attempts to deal with transracial adoptions have not been considered as spectacularly successful, especially in the case of MEPA. Nevertheless, efforts have been made to limit the routine consideration of race and ethnicity in adoption, with the result that black children may be remaining for shorter periods in undesirable out-of-home placements. (National data are not yet able to demonstrate clear trends.) However, DHHS guidance still permits consideration of race and ethnicity in specific cases, with the apparent concession that some black children may need a black family for the realization of the child's best interests.

The burden is on forensic psychiatrists and other mental health professionals who perform adoption evaluations to point out cogently and logically two points: first, whether race is a factor that is relevant in the adoption evaluation; and second, whether there is something unique or particular about that adoption context that requires race to be considered. It will require special argumentation for the evaluator to claim that a particular black child could benefit more from placement with a black family than with a non-black family. As stated earlier, the evidence is clear that black children can do well in transracial placements. The pointed objective, therefore, in future evaluations will be to show that a particular black child has such unique and special needs that he or she deserves particular consideration for placement in a black family. It will be interesting to see whether our forensic colleagues, in striving for objectivity, will consider the factor of race in their evaluations only when something unique about that particular adoption context cries out for race to be considered so that the best-interest-of-the-child standard can be met. It seems clear that forensic professionals must be careful not to state that they routinely consider race in their adoption evaluations unless they intend to argue clinically that race is always relevant. And even then, they should be cautious about not articulating a general preference for inracial over transracial adoptions.

Despite federal statutory attempts to remove race as a controlling factor in adoption and foster care placement decisions, the debate over transracial adoption is not over. Indeed, strains of the debate are evidenced in the statutes and their implementation guidelines and the argument continues among our mental health colleagues. . . .

EZRA E. H. GRIFFITH is deputy chair of clinical affairs and a professor of psychiatry and African American studies at Yale University, School of Medicine.

RACHEL L. BERGERON is an assistant clinical professor of psychiatry at Yale University, School of Medicine.

**Elizabeth Bartholet and
Diane H. Schetky**

 **NO**

Commentary: Cultural Stereotypes Can and Do Die: It's Time to Move on with Transracial Adoption

Ezra Griffith and Rachel Bergeron write in their article, "Cultural Stereotypes Die Hard: The Case of Transracial Adoption," that the controversy that has long surrounded transracial adoption is ongoing and that the law is significantly ambiguous. Accordingly, they say that psychiatrists and other mental health professionals are faced with a challenge in deciding on the role that race should play in adoption evaluations for purposes of foster and adoptive placement decisions.

I agree that the controversy is ongoing, but think that the law is much clearer than Griffith and Bergeron indicate and that it provides adequate guidance as to the very limited role that race is allowed to play. However, because of the ongoing controversy, many players in the child welfare system are committed to law resistance and law evasion. The challenge for mental health professionals is to decide how to respond to conflicting pressures and whether to use their professional skills to assist in good faith implementation of the law or in efforts to undermine the law. The challenge is a real one, because those committed to undermining the law do so in the name of the ever popular best-interests-of-the-child principle, arguing that best practices require consideration of race in placement decisions. However, in my view the choice should be clear, not simply because the law exists, but because the law takes the right position—right both for children and for the larger society.

Griffith and Bergeron acknowledge that, after a period in which race-matching was common and court-made law allowed at least some regular use of race in the placement process, the U.S. Congress passed laws governing these matters: the 1994 Multiethnic Placement Act and the 1996 amendments to that Act (here referred to collectively as MEPA and, when it is important to distinguish between the original 1994 Act and the amended Act, referred to as MEPA I and MEPA II, respectively). However they say that these laws "may still leave the door open to continued race-matching. . . ." They go on to say:

> [E]ven though the statutory attempts were meant to eliminate race as a controlling factor in the adoption process, their implementation has left

room for ambiguity regarding the role that race should play in adoption proceedings. Consequently, even though the statutes were intended to eliminate adoption delays and denials because of race-matching, they may have allowed the continued existence of a cultural stereotype—that black children belong with black families—and may have facilitated its continued existence.

Griffith and Bergeron accurately describe how MEPA I allowed the use of race as one factor in placement, so long as it was not used categorically to determine placement or to delay or deny placement:

> An agency . . . may consider the cultural, ethnic, or racial background of the child and the capacity of the prospective foster or adoptive parents to meet the needs of a child of this background as one of a number of factors used to determine the best interests of a child.

And they describe how MEPA II removed that section of the law, and made related amendments designed to limit the use of race. They note that the U.S. Department of Health and Human Services (DHHS), the MEPA enforcement agency, interprets the law to require strict scrutiny as the standard by which to judge use of race in placements and quote one of the guidance memoranda issued by DHHS. . . .

But they conclude that the DHHS guidance "seemed to frame the possibility for adoption agencies to continue the practice of race-matching," and "allows for discussions with prospective adoptive or foster care parents about their feelings, preferences, and capacities regarding caring for a child of a particular race or ethnicity." They go on to cite the positions of the National Association of Black Social Workers, the Child Welfare League of America, the National Association of Social Workers, and some others, all arguing for a systematic preference for race-matching.

While Griffith and Bergeron raise some questions about the wisdom of assumptions made by race-matching proponents that all blacks will be culturally competent to raise black children in a way that no whites will be, they conclude with a message that seems to emphasize the difficulty of the challenge faced by mental health professionals in deciding just how much weight to give race in their placement evaluations. They state that MEPA has not been considered "spectacularly successful," and that DHHS guidance permits some consideration of race in specific cases. . . .

In their final two paragraphs Griffith and Bergeron cite the Adoption and Race Work Group, assembled by the Stuart Foundation, as evidence of the ongoing debate within the mental health community, noting its conclusion that "race should not be ignored when making placement decisions and that children's best interests are served—all else being equal—when they are placed with families of the same racial, ethnic, and cultural background as their own."

There are several problems with the message that this article by Griffith and Bergeron sends to their colleagues. First, the law is much clearer than they indicate. MEPA II did, as they point out, eliminate the provision in MEPA I that had allowed race as a permissible consideration. MEPA II also eliminated related language indicating that some use of race might be permissible—language in MEPA I forbidding agencies to "categorically deny" placement, or delay or deny placement "solely" on the basis of race—and substituted language that tracked the language of other civil rights statutes, simply prohibiting discrimination. As I discuss elsewhere:

> The intent to remove race as a factor in placement decisions could hardly have been made more clear. The legislative history showed that the race-as-permissible-factor provision was removed precisely because it had been identified as deeply problematic. The simple antidiscrimination language substituted had been consistently interpreted in the context of other civil rights laws as forbidding *any* consideration of race as a factor in decision-making, with the increasingly limited exception accorded formal affirmative action plans.

While it is true that DHHS issued a 1997 Guidance Memorandum allowing consideration of race in some circumstances, that Guidance makes clear that race cannot be used in the normal course but only in exceedingly rare situations. . . .

Moreover, when the Guidance states that use of race in placement is governed by the strict scrutiny standard, it invokes a standard known in the legal world as condemning as unconstitutional under the Federal Constitution almost all race-conscious policies.

MEPA's prohibition of racial matching is controversial within the child welfare world, with some arguing for its repeal and others for "interpretations" that would allow for race-matching in blatant disregard for the clear meaning of the law. The positions taken by the Child Welfare League of America, the National Association of Social Workers, and the National Association of Black Social Workers, cited by Griffith and Bergeron, illustrate these organizations' disagreement with the law. The Report issued by the Stuart Foundation's Adoption and Race Work Group, relied on by Griffith and Bergeron in their concluding paragraphs, illustrates the commitment by many who disagree with the law to evade its restrictions. As I wrote when asked for my comments on this Group's preliminary draft report, which became the final report with no significant changes in tone or substance:

> From start to finish [the Report] reads like a justification for the present race-matching system, and an argument for continuing to implement essential features of that system in a way designed to satisfy the letter but not the spirit of [MEPA]. . . .
>
> The general thrust of the Report in terms of policy direction, together with its specific Recommendations, read to me like the advice prepared by clever lawyers whose goal it is to help the client avoid the clear spirit of the law. The general idea seems to be to tell those in a position to make and implement policy, that this is a bad law, based on a misunderstanding of the needs of black children, but that since it is less than crystal clear, it will be possible to retool and reshape current policies and practices so that they look quite different but accomplish much the same thing.

The fact that there is ongoing controversy about and resistance to this law matters. Law is not self-enforcing. It relies on people, nonprofit organizations, and government entities to demand enforcement.

However, just as controversy affects law, so law also affects controversy. The fact that federal law now states that race-matching is equivalent to race discrimination matters in a nation that has committed itself in significant ways to the proposition that race discrimination is wrong. Moreover this particular law mandates powerful penalties, specifying an automatic reduction of a set percentage of the federal funds provided to each state for foster and adoption purposes, for any finding of violation. This changes the risk assessment enterprise for typically risk-averse bureaucrats. Acting illegally can get you into trouble, especially if millions of dollars of financial penalties are at stake. While in the years after MEPA's passage I was one of the most vocal critics of the absence of MEPA enforcement activity, as the years went by I began to get the sense in my travels around the country speaking on these issues that social work practice was adjusting, albeit slowly, to MEPA's demands.

The dramatic new development is on the enforcement front. The U.S. Department of Health and Human Services (DHHS), designated as the enforcement agency for MEPA, has finally moved beyond the tough-sounding words that it issued providing interpretive guidance, to take action—action in the form of decisions finding states in violation of the law and imposing the financial penalties mandated by MEPA for such violations. Griffith and Bergeron make no mention of this development, but it seems likely to have a major impact on child welfare agencies nationwide and accordingly seems likely to change the context in which mental health professionals will work in making placement evaluations and the pressures on them with respect to the race factor. The first such enforcement decision involved Hamilton County, Ohio. In 2003, after a four-and-one-half-year investigation, DHHS's Office for Civil Rights (OCR) issued a Letter of Findings, concluding that Hamilton County and Ohio had violated MEPA as well as Title VI of the 1964 Civil Rights Act (42 U.S.C. Sec. 2000(d)), and DHHS's Administration for Children and Families (ACF) issued a Penalty Letter imposing a $1.8 million penalty. In its extensive Letter of Findings, DHHS confirmed that under MEPA as well as Title VI, strict scrutiny is the standard, and child welfare workers have extremely little discretion to consider race in the placement process. DHHS found that MEPA prohibits any regular consideration of race in the normal course, any regular consideration of race in the context of a transracial placement, and any differential consideration of transracial as compared with same-race placements. Moreover, the Letter stated that MEPA prohibits the variety of policies and practices used to assess transracial placements with a view toward the prospective parents' apparent ability to appropriately nurture the racial heritage of other-race children. More specifically, DHHS found illegal administrative rules requiring that: (1) home-studies of prospective adoptive parents seeking "transracial/transcultural" placements include a determination of whether a prospective parent is able to "value, respect, appreciate and educate a child regarding a child's racial, ethnic and cultural heritage, background and language and . . . to integrate the child's culture into normal daily living patterns"; (2) assessments be made of the racial composition of the neighborhood in which prospective families live; and (3) prospective parents prepare a plan for meeting a child's "transracial/transcultural needs." DHHS stated that, in enacting MEPA II, Congress "removed the bases for arguments that MEPA permitted the routine consideration of race, color, or national origin in foster or adoptive placement, and that MEPA prohibited only delays or denials that were categorical in nature." In the consideration of particular Hamilton County cases, DHHS regularly faulted child welfare workers for demanding that home-studies reflect a child's cultural needs, asking for additional information on racial issues, and inquiring into and relying on prospective parents' statements about their racial attitudes (e.g., intention to raise the child in a "color-blind" manner), the degree of contact they had with the African-American community, the level of racial integration in their neighborhood or school system, their plans to address a child's cultural heritage, their level of realism about dealing with a transracial placement, the adequacy of their training in areas like hair care, their unrealistic expectations about racial tolerance, their apparent ability to parent a child of another race,

their willingness to relocate to a more integrated community, their apparent ability to provide a child with an understanding of his heritage, and their readiness for transracial placement.

In rejecting one of Ohio's defenses, based on allegedly inadequate advice on the operation of MEPA, DHHS found that the guidance issued in the form of various memoranda from 1995 through 1998 was fully adequate in clarifying the prohibition against any special requirements related to transracial placements.

The subsequent DHHS decision imposing the $1.8 million penalty took issue additionally with Ohio's apparent attempt to circumvent the law by a new administrative rule providing that an agency determination that race should be considered would trigger a referral for an opinion from an outside licensed professional (psychiatrist, clinical psychologist, social worker, or professional clinical counselor). The professional was to be required to provide an "individual assessment of this child that describes the child's special or distinctive needs based on his/her race, color, or national origin and whether it is in the child's best interest to take these needs into account in placing this child for foster care or adoption." DHHS faulted the process for signaling to the professional that the agency thinks race should be a factor, for the professional's lack of training regarding the legal limitations on considering race and for asking the professional whether race should be considered, while failing to require any finding by the professional: "that there is a compelling need to consider race; that such consideration is strictly required to serve the best interests of the child; and that no race-neutral alternatives exist." DHHS also noted that Ohio had indicated its desire for state approval to obtain opinions from professionals known to be opposed to transracial adoptions. DHHS concluded that the rule was "readily susceptible to being used to foster illegal discrimination."

In 2005, DHHS made a second enforcement decision, involving South Carolina, with OCR issuing a Letter of Findings concluding that the state's Department of Social Services had violated both MEPA and Title VI, and ACF issuing a Penalty Letter imposing a penalty of $107,481. In its Letter of Findings in this case, DHHS again emphasized that strict scrutiny is the standard and that the law forbids any regular consideration of race, allowing its consideration only on rare occasions and even then only to the degree it can be demonstrated to be absolutely necessary. DHHS found illegal South Carolina's practice of treating prospective parent racial preferences with greater deference than other preferences: "By treating race differently from all other parental preferences . . . [the agency] establishes its own system based on racial preference. . . ." DHHS also found illegal the agency's practice of deferring to birth parents' racial preferences, stating that the law requires agencies to make placement decisions "independent of the biological parent's race, color or national origin preference." Furthermore, DHHS found illegal the agency's practice of treating transracial adoptions with greater scrutiny, faulting, for example, the inquiries into prospective parents' ability to adopt transracially, and ability to nurture a child of a different race, as well as inquiries into the racial makeup of such parents' friends, neighborhoods, and available schools. And finally, DHHS found to be illegal various other ways in which the agency took race into consideration, including use of race as a "tie-breaking" factor, matching for skin tone, and use of young children's racial preferences—"the routine deference to and wide range of reasons given for . . . following the same-race preferences of young children undermines any claim that these placement decisions are truly individualized." In addition, DHHS made findings of violations in several individual cases, including that of a black couple interested in adopting a Hispanic child, in which the agency was faulted for inquiry into the couple's ability to meet the child's cultural needs. DHHS specified that any acceptable corrective action plan by the state would have to include, *inter alia*, support and encouragement for parents interested in adopting transracially, the creation of progressive disciplinary action, including termination, for staff continuing to use race improperly, the development of whistle-blower protection for staff who reported the use of race by others, and monitoring and reporting requirements designed to ensure future compliance with the law. The ACF Penalty Letter noted that, having reviewed and concurred in the OCR's Letter of Findings, it was imposing the penalty mandated by MEPA.

While these are the only cases in which Letters of Findings and Penalty Letters have been issued, DHHS's OCR has engaged in compliance efforts in several other cases, resulting in agreements by various state agencies to modify their practices in accord with OCR's demands. In addition DHHS's ACF has through various policy statements reenforced its commitment to rigorous enforcement of MEPA.

DHHS's recent enforcement action constitutes a shot across the bow for all state agencies involved in foster and adoptive placement throughout the nation. The opinions in the two cases in which financial penalties were imposed are as clear as they can be that, at the highest ranks, DHHS believes that MEPA and the various MEPA-related guidance memoranda that DHHS has issued mean that race cannot lawfully be taken into account in any routine way in placement decisions, that it is only in the exceptional cases that race can be considered, and even then that authorities will have to be very careful to demonstrate that compelling necessity demands such consideration, consistent with the strict scrutiny standard.

While DHHS guidance had in my view made all this clear previously, the fact that OCR has now taken enforcement action finding MEPA violations, with ACF imposing financial penalties, raises the stakes in a way that agency directors and agency workers will not be able to ignore. Penalties for MEPA violations are mandated under the law, and they are very severe, reducing by set percentages the federal funds on which states are absolutely dependent to run their child welfare systems. A 1997 DHHS Guidance Memorandum noted that in some states MEPA's penalties could range up to more than $3.6 million in a given quarter and could increase to the $7 to $10 million range for continued noncompliance. State agencies act at their peril in ignoring this law. So, too, do agency workers, since their supervisors are not likely to be pleased with action that puts the state's child welfare budget at risk.

Some will no doubt continue to resist and evade the law, but I predict that such conduct will diminish over time as the law becomes more established in people's minds as simply part of the nation's basic civil rights commitment. While some have called for MEPA's repeal there has been no significant move in this direction.

My hope is that mental health professionals will join ranks with those interested in following the law in good faith, rather than with those interested in evading its mandate. I say this not simply because MEPA is the law, but because I believe it is a good law, one that serves the interests both of children and of the larger society. Griffith and Bergeron note that black children "can" do well in white families, but I believe the social science evidence provides much stronger support for MEPA than that. By now, there is a significant body of studies on transracial adoptees, many of which are good, controlled studies, comparing them to same-race adoptees. My review of these studies and that of others besides me, reveals no evidence that any harm comes to children by virtue of their placement across color lines. By contrast, there is much evidence that harm comes to children in foster or institutional care when they are delayed in adoptive placement or denied adoption altogether, and there is much evidence that race-matching policies result in such delay and denial. In addition, there is evidence that even when child welfare systems purport to use race as only one factor in decision-making, rather than as a categorical factor justifying delay and/or denial of adoptive placement, race ends up being used in ways that result in just such delay and denial. This latter was, of course, the main reason Congress amended MEPA I to eliminate race as a permissible consideration—Senator Metzenbaum, the law's sponsor, became convinced that MEPA I was not succeeding in eliminating the categorical use of race because its permission to use race as one factor was being abused, something that many of us who supported MEPA II had thought was inevitable, based on experience.

So, it seems to me clear that MEPA serves the interests of children, by helping black children in particular to find placements in loving homes of whatever color as promptly as possible. MEPA also seems to me to serve the interests of the larger society, by combating in a small but significant way the notion that race should divide people. Race-matching is the direct descendant of white supremacy and of black separatism. For the state to promote the formation of same-race families and discourage the formation of interracial families, as it does when it endorses race-matching, is wrong in my view for the same reasons that barriers to interracial marriage were wrong. The U.S. Supreme Court struck down those marriage barriers in 1967 in *Loving v. Virginia.* Congress took an important step in passing MEPA II to bring our nation's child welfare policies in line with the rest of our civil rights regimen. This law makes the statement that while race, of course, does matter in myriad ways in our society, it does not and should not define people's capacity to love each other.

≈✿≈

Commentary: Transracial Adoption—Changing Trends and Attitudes

. . . The increase in transracial adoptions of African-American children in the United States arose in response to the paucity of white babies available for adoption and pressures on public agencies to free children in foster care for adoption. The majority of single teenage mothers now choose to keep their babies. There is increased use of kinship care or adoption, and heightened use of birth control, all of which result in fewer newborn babies being available for adoption. In my state of Maine, the rate of teenage pregnancies has plummeted and is now one of the lowest in the nation. The option of seeking infants from abroad is fraught with uncertainty—concerns about health problems and attachment disorders, delays, expenses, and policies regarding adoptions by foreigners that keep shifting in many nations. Yet another attraction for parents considering adopting African-American babies is the shorter waiting period.

In many parts of the United States and other countries, communities have become more accepting of racially mixed families. In as much as African-American children tend to stay longer in out-of-home care than do white children, freeing them for adoption by white families became a means of alleviating this situation. In the 1990s, public agencies were under a mandate to hasten the exit of children from foster care into permanent care and the Adoption and Safe Families Act of 1995 offered incentives to states that increased adoption of children in foster care. This, combined with the Multiethnic Placement Act, resulted in a dramatic decrease in the number of children in foster care and those awaiting adoption. As of 2001, 14 percent of all adoptions were transracial, although most of them were international adoptions.

As noted by Griffith and Bergeron, the pendulum of statutes regarding transracial adoptions has been swinging like the chapper of a ringing bell. The common thread that runs throughout these debates and dialogues is the concept of adhering to the child's best interests. This guidepost dates back to a 1925 decision by judge Cardozo who first coined the term *best interests.* Goldstein *et al.* would

later elaborate on this concept in their book, *Beyond the Best Interests of the Child,* in which they applied psychoanalytic concepts to the resolution of custody disputes. The best-interest standard has held up well over time and continues to be used by courts in determining child custody determinations. Most states further delineate a list of factors to be considered in making custody recommendations to the court.

Caseworkers and forensic mental health professionals have always had to be mindful of their potential biases in making custody recommendations. Such biases might pertain to potential adoptive parents' socioeconomic status, education, lifestyle, or sexual orientation. The issue of transracial adoptions may bring out even stronger feelings that threaten the objectivity of those making recommendations and final decisions about adoptions. Resistance to transracial adoptions is reminiscent of the opposition to adoption by same-sex couples. There used to be great concern that children adopted into these families would be stigmatized, proselytized into the gay lifestyle, and deprived of adequate role models. Some professionals in child welfare were adamantly opposed on moral grounds. And yet, follow-up studies have consistently shown that children raised by same-sex couples are no different from children raised by heterosexual parents. Eventually, adoption agencies began to see same-sex couples as a valuable resource for hard-to-place children such as those with AIDs or other serious medical or mental problems and older children with histories of failed adoptions. With time, society has become more accepting of these alternative families and their children. These families have, in turn, demonstrated their parenting skills with some of the most challenging children.

Griffith and Bergeron raise the question of the importance of African-American culture in the adoptee's life. I recall many years ago testifying in the Northwest regarding the placement of a child who was part Native American and part Latino. Strong arguments were put forth on the importance of preserving his Native-American heritage, yet no one was arguing for his Latino heritage. Concern for the well-being of African-American children unable to be returned to their birth parents is a relatively new phenomenon. Certainly, few people advocated for them or for white children in the mid-20th century when it was not unusual for children to languish in foster care for up to five years and then be too old or too emotionally damaged to be deemed adoptable. The hue and cry of professionals opposed to transracial adoption was in part related to fears that African-American children raised by whites would not be able to defend themselves against prejudice in a racist society. However, one must also ask whether life in the impermanence of foster care with multiple placements and the risk of further abuse or neglect better prepare them to live in a racist society. Of note, private adoption agencies began placing African-American children with white families long before public agencies did so, as the costs of recruiting African-American families was too high. The numbers were small, but there was little protest and somehow this practice passed under the radar screen.

Norris and Ferguson note that the 1960s and 1970s saw the decimation of many minority families due to substance abuse, incarceration, the HIV epidemic, higher mortality rates, and unemployment due to racism. The net result of these forces was more children of color in foster care. In addition, African-American families often failed to meet the criteria for adoption eligibility. The Adoption Assistance and Child Welfare Act of 1980 provided some relief to families that could not afford to adopt. Simon conducted a 20-year study of 200 white parents and their predominantly African-American adopted children and found that most of the children were happy with their racial identity and racial awareness and happy with themselves. Twenty percent of the group studied experienced some problems in their preteen and adolescent years. This is not a very high percentage, considering the problems faced by most teens and, in particular, adopted teens who have a more difficult time coming to terms with their identity as they approach this phase of development.

The problems faced by children in transracial families should be approached on a developmental level. Ethnoracial awareness does not begin until sometime between the ages of three and five years. My eldest son who, at age three, would insist that our African-American nanny was part of our family and shared our last name brought this point home to me. One day, he was looking out the window at the park across the street and said excitedly, "Mommy, look! There are three black people out there!" Thinking he finally was beginning to note racial differences, I looked out the window and saw three nuns walking in their black habits. As adopted children become aware that their color is different from that of their parents, this might actually facilitate conversations about adoption earlier than in homogenous families, and there is less likely to be secrecy about the adoption.

As noted, problems with racial identity may not surface until adoptees enter their preteen and adolescent years. White families who welcome African-American children into their homes to play with their children may become less welcoming once their children are of dating age. African Americans raised in predominantly white communities may have difficulty fitting in with other African Americans once they leave home. I treated an African-American teenager from an affluent white community where she was well accepted in her predominantly white high school. She related how difficult she found it relating to the African-American students at her college who viewed her as an "Oreo": black on the outside and white inside. She commented on how she had felt like neither fish nor fowl in her new environment. Although not adopted, she faced dilemmas similar to those faced by adoptees who grew up in cultures where they are very much in the minority.

For many years, adoption agencies tried to match children with families who shared similar physical attributes. This effort coincided with secrecy about adoption, the shame of infertility, and even the need to protect a child from knowledge of his illegitimacy. Families now speak more openly of adoption and even practice open adoptions. My brother was carefully matched to my family's phenotype, but aside from both of us being tall and Anglo-Saxon in appearance, we have little in common. Biological siblings may look very different from one another and even their parents. Why must there be so much emphasis on sameness? Rainbow families have demonstrated that there is much more to being family than external appearances. Diversity might actually facilitate individuation and separation in children.

Cultural competence and capacity are routinely screened for in white parents wishing to adopt African-American children. In addition, there are many books and Web sites available to help these parents, once they have been approved to adopt, on how best to raise children of a different race and preserve their cultural roots. There is much emphasis on the need for adoptive parents to expose their adopted children to their African-American culture. While I do not take issue with this, I think there is a much broader need to instill appreciation of African-American culture among all school children and their parents. Tolerance, understanding, and respect should be taught early and reinforced at home. The magazine *Teaching Tolerance* published by the Southern Poverty Law Center has had significant impact on our school systems in this regard. Our culture is rapidly changing, and the fear that African Americans in white families will not be able to handle discrimination seems like an outdated notion. The onus should not be put on adoptees to learn to deal with discrimination but rather on society to end discrimination. African-American children in white families may play an important role in helping other children and their parents overcome racial stereotypes.

ELIZABETH BARTHOLET is the Morris Wasserstein Public Interest Professor of Law and faculty director of the Child Advocacy Program at the Harvard Law School.

DIANE H. SCHETKY is a forensic child and adolescent psychiatrist and clinical professor of psychiatry at the Maine Medical Center.

EXPLORING THE ISSUE

Do Federal Laws Make Transracial Adoptions More Commonplace?

Critical Thinking and Reflection

1. Griffith and Bergeron believe that transracial adoption should be less commonplace because more and more children are being considered "special cases." Define what makes a child a special case and why it would be harmful for children in these special cases to be adopted transracially.
2. Bartholet suggests that by allowing race as a factor in adoptions, American society is allowing racial discriminations, which our country has been fighting to eliminate. Support or refute this statement and explain why making reference to content from the articles.
3. Take a stance, pro or con, regarding transracial adoption. Explain your position citing evidence from either the Griffith and Bergeron or the Bartholet selections to support your position.

Is There Common Ground?

The Multiethnic Placement Act is intended to provide an effective support for transracial adoption. It seeks to eliminate the consideration of race in the placement of children except in exceptional cases. Legislation such as this is intended to protect the interests of adoptees and their prospective parents. However, do prospective parents usually prefer children of their own race? Or, are adopting parents pleased to have a child—of any race—to love and rear? Do you believe, as suggested in the NO selection, that as respect for all minority cultures and tolerance for diversity continue to pervade our society, the need for "best interest" legislation such as this act may become unnecessary? Will our society ever evolve to the degree that there would never be extenuating circumstances in which children placed for adoption need to be adopted by parents of the same race?

There are many children in need of adoption, and most are minority children. The goal of adoption is to get children out of institutions and orphanages and into loving and caring homes. The vast majority of the literature on transracial adoption finds little to suggest that it harms children when they are adopted by parents of a different race. The National Association of Black Social Workers (NABSW) seems to be the ones who are most vociferous in denouncing transracial adoption. Is this a form of discrimination, to prevent Anglo-Americans from adopting a minority child who is of a different race?

Although the efficacy of transracial adoption has been well established in the research literature, the controversy continues as to whether or not it should be widely practiced. Many feel that the issue should be laid to rest—once and for all—because children thrive more effectively in adoptive homes than in institutions. And, there are simply not enough same-race minority families to adopt children of the given race. Others suggest that although we as a society make overtures to being nondiscriminating, the

practice still occurs in adoptions despite the law. Also, in some cases, people believe it is necessary to consider race in placing children. It seems clear that those on either side of the issue would agree, however, on two fundamental goals: (1) to decrease the amount of children in institutions and orphanages and (2) to place children in adoptive homes that will best meet their physical and emotional needs. The problem seems to be in the differing points of view as to how to best achieve these goals.

Create Central

www.mhhe.com/createcentral

Additional Resources

Child Welfare Information Gateway. Transracial and Transcultural Adoptions. Retrieved on April 7, 2011, from www.childwelfare.gov/pubs/f_trans.cfm

This website defines and discusses reasons for transracial adoptions and expert opinions on their impact on children.

Issues in Transracial Adoption. Retrieved on April 7, 2011, from http://userpages.umbc.edu/~mmcman1/

This website discusses the various issues that must be taken into consideration when considering transracial adoptions.

Morrison, A. (2004) Transracial Adoption: The Pros and Cons and the Parents' Perspective. *Harvard BlackLetter Law Journal*, 20, pp. 163–202. Retrieved on April 7, 2011, from www.law.harvard.edu/students/orgs/blj/vol20/morrison.pdf

This is an article posted online that discusses some of the pros and cons of transracial adoptions, as well as the parents' perspectives on these types of adoptions.

Internet References . . .

Adoptive Families

www.adoptivefamilies.com/transracial-adoption.php

The Adoption History Project. Retrieved on April 7, 2011

This website describes the history of transracial adoptions in America.

http://pages.uoregon.edu/adoption/topics /transracialadoption.htm

Unit 2

UNIT

Early Childhood

The period of early childhood is sometimes referred to as the preschool years. It generally encompasses ages two or three through four or five. This is a time when children become much more adept at taking part in physical activities, satisfying curiosities, and learning from experience. It is also a time when parents who think they have finally figured their children out realize that they have to adapt what they have been doing and learn new skills to deal with the new skills their children are acquiring. Preschoolers play more frequently with other children, become increasingly skilled in daily tasks, and are much more responsive to people and things in their environment. Many children begin school during their preschool years, an experience that gives them their first extended contacts with a social institution other than the family. Changing attitudes about discipline, family size, divorce, and the mass media all have implications for a child's development. This section examines some of the choices families make in rearing their preschool children.

Selected, Edited, and with Issue Framing Material by:
Kourtney Vaillancourt, *New Mexico State University*

ISSUE

Is Spanking Detrimental to Children?

YES: Rupert Shepherd, from "Spanking Children Can Cause Mental Illness," *Medical News Today* (July 2012)

NO: CTV.ca News Staff, from "Contentious Study Says Spanking May Benefit Children," (January 7, 2010)

Learning Outcomes

After reading this issue, you should be able to:

- List some of the arguments in favor of, and opposed to, spanking.
- Describe some of the negative effects that can come from spanking children.
- Identify the difference between mild spanking and physical abuse.

ISSUE SUMMARY

YES: Rupert Shepherd discusses findings from the American Academy of Pediatrics that state spanking can cause children to have an increased risk of mental problems as they age.

NO: CTV News Staff reports on a study that argues children who are spanked might grow up to be happier and more productive than children who are not spanked.

The topic of spanking, also known as corporal punishment, provokes highly emotional responses from family practitioners, parents, researchers, and children. There seems to be no one who is neutral about the subject, especially children. It would be interesting to ask children about their feeling toward spanking. Were you spanked as a child? What was used to spank you? Bare hand? Hairbrush? Ruler? Belt? The list could go on and on. Do you think the spankings negatively affected you, or did they teach you how to act appropriately? The following quotes are often used in relationship to spanking: "Spare the rod and spoil the child. I was spanked and I turned out OK. Kids need to be spanked to show them who's boss."

If you were not spanked, what was used to correct your misbehavior? Was the misbehavior explained? Was your correct behavior rewarded and your misbehavior punished? What about children who were not spanked or corrected in any way? Are they considered spoiled or out of control? Perhaps verbal abuse or a slap to the face was used to correct your behavior, or maybe you were ignored altogether. These techniques are considered similar to spanking in that they can become abusive or neglectful.

Ninety-four percent of American parents report spanking their children by the time their children are 3 years old. Although spanking is a popular form of discipline in the United States, several countries have outlawed spanking and the physical punishment of children: Austria, Croatia, Cyprus, Germany, Israel, Italy, Latvia, Norway, Denmark, Sweden, and Finland. Proponents of spanking point out that these countries' rates of child abuse have not declined as a result of banning spanking.

Corporal punishment is associated with family violence and child abuse. These are the stories often found in the media about parents injuring or even killing their children as a result of physical punishment. Although the media exploits these situations and makes the public feel outraged that children are treated this way, one must remember these are extreme cases. Most families feel they use spanking judiciously and do not consider it abusive.

Ultimately, spanking is used as a teaching tool and a way to solve problems. Parents see children misbehave, look for a way to gain the children's attention immediately, and spank them. Parents believe that by inflicting pain, they are changing children's behavior and solving the problem of misbehavior. Opponents of spanking ask the question of how children will change misbehavior if they are not taught what *to do* versus what *not to do*. In addition, the message is sent that I am bigger than you so I can solve this problem by hitting you.

In the YES selection, Rupert Shepherd reports that children who are spanked have been found to have increased risk for mental disorders when they grow older.

He purports that between 2 and 7 percent of mental disorders were linked in some way to physical punishment. In the NO selection, CTV News Staff in Canada reports on a study that refutes the notion that spanking is detrimental. In this study, physical discipline was associated with increased school grades, optimism, and ambition.

YES

Rupert Shepherd

Spanking Children Can Cause Mental Illness

American Academy of Pediatrics, which is already opposed to using physical punishments on children, has released a new study today, backing their stance and reinforcing the belief that spanking children belongs firmly in the past.

The study, named "Physical Punishment and Mental Disorders: Results from a Nationally Representative U.S. Sample," is released in the August edition of *Pediatrics*, which is online July 2nd.

It states clearly that **children who are spanked, hit or pushed have an increased risk of mental problems when they grow older.** The research seems to show that the effect can range from mood and anxiety disorders to drug and alcohol abuse.

Afifi, an assistant professor of epidemiology in the Department of Community Health Sciences at the University of Manitoba, Canada, clarified to *USA Today*:

> "There is a significant link between the two . . . Individuals who are physically punished have an increased likelihood of having mental health disorders. . . . [the studies findings confirm that] physical punishment should not be used on any child, at any age,"

She goes on to state that between 2% and 7% of mental disorders found in the study were linked to physical punishment.

The study involved a large number of subjects with data collected from some 35,000 non-institutionalized adults in the USA. Around 1,300 of the subjects confirmed that they had, at sometime, or regularly been *"pushed, grabbed, shoved, slapped or hit by your parents or any adult living in your house."*

The aim was not to look at more aggressive physical or sexual abuse, emotional abuse, neglect, but rather to identify the link between light deliberate punishment and Axis I and II mental disorders.

Axis I is defined as clinical disorders, including major mental disorders, learning disorders and substance use disorders, while Axis II relates to: personality disorders and intellectual disabilities (although developmental disorders, such as Autism, were coded on Axis II in the previous edition, these disorders are now included on Axis I).

The study has been criticized, however, with Robert Larzelere, of Oklahoma State University, Stillwater stating to *USA Today* that:

> "Certainly, overly severe physical punishment is going to have adverse effects on children . . . But for younger kids, if spanking is used in the most appropriate way and the child perceives it as being motivated by concern for their behavior and welfare, then I don't think it has a detrimental effect."

His own 2005 research showed that when light spanking is used appropriately, rather than wantonly and where it only serves to back up non-physical discipline, such as talking sternly to the child or enacting some kind of punishment or removal of privileges, it does, in fact, prove very effective at removing non-compliant behavior.

He goes on to state that the current study "does nothing to move beyond correlations to figure out what is actually causing the mental health problems. . . . The motivation that the child perceives and when and how and why the parent uses (spanking) makes a big difference. All of that is more important than whether it was used or not."

This would probably concur with the ideals of many mentally balanced and well educated parents, who would do anything to avoid having to get physical with their children, but ultimately, in the appropriate moment, with the correct words and mood, find that spanking can be useful and not cause long term detriment.

Afifi's report concludes that the findings inform the ongoing debate around the use of physical punishment and provide evidence that harsh physical punishment, independent of child maltreatment, is related to mental disorders.

RUPERT SHEPHERD writes articles for *Medical News Today*.

CTV.ca News Staff

 **NO**

Contentious Study Says Spanking May Benefit Children

A new U.S. study that has drawn criticism from rights advocates says children who are spanked may grow up to be happier, more productive adults.

Researchers at Calvin College, a Christian school in Michigan, surveyed 2,600 people and included interviews with 179 teenagers. They concluded that children spanked by their parents may perform better at school and grow up to be happier than those who don't receive such punishment.

Teenagers who were spanked up to age six reported that they were more successful in school, more interested in attending university, more likely to work as volunteers and more positive about life, the researchers say.

Psychologist Marjorie Gunnoe, the study's lead researcher, interviewed people between ages 12 and 18. The study examined their responses on a questionnaire concerning how they were disciplined as children, and compared the responses to their conduct as teenagers.

The study, which hasn't been published yet, focused on a number of "good" and "bad" behaviours, such as optimism about the future and anti-social conduct. Teenagers who were spanked between two and six years of age performed slightly better on the positive behaviours—but no worse on the negative measures—than those who had never been spanked.

Another finding was that young people who were still being spanked when they were in their teens, displayed behavioural problems.

The study was not intended to encourage parents to strike their children, Gunnoe reportedly said, but to dissuade government from banning the practice.

However, Grant Wilson, president of the Canadian Children's Rights Council, criticised the study and said spanking should be banned.

"Canada is a country that should have eliminated this quite a while ago," he told CTV News Channel. "If you look at the polls, parents are generally speaking against hitting children for the purpose of disciplining them."

"It is contradictory to say to a child 'it's ok for a parent, a big person, to hit you and cause you physical pain,' and then 'you should go out and play with your friends and not hit them,'" he said.

However, Andrea Mrozek, with the Institute of Marriage and Family Canada, said spanking children can be positive if used "appropriately."

"There's a certain age range where it's appropriate and in fact may even be necessary to prevent greater harm to a child," Mrozek said.

"When you have legislature step in and tell parents how to be parents, I think it's extremely detrimental," she added.

Spanking is prohibited in many countries, particularly in Europe. It's legal in the U.S. and Canada, under certain circumstances.

CTV.CA NEWS STAFF is Canada's 24-hour all-news network.

EXPLORING THE ISSUE

Is Spanking Detrimental to Children?

Critical Thinking and Reflection

1. Explain the effects of corporal punishment on the parent–child relationship. List and explain one positive and one negative reaction to corporal punishment.
2. Explain the connection between mental health and corporal punishment, according to Shepherd.
3. Explain the reasons that CTV says spanking may actually be beneficial to children.

Is There Common Ground?

There is a real debate over what mild spanking is and how it fits into the overall parenting discipline technique. Child development experts agree that reasoning, talking, and listening to children teaches them how to distinguish right from wrong and preserves their positive self-image. They admit this approach takes more time and effort but that in the long run, it is more effective and leads children to a better adjusted adulthood. What might be some reasons that parents do not report using these techniques as frequently as spanking?

There are authorities in child development who believe spankings, when properly administered and within the context of a loving home, are effective in shaping children's behavior. Most agree to spank from about 2 years of age until puberty and to only use an open hand and never use objects to hit children. They urge parents to explain to their children why they are being spanked. Do you believe that this can make a difference in the outcomes of spanking on children? Why or why not?

Are spankings useful and justified, or is there a fine line between spanking and child abuse? Is it likely that parents who spank will cross that line to abuse in the heat of the moment? Is it really possible to spank with appropriate force and with logical thought? Can studies on the effects of spanking be designed to answer these questions? With all the studies already conducted, methodology and definitions are still being debated. It appears that there are many critical variables that need to be quantified before conducting research on the subject. In the meantime, parents are presented with the dilemma of how best to guide and discipline their children from childhood to becoming responsible adults. If you were advising a parent, what would you suggest?

Create Central

www.mhhe.com/createcentral

Additional Resources

Henderson, T. (2010). Researcher Says a Little Spanking Is Good for Kids. Retrieved on April 7, 2011, from www.parentdish.com/2010/01/05/researcher-says -a-little-spanking-is-good-for-kids/

This article discusses some reasons why a little bit of spanking can be beneficial for children

Hunt, J. (1997). The Natural Child Project: Ten Reasons Not to Hit Your Kids. Retrieved on April 7, 2011, from www.naturalchild.org/jan_hunt/tenreasons.html

This website lists reasons that spanking should not be used on children.

Shute, N. (2008). A Good Parent's Dilemma: Is Spanking Bad? Retrieved on April 7, 2011, from http://health.usnews.com/health-news/family-health/ articles/2008/06/12/a-good-parents-dilemma-is- spanking-bad

This article posted online discusses research about the effects of spanking on children.

Internet References . . .

Parents.com

www.parents.com/kids/discipline/spanking/

PsychCentral

http://psychcentral.com/blog/archives/2012/08/16 /why-shouldnt-you-spank-your-kids-heres-9-reasons/

Selected, Edited, and with Issue Framing Material by:
Kourtney Vaillancourt, *New Mexico State University*

ISSUE

Are Fathers Really Necessary?

YES: CIViTAS: The Institute for the Study of Civil Society, from "How Do Fathers Fit In?" December, 2001

NO: Peggy Drexler and Linden Gross, from "Good News from the New Home Front," *Raising Boys Without Men* (Rodale Books, 2005)

Learning Outcomes

After reading this issue, you should be able to:

- Identify the arguments posed in favor of and in opposition to the importance of a father's involvement in a child's life.
- Critique the type of research that each article reported on, identifying the strengths and weaknesses of the approach.
- List differences that can be found between homes where fathers are present versus those where they are not.

ISSUE SUMMARY

YES: CIViTAS: The Institute for the Study of Civil Society identifies how fathers fit into a family and the unique strengths that they contribute to family life.

NO: Peggy Drexler, assistant professor of psychology in psychiatry and special features editor, and Linden Gross assert that women are capable of raising children without a father figure in the home. Their book is based on Drexler's research that compared boys from female-headed households with boys from traditional mom-and-dad families.

There has been a dramatic rise in single-parent homes in the United States in the past 20 years. A more dramatic increase is the number of children being raised by men. Since the 1990 census, households headed by single fathers have risen from 1.3 million homes in 1990 to over 2.5 million in 2006. Because of this increase, an issue that has confronted researchers revolves around the necessity of the two-parent family. Specifically, are both mothers and fathers necessary to raise children effectively?

Children need nurturing, guidance, and economic security. Must they receive these things from both a father and a mother? Some scholars argue that children need active involved fathers throughout their childhood and adolescence. If this does not occur, children may be more prone to involvement in crime, premature sexual activity, out of wedlock childbirth, lower educational achievement, depression, substance abuse, and poverty.

Other scientists question whether the ability to meet children's needs is gender specific. Although few would argue that it is more challenging to raise a child in a single-parent home, well-socialized and successful children have come from single-parent homes that are male as well as female headed. Females head the vast majority of single-parent homes. In fact, there are over 10.4 million single mothers raising children in the United States today.

Another consideration is the increase in adoption by gay and lesbian parents in two-parent homes. Although children may face emotional challenges in dealing with the prejudice associated with being raised in these particular households, one might ask how this arrangement works. Is there evidence that children need both a male and a female parent? Many scientists argue that there is little, if any, scientific evidence that both a female and a male must raise children.

Although there is no consensus on whether or not children need both mothers and fathers to raise them, there is a concern that society makes it difficult for dads to be involved in their children's lives. Philip Cowan and Carolyn Cowan describe six institutional barriers to father involvement in the Family Focus on Fatherhood (National Council on Family Relations, 2009). The six barriers are culturally based gender role stereotypes, government child support programs, social science research, the workplace, family service agencies, and focus on coparents. Overcoming these barriers will not happen from attending a single workshop or reading one memo, but will need the ongoing support of educators and agency personnel.

Philip Cowan and Carolyn Cowan suggest specific ideas to increase father involvement: realize that fathers are motivated to be with their children, but are often prevented from doing so; add emotional support to monetary support in child support mandates; encourage mothers who are the gatekeepers to involve dads with their children; and ask workplaces to implement flex-time schedules for dads. Natasha Cabrera, Jacqueline Shannon, and Catherine Tamis-LeMonda conducted research based on observations versus survey data. They found that fathers with at least a high school education were more supportive than fathers with fewer resources and had a positive effect on children's emotional and cognitive development.

As you read the following selections, consider your family of orientation. Was your upbringing an optimal situation? Did the role that your father played have a positive or negative effect on your life?

**YES** CIViTAS: The Institute for
the Study of Civil Society

How Do Fathers Fit In?

Two Heads Are Better Than One

Richness of Care

A child who has both a mother and a father benefits from an increased richness of care. In other words, children with both a mother and a father can benefit from *more* caring, as well as a *variety* of caring styles.

Bridges to the World

Through their fathers and mothers, children have access to a vast network including grandparents, cousins, aunts and uncles, friends of the family, work colleagues, community organisations, faith communities, and even personal histories. Fathers and mothers provide "bridges" to all these aspects of the outside world, providing more experiences for children as well as practical opportunities such as job possibilities.

Mothers Benefit from Fathers' Support

If a mother can count on her children's father to help with keeping the house clean and in good repair, caring for the children, paying the bills, and planning for the future, she probably will be a happier, more effective parent. The support a mother receives from her child's father can even help her be more competent and sensitive when feeding her baby. Mothers seem to gain the most security when they are married and know the father is committed to a lifelong relationship to her and their child.[1]

Breadwinning

Today, most families rely upon the incomes of both mothers and fathers. However, fathers still provide the lion's share of income. Fathers are either the sole earners or the main earners in two-thirds of two-parent households. Moreover, fathers' earnings are uniquely linked to many positive results for children, even when mothers' earnings are taken into consideration.[2]

Complementary Roles

It often is useful, as well as accurate, to generalise about *average* differences between men and women. Whether these differences are due more to inborn biological chemistry, or social pressures, or some combination of the two, is much debated.

It is generally agreed that men and women should no longer be regarded as "opposites." The important thing to remember is that mothers and fathers often bring different strengths and styles to their parenting roles. These roles complement each other, meaning that they are not interchangeable and are each necessary for healthy childrearing. . . .

How Fathers Influence Children as They Grow

In the past, psychologists studying the development of children focused almost exclusively on children's relationships with their mothers. Today, they have come to agree that fathers play a unique and crucial role in nurturing and guiding children's development. Many experts now believe that fathers can be just as nurturing and sensitive with their babies as mothers.[3] As their children grow, fathers take on added roles of guiding their children's intellectual and social development. Even when a father is "just playing" with his children, he is nurturing their development.

Fathers and Babies

Babies need predictability and security, which they get when their mother and father respond consistently, promptly, and appropriately to their cries, smiles and other signals. As a baby develops a relationship with his or her mother and father, he comes to prefer them to other adults, in a process known as *attachment*. Psychologists agree that babies with secure attachments to their parents have better chances to develop into happy, successful, and well-adjusted children and adults.[4] Mothers tend to be relied upon more than fathers for the comfort and security components of attachment, primarily because they are usually the infant's main caregiver.[5] Babies also form attachments to their fathers, who tend to be just as responsive to their babies' bids for attention as mothers.[6] When fathers spend more time with their babies, they get to know exactly what each of their baby's signals mean. This familiarity allows fathers to respond *sensitively*, meaning that they know when their baby is hungry rather than when he just wants a change of scenery.[7]

The effects of attachment on children are broad and long-lasting. For example, one study found that primary school children scored higher on tests of *empathy*—the ability to see a situation from another person's viewpoint—if they had secure attachments to their fathers during infancy. These children were able to recognize how other children felt and took steps to make them feel better.[8]

Both mothers and fathers encourage their babies to investigate the world, manipulate objects, and explore physical relationships.[9] However, mothers and fathers have different styles of relating. Mothers tend to speak soothingly and softly in repetitive rhythms to their infants and snugly hold them. Fathers tend to provide more verbal and physical stimulation, by patting their babies gently and communicating to them with sharp bursts of sound. As babies grow older, many come to prefer playing with their fathers who provide unpredictable, stimulating, and exciting interaction.[10] This stimulation is important because it fosters healthy development of the baby's brain and can have lasting effects on children's social, emotional, and intellectual development. Infants with involved fathers tend to score higher on tests of thinking skills and brain development.[11]

Both the mother and the father are important to an infant's development in special ways. For example, in one study, baby boys whose fathers engaged in physically playful, affectionate and stimulating play during infancy were more popular later as school children. Mothers influenced their sons' popularity through a different route, by providing verbal stimulation.[12]

Fathers and Small Children

When babies become toddlers, parents must go beyond nurturing them and begin to address two additional needs: supporting their toddler's exploration and setting appropriate limits for the child. Through playing with their toddlers, fathers take a special role in achieving these two goals. Children learn from them how to solve problems and how to get along with others.[13]

Fathers spend a larger proportion of their time playing with their young children than mothers do, and they tend to be more boisterous and active in their play.[14] Most children enjoy this kind of play. Even if their fathers spend less time with them than their mothers, fathers become *salient*, or meaningful and special, to their children through play.[15]

When fathers play with their toddlers, they are not just entertaining them. They are providing a safe, yet challenging arena for toddlers to learn how to interact with the world and with others. Through rough-and-tumble play, fathers create obstacles for their children and demand respect for limits and boundaries. At the same time, they challenge their children and encourage them to explore their own strength, their ability to do new things, and their impact on the world around them. Toddlers who must work out for themselves how to achieve goals—such as retrieving a ball that is just out of reach in their father's hand or wrestling their father to the ground—are practicing important problem-solving skills. In fact, when fathers

are good at playing with their young children, these children score higher on tests of thinking and problem-solving skills.[16]

Playing with fathers also helps children develop emotional knowledge, so that they can identify their own emotions, acknowledge the emotional experiences of others, and describe the causes of emotions. Toddlers must also learn *emotional regulation,* the ability to express emotions responsibly and control their behaviour. To understand how much emotional regulation develops during early childhood, one can picture a toddler in the midst of an angry temper tantrum, holding his breath until he gets his way. Contrast this with a four-year-old who feels frustrated that the rain has ruined his plans to play football, yet moves beyond those feelings and engages in a board game with his sister instead. When children understand their emotions and know how to control them, it makes them more popular with other children.[17]

The father's influence on emotional development is not limited to play, but also comes through direct teaching and daily interaction. Studies have shown that, when fathers are affectionate and helpful, their children are more likely to get on well with their brothers and sisters.[18] When children have fathers who are emotionally involved—that is, they acknowledge their children's emotions and help them deal with bad emotions—they score higher on tests of "emotional intelligence." Moreover, they tend to have better relationships with other children and behave less aggressively. Fathers' involvement in their young children's care can even last well into adulthood.[19] Mothers seem to have much less impact in this area of emotional regulation and peer relationships than fathers. It really is fathers who can have a major influence on helping their children build strong social relationships during childhood and later in life.

Fathers of Children at Primary School

Learning to Meet Challenges

As children reach school age, they begin to grapple with learning more adult-like skills, testing them out in new environments, and dealing with the feelings evoked by successes and failures. A sense of *industry,* or a belief that he or she can accomplish a goal or master a skill, is important to a child's developing sense of self-esteem. Fathers seem to be key teachers in this area. As one expert puts it, "the quality of the father's involvement during this period is a crucial factor in determining whether the child develops the confidence and competence to meet new challenges in a positive manner."[20]

One reason that fathers have such an influential role at this time is because they tend to challenge their children to try new experiences and to become more independent. Challenged children have more opportunity to develop problem-solving skills. In one study, children whose fathers expected them to handle responsibilities, such as carrying scissors, crossing the street, or taking a bath alone, scored higher in tests of thinking skills.[21] Accomplishing tasks at this age is so important, and fathers' involvement is so crucial, that fathers have a larger influence on their children's self-esteem at this age than do mothers.[22]

By encouraging children to take on new challenges, fathers help them not only to learn new skills, but also to take responsibility for their own actions.[23] Fathers with a strong commitment to their family provide a model of responsible behaviour for their children. These children have an *internal sense of control*, which means that they are more likely to believe that their successes and failures are due to their own efforts rather than due to external factors. These children tend to take more responsibility for their actions and rarely blame others for their mistakes.[24]

Fathers usually have a positive influence on their children's sense of industry, competence, and responsibility. However, if a father discourages his children and intrudes on potential learning situations by being too restrictive or imposing his own solutions, he will have a bad influence on his children. Whether this type of paternal behaviour is motivated by a desire to protect his child, by feelings of impatience or frustration, or by his lack of trust in the child, it can hamper children's development of creativity, motivation, and problem-solving skills, making them less responsible and more dependent.[25]

Achieving in School

Generally speaking, the more actively involved and interested a father is in his children's care and education, the more intellectually developed his children are.[26] Why should this be the case? One reason is that, when fathers are involved, they tend to provide better economic support for their children. Children with better economic support have access to more educational resources and have better opportunities to learn. For example, in two-parent families, the more the father earns, the better his children do at school, even when mothers' earnings are taken into consideration.[27] Another reason that fathers influence intellectual development is that, when their children are school-aged, fathers spend a good deal of time helping them with studies. This level of commitment has an impact on children's academic success. In one study, four- and five-year-old boys scored higher in maths tests when fathers encouraged skills like counting and reading.[28] In another study, the level of a father's involvement in his child's academic studies predicted success later in life. One expert even found that the amount of time fathers spend with their children has a direct link with maths skills.[29]

The influence fathers have on their children's intellectual development is not limited specifically to helping with school work. Fathers can have a positive influence on their children's thinking skills by participating in social activities and sports as well.[30] One study found that children whose fathers encouraged them in sport and fitness activities were more successful in school and in their careers later in life. This held true for daughters as well as sons.[31]

Getting on in Life

A father's involvement during his children's school years has other positive outcomes. The first years of school can be difficult for children, but fathers can help their children adjust.[32] When fathers are supportive, their children have fewer problems at school such as excessive absence or poor exam results. This holds true even after taking into consideration the influence of the children's mothers.[33] Even when fathers provide only limited attention, warmth, and affection, and are not around all of the time, their children benefit from their influence in terms of adjusting to new experiences, having stable emotions, and knowing how to get along with others.[34] For children with Attention Deficit/Hyperactivity Disorder (ADHD), supportive fathers can have a stronger positive influence on their adjustment to school than mothers.[35]

Moral development is another area where fathers have special influence. How do fathers influence their children's moral development? First, by directly providing guidance and direction. When fathers share their plans, activities, and interests, their children are better behaved in school. When fathers emphasise how behaviour can affect other people's feelings, their school-aged daughters are regarded as very unselfish by classmates. The mere presence of a father helped boys in one study to develop patience by waiting for things they wanted. These children chose to delay a small reward of sweets for a week in order to receive a larger reward of sweets.

Fathers also influence their children's moral development by providing models for their children. In one study, boys who felt similar to, admired, and wanted to resemble their fathers scored higher on tests of personal moral judgement, moral values, and rule-following. However, boys who did not identify strongly with their fathers showed reluctance to accept blame or guilt when they misbehaved. These boys also tended to have problems with self-control and were more aggressive in school.[36] The father's special influence on his school-aged children's development of personal morality lasts into adulthood. Adults whose fathers had been highly involved when they were children were more tolerant and understanding and engaged in more socially responsible behaviour than those with less involved fathers.[37]

Fathers and Teenagers

One of the main tasks for adolescents and teenagers is to develop their personal identity and deepen their relationships with their friends, while also maintaining a strong connection to their families. Teenagers spend more time away from their parents and look to their friends for cues on how to dress and which parties to go to. However, mothers and fathers continue to have a strong influence, especially upon their children's beliefs, values, and plans for the future.

Adolescence is often a time of increased conflict between children and their parents, especially their mothers.

This might be because teenagers spend more time with their mothers than their fathers, or because mothers tend to take issue with aspects of behaviour that touch on teenagers' sense of personal identity, such as clothing or body piercing.

Although teenagers rely more upon their mothers for emotional support, the relationship with fathers continues to be important. Teenagers rely more upon their fathers for conversation, advice, and just "being there."[38] Adolescents who felt their fathers were "available" to them had fewer conflicts with their friends.[39]

Unfortunately, some fathers seem to withdraw from their teenagers. Whether this is due to his concern for instilling independence in his children, or due to changes and stresses he is experiencing in his own life, a reduction in a father's availability and guidance during his children's adolescence can have bad consequences. This is especially the case for daughters. As noted above, fathers' involvement was important to both sons' and daughters' self-esteem when they were in primary school. However, for 15–16 year old girls, the level of a mother's involvement seems to have more influence.[40] Teenage girls find it easier to talk to their mothers, which can make fathers feel as if they are not needed. However, this is not the case. Teenage girls may find self-esteem in their relationships with mothers, but they find guidance about how to relate to others and how to plan for the future from their fathers.

How Fathers Fit into the Family
The Family System

Social scientists often emphasise the role of fathers in the *family system*, and how their actions affect the entire environment and context in which a child grows. One of the most important ways a father influences that environment is in his interaction with his children's mother. This is because the relationships which children observe and experience at an early age influence their own relationships later in life. It is also because family relationships are interrelated—the way that mothers and fathers interact affects the mother–child relationship as well as the father–child relationship. Because of this interrelatedness, parents who have a strong and happy relationship have a head-start to being good parents.[41]

Nonresident Fathers

Statistics about children who do not live with their fathers can be grim. On almost every outcome that has been tested, including educational achievement, self-esteem, responsible social behaviour, and adjustment as adults, children do better when they live with both of their parents. Family instability and financial problems do contribute to the poor outcomes for children from broken homes. However, as one scholar who reviewed 28 studies of father absence states: "the major disadvantage related to father absence for children is lessened parental attention."[42]

Non-resident fathers can face special challenges in contributing positively to their children's development. Fathers who do not live with their children simply are less available to nurture, guide, and provide for their children. In cases of divorce, some mothers limit the time children have with their fathers. Fathers who were never married are even less likely than divorced fathers to keep in contact with their children. Moreover, the large geographic distances that exist between some children and their fathers make close relationships difficult to maintain. Either parent or both may form new relationships and have children with other people. In many cases, the entire family enjoys a lower standard of living when they live apart.

Despite these disadvantages, non-resident fathers can still make a difference for their children. The most obvious route of influence is by providing adequate financial support. Studies show children whose fathers pay child support do better in school and have fewer behaviour problems.[43] Children who feel close to their non-resident fathers also tend to do better. And, when non-resident fathers are able to use their time with their children wisely by helping with homework, setting and enforcing rules, and supervising their children, children can benefit a great deal.[44]

Married or Cohabiting Fathers

The role of marriage as a foundation for family life has become controversial. More and more people are cohabiting or living together before marriage or as an alternative to marriage. More couples also are having children without marrying. Some people say that marriage is "just a piece of paper" and does not make any difference to the couple or their children. For some couples, this might be the case. However, studies have shown that the majority of cohabiting couples are less committed than married couples, even if they have children. In fact, only 36% of children born to cohabiting couples are likely to live with both their mother and their father for their entire childhood, compared to 70% of children born within marriage.[45] It is for this reason that many supporters of the father's role in raising children also support marriage for fathers.[46]

Good Fathering Is Good Parenting

Most children do best when their mothers and fathers engage in what developmental psychologists call *authoritative parenting*. This style of parenting involves spending time with children, providing emotional support, giving everyday assistance, monitoring children's behaviour, and providing consistent, fair and proportionate discipline.[47] This can be contrasted with *permissive* parenting, in which parents avoid setting standards and limits, and *authoritarian* parenting, in which parents are harsh and rigid in their discipline and fail to respect their child's point of view. Neither of these parenting styles have as positive an influence on children's development as authoritative parenting.

Authoritative, or "good parenting," may be expressed in different styles. While mothers tend to provide more emotional warmth for their children, fathers provide a strong sense of security. While children usually can depend on their mothers for unconditional love, they often must earn their father's approval. While mothers soothe their children more often, fathers often provide more stimulation.

All parents—both mothers and fathers—have important roles in rearing their children. Better appreciation of where fathers fit in will lead to happier and more productive children.

References

1. Pleck, J.H., *Working Wives and Family Well-Being*, Beverly Hills, CA: Sage, 1984; Durrett, M.E., Otaki, M. & Richards, P., 'Attachment and the mother's perception of support from the father', *International Journal of Behavioral Development*, 7, 1984, pp. 167–176; Goldberg, W.A. & Easterbrook, M.A., 'The role of marital quality in toddler development', *Developmental Psychology, 20*, 1984, pp. 504–514; Cummings, E.M. & Watson O'Reilly, A., 'Fathers in family context: Effects of marital quality on child adjustment', in Lamb, M.E. (ed.), *The Role of the Father in Child Development*, 3rd ed., New York: John Wiley & Sons, Inc., 1997; Parke, R.D., Power, T.G. & Gottman, J., 'Conceptualizing and quantifying influence patterns in the family triad', in Lamb, M.E., Suomi, S.J. & Stephenson, G.R., (eds.), *Social Interaction Analysis: Methodological Issues*, Madison, WI: University of Wisconsin Press, 1979, pp. 231–252.

2. Burghes, L., Clarke, L. & Cronin, N., *Fathers and Fatherhood in Britain*, London: Family Policy Studies Centre, 1997, pp 46–48; Amato, P., 'More than money?: Men's contributions to their children's lives', in Booth, A. & Crouter, N. (eds.), *Men in Families: When do They Get Involved? What Difference Does it Make?*, Mahwah, NJ: Erlbaum, 1998, pp. 241–278.

3. Pruett, K., *The Nurturing Father*, New York: Warner Books, 1987.

4. Bowlby, J., *Attachment and Loss: Vol 1. Attachment*, New York: Basic Books, 1969; Ainsworth, M., Blehar, M., Waters, E. & Wall, S., *Patterns of Attachment*, Hillsdale, NJ: Erlbaum, 1978; De Wolff, M. & van IJzendoorn, M., 'Sensitivity and attachment: A metaanalysis on parental antecedents of infant attachment', *Child Development*, 68, 1997, pp. 571–591; Pederson, D. & Moran, G., 'Expressions of the attachment relationship outside of the strange situation', *Child Development*, 67, 1996, pp. 915–927.

5. Cox, M.J., Owen, M.T., Henderson, V.K. & Margand, N.A., 'Prediction of infant-father and infant-mother attachment', *Developmental Psychology*, 28, pp. 474–483.

6. Lamb, M., Frodi, A., Hwang, C. & Steinberg, J., 'Mother- and father-infant interactions involving play and holding in traditional and non-traditional Swedish families', *Developmental Psychology*, 18, 1982, pp. 215–221; De Wolff van IJzendoorn, 'Sensitivity and attachment', *Child Development*, 1997.

7. Lamb, M.E., 'The development of father-infant relationships', in Lamb (ed.), *The Role of the Father in Child Development*, 3rd edition, 1997, pp. 104–120.

8. Biller., H.B., *Fathers and Families: Paternal Factors in Child Development*, Westport: Auburn, 1993; Biller, H.B. & Trotter, R.J., *The Father Factor*, New York: Simon & Schuster, 1994.

9. Teti, D.M., Bond, L.A. & Gibbs, E.D., 'Mothers, fathers, and siblings: A comparison of play styles and their influence upon infant cognitive level', *International Journal of Behavioral Development*, 11, 1988, pp. 415–432; Power, T. G., 'Mother- and father-infant play: A developmental analysis', *Child Development*, 56, 1985, pp. 1514–1524; Yogman, M., 'Games fathers and mothers play with their infants', *Infant Mental Health Journal*, 2, 1981, pp. 241–248.

10. Clarke-Stewart, K.A., 'And Daddy makes three: The father's impact on mother and young child', *Child Development*, 49, 1978, pp. 466–478; Crawley, S.B. & Sherrod, R.B., 'Parentinfant play during the first year of life', *Infant Behavior and Development*, 7, 1984, pp. 65–75; Lamb, M.E., 'Father-infant and mother-infant interaction in the first year of life', *Child Development*, 48, 1977, pp. 167–181; Clarke-Stewart, K.A., 'The father's contribution to children's cognitive and social development in early childhood', in Pedersen, F.A. (ed.), *The Father-Infant Relationship: Observational Studies in a Family Setting*, New York: Preaeger, 1980, pp. 111–146.

11. Radin, N., 'Primary caregiving fathers in intact families', in Gottfried, A.E. & Gottfried, A.W. (eds.), *Redefining Families*, New York: Plenum Press, 1994, pp. 11–54.; Radin, N., 'The influence of fathers upon sons and daughters and implications for school social work', *Social Work in Education*, 8, 1986, pp. 77–91; Nugent, J.K., 'Cultural and psychological influences on the father's role in infant development', *Journal of Marriage and the Family*, 53, 1991, pp. 475–585.

12. MacDonald, K. & Parke, R.D., 'Bridging the gap: Parent-child play interaction and peer interactive competence', *Child Development*, 55, 1984, pp. 1265–1277.

13. Parke, R.D. & Buriel, R., 'Socialization in the family: Ethnic and ecological perspectives', in Damon, W. & Eisenberg, N. (eds.), *Handbook of Child Psychology: Vol 3. Social, Emotional, and Personality Development*, 5th ed., New York: Wiley, 1998, pp. 463–552.

14. MacDonald & Parke, 'Bridging the gap', *Child Development*, 1984; Collins, W.A. & Russell, G., 'Mother–child and father–child relationships in middle childhood and adolescence: A developmental analysis', *Developmental Review*, 11,

1991, pp. 99–136; Bronstein, P., 'Difference in mothers' and fathers' behaviors toward children: A cross-cultural comparison', *Developmental Psychology*, 20, 1984, pp. 995–1003.

15. Lamb, M.E., Frodi, A.M., Hwang, C.P. & Frodi, M., 'Varying degrees of paternal involvement in infant care: Attitudinal and behavioural correlates', in Lamb, M.E. (ed.), *Nontraditional Families: Parenting and Child Development*, Hillsdale: Erlbaum, pp. 117–137.

16. Radin, 'Primary caregiving fathers in intact families', 1994; Radin, 'The influence of fathers', *Social Work in Education*, 1986; Nugent, 'Cultural and psychological influences', *Journal of Marriage and the Family*, 1991.

17. Cassidy, J., Parke, R.D., Butkovsky, L. & Braungart, J., 'Family-peer connections: The roles of emotional expressiveness within the family and children's understanding of emotions', *Child Development*, 63, 1992, pp. 603–618; Parke, R.D., MacDonald, K.D., Beitel, A. & Bhavnagri, N., 'The role of the family in the development of peer relationships', in Peters, R.D. & McMahon, R.J. (eds.), *Marriages and Families: Behavioral Treatments and Processes*, New York: Brunner/Mazel, 1988.

18. Volling, B. & Belsky, J., 'The contribution of mother-child and father-child relationships to the quality of sibling interaction: A longitudinal study', *Child Development*, 63, 1992, pp. 1209–1222.

19. Gottman, J.M., Katz, L.F. & Hooven, C., *Meta-Emotion: How Families Communicate Emotionally*, Mahwah, NJ: Erlbaum, 1996; Parke, R.D. & Brott, A.A., *Throwaway Dads: The Myths and Barriers That Keep Men from Being the Fathers They Want to Be*, Boston: Houghton Mifflin Company, 1999, pp 6–7; Koestner, R.S., Franz, C.E. & Weinberger, J., 'The family origins of empathic concern: A 26-year longitudinal study', *Journal of Personality and Social Psychology*, 61, 1990, pp. 586–595.

20. Biller, *Fathers and Families*, 1993.

21. Clarke-Stewart, 'And Daddy makes three', *Child Development*, 1978; Clarke-Stewart, 'The Father's contribution', in Pedersen (ed.), *The Father-Infant Relationship*, 1980.

22. Amato, P.R., 'Marital conflict, the parent-child relationship, and child self-esteem', *Family Relations*, 35, 1986, pp. 403–410.

23. Biller, H.B. & Solomon, R.S., *Child Maltreatment and Paternal Deprivation: A Manifesto for Research, Prevention, and Treatment*, Lexington, MA: Lexington, 1986.

24. Radin, 'Primary caregiving and rolesharing fathers of preschoolers', in Lamb (ed.), *Nontraditional Families*, 1982, pp. 173–208; Sagi, A., 'Antecedents and consequences of various degrees of paternal involvement in childrearing: The Israeli Project', in Lamb (ed.), *Nontraditional Families*, 1982.

25. Biller, H.B., 'Fatherhood: Implications for child and adult development', in Wolman, B.B. (ed.), *Handbook of Developmental Psychology*, Englewood Cliffs, NJ: Prentice-Hall, 1982, pp. 702–725; Biller & Solomon, *Child Maltreatment*, 1986.

26. Radin, 'Primary caregiving fathers', 1994; Radin, 'The influence of fathers', *Social Work in Education*, 1986; Nugent, 'Cultural and psychological influences', *Journal of Marriage and the Family*, 1991.

27. Kaplan, H.S., Lancaster, J.B. & Anderson, K.G., 'Human parental investment and fertility: The life histories of men in Albuquerque', in Booth & Crouter (eds.), *Men in Families*, 1998, pp. 55–109.

28. Radin, N., 'The role of the father in cognitive, academic and intellectual development', in Lamb, M.E., (ed.), *The Role of the Father in Child Development*, 2nd ed., New York: Wiley, 1981, pp. 379–427.

29. Snarey, J., *How Fathers Care for the Next Generation: A Four Decade Study*, Cambridge, MA: Harvard University Press, 1993; Radin, 'Primary caregiving fathers', 1994; Radin, 'The influence of fathers', *Social Work in Education*, 1986.

30. Biller, *Fathers and Families*, 1993; Biller & Trotter, *The Father Factor*, 1994.

31. Snarey, *How Fathers Care for the Next Generation*, 1993.

32. Barth, J.M. & Parke, R.D., 'Parent-child relationship influences on children's transition to school', *Merrill-Palmer Quarterly*, 39, 1992, pp. 173–195.

33. Browne, C.S. & Rife, J.C., 'Social, personality, and gender differences in at-risk and not-at-risk sixth grade students', *Journal of Early Adolescence*, 11, 1991, pp. 482–495; Amato, P.R. & Booth, A., *A Generation at Risk: Growing up in an Era of Family Upheaval*, Cambridge, MA: Harvard University Press, 1997; Franz, C.E., McClelland, D. & Weinberger, J., 'Childhood antecedents of conventional social accomplishment in midlife adults: A 36-year prospective study', *Journal of Personality and Social Psychology*, 60, 1991, pp. 586–595; Snarey, *How Fathers Care for the Next Generation*, 1993.

34. Reuter, M.W. & Biller, H.B., 'Perceived paternal nurturance-availability and personality adjustment among college males', *Journal of Consulting and Clinical Psychology*, 40, 1973, pp. 339–342; Biller, H.B., 'Fatherhood: Implications for child and adult development', in Wolman (ed.), *Handbook of Developmental Psychology*, 1982, pp. 702–725; Biller, *Fathers and Families*, 1993.

35. Barkley, R.A., *Hyperactive Children: A Handbook for Diagnosis and Treatment*, New York: Guilford, 1981; Margalit, M., 'Perception of parents' behavior, familial satisfaction, and sense of coherence in hyperactive children', *Journal of School Psychology*, 23, 1985, pp. 355–364.

36. Hoffman, M.L., 'Father absence and conscience development', *Child Development*, 4, 1975, pp. 400–406; Hoffman, M.L., 'The role of the father in moral internalization', in Lamb (ed.), *The Role of the Father in Child Development*, 2nd ed., 1981, pp. 359–378; Mischel, W., 'Father absence and delay of gratification', *Journal of Abnormal and Social Psychology*, 62, 1961, pp 116–124.

37. McClelland, D.C., Constantin, C.A., Regalado, D. & Stone, C., 'Making it to maturity', *Psychology Today*, 12, 1978, pp. 42–46; Biller, *Fathers and Families*, 1993.; Biller & Trotter, *The Father Factor*, 1994; Block, J., *Lives Through Time*, Berkeley, CA: Bancroft, 1971; Appleton, W.S., *Fathers and Daughters*, New York: Doubleday, 1981.

38. Catan, L., Dennison, C. & Coleman, J., *Getting Through: Effective Communication in the Teenage Years*, London: Trust for the Study of Adolescence & the BT Forum, 1997; O'Brien, M. & Jones, D., 'Young people's attitudes to fatherhood', in Moss, P. (ed.), *Father Figures: Fathers in the Families of the 1990s*, Children in Scotland, HMSO, 1995; O'Brien, M. & Jones, D., 'The absence and presence of fathers: Accounts from children's diaries,' in Bjornberg, U. & Kollind, A-K. (eds.), *Men's Family Relations*, Gothenburg: University of Goteborg Publications, 1996.

39. Lieberman, M., Doyle, A.B. & Markiewica, D., 'Developmental patterns in security of attachment to mother and father in late childhood and early adolescence: Associations with peer relations', *Child Development*, 70, 1999, pp. 202–213.

40. Amato, P., 'Father involvement and the self-esteem of children and adolescents', *Australian Journal of Sex, Marriage, and Family*, 7, 1986, pp. 6–16.

41. Cummings, E.M. & O'Reilly, A.W., 'Fathers in family context: Effects of marital quality on child adjustment', in Lamb (ed.), *The Role of the Father in Child Development*, 3rd ed., 1997, pp. 49–65; Parke & Buriel, 'Socialization in the family', in Damon & Eisenberg (eds.), *Handbook of Child Psychology, Vol. 3 Social, Emotional, and Personality Development*, 5th ed., 1998, pp. 463–552; Henggeler, S.W., Edwards, J.J., Cohen, R. & Summerville, M. B., 'Predicting changes in children's popularity: The role of family relations', *Journal of Applied Developmental Psychology*, 12, 1992, pp. 205–218; Isley, S., O'Neil, R. & Parke, R.D., 'The relations of parental affect and control behavior to children's classroom acceptance: A concurrent and predictive analysis', *Early Education and Development*, 7, 1996, pp. 7–23.

42. Shinn, M., 'Father absence and children's cognitive development', *Psychological Bulletin*, 85, 1978, pp. 295–324.

43. McLanahan, S.S., Seltzer, J.A., Hanson, T.L. & Thomson, E., 'Child support enforcement and child well-being: Greater security or greater conflict?', in Garfinkel, I., McLanahan, S.S. & Robins, P.K. (eds.), *Child Support and Child Well-Being*, Washington, DC: Urban Institute, 1994, pp. 285–316; Graham, J.W., Beller, A.H. & Hernandez, P.M., 'The effects of child support on education attainment', in Garfinkel, McLanahan, & Robins (eds.), *Child Support*, 1994, pp. 317–354; Knox, V.W. & Bane, M.J., 'Child support and schooling', in Garfinkel, McLanahan, & Robins (eds.), *Child Support*, 1994, pp. 285–316; Amato, P. & Gilbreth, J.G., 'Nonresident fathers and children's well-being: A meta-analysis', *Journal of Marriage and the Family*, 61, 1999, pp. 557–573. King, V., 'Nonresident father involvement and child well-being: Can Dads make a difference?', *Journal of Family Issues*, 15, 1994, pp. 78–96.

44. Furstenberg, F.F., Jr. & Cherlin, A.J., *Divided Families*, Cambridge, MA: Harvard University Press, 1991.

45. Ermisch, J. & Francesconi, M., 'Patterns of household and family formation', in Berthoud, R. & Gershuny, J. (eds.) *Seven Years in the Lives of British Families: Evidence on the dynamics of social change from the British Household Panel Survey*, London: The Policy Press, 2000.

46. Blankenhorn, D., *Fatherless America: Confronting our Most Urgent Social Problem*, New York: Basic Books, 1995; Popenoe, D., *Life Without Father*, New York: Free Press, 1996; Horn, W.F., *Father Facts*, Lancaster, PA: National Fatherhood Initiative, 1995.

47. Baumrind, D., 'Authoritarian versus authoritative parental control', *Adolescence*, 3, 1968, pp. 255–272; Parke & Buriel, 'Socialization in the family', in Damon & Eisenberg (eds.), *Handbook of Child Psychology, Vol. 3. Social, Emotional, and Personality Development*, 5th ed., 1998, pp. 463–552.

CIVITAS: THE INSTITUTE FOR THE STUDY OF CIVIL SOCIETY is an organization who provides research and educational work with the aim of facilitating informed public debate about issues that are relevant today, along with producing objective publications, seminars, and conferences geared toward mutual learning and open discussion.

**Peggy Drexler and
Linden Gross**

Good News from the New Home Front

"I'm gonna make a club, and my friends can be in
my club no matter what they wear."

— 4½-year-old Quentin

TWO-AND-A-HALF-YEAR-OLD QUENTIN was kicked in the
shins by another little boy on the playground. Crying, he
ran over to the yard monitor for comfort, then, of his own
volition, approached the little boy who had kicked him. "I
do not like what you did, Martin," he told him in a voice
full of emotion. "I would not kick you—you should never
kick, and that's the truth!" Rather than impulsively kick-
ing back, as many boys his age might have done, Quentin
was using his words effectively at an exceptionally young
age. A couple of years later, when Quentin found himself
excluded from a group of other boys because he was wear-
ing the wrong shoelaces, he announced, "I'm gonna make
a club, and my friends can be in my club no matter what
they wear."

Eight-year-old Mac was already a talented cartoonist
who was into music, sports, math, and language arts. He
developed an especially close friendship with his buddy
Alec. The two would sit with their arms around each other
in the car when one of their parents drove them to soccer
games or the playground. Later, after playing rough and
tough together, they would read a book side by side and
just talk to each other. Then Alec transferred to another
school. "It was lonely, like cloud rain," Mac recalled. "You
know how a rainy day makes you feel bad? It was like
that."

Quentin and Mac are both being raised in households led by women. Quentin is the son of two lesbians,
Mac's mother gave birth to him as a single woman, using
a anonymous donor, and is parenting him on her own.
Like nearly all of the boys I interviewed for my study of
sons parented solely by women, both Quentin and Mac
exhibited striking levels of stability, independence, creativity, and caring. As I will show in this chapter, these
mom-raised sons are avatars of a new social moment, one
that is producing boys who promise to become good, even
exceptional, men.

Focusing on how these children view themselves, the
studies that became this book were the first to investigate
lesbian couples and their sons in their own homes and
as they lived their lives. To my knowledge, no researchers
had previously introduced themselves so intimately into
the lives of gay and lesbian families to perform what child

psychoanalyst Anna Freud called "direct observation"—
establishing a sustained involvement with a person or
family that is maintained long enough so that the observer
has some basis in experience, in words heard and actions
witnessed, for coming to more general conclusions. My
similar research of single mothers raising sons (of women
who were widowed, divorced, or separated and their sons
whose fathers were otherwise to on the scene) is unique in
this very new field of study.

I began my work by examining the elementary- and
junior-high-school-age sons of lesbians in planned, intact,
stable, two-parent relationships in the San Francisco Bay
Area—first comparing their moral development with
that of boys from two-parent heterosexual families. I also
explored how these boys grow up with a sense of their own
masculinity with no father around. How do they react to
not having a father—indeed, in many cases, having only
an anonymous *seed daddy*? Coming from America's newest
and fastest-growing sector of minority families, how did
they deal with teasing and harassment from other children? Were they developing the kind of moral spine that
our culture believes it is up to fathers to provide?

Just to give you a taste of some of those findings:
The two groups of boys showed no significant differences
in their moral reasoning, and both sets of parents showed
no significant difference in their basic beliefs regarding
moral behavior. However, when I subjected the parental
attitudes data to a sophisticated measure of statistical analysis, I found that lesbian mothers scored higher on the
moral attitude scale than their heterosexual counterparts
and were more likely to create opportunities for their sons
to examine moral and values issues. They were also more
likely to talk about morality in terms of broader social
implications. The Rasch analysis also suggested that there
was a positive correlation between the lesbian-led families'
parental attitudes about moral issues and the rate of moral
development in their sons.

It turned out, however, that the nonbiological
mothers (I call them *social mothers* throughout this
book) and the fathers in the heterosexual couples were
more likely to teach their sons by talking about principles and what ought to be. The biological mothers, in
both groups, tended to teach their sons ethical behavior
using emotional and empathic language. The heterosexual fathers and social mothers more readily praised their
sons. The biological mothers in both samples were more
worried about their sons than the social mothers and

heterosexual fathers. But by and large the similarities between the couples outweighed the differences, with a couple of notable exceptions.

My findings revealed that the sons of two-mother families spent less time with an outside caregiver than those of two-parent families. "We don't like the concept of having our children in the care of other people, however lovely, for long periods of time," a lesbian social mom told me. My study showed that not only did these mothers spend more time with their children; they shared parenting responsibilities fairly equally. That didn't go unnoticed by other mothers around them. "In some ways I'm jealous of your relationship," Christine Carson, a 41-year-old married professor and mother of two, told the lesbian mother of one of her son's friends, "because you two tackle this thing [raising children] 50–50."

I did not use questionnaires, but for the first phase of my study, I did rely on objective or standardized measures to ascertain if there were any differences in the moral development of boys from two-mother homes and their counterparts being raised by a mother and father.

A vast majority of studies have concluded that the sons and daughters of gays and lesbians are no more anxious, depressed, insecure, or prone to emotional troubles than the children of heterosexuals.

Michael Lamb, Ph.D., chief of the section on Social and Emotional Development of the National Institute of Child Health and Human Development, has also asserted that being raised by gay parents would not have negative consequences for children. "It's become clear that the absence of a male figure is really not important," Dr. Lamb said. Louise Silverstein, Ph.D., and Carl Auerbach, Ph.D., have agreed with that assessment, concluding that children don't necessarily require an adult male as one of their caregivers.

Still, in the present climate of bias, any differences found in the children of homosexual parents have been equated with deficit.

Charting the moral development of the boys was complicated because it required me to analyze the verbal responses of these children, taking into account developmental-stage issues and levels of sophistication, as well as beliefs about morality. Children share two worlds, one with parents and other adult authorities, and another with peers and friends. The relationships in each world contribute equally, but differently, to children's development. To function successfully in the world, children need to discover why and under what circumstances they have to obey authority figures and how to handle conflict with their peers—including issues of sharing and fairness, such as who gets what when, why, and under what circumstances. By examining how boys from two-parent lesbian families thought about and made use of moral principles with both adults and peers, I was able to ascertain whether these boys were the same as or different from those reared in more conventional families. In addition, in both groups I evaluated the families' parental teaching methods about

morality, parental time spent with the boys, and important figures in their lives from birth to their present age.

My original query (and the subject of my dissertation) was intended to establish whether and how the sons of lesbians developed moral character without the presence of a moralizing father figure. Hearing of my proposed work, some of the faculty and my fellow students laughed at me, wondering how I would actually find enough planned, two-parent lesbian families raising sons between the ages of 5 and 9 to perform a direct observation. I admit that I shared their concern. But even as early as 1996, it turned out that these families were everywhere. Word of my study spread, and I ended up with a waiting list of two-mother lesbian families from all over the San Francisco Bay Area, and a few more from across the country, who were raising sons. In a nation still preoccupied with issues of single mothers, lesbian and gay parents were flying under the cultural radar.

Like many straight people of my generation, I had very little firsthand knowledge of gay and lesbian lives. Having lived first in New York and then in San Francisco for 18 years, I knew many gay and lesbian people, but I had never explored their issues and circumstances in any systematic way. I worried about how I would be received by the lesbian-headed families I planned to study. Would they wonder if I was a lesbian, and if they found out I was not, would they accept me? Would they perceive me as violating their hard-won turf, or think me primed to be judgmental of their parenting? But only 1 out of the 32 lesbian mothers I interviewed asked me if I was a lesbian. Most of the lesbian mothers I interviewed—as well as the single mothers by choice that I went on to study— said they felt like pioneers in uncharted territory. They embraced any psychological exploration that would help them raise their sons well. All the lesbian mothers I interviewed welcomed me into their homes, proved extremely cooperative and eager to talk with me, and trusted me. The frank, wide-ranging conversations we shared readily normalized our differences. I learned that I did not have to be concerned about asking honest questions. In fact, the mothers were asking themselves the same questions about their sons' development.

This study centered on two-mother lesbian couples who had given birth to sons they were raising in intact, two-parent households. None of these 16 boys had a father on the premises. Many of them did not even know the names of their fathers—nor did their mothers. Thanks to the technological revolution of anonymous-donor insemination, the identity of a founding father may not even be part of the basic proposition of a two-mother family or a single-mother family.

Once a technology that served mostly married couples, donor insemination is now a practice that assists unmarried women, both straight and gay, and thereby yields many different sorts of families. The fathers of sons I studied were unknown donors, only some of whom wanted their identities to be revealed to their offspring;

known donors; or donors who were family friends or relatives of nonbiological mothers. In one situation, a child shared a known donor with a classmate, and in another the father of a classmate was the donor. Whether or not a donor has a social father relationship with his child, he usually has surrendered his legal paternal rights. The relationships vary. In Thomas's case, "I see Chris, like, once every month. I guess he's my dad, but he's mostly my uncle. I don't think he's a parent, exactly, but we have a lot of fun going to the zoo and stuff." Nathan, another boy in the study, saw his own donor father infrequently at best. However, his sister's donor father actively participated in family activities on a weekly and sometimes daily basis.

Because lesbians are constructing families that do not fit standard legal definitions, they cannot usually adopt as couples but must instead undertake single-parent adoptions. Lesbian couples have generated the revolutionary concept of the social mother—the parent who has no genetic connection with the son she helps to raise, who may or may not have a legal relationship with him, but who possesses a vital emotional bond. Talking about his social mother, Nathan said, "It was Stephanie who taught me to play basketball. So when I get to play in the NBA, I'll invite her to the games."

It takes strong women to build a family from scratch. The lesbians I studied were mostly white-collar workers who had succeeded as businesspeople or in their professions. These lesbian moms were "social saboteurs," women who were living and raising children outside the dominant culture in conscious, courageous ways. From coming out as lesbians to deciding to have children, they exhibited the will and temperament to buck prevailing notions and create their own family structures, with very few models from which to work. Moreover, they were very conscious that they were on the cutting edge of a social movement. "Mostly we just have a normal home with Nathan and Beth," said Stephanie Goldman, 10-year-old Nathan's social and adoptive mother and 8-year-old Beth's biological mother. "We go to work, take the kids to ballet lessons and soccer games. But you can't help but realize that beyond your own domestic sphere, you're doing something really new and significant."

I have come to think that this sense of significance informed the parenting style of the mothers I studied. But other factors contributed to their mindfulness. We all know that it's better to be wanted than not, and adoptive parents often repeat that being chosen makes for a very special child. The very nature of parenthood through donor insemination means that children are thought about and brought into the world with care and preparation. Women who are inseminated—and who adopt—must think hard and long before making a family. The children brought into families in these ways are not accidents, and they are not surprises because so much planning has gone into their births. Since many of these women were older, the testing they had undergone had provided information about the sex of the baby (or

babies) early, and so they had had more time to begin the mental preparation for having sons or daughters.

In addition to being older, these lesbian mothers tended to be better educated and more financially secure than average moms. They had the wherewithal to develop a parenting style that was both intense and considered. The developmental advantages this offered may help to explain why their sons were so remarkable.

The families who participated in my study turned out to be an extremely stable group. The couples had been together from 8 to 22 years and had lived at the same address for an average of 5½ years. They were predominantly White, middle- to upper-middle-class, and highly educated. I have been asked why there were almost no people of color in my study. Like mine, most research in this area has concerned a primarily White and privileged population. Lesbian identity among socioeconomically subordinate groups is generally less visible or less affirmed than it is among more prosperous, White, educated, urban populations. Ethnographic evidence suggests that closeted lesbian and gay people of color often value racial solidarity over sexual adhesiveness. Racial/ethnic allegiances may deter disproportionate numbers of people of color from coming out.

After my research was completed and analyzed, and my dissertation written, defended, and accepted, I found myself continuing to think about the sons of the two-mother families I had come to know. The boys stayed in my mind, and I wanted to learn more about them. So I went back to the families I had interviewed and did further research on them, using the same methods I had for my initial study. I wanted to explore the larger issues of the parenting these boys received and how they were forming their identities as boys at home and in the world. Throughout my studies, I was known to these children as a psychologist who came into their homes, talked with them, played games with them, drew with them, and was very interested in what it felt like to be a boy growing up and to come from an alternative family. I also had plenty of questions to ask these boys' mothers.

This time my questions were even more far-reaching. What kind of parents did lesbians make, anyway? What kind of values did they hold up and try to see their sons live out? What were the children of these families like as they grew up? Were the gay and lesbian families representative of families in our society?

I also wanted to look at the major problems and challenges these families faced. Was one mommy more real than the other? In the absence of the standard mom-dad dynamic to divide up the tasks of parenting, which roles did lesbian mothers take on, and how did their sons relate to two female authority figures? What were the fears, worries, and desires of children of gay and lesbian families? Did they look at other, more "normal" families with envy, fear, or even contempt? Was it possible that they felt special having two moms? Might they even have seen benefits accrued as the result of having the extra mom that other children lacked?

My work took me into these families' homes over the course of several years. Spending hour after hour with the boys and their mothers, I encouraged them to talk about the specifics of their lives growing up with two mothers and no "everyday father." When conversation lagged, I played games or had the boys talk about the drawings they made for me. I gathered information through notes, tape-recorded conversations, and summaries of observations.

When I first began visiting the boys, I was on an intellectual journey, seeking to explore a specific psychological and moral issue. But like many journeys, mine was full of twists and turns, and my destination turned out to be different from what I had expected. It became a journey of the heart as well as the mind. It led me beyond the basic questions of my research into the broader and even more compelling issues of maverick mothers of all sorts, women who were raising sons on their own.

After I finished the second stage of research with the sons of lesbians, I happened to be talking to Kamala, a heterosexual single mother by choice who had two sons in their early teens enrolled in my daughter's school. She told me that when she asked one of her sons to define the most important part of being a boy, he replied, "Taking care of others." She was proud of him for that because caregiving is not usually associated with teenage boys. Kamala's comment spurred me to see whether what I had witnessed in the sons of lesbians was also true of boys raised by single mothers. I set out to intensively interview 30 single mothers by choice who were raising sons all across the country, in places like Arkansas, California, Louisiana, New York, North Carolina, and Texas. I also interviewed 30 mothers who were single by circumstance—such as the death of a partner, separation, divorce, or the complete abrogation of a partner's parental responsibilities—who were raising sons without a father present in the home.

Like the lesbian couples who had chosen to have children, the single mothers by choice were highly motivated, successful, self-supporting career women. Though geographic considerations prevented me from meeting many of their sons, their views about raising boys turned out to be very similar to those of the lesbian mothers I interviewed. They were dedicated to their beliefs in non-sexist parenting and said they accepted who their sons were rather than consciously molding them into what they thought their boys should be. They believed in open communication and respect for differences, but they enforced firm limits and sought to instill a high sense of personal, intrafamilial, and social responsibility in their sons. "You are my emissaries," single mom Anna Malicki, 43, would tell her sons. She kept Matthew, 12, and Eddie, 14, in line by making it clear that they represented her best self out in the world.

At home, the sons of both single- and two-mother families were expected to be participatory members of the household, doing chores and fulfilling other age-appropriate responsibilities. By the time he was 6, Quentin was already earning his allowance by pulling the sheets off the beds, helping with the washing on Saturdays, bagging the newspapers for recycling, setting the table at night, and even washing the salad for dinner. "What we say to him is 'Everybody works in this family. We all work. Nobody gets to sit and be waited on,'" his co-mom, Sarah, told me. "He likes having a role in the family and having jobs that are his. I think it's important to a kid to feel like he's got a role and he's part of the team."

These mothers' high expectations stretched past action to interaction. "The guidelines we set up for behavior—treat each other with respect and kindness—extend outward from our family to our neighbors and friends," one social mom told me.

Single mothers and co-moms fostered independence in their sons, encouraging them to do whatever they could by themselves, from sounding out letters and writing their names to closing the car door and carrying their dishes to the sink. They facilitated this process by providing the tools their sons needed. Single mom Deborah Iverson, for example, made cleanup easier for her three sons by storing little dustpans and whisk brooms under each sink and in the playroom. These mothers also worked to keep their boys connected with their parents and siblings, encouraging free expression of a broad range of feelings. Those sons that I did meet—both grown men and younger boys—reminded me of the sons of lesbians I had come to know so well.

During the time I spent as a gender scholar at Stanford University, I evaluated my clinical data and the sons' and mothers' narratives. Patterns and categories began to jump out at me. To interpret my research, I also drew on my personal experience as both a biological mother and an adoptive mother happily married to a very busy man and a good father. My own experience would serve as a one-woman control group representing married mothers, and as a useful example of a mother who found her maternal role and her relation to fatherhood to be continually evolving.

My study determined, essentially, that boys will be boys. I found sons raised in woman-headed homes to be astonishingly deft at answering questions about—or simply figuring out for themselves—how to be boys. Their mothers were also very good at instilling male confidence in their sons. These boys readily engaged in the task of relating to their parents, siblings, and the men in their lives. Whether they grew up in single-mother families or lesbian-led nuclear families, these boys had an innate and astonishing ability to get what they needed in order to establish a strong and resilient sense of their own masculinity. [I also] tell of my experiences and show how these maverick mothers worked to nurture their sons' development and the various ways in which the boys exhibited their masculinity. You will see that they were acutely aware of the very process of becoming manly and that their mothers fostered this awareness.

The boys in my study were not sissies or mama's boys. Nor did they compensate for the lack of a father figure by becoming overly aggressive. Other studies have shown that sons raised in lesbian households are no more likely to become homosexual than they would if raised in heterosexual families.

But how could they be so boyish without fathers as role models? In the first phase of my study of lesbian and heterosexual families, I found that lesbian mothers reported that their sons had fewer male role models than their heterosexual counterparts did. Yet when I began to meet with the boys biweekly over a 2-year period, I saw that those boys actually had more male figures in their lives than did boys from heterosexual families, where the father was often the sole male in their lives.

Boys raised in mother-only families were remarkably resourceful in securing role models for their masculinity. They searched out teachers, friends of the family, coaches, and neighbors. If the boys were having trouble finding these men, their mothers stepped in to help. Most of the boys were fascinated by sports figures, and they had precocious knowledge of the details of the lives of their heroes. They were especially intrigued by the lives of two-generation athletes, taking special pleasure in following those father-son duos. Since the boys themselves had a big say in the choice of males they admired, they were able to select men whose interests and personalities were in harmony with their own. They gave short shrift to those who were unkind or authoritarian, whether blood relatives or not.

Still, I assumed that the boys I studied must have suffered from the stigma of being raised in unconventional families. Not necessarily. I found that their mothers made serious efforts to help their sons deal constructively with the prejudice they faced, thereby helping them develop significant strengths. Perhaps as a result, maverick mothers' sons seemed to have an easy time thinking independently and standing up for what they believed. They had an advantage when it came to acquiring moral standards and courage.

These boys were remarkably sophisticated about the world and about themselves. They were unusually able to articulate their concerns and their joys. Over the years I spent with them, I learned to expect—and to appreciate—the high degree of emotional savvy they exhibited. I call them *head-and-heart boys,* you will see how they dealt with the vicissitudes of their lives, navigated the shoals of complex family situations, and grew into strong and sensitive young men.

Throughout my work with the boys, it seemed clear to me that their essential boyishness was hardwired (and most biological research into gender substantiates my observations). But I needed to understand the dynamics of the nurturing environment. I listened to many single, widowed, divorced, and lesbian mothers tell me about their ups and downs and their boy-rearing strategies. Almost universally, I found a commitment on their part to talk and talk and talk with their sons. The communication imperative proved to be another big lesson of my research.

We have been raised in a society where mother-son closeness is approached with suspicion. I wanted to find out if this trepidation—especially of maverick mother families and their sons—was warranted. Simply put, it isn't. I found that the combination of closeness and conversation led to a natural intimacy between mother and son that continued throughout their lives. A major factor in this connectedness was the mother's ability to acknowledge mistakes to her son, to let him know what she was feeling, and her determination to treat her son's feelings with respect. By admitting to being only human, these mothers encouraged their sons' humanity. And by taking their sons seriously, they imbued them with self-respect. This clearly constituted a healthy version of mother-son closeness.

I also wanted to know how these single or lesbian mothers went about creating a family setting for their sons. [I also discuss] "Collected Families," [which] tells stories of moms who carved out rich and varied environments for their children from all the parts of their lives: blood relations, friends, colleagues, community organizations, and special groups for single moms. These families reminded me of the Advent calendar, on which each day until Christmas you open another window and see a different scene. It could be soccer with Mom, piano in the afternoon with Grandma, and a tutoring session with a donor dad across town, or perhaps dinner with him, his wife, and their teenage son. A complex summons to adulthood looms for these boys. The challenges they face are also the ones that most preoccupy America's moral arbiters—namely, are sons (even more than daughters) from alternative families equipped to come to terms with their own sexuality? Can they reconcile their sexuality with that of their parents without undue confusion? And most important, can they navigate the larger world without protection from their parents or the communities in which they were raised?

"I admit, sometimes I wonder if Evan would be better equipped for the world if he had an everyday dad around," Vivian told me. "And sure, I worry about what Evan is going to face when he's on his own. When they hear he was raised by two mothers, will they ever vote for him for president?" Vivian shrugged and rolled her eyes. For his part, Evan was pretty sure he'd still get to play first base for the San Francisco Giants.

From the evidence offered by their childhoods, I believe these boys will have the social and psychological equipment they need to become steady, inquisitive, well-balanced teenagers able to reconcile the conflicting demands they will face. All of these boys will be strongly supported by their mothers as they venture toward their independent sexuality. "As a young boy and then as a teenager, I did all the same things every normal son does: play sports, have girlfriends, break curfew, have parties when my parents were away," 34-year-old Gene Leighton, son of a lesbian mom and a straight dad, told me. Gene's mom divorced his dad when Gene was 8 and formed a life partnership with another woman. "Like most teenagers, I was confused about a lot of things, but my sexual preference was not one of them," Gene added. "In that sense my growing up was perfectly normal."

Certainly, sons of gay parents will have to establish the terms of their sexuality with more self-consciousness than most other teenage boys will. If my experience with sons in lesbian-led families is any indication about how these boys feel about women, they will probably be able to relate to other females with great respect and openness. In fact, they may grow up to be the strong yet open-hearted men women are purported to want to marry. As lesbian

co-mom Sarah confided to me with amused pride about her 12-year-old son, "Quentin is going to make some woman a great husband someday. He'll be a great catch."

Peggy Drexler is an assistant professor of psychology in psychiatry at Weill Medical College of Cornell University.

Linden Gross is a former special features editor for the *Los Angeles Times* and a ghostwriter for several books.

EXPLORING THE ISSUE

Are Fathers Really Necessary?

Critical Thinking and Reflection

1. How do lesbian mothers differ from the "average" mother?
2. How has the focus of "strengthening father's effects on families" changed over the years?
3. What do you think is the best way to encourage father involvement? Give three reasons for your answer.
4. What are the three main demographic trends that have increased the likelihood that children will live apart from at least one of their biological parents? Do you think these trends can be reversed? Why or why not?

Is There Common Ground?

What role does the father play in the development of a child? Is it the role of dad and what society says he should be that becomes important to the child rather than how the father treats his child? Or, is it that important? If the former is true, then anyone, regardless of how he or she treats the child, will be important to the child. We often see evidence of this phenomenon in dealing with abused children. No matter what the abuse, most children in this situation want to stay at home with abusive fathers rather than be placed in foster care. When confronted with "telling on" their fathers, children will not say what abuse occurred for fear of losing their father's love and being separated from him.

If it is true that the role of dad and what society says he should be is what is important to the child, the quality of interaction and events that children share with their fathers becomes critical to their development. Then why could women not play that role? Women can interact with children in nearly all the same ways that men can. Women can just as easily accompany children to baseball games, act as the soccer coach, or attend the school play, as can men. Thus, the question might not be "Are fathers really necessary?" but "Are men really necessary for the positive development of children?" To many, this would not only mean an assault on the role of fatherhood, but would also constitute an attack on men in general.

As with most issues, extremes on either side make less sense than the middle ground. Child development experts would probably agree that the more adults, both male and female, involved in a child's life, the better. Having a variety of people in one's life brings a variety of experiences and an extensive social network that can benefit children throughout their lives.

Currently, significant research on fathering is being conducted. Soon, scientists will be able to make more definitive statements about how mothers and fathers influence a child's life. Perhaps, one can conclude that as a society, we are all responsible for fathering and mothering. This is especially true for families that do not have the choice of raising children in a two-parent home due to divorce or the death of a spouse. We must continue to strive to find ways to support all families so that children will experience the optimal growth and development that they all deserve.

Create Central

www.mhhe.com/createcentral

Additional Resources

National Organization of Single Mothers, Inc. Retrieved on April 8, 2011, from http://singlemothers .org/cms/index.php

The National Organization of Single Mothers, Inc., is an organization dedicated to "helping single moms by choice or chance face the daily challenges of life with wisdom, wit, dignity, confidence, and courage."

Parade. Obama's Father's Day Speech. Retrieved on April 8, 2011, from www.parade.com/news/2009/06/ barack-obama-we-need-fathers-tostep-up.html

This website provides the full text of President Barack Obama's June 21, 2009, Father's Day speech.

The Family Economic Strategies. Retrieved on April 8, 2011, from www.sixstrategies.org/

The Family Economic Self-Sufficiency Project describes six strategies that families, especially women, can follow as they move from welfare to self-sufficiency. See the "Setting the Standard for American Working Families" report.

Work and Family: National Partnership for Women and Families. Retrieved on April 8, 2011, from www.nationalpartnership.org

This public education and advocacy site aims "to promote fairness in the workplace, quality health care, and policies that help women and men meet the dual demands of work and family." This site includes a wealth of information about relevant public policy issues, including the Family Medical Leave Act.

Internet References . . .

The Atlantic

www.theatlantic.com/magazine/archive/2010/07/are
-fathers-necessary/308136/

Psychology Today

www.psychologytoday.com/blog/the-long-reach
-childhood/201106/the-importance-fathers

Selected, Edited, and with Issue Framing Material by:
Kourtney Vaillancourt, *New Mexico State University*

ISSUE

Does Divorce Create Long-Term Negative Effects for Children?

YES: **Elizabeth Marquardt**, from "The Bad Divorce," *First Things* (February 2005)

NO: **Constance Ahrons**, from "No Easy Answers: Why the Popular View of Divorce Is Wrong," *We're Still Family: What Grown Children Have to Say About Their Parents' Divorce* (HarperCollins, 2004)

Learning Outcomes

After reading this issue, you should be able to:

- List and discuss some of the problems that children of divorce may face.
- Describe resiliency and the lessons that children learn from divorce.
- Understand some of the complicating factors that make it difficult to determine definitively how divorce affects children.

ISSUE SUMMARY

YES: Elizabeth Marquardt, author and director of the Center for Marriage and Families, states that divorce is a tragedy, which has negative lifelong effects on children. She specifically argues against the data collection method that Constance Ahrons used in her current study.

NO: Constance Ahrons, author, therapist, and co-chair of the Council on Contemporary Families, believes that the idea that children of divorce end up troubled and unable to form adult attachments is a myth. Her research found that children of divorce were strong, wise, and had close family relationships.

How does divorce affect children? Do they perceive it as positive or negative? How would their lives differ if their parents had worked out their problems and stayed together, even if only for the sake of the children? How do children from divorced families differ from those in intact homes—happy or unhappy? Do both groups have similarities, or are they significantly different? These are questions researchers ask when they study the effects of divorce on children.

According to some studies, children from divorced homes are more likely to divorce themselves. Other studies indicate that the quality of the home postdivorce is more likely to affect children's development than the actual divorce event. Is society setting children up for subsequent failed marriages by condoning divorce? Or is divorce simply a solution to the problem of choosing the wrong partner, giving individuals a way of correcting that mistake? Does the divorce spell disaster for children as they grow into adulthood, or are there other explanations for the problems, which children from divorced homes might exhibit?

As the divorce debate evolved from the 1960s to the 1980s, some professionals viewed divorce as an acceptable alternative to living in an unhappy home, while others saw divorce as having devastating effects on children and the family. In the 1990s, a movement to do away with no-fault divorce also spawned a renewed interest in the effects of divorce on children. Family scientists, therapists, and researchers questioned the belief that children eventually adjust to the effects of divorce and that it is better for children to live in a divorced home than in an unhappy, intact home. In the 2000s, longitudinal data on divorce's effects presented conflicting conclusions with more questions than answers to the issue.

There are numerous studies on the effects of divorce on children. Some show that children benefit from divorce while others show it is the worst thing that ever happened. On the positive side, children from divorced homes reap benefits as a consequence of their divorce experience, particularly if parents model responsible coping skills. Some children do better in a home without the constant tension and fighting found in an unhappy intact home. These children appear more mature, more realistic about life, and more flexible.

Problems for children in divorced families are well documented. For these children, parents split physically and legally, but not emotionally. These family members might ride an emotional rollercoaster for years after the initial divorce decree. One parent pitted against the other with the child in the middle is all too common for divorced families. Family turmoil may result in children doing poorly in school, beginning to have sex at an early age, and displaying delinquent behavior. Children have no say in the divorce, but must live with the instability and confusion that occurs after the breakup.

If parents decide to divorce, there are things they can do to keep the divorce more healthy according to family life educators. They suggest not putting the other parent down in front of the children. This helps maintain some sense of stability and civility for the children. Seek outside help for the emotional turmoil associated with divorce, rather than using the children as a "sounding board." Make sure any heated discussions with the other parent are held in private where the children cannot hear. Also, try to accept the other parent's new mate so that children do not feel they are betraying the other parent when visiting the new family.

In the following selections, arguments are made about the long-term effects of divorce on children. Based on research and personal experience, Elizabeth Marquardt feels divorce is "bad" for children. She believes that the types of questions Constance Ahrons asked in her survey led participants to report a positive view of divorce even if they felt differently. Elizabeth Marquardt describes children of divorce as grieving losses following their parents' divorce and negatively affected by the fractured family life that follows divorce. Constance Ahrons interviewed 98 divorced couples in 1992. In the current article, she reports on interviews with the same parents' 173 grown children. Based on the grown children's responses, she believes the divorce was a "good" event and that children learned positive life lessons from it.

According to Elizabeth Marquardt, children of divorce feel a loss of security and confidence when their parents divorce. They are damaged by the event and never recover from the fractured family system they endure. She believes that the conclusions Constance Ahrons drew were inaccurate and based on faulty research methods. Constance Ahrons found that children emerged from divorce wiser, stronger, and with a greater appreciation for strong family relationships.

YES ↵

Elizabeth Marquardt

The Bad Divorce

It is often said that those who are concerned about the social and personal effects of divorce are nostalgic for the 1950s, yearning for a mythical time when men worked, women happily stayed home baking cookies for the kids, and marriages never dissolved. Yet often the same people who make the charge of mythology are caught in a bit of nostalgia of their own, pining for the sexual liberationism of the 1970s, when many experts began to embrace unfettered divorce, confident that children, no less than adults, would thrive once "unhappy" marriages were brought to a speedy end.

Constance Ahrons, who coined the term "the good divorce" in the title of an influential 1992 book that examined ninety-eight divorcing couples, is very much a member of the latter camp. In her new book, *We're Still Family: What Grown Children Have to Say about Their Parents' Divorce*, Ahrons returns to those ninety-eight couples to survey their now-grown children. The result is a study based on telephone interviews with 173 young adults from eighty-nine families that tries to advance the idea it is not divorce itself that burdens children but rather the way in which parents divorce. As in her earlier book, Ahrons argues that the vocabulary we use to discuss divorce and remarriage is negative; she would prefer that we regard divorced families as "changed" or "rearranged" rather than broken, damaged, or destroyed. She claims that upbeat language will, above all, help children feel less stigmatized by divorce. Both of her books offer many new terms, such as "binuclear" and "tribe," to describe divorced families. The specific novelty of the new book is Ahrons' claim that her interviewees view their parents' divorces in a positive light.

It is with delight, then, that Ahrons shares surprising new findings from her on-going study. According to Ahrons, over three-quarters of the young people from divorced families who she interviewed do not wish their parents were still together. A similar proportion feel their parents' decision to divorce was a good one, that their parents are better off today, and that they themselves are either better off or not affected by the divorce. To general readers who have been following the debates about children of divorce in recent years, such findings might sound like big news. But there are problems.

According to Ahrons, over three-quarters of the young people whom she interviewed do not wish that their parents were still together. A similar proportion feel that their parents' decision to divorce was a good one, that their parents are better off today, and that they themselves are either better off because of the divorce or have not been affected by it. Statistically, that sounds overwhelmingly convincing. But an answer to a survey question tells us very little unless we have a context for interpreting it and some grasp of the actual experiences that gave rise to it.

Like those whom Ahrons interviewed, I grew up in a divorced family, my parents having split when I was two years old. Like Ahrons, I am a researcher in the field, having led, with Norval Glenn, a study of young adults from both divorced and intact families that included a nationally representative telephone survey of some 1,500 people. As someone who studies children of divorce and who is herself a grown child of divorce, I have noticed that the kinds of questions that get asked in such studies and the way the answers are interpreted often depend on whether the questioner views divorce from the standpoint of the child or the parent.

Take, for example, Ahrons' finding that the majority of people raised in divorced families do not wish that their parents were together. Ahrons did not ask whether as children these young people had hoped their parents would reunite. Instead, she asked if they wish today their parents were still together. She presents their negative answers as gratifying evidence that divorce is affirmed by children. But is that really the right conclusion to draw?

Imagine the following scenario. One day when you are a child your parents come to you and tell you they are splitting up. Your life suddenly changes in lots of ways. Dad leaves, or maybe Mom does. You may move or change schools or lose friendships, or all of the above. Money is suddenly very tight and stays that way for a long time. You may not see one set of grandparents, aunts, uncles, and cousins nearly as much as you used to. Then, Mom starts dating, or maybe Dad does. A boyfriend or girlfriend moves in, perhaps bringing along his or her own kids. You may see one or both of your parents marry again; you may see one or both of them get divorced a second time. You deal with the losses. You adjust as best you can. You grow up and try to figure out this "relationship" thing for yourself. Then, some interviewer on the telephone asks if you wish your parents were still together today. A lifetime of pain and anger and adjustment flashes before your eyes. Any memory of your parents together as a couple—if you can

Marquardt, Elizabeth. From *First Things*, February 2005. Copyright © 2005 by Institute on Religion and Public Life. Reprinted by permission.

remember them together at all—is buried deep under all those feelings. Your divorced parents have always seemed like polar opposites to you. No one could be more different from your mother than your father, and vice versa. "No," you reply to the interviewer, "I don't wish my parents were still together." Of course, one cannot automatically attribute such a train of thought to all of Ahrons' interview subjects. Still, it is plausible, and it might explain at least some of the responses. But Ahrons does not even consider it.

Ahrons tells us that the vast majority of young people in her study feel that they are either better off or not affected by their parents' divorce. For a child of divorce there could hardly be a more loaded question than this one. The generation that Ahrons is interviewing grew up in a time of massive changes in family life, with experts assuring parents that if they became happier after divorce, their children would as well. There wasn't a lot of patience for people who felt otherwise—especially when those people were children, with their aggravating preference for conventional married life over the adventures of divorce, and their tendency to look askance at their parents' new love interests.

However, a child soon learns the natural lesson that complaining about a parent's choices is a surefire way to be ignored or worse, and that what parents want above all is praise for those choices. Few things inspire as much admiration among divorced parents and their friends as the words of a child reassuring them that the divorce was no big deal—or even better, that it gave the child something beneficial, like early independence, or a new brother or sister. Parents are proud of a resilient child. They are embarrassed and frustrated by a child who claims to be a victim. And who among us wants to be a victim? Who would not rather be a hero, or at least a well-adjusted and agreeable person? When the interviewer calls on the telephone, what will the young adult be more likely to say? Something like "I'm damaged goods"? Or "Yes, it was tough at times but I survived it, and I'm stronger for it today." It is the second reply that children of divorce have all their lives been encouraged to give; and the fact that they are willing to give it yet again is hardly, as Ahrons would have it, news.

Thus, Ahrons' statistics on their own hardly constitute three cheers for divorce. Far more meaningful and revealing are the extended quotations from interview subjects with which the book is liberally studded. She writes, for instance, that Andy, now thirty-two, sees "value" in his parents' divorce. Why? Because:

> "I learned a lot. I grew up a lot more quickly than a lot of my friends. Not that that's a good thing or a bad thing. People were always thinking I was older than I was because of the way I carried myself."

Treating a sad, unfortunate experience (like being forced to grow up more quickly than one's peers) as something neutral or even positive is merely one example of what can happen when a person attempts to conform to a culture that insists that divorce is no big deal. To take such an ambivalent response as clear evidence that divorce does no damage, as Ahrons does is inexcusable.

Ahrons cheerfully reports other "good" results of divorce. Here for example is Brian, whose parents split when he was five:

> "In general, I think [the divorce] has had very positive effects. I see what happens in divorces, and I have promised myself that I would do anything to not get a divorce. I don't want my kids to go through what I went through."

Tracy, whose parents divorced when she was twelve, sees a similar upside to divorce:

> "I saw some of the things my parents did and know not to do that in my marriage and see the way they treated each other and know not to do that to my spouse and my children. I know [the divorce] has made me more committed to my husband and my children."

These are ringing endorsements of divorce as a positive life event? Like the testimony of a child who's learned a painful but useful lesson about the dangers of playing with fire, such accounts indicate that the primary benefit of divorce is to encourage young people to avoid it in their own lives if at all possible.

Then there are the significant problems with the structure of Ahrons' study itself. While the original families were recruited using a randomized method, the study lacks any control group. In other words, Ahrons interviewed plenty of young people from divorced families but spoke to no one of similar ages from intact families. So she really can't tell us anything at all about how these young people might differ from their peers.

Rather than acknowledging that her lack of a control group is a serious limitation, Ahrons sidesteps the issue. In several places she compares her subjects to generalized "social trends" or "their contemporaries" and decides, not surprisingly, that they are not all that different. Thus, Ahrons notes that many of the young people from divorced families told her they frequently struggled with issues of "commitment, trust, and dealing with conflict," but on this finding she comments, "These issues are precisely the ones that most adults in this stage of their development grapple with, whether they grow up in a nuclear family or not." Never mind that she has not interviewed any of those other young people, or cited any studies to back up her contention, or acknowledged the possibility that, while all young people do have to deal with these kinds of interpersonal issues, some have a much harder time doing it than others. Ahrons instead wholly dismisses the pain expressed by the children of divorce and assures us that they are simply passing through a normal development phase.

When it comes to her conclusions, Ahrons claims that "if you had a devitalized or high-conflict marriage, you can take heart that the decision to divorce may have been the very best thing you could have done for your children." While research does show that children, on average, do better after a high-conflict marriage ends (the same research, by Paul Amato and Alan Booth, also shows that only one-third of divorces end high-conflict marriages), no one—Ahrons included—has shown that children do better when an adult ends a marriage he or she perceives as "devitalized." Children don't much care whether their parents have a "vital" marriage. They care whether their mother and father live with them, take care of them, and don't fight a lot. . . .

Ahrons also remains preoccupied with the concept of stigma. She writes, for instance, that we are seeing "progress" because a high divorce rate has the effect of reducing the stigma experienced by children of divorce. That's all well and good, but one wonders why Ahrons gives stigma so much attention while saying nothing about a far more damaging social problem for children of divorce—namely, silence. Consider my own experience. The type of family in which I grew up was radically different from the intact family model. Yet no one around me, not even therapists, ever once acknowledged that fact. Never mind that my beloved father lived hours away, or that the mother I adored was often stressed as she tried to earn a living while also acting as a single parent. I was left to assume, like many children of divorce, that whatever problems I struggled with were no one's fault but my own. The demand that children of divorce keep quiet and get with the program puts them in the position of protecting adults from guilt and further stress—effectively reversing the natural order of family life in which the adults are the protectors of children.

Ahrons is remarkably unsympathetic to the children on whom this burden is laid. What do children of divorce long for? According to Ahrons, they nurture unrealistic hopes for "tidy," "perfect" families. She uses these words so frequently—the first term appears at least six times in the book and the second at least four times—that she sometimes appears to be portraying children of divorce as weird obsessives. Speaking directly to children of divorce, Ahrons offers the following advice: "You may not have the idyllic family you dreamed of . . . [but] often the only thing within our control is how we perceive or interpret an event." "For example, you can choose to see your family as rearranged, or you can choose to see it as broken." Indeed, the curative powers of social constructivism are nothing

short of miraculous. Encouraging readers to stop using the descriptive term "adult child of divorce," she asserts that "it's a stigmatizing label that presumes you are deficient or traumatized. . . . If you have fallen prey to using it to explain something about yourself, ask yourself if it is keeping you from making changes that might bring you more satisfaction in your life." Apparently, coming to grips with one's family history and the deepest sources of one's sadness and loneliness is the worst thing a child can do. . . .

Ahrons surely knows more about the tragedies of divorce than her thesis allows her to admit. She has studied divorced families for years. She has worked with them as a clinician. She has been through divorce herself. Yet she inevitably follows up heartbreaking observations of interviewees with the confident assertion that everyone involved would be so much happier if only they talked themselves out of— and even walked away from—their anguish. As she writes in one (unintentionally haunting) passage, "Over the years I have listened to many divorcing parents in my clinical practice talk about how much they look forward to the day when their children will be grown and they won't have to have anything more to do with their exes." Is it possible to image a sadder or more desperate desire than this one—the longing for one's children to grow up faster so that relations with one's ex-spouse can be more effectively severed? In such passages it becomes obvious that all of Ahrons' efforts to explain away the tragedy of divorce and its legacy are in vain. In the end, the theory collapses before reality.

Ahrons' poorly structured study and far too tendentious thesis are of no help to us in thinking through our approach to divorce and its consequences. Children of divorce are real, complex people who are deeply shaped by a new kind of fractured family life—one whose current prevalence is unprecedented in human history. These children are not nostalgic for "tidy," "perfect," "idyllic" families. They grieve the real losses that follow from their parents' divorce. They don't need new words to describe what they've been through. Ordinary words will serve quite well—provided that people are willing to listen to them.

ELIZABETH MARQUARDT is the director of the Center for Marriage and Families and authored *Between Two Worlds: The Inner Lives of Children of Divorce* (Crown, 2005).

Constance Ahrons  **NO**

No Easy Answers: Why the Popular View of Divorce Is Wrong

Although it may appear strange, my exhusband's untimely death brought his second and first families closer together. I had mourned at his funeral and spent time with his family and friends for several days afterward. A different level of kinship formed, as we—his first and second families—shared our loss and sadness. Since then, we have chosen to join together at several family celebrations, which has added a deeper dimension to our feelings of family.

You may be thinking, "This is all so rational. There's no way my family could pull this off." Or perhaps, like the many people who have shared their stories with me over the years, you are nodding your head knowingly, remembering similar occasions in your own family. The truth is we are like many extended families rearranged by divorce. My ties to my exhusband's family are not close but we care about one another. We seldom have contact outside of family occasions, but we know we're family. We hear stories of each other's comings and goings, transmitted to us through our mutual ties to my daughters, and now, through grandchildren. But if many families, like my own, continue to have relationships years after divorce, why don't we hear more about them?

Quite simply, it's because this is not the way it's supposed to be. My family, and the many others like mine, don't fit the ideal images we have about families. They appear strange because they're not tidy. There are "extra" people and relationships that don't exist in nuclear families and are awkward to describe because we don't have familiar and socially defined kinship terms to do so. Although families rearranged and expanded by divorce are rapidly growing and increasingly common, our resistance to accepting them as normal makes them appear deviant.

Societal change is painfully slow, which results in the situation wherein the current realities of family life come into conflict with our valued images. Sociologists call this difference "cultural lag," the difference between what is real and what we hold as ideal. This lag occurs because of our powerful resistance to acknowledging changes that challenge our basic beliefs about what's good and what's bad in our society.

Why Good Divorces Are Invisible

Good divorces are those in which the divorce does not destroy meaningful family relationships. Parents maintain a sufficiently cooperative and supportive relationship that allows them to focus on the needs of their children. In good divorces children continue to have ties to both their mothers and their fathers, and each of their extended families, including those acquired when either parent remarries.

Good divorces have been well-kept secrets because to acknowledge them in mainstream life threatens our nostalgic images of family. If the secret got out that indeed many families that don't fit our "mom and pop" household ideal are healthy, we would have to question the basic societal premise that marriage and family are synonymous. And that reality upsets a lot of people, who then respond with familiar outcries that divorce is eroding our basic values and destroying society.

Although we view ourselves as a society in which nuclear families and lifelong monogamous marriages predominate, the reality is that 43 percent of first marriages will end in divorce. Over half of new marriages are actually remarriages for at least one of the partners. Not only have either the bride or groom (or both) been divorced but increasingly one of them also has parents who are divorced.

Families are the way we organize to raise children. Although we hold the ideal image that marriage is a precursor to establishing a family, modern parents are increasingly challenging this traditional ideal. Families today arrange—and rearrange—themselves in many responsible ways that meet the needs of children for nurturance, guidance and economic support. Family historian Stephanie Coontz, in her book *The Way We Never Were*, shows how the "tremendous variety of workable childrearing patterns in history suggests that, with little effort, we should be able to forge new institutions and values."

One way we resist these needed societal changes is by denying that divorce is no longer deviant. We demean divorced families by clinging to the belief that families can't exist outside of marriage. It follows then that stories of healthy families that don't fit the tidy nuclear family package are rare and stories that show how divorce destroys families and harms children are common. In this way, bad divorces appear to represent the American way of divorce and good divorces become invisible.

Messages That Hinder Good Divorces

When the evils of divorce are all that families hear about, it makes coping with the normal transitions and changes that inevitably accompany divorce all the more difficult. Negative messages make children feel different and lesser, leading to feelings of shame and guilt. Parents who feel marginalized in this way are less likely to think about creative solutions to their problems. That all of this unnecessary anxiety is fueled by sensationalized reports of weak findings, half-truths and myths of devastation is deplorable. Only by sorting out the truths about divorce from the fiction can we be empowered to make better decisions, find healthy ways to maintain family relationships, and develop important family rituals after divorce. Let's take a close look at the most common misconceptions about divorce.

Misconception 1: Parents Should Stay Married for the Sake of the Kids

This is a message that pervades our culture, and it rests on a false duality: Marriage is good for kids, divorce is bad. Underlying this premise is the belief that parents who divorce are immature and selfish because they put their personal needs ahead of the needs of their children, that because divorce is too easy to get, spouses give up on their marriages too easily and that if you're thinking about divorcing your spouse, you should "stick it out till the kids are grown." A popular joke takes this message to its extreme. A couple in their nineties, married for seventy years, appears before a judge in their petition for a divorce. The judge looks at them quizzically and asks, "Why now, why after all these years?" The couple responds: "We waited until the children were dead."

The research findings are now very clear that reality is nowhere near as simple and tidy. Unresolved, open interparental conflict between married spouses that pervades day-to-day family life has been shown again and again to have negative effects on children. Most experts agree that when this is the case it is better for the children if parents divorce rather than stay married. Ironically, prior to the initiation of no-fault legislation over twenty years ago, in most states this kind of open conflict in the home was considered "cruel and inhumane" treatment and it was one of the few grounds on which a divorce would be granted—if it could be proved.

But the majority of unsatisfying marriages are not such clearcut cases. When most parents ask themselves if they should stay married for the sake of their children, they have clearly reached the point where they are miserable in their marriages but wouldn't necessarily categorize them as "high-conflict." And here is where, in spite of the societal message, there is no agreement in the research findings or among clinical experts. That's because it's extremely complex and each individual situation is too different to allow for a "one-size-fits-all" answer.

A huge list of factors comes into play when assessing whether staying married would be better for your kids. For example,

- Is the unhappiness in your marriage making you so depressed or angry that your children's needs go unmet because you can't parent effectively?
- Do you and your spouse have a cold and distant relationship that makes the atmosphere at home unhealthy for your children?
- Do you and your spouse lack mutual respect, caring or interests, setting a poor model for your children?
- Would the financial hardships be so dire that your children will experience a severely reduced standard of living?

Add to this your child's temperament, resources and degree of resilience, and then the personal and family changes that take place in the years after the divorce, and you can see how the complexities mount.

It is a rare parent who divorces *too easily*. Most parents are responsible adults who spend years struggling with the extremely difficult and complex decision of whether to divorce or stay married "for the sake of the children." The bottom line is that divorce is an adult decision, usually made by one spouse, entered into in the face of many unknowns. Without a crystal ball, no one knows whether their decision will be better for their children. As you read further in this book, however, you may gain some perspective on what will be most helpful in your situation, with your children, by listening carefully to the reactions and feelings of various children of divorce *as they have changed over twenty years.*

Misconception 2: "Adult Children of Divorce" Are Doomed to Have Lifelong Problems

. . . The truth is that, for the great majority of children who experience a parental divorce, the divorce becomes part of their history but it is not a defining factor. Like the rest of us, most of them reach adulthood to lead reasonably happy, successful lives. Although children who grew up with divorced parents certainly share an important common experience, their ability to form healthy relationships, be good parents, build careers, and so on, are far more determined by their individual temperaments, their sibling relationships, the dynamics within their parents' *marriages* and the climate of their *postdivorce* family lives.

Misconception 3: Divorce Means You Are No Longer a Family

There's this myth that as long as you stay married your family is good but as soon as you announce you're separating, your family is thrown into the bad zone. Your family goes from being "intact" to being "dissolved," from two-parent to single parent, from functional to dysfunctional. Even though we all know that people don't jump from happy marriages right into divorce, there is an assumption that the decision to separate is the critical marker. It doesn't seem to matter whether your marital relationship was terrible, whether you were miserable and your children troubled. Just as long as you are married and living together in one household, the sign over the front door clearly states to the world, "We're a normal family."

The inaccurate and misleading message that divorce destroys families and children because it hides and denies all the positive ways that families can be rearranged after divorce. It sends the destructive message to children that divorce means they only get to keep one parent and they will no longer be part of a family. Although two-parent first-married households now represent less than 25 percent of all households, and an increasing number of children each year are raised by unmarried adults, many people cling to the belief that healthy families can only be two-parent married families and social change is always bad and threatening to our very foundations. . . .

⸻ ⟨◍⟩ ⸻

The truth is that although some divorces result in family breakdown, the vast majority do not. While divorce changes the form of the family from one household to two, from a nuclear family to a binuclear one, it does not need to change the way children think and feel about the significant relationships within their families. This does not mean that divorce is not painful or difficult, but over the years, as postdivorce families change and even expand, most remain capable of meeting children's needs for family.

Misconception 4: Divorce Leaves Children without Fathers

This message is linked closely with the preceding one because when we say that divorce destroys families we really mean that fathers disappear from the family. The myths that accompany this message are that fathers are "deadbeat dads" who abandon their kids and leave their families impoverished. The message strongly implies that fathers don't care and are unwilling or unable to make continuing commitments to their children. While this reflects the reality for a minority of divorced fathers, the majority of fathers continue to have loving relationships with their children and contribute financially to their upbringing. . . .

Misconception 5: Exspouses Are Incapable of Getting Along

. . . Although we have come to realize that parents who divorce still need to have some relationship with one another, the belief that it's not really possible still lingers.

In fact, when exspouses remain friends they are viewed as a little strange and their relationship is suspect. Yet, the truth is that many divorced parents *are* cooperative and effective coparents. Like good divorces and involved fathers, they are mostly invisible in the media. . . .

Misconception 6: Divorce Turns Everyone into Exfamily; In-Laws Become Outlaws

When it comes to the semantics of divorce-speak, all of the kinship ties that got established by marriage dissolve abruptly. On the day of the legal divorce, my husband and all of his relatives suddenly became exes. But even though the kinship is *legally* terminated, meaningful relationships often continue. My friend Jan, during her fifteen-year marriage, formed a very close relationship with her mother-in-law. Now, twenty years later, she still calls her eighty-two-year-old exmother-in-law "Mom," talks with her several times a week and has dinner with her weekly. Exmother-in-law is certainly not an adequate description of this ongoing relationship.

As a culture we continue to resist accepting divorce as a normal endpoint to marriage even though it is an option chosen by almost half of those who marry. It is this cultural lag, this denial of current realities that causes the inaccurate language, not only for the family ties that continue but also for the family we inherit when we, our former spouses, our parents or our children remarry. Kinship language is important because it provides a shorthand way for us to identify relationships without wading through tedious explanations. . . .

Misconception 7: Stepparents Aren't Real Parents

. . . Children and their new stepparents start off their relationships with two strikes against them. They have to fight an uphill battle to overcome negative expectations, and they have to do so without much help from society. Since almost 85 percent of the children with divorced parents will have a stepparent at some time in their lives, it is shocking that we know so little about how these relationships work. Clearly, societal resistance to recognizing the broad spectrum of postdivorce families has hindered the development of good role models for stepchildren and their stepparents.

Painting a False Picture

Taken together, these negative messages paint a false picture of divorce, one that assumes family ties are irretrievably broken so that postdivorce family relationships appear to be nonexistent. Despite these destructive messages, many divorced parents meet the needs of their children by creating strong families after divorce. Without a doubt, divorce is painful and creates stress for families, but it is important to remember that most recover, maintaining some of their kinship relationships and adding new ones over time.

By making good divorces invisible we have accepted bad divorces as the norm. In so doing, children and their divorced parents are being given inaccurate messages that conflict with the realities they live and make them feel deviant and stigmatized. It is time we challenge these outdated, ill-founded messages and replace them with new ones that acknowledge and accurately reflect current realities.

The Distortions of Oversimplifying

Just a little over a decade ago, in January 1989, the *New York Times Magazine* ran a cover story called "Children after Divorce," which created a wave of panic in divorced parents and their children. Judith Wallerstein and her coauthor, Sandra Blakeslee, a staff writer for the *New York Times*, noted their newest unexpected finding. Calling it the "sleeper effect," they concluded that only ten years after divorce did it become apparent that girls experience "serious effects of divorce at the time they are entering young adulthood."

When one of the most prestigious newspapers in the world highlights the findings of a study, most readers take it seriously. "That 66 percent of young women in our study between the ages of nineteen and twenty-three will suffer debilitating effects of their parents' divorce years later" immediately became generalized to the millions of female children with divorced parents. The message—just when you think everything may be okay, the doom of divorce will rear its ugly head—is based on a *mere eighteen out of the grand total of twenty-seven women* interviewed in this age group. This detail wasn't mentioned in the fine print of the article but is buried in the appendix of the book that was scheduled for publication a month after the *New York Times* story appeared. And it is on this slim data that the seeds of a myth are planted. We are still living with the fallout.

In sharp contrast to Wallerstein's view that parental divorce has a powerful devastating impact on children well into adulthood, another psychologist made headlines with a completely opposite thesis. In her book, *The Nurture Assumption: Why Children Turn Out the Way They Do*, Judith Rich Harris proposes that what parents do makes little difference in how their children's lives turn out. Half of the variation in children's behavior and personality is due to genes, claims Harris, and the other half to environmental factors, mainly their peer relationships. For this reason, Harris asserts parental divorce is not responsible for all the ills it is blamed for.

These extreme positions—of divorce as disaster and divorce as inconsequential—oversimplify the realities of our complex lives. Genes and contemporary relationships notwithstanding, we have strong evidence that parents still make a significant difference in their children's development. Genetic inheritance and peer relationships are part of the story but certainly not the whole story.

Sorting Out the Research Findings

Drawing conclusions across the large body of research on divorce is difficult. Studies with different paradigms ask different questions that lead to different answers. A classic wisdom story shows the problem. Three blind men bumped into an elephant as they walked through the woods. They didn't know what it was, but each prided himself on his skill at "seeing." So one blind man reached out and carefully explored the elephant's leg. He described in great detail the rough, scratchy surface that was huge and round. "Aha, this is an ancient mighty tree. We're in a new forest." "No, no," said the blind man who had taken hold of the elephant's trunk. "We're in great danger—this is a writhing snake, bigger than any in our hometown. Run!" The third man laughed at them both. He'd been touching the elephant's tusk, noticing the smooth hard surface, the gentle curve, the rounded end. "Nonsense! We have discovered an exquisitely carved horn for announcing the emperor's arrival."

The blind men described what they "saw" accurately. Their mistake was to claim that what they saw was the whole. Much like the three blind men, researchers see different parts of the divorce elephant, which then frames their investigations.

It should come, then, as no surprise that reports of the findings about divorce are often contradictory and confusing. It is impossible for any study to take account of all the complexities of real life, or of the individual differences that allow one family to thrive in a situation that would create enormous stress, and frayed relationships, in another. But it is in these variations that we can begin to make sense of how divorce impacts the lives of individuals and families.

Facing Reality

Hallmark Cards recently launched a line of greeting cards called "Ties That Bind" aimed at various nontraditional unions—from stepfamilies to adopted child households to unmarried partnerships. "Our cards reflect the times," says Marita Wesely-Clough, trend group manager at Hallmark. "Relationships today are so nebulous that they are hard to pin down, but in creating products, we have to be aware that they are there. Companies need to respect and be sensitive to how people are truly living their lives now, and not how they might wish or hope for them to live."

Advertising agencies and marketing services make it their business to assess social realities. To sell their products, they have to evaluate the needs and desires of their potential consumers. They do not share the popular cultural anxiety about the changes in families. Instead they study them and alter their products to suit. Policy makers would do well to take some lessons from them and alter their preconceived notions about families to reflect current realities.

While the political focus today is on saving marriages and preserving traditional family values, Americans in large numbers are dancing to their own drummers.

They're cohabiting in increasingly large numbers, having more children "out of wedlock" and engaging in serial marriages. While the rates of divorce have come down from their 1981 highs, they have leveled off at a high rate that is predicted to remain stable. To meet the needs of children and parents, we need to burst the balloon about idealized families and support families as they really live their lives. And that means we have to face the true complexities of *our* families and not search for simple answers.

As you read this book, keep in mind that we can all look back on our childhoods and note something about our mothers or fathers or sisters or brothers that has had lasting effects on our personalities. If you are looking to answer the question of whether a parental divorce results in children having more or less problems than children who grew up in other living situations, you will be disappointed. Nor will you find answers to whether the stresses of divorce are worse for children than other stresses in life. However, you will find answers here to questions about how and why individual children respond in different ways to the variations in their divorced families.

Divorce is a stressful life event that requires increased focus on parenting. The effort and care that parents put into establishing their postdivorce families are crucial and will pay off over the years in their many benefits to the children. But remember, families are complex, and if you find easy answers, they are likely to be wrong.

Constance Ahrons is cochair of the Council on Contemporary Families. She is a therapist and author of three books. She is Professor Emerita from the Department of Sociology and former director of the Marriage and Family Therapy Doctoral Training Program at the University of Southern California in Los Angeles.

EXPLORING THE ISSUE

Does Divorce Create Long-Term Negative Effects for Children?

Critical Thinking and Reflection

1. How do you think the media depicts divorce in the United States? Do you think it provides an accurate depiction, a harsher depiction, or a sugar-coated one?
2. Based on what you read in these articles, how accurate do you think the depictions are?
3. Provide examples of movies, television shows, books, and/or magazine articles in making your points.

Is There Common Ground?

When parents find that they are no longer happy in a marriage, which choice is better for their children? Should they stay together to maintain an intact home for their children even though there may be constant conflict? Or should they divorce, creating two households for their children, with the hope that they will find happiness either as a single person or remarried to someone new? How will a remarriage, in addition to a divorce, affect their children? Obviously, there are no easy answers to these questions as the opposing selections clearly indicate. One thing researchers know for sure is that no matter what traumatic event happens to children, whether it is a divorce, death of a parent, or natural disaster, the support and modeling of appropriate behavior by important adults in the child's life is critical. Children who have someone to talk to, who will listen to and guide the child, can make a significant difference in the way children adapt to negative life events.

Perhaps the answer is in making sure parents never have to face trying to end a marriage by divorce. Authors from each selection disagree on the long-term effects of divorce, but would probably agree on society making more of an effort to strengthen marriage to reduce the incidence of divorce. Strengthening marriage by providing marriage

education for adolescents would help children learn how intact marriages work. Information on how to deal with current issues of balancing work and family as well as how to deal with conflict could be taught. This education could provide needed support to young adults as they choose marriage partners and help them develop healthy expectations of marriage.

Create Central

www.mhhe.com/createcentral

Additional Resources

American Men's Studies Association. Retrieved on April 8, 2011, from http://mensstudies.org

The American Men's Studies Association is a not-for-profit professional organization of scholars, therapists, and others interested in the exploration of masculinity in modern society.

Eleoff, S. (2003). Divorce Effects on Children. Retrieved on April 7, 2011, from www.childadvocate.net/divorce_effects_on_children.htm

This is an article posted online that discusses some of the ramifications of divorce.

Internet References . . .

Feminist Majority Foundation. Retrieved on April 8, 2011

The Feminist Majority Foundation website provides affirmative action links, resources from women's professional organizations, information for empowering women in business, sexual harassment information, and much more.

www.feminist.org

Helpguide.org. Children and Divorce: Helping Your Kids Cope with the Outcomes of Divorce. Retrieved on April 7, 2011

This website provides information for parents to help them work with their children during a divorce.

www.helpguide.org/mental/children_divorce.htm

Kid's Health—A Kid's Guide to Divorce. Retrieved on April 7, 2011

This website provides information that kids can easily understand about divorce.

http://kidshealth.org/kid/feeling/home_family/divorce.html

Selected, Edited, and with Issue Framing Material by:
Kourtney Vaillancourt, *New Mexico State University*

ISSUE

Is Viewing Television Violence Harmful for Children?

YES: Mark Sappenfield, from "Mounting Evidence Links TV Viewing to Violence," *The Christian Science Monitor* (2002), www.CSMonitor.com

NO: John Grohol, from "TV, Violence & Children: More Weak Pediatrics Studies" (Psych Central, 2013), psychcentral.com

---

Learning Outcomes

After reading this issue, you should be able to:

- Identify some of the effects that television viewing is believed to have on children.
- Discuss the reasons why some researchers believe that violence on television is causing an increase in aggressive behaviors in children.
- Discuss the reasons why some researchers believe that television watching has not been studied in the correct way to support the negative effects that are reported.

ISSUE SUMMARY

YES: Mark Sappenfield, writer for *The Christian Science Monitor,* describes a new scientific report that links television viewing with violent behavior, even in adults.

NO: John Grohol, an author, researcher, and expert in mental health online, asserts that the studies that condemn television watching in children fail to consider a myriad of factors involved with children that might also be the cause of negative outcomes.

Almost everyone has access to television (TV). There is hardly any other factor so pervasive in our society as television viewing. What is the relationship of TV viewing to violent acts? Those who believe that TV viewing is the root of all evil support unplugging the "boob tube" and going back to the good old days of reading, listening to the radio, and swapping stories while sitting by the fireplace. At the other end of the continuum, those who argue that TV is merely the next evolution of communication technology would promote going with the flow, grinning and bearing TV for it is surely here to stay, and stop worrying about TV.

There are numerous studies on children who watch violent TV shows, as well as on the amount of TV children watch. Some research suggests that children who spend excessive amounts of time watching TV tend to do poorly in school. Other studies show that children who spend moderate amounts of time in front of the set perform better scholastically than those who watch no TV at all. Children are more likely to be overweight when they watch

TV versus playing actively. If children are watching TV to excess, they are not communicating with adults in the family and are not learning family values.

The debate over TV violence rages on. Ask any group of people you meet today about violence in contemporary society. The responses will be remarkably similar. "Violence is in epidemic proportions. There is a lot more violence out on the streets now than when I was a kid. It's just not safe to be out anymore. We live in such violent times." The anecdotes and nostalgia about more peaceful times seem to be endless. The unison in which society decries the rise in violence begins to disintegrate, however, when one attempts to discern causes for the increases in crimes like murder, rape, robbery, and assault.

One segment of society that is regularly targeted as a contributing cause to the rise in violence is the media, particularly TV programming. A common argument is that TV is much too violent, especially in children's programming. It has been suggested, for example, that a child will witness in excess of 100,000 acts of simulated violence depicted on TV before graduating from elementary school! Lower socioeconomic status children may view even more hours of violent TV. Many researchers suggest that this TV violence is at least in part responsible for the climbing rates of violent crime, since children tend to imitate what they observe in life.

On the other side, critics argue that it is not what is on TV that bears responsibility for the surge in violence. Programming is merely reflective of the level of violence in contemporary society. The argument is that while TV watching may be associated with violence, it does not mean that it causes violence. As an example, the critics suggest that we have known for some time that aggressive children tend to watch more aggressive TV programming. However, does the aggression predispose an interest in aggressive programming, or does the programming cause the aggression? This is a question that sparks hotly contested debates.

Those who believe TV viewing is at least partly responsible for aggressive behavior in children want the U.S. Congress to more closely regulate the ratings, viewing times, and amount of violence that can be shown on American TV. Those on the other side of the issue point to the infringement on First Amendment rights of freedom of expression if such intense regulation is imposed on the media.

Other factors that contribute to the issue of TV viewing and violence are the types of programs and commercials that children watch. School-aged children are the most targeted when it comes to advertising. There are more commercial breaks per hour for children's programming than for other types of programs. Additionally, with the widespread access to cable TV, children can watch violent adult programming, many times in unsupervised homes.

Several organizations have emerged to address the issue of TV violence and its effects on society. The Center for Media Literacy provides practical information to children and adults by translating media literacy research and theory into easy-to-read resources. They also provide training and educational tools for teachers, youth leaders, parents, and caregivers of children. The National Institute on Media and the Family sponsors "Media Wise," which educates and informs the public, as well as encourages practices and policies that promote positive change in the production and use of mass media. According to their mission statement, they do not advocate censorship of any kind. They are committed to partnering with parents and other caregivers, organizations, and corporations in using the power of the free market to create healthier media choices for families, so that there are healthier, less violent communities. What should be done to effectively address this problem? Is it realistic to revert back to the days prior to the TV era? Or should we just relax and stop worrying about TV? After all, children are resilient; they can eventually understand TV's impact on their lives just as we adults have. Anyone reading this book grew up with the "magic" box and probably turned out OK.

The two articles that follow are typical of the debate centered around violence and TV as it affects children. In the YES article, Mark Sappenfield describes a study that links violent behavior and television viewing, even among adults. He details the evidence, which he refers to as "overwhelming" that explains how the two are linked. In the NO article, John Grohol identifies aspects of children's lives, such as social support, that are not included in the studies that condemn television watching for children. He argues that there are multiple factors involved in a child's outcome and blaming television solely is simply not justified.

YES

Mark Sappenfield

Mounting Evidence Links TV Viewing to Violence

A new scientific report released today says television can affect violent behavior even among adults.

For much of the past half century, the link between watching violence on television and violent behavior in everyday life has seemed an open question embraced by one study, rejected by another, and largely left unanswered by years of congressional inquiries.

That, however, is rapidly changing. To a growing number of scientists and psychiatrists, the correlation between the two is no longer a point of debate, it is an established fact.

A study released today in the journal *Science* adds to a large body of work that suggests some sort of connection. Already, six major pediatric, psychiatric, and medical associations have said that the evidence of a link is overwhelming, citing more than 1,000 studies in the past 30 years.

As a result, the debate is increasingly splintering into a fight that echoes the recent antitobacco or global-warming campaigns, as a preponderance of scientists square off against a besieged industry and a smattering of contrarian colleagues.

Many Americans are not yet convinced. On average, children still watch three hours of television a day, and calls to regulate the industry have resulted only in minor tweaks like the current ratings system. But with the scientific community presenting a more unified front and casting the issue as one of public health, not taste[,] the pressure for more change is gaining momentum.

"Clearly, with more exposure [to media violence, children] do become desensitized, they do copy what they see, and their values are shaped by it," says Susan Villani, a Baltimore, Md., psychiatrist who has reviewed the past 10 years of study on the subject.

Not even the most ardent critic of TV violence argues that images of gunplay and kung fu are the sole causes of youth violence. Yet they can be significant. One study last year found a 25 percent decrease in violence in a San Jose, Calif., grade school where kids received classroom lessons in media awareness and were asked to watch only seven hours of TV a week for several months. Another in North Carolina showed that teenage boys who regularly watched professional wrestling were 18 percent more likely to get into a physical confrontation with a date.

TV's Effect on Adult Behavior

Today's study, experts say, is particularly interesting for several reasons. It is the first survey of its scope to provide evidence that violent behavior is associated with television viewing beyond childhood well into adolescence and adulthood. In addition, it claims a connection even when other factors such as childhood neglect and low family income are taken into account.

"What this study serves to do is remove some of these variables," says Michael Brody of the American Academy of Child and Adolescent Psychiatry.

Adolescents who watched more than one hour a day of television regardless of content were roughly four times more likely to commit aggressive acts toward other people later in their lives than those who watched less than one hour. Of those who watched more than three hours, 28.8 percent were later involved in assaults, robberies, fights, and other aggressive behavior.

The study, led by Jeffrey Johnson of Columbia University in New York, followed 707 participants in upstate New York for 17 years, recording their TV viewing habits and tracking their behavior through periodic interviews and public documents.

What it did not do, say critics, is prove that the television viewing necessarily caused the violence. The comment goes to the heart of the debate over the issue: Does TV play a part in making violent people, or are violent people naturally inclined to watch violence on TV?

"I don't think there is any link at all," says Jonathan Freedman, a professor at the University of Toronto who disputes the statistic that thousands of studies have shown a link between television violence and violent behavior.

Doubts Within TV Industry

Members of the broadcasting industry share Mr. Freedman's skepticism of such media studies. "They spark a lot of interest, but nothing definite comes out that can establish a direct link," says Dennis Wharton of the National Association of Broadcasters in Washington.

The industry also touts their cleaner fare: A recent study by the Center for Media and Public Affairs in Washington found a 29 percent drop in TV violence last season compared with 1998–99.

Aspects of the criticism find broader support. It's true that some kids might be able to watch TV all day and not commit a single violent act. But some psychiatrists say that merely begs for more research about who might be influenced by TV and how.

But most also insist that the vast majority of studies support a link. Granted, no study can definitively say that TV caused a violent act; it can only infer. But the results of one of the most researched areas in social science are

pretty consistent, says professor Craig Anderson of Iowa State University in Ames. "It doesn't matter how you study it, the results are the same," says Mr. Anderson.

Plus, for many, it's simply a matter of common sense. "If television doesn't influence kids, then why are so many people spending so many billions of dollars to advertise," says Dr. Brody. "It's not the sole cause, but even if it represents 10 percent of the reason [for violence], somebody should look at this."

MARK SAPPENFIELD is a staff writer for *The Christian Science Monitor*. Mark joined the *Monitor* in 1996 and has since written from Boston, the San Francisco Bay Area, the Pentagon, and India. In addition to reporting from Pakistan and Afghanistan during his time in South Asia, Mark has also written on issues of sports and science. He has covered five Olympic Games and attended various events at NASA's Jet Propulsion Laboratory, including the landing of the Mars rover Opportunity.

John Grohol

TV, Violence & Children: More Weak Pediatrics Studies

Did you know that simply watching TV causes harm to children? Well, that's what the American Academy of Pediatrics would have you believe. And yet, here we are in the sixth decade since TV became popular, and we have not yet seen the end of the world based upon multiple generations that grew up with television as a mainstay

The latest issue of *Pediatrics* has two studies—and a bonus editorial!—that suggests television viewing by children is associated with greater criminality and antisocial personality, and that a child's behavior can be modified by simply changing what they're watching.

Pediatrics is the mouthpiece for the American Academy of Pediatrics. And while it's ostensibly an objective, scientific journal, it continually publishes weak research—especially on the effects of TV and children.

Let's check out the latest . . .

The first study (Robertson, et al., 2013) followed 1,037 New Zealand children over the course of their early lives, from ages 5 to 26. Parents were asked how much time their children spent watching TV, until age 13, when the children themselves were asked directly. Then they looked at some other factors—like criminal convictions, antisocial personality disorder, IQ, and the socio-economic status of the families. Parental control was also measured twice—at ages 7 and 9—by asking the mom about what kinds of rules and procedures were used to run family life.

From this data, the researchers found that those with more criminal convictions or with antisocial personality traits watched significantly more TV as children.

But here's all the things the researchers **did not** measure:

- Social peer network and social support
- Relationships and quality of relationships with friends
- Existence of other mental disorders (because the researchers only focused on antisocial personality disorder)
- Parental marital status
- Parental relationship quality
- Parental role modeling behavior
- History of criminal convictions within the immediate family
- Limited understanding of family dynamics from just two data points, and just from the perspective of the mother

- Religion and moral upbringing
- Amount of time spent in creative play
- Amount of time attending or participating in sports
- And so on . . .

As you can see, the list of alternative explanations for this correlational relationship is *voluminous*. Without controlling for as many variables as possible in a child's environment, **there is no reasonable way you can isolate a single variable.** And without measuring the kinds of things in the list above (among others) you'd have no way to determine if one of those might provide a more reasonable—or at least alternative—explanation.

While two variables can often be associated with one another, an association rarely tells you much. Especially in this case, where the researchers never bothered to ask or measure what type of TV programs the children actually watched. For all we know, they could've all been heavy viewers of *The Waltons*. It seems incomprehensible that in a study that purports to study the importance of TV watching's effects on children such an oversight could've been made.

Only buried at the end of the study do you find this acknowledgment:

> As with any observational research, we cannot prove that television viewing causes antisocial behavior, but the study has a number of features that enable us to make causal inferences. [. . .]
> [It] is also possible that other unmeasured factors associated with the milieu in which television viewing occurs may explain the observed relationship.

Yes, of course it may. Which means you can't say anything about causation. So why do they then contradict themselves in the abstract of the study?

> The findings are consistent with a causal association and support the American Academy of Pediatrics recommendation that children should watch no more than 1 to 2 hours of television each day.

And people wonder why social scientists often get a bad name in science?

That's Okay, You Can Watch This on TV Instead

But hey, maybe it *does* matter what your child actually watches on TV. Let's look at study 2 (Christakis, et al., 2013):

> We devised a media diet intervention wherein parents were assisted in substituting high quality prosocial and educational programming for aggression-laden programming without trying to reduce total screen time. We conducted a randomized controlled trial of 565 parents of preschool-aged children ages 3 to 5 years recruited from community pediatric practices. Outcomes were derived from the Social Competence and Behavior Evaluation at 6 and 12 months.

The researchers found about a 2 point difference in the Social Competence and Behavior Evaluation (SCBE) scale between the two groups. This was a statistically significant difference (in their regression analysis according to the researchers).

However, it was a meaningless difference in the real world. The SCBE is a scale scored from 1 to 6 on 30 questions, resulting in a possible overall score of 180.

After 6 months, the control group scored a 106.38 versus a 108.36 of the intervention group. That's an average change of just two of the 30 questions changing just one point in the positive direction. (A similar point difference was seen at the 1 year followup mark.)

Their original hypothesis was to find a significant change in all the subscales and the overall score of the SCBE— that's four scales:

> We hypothesized that the intervention would increase the overall score and each of the 3 sub-scale scores.

After one year, all they found was a statistically significant change in one subscale score and the overall score. So were the researchers cautiously optimistic in their findings' discussion, considering the tiny increases they found in the intervention group?

> We demonstrated that an intervention to modify the viewing habits of preschool-aged children can **significantly enhance** their overall social and emotional competence and that low-income boys may derive the greatest benefit.

Not , "we found support for . . ." or "on one single measure of social and emotional competence . . ."

The apparently lack of objectivity displayed here is, in my opinion, simply astounding.

Should your child spend 5 hours a day in front of the TV? In general, probably not. Nor should they spend 5 hours a day playing sports, a video game, or eating bananas. This is called "common sense," and no amount of psychological research—good or bad—can infuse it into parents who don't care how they raise their children. Why researchers insist on pursuing this questionable line of inquiry is beyond me.

References

Christaskis, D.A., et al. (2013). Modifying Media Content for Preschool Children: A Randomized Controlled Trial. *Pediatrics.* doi: 10.1542/peds.2012-1493

Robertson, L.A., McAnally, H.M. & Hancox, R.J. (2013). Childhood and Adolescent Television Viewing and Antisocial Behavior in Early Adulthood. *Pediatrics.* doi: 10.1542/peds.2012-158

JOHN GROHOL is the founder & CEO of Psych Central. He is an author, researcher, and expert in mental health online, and has been writing about online behavior, mental health and psychology issues—as well as the intersection of technology and human behavior—since 1992. Dr. Grohol sits on the editorial board of the journal *Cyberpsychology, Behavior and Social Networking* and is a founding board member and treasurer of the Society for Participatroy Medicine.

EXPLORING THE ISSUE

Is Viewing Television Violence Harmful for Children?

Critical Thinking and Reflection

1. Sappenfield asserts throughout his selection that violent television programming increases aggressive behavior. Do you agree with this assertion? Why, or why not?
2. Because television is in virtually every household in America, is it reasonable to think that television programs could ever be regulated? Explain your answer.
3. Grohol argues that there are multiple alternative explanations for children's outcomes besides just television viewing. Which of these alternatives do you think contributes the MOST to children's development and why?

Is There Common Ground?

There are numerous studies on children who watch violent television (TV) shows, as well as on the amount of TV children watch. Some research suggests that children who spend excessive amounts of time watching TV tend to do poorly in school. Other studies show that children who spend moderate amounts of time in front of the set perform better scholastically than those who watch no TV at all. Children are more likely to be overweight when they watch TV versus playing actively. If children are watching TV to excess, they are not communicating with adults in the family and are not learning family values. Logically, there must be middle-ground solutions to the issue of children, TV viewing, and violence.

Ideally, society could move past this dichotomy of thinking TV as simply good or bad. TV viewing could be thought of as an active endeavor rather than a passive one. Parents could become more involved with their children as they watch TV by controlling the amount and type of TV shows their children are watching. Through modeling, parents could teach children to be skeptical about TV advertisements, point out the differences between fantasy and reality, and argue that the moral values being portrayed on the tube are different from values that are important to the parents.

Create Central

www.mhhe.com/createcentral

Additional Resources

American Academy of Pediatrics. Smart Guide to Kids Television. Retrieved on April 11, 2011, from www.fcctf.org/pdf%20files/Parenting%20info%20pdfs /Smart%20Guide%20to%20Kids%20TV.pdf

This website provides guidance for parents on how to handle their child(ren)'s television viewing.

KidsHealth. How TV Affects Your Child. Retrieved on April 11, 2011, from http://kidshealth.org/parent /positive/family/tv_affects_child.html

This website discusses the impact that television viewing can have on children.

PBS Parents. Children and Media. Retrieved on April 11, 2011, from www.pbs.org/parents /childrenandmedia/article-faq.html

This website addresses the most common questions that parents of children under three have about television viewing.

The University of Maine, Cooperative Extension Publications. Children, Television, and Screen Time. Retrieved on April 11, 2011, from http://umaine.edu /publications/4100e/

This website discusses the impact that television viewing can have on children, in addition to suggestions for what parents can do and alternatives to television viewing.

Internet References . . .

Family: Single Parenting

This Single Parenting page of ParentsPage.com focuses on issues concerning single parents and their children.

www.ivillage.com/parenting /search?q=single+parenting

National Institute on Out-of-School Time

Directed by the Wellesley College Center for Research on Women, this National Institute on Out-of-School Time project aims to improve the quality and quantity of school-age child care nationally.

www.niost.org

Action for Healthy Kids

This is a nonprofit organization formed specifically to address the epidemic of overweight, undernourished, and sedentary youth by focusing on changes at school.

The organization's goal is to improve children's nutrition and increase physical activity, which will in turn improve their readiness to learn.

http://www.actionforhealthykids.org

Unit 3

UNIT

Middle Childhood

*M*iddle childhood, or school age, is the period from ages five through twelve. The rate of a child's growth that has been relatively steady prior to this point generally declines until the later part of this stage of development. Perhaps the most important experience during middle childhood is schooling. As a child progresses through this stage, new significant others outside the family emerge in the child's life. Children gain a broader understanding of the similarities and differences among them. The peer group (especially same-sex peers), teachers, and media personalities take on increased importance for the child. This section examines issues related to schooling, language development, and self-care.

Selected, Edited, and with Issue Framing Material by:
Kourtney Vaillancourt, *New Mexico State University*

ISSUE

Does Marriage Improve Living Standards for Children?

YES: Wade F. Horn, from "Healthy Marriages Provide Numerous Benefits to Adults, Children, and Society," *Insight* (March 18, 2002)

NO: Stephanie Coontz and Nancy Folbre, from "Marriage, Poverty, and Public Policy," *The American Prospect* (March 19, 2002), www.prospect.org

---

Learning Outcomes

After reading this issue, you should be able to:

- List and discuss the benefits to marriage that researchers have identified.
- List some of the ways that living standards for children can be improved.
- Discuss some of the reasons that marriage is considered by some to be detrimental to poor people.

ISSUE SUMMARY

YES: Wade F. Horn, from the Marriage Initiative for President George W. Bush, asserts that marriage can remedy the ills of society, including family poverty and poor living standards for children.

NO: Stephanie Coontz, author and family advocate, and Nancy Folbre, professor of economics at the University of Massachusetts, contend that improving the living standards of children is a complicated issue, which needs to be approached from many different angles in order to make improvements.

There is no doubt that living with two parents who are married and who want to be together, is good for children, psychologically and economically. Having two married parents means that there is a possibility for two incomes, which would provide a higher standard of living for children and would make it more likely that the children will not grow up in poverty. Presently, the majority of children living in poverty live with a single parent, usually their mom.

And yet, is the issue that simple? Should we merely request or require that parents marry? Will that make everything all right? Will children's living standards improve if their parents get married? One-third of poor children live within a two-parent family. If the premise that marriage improves living standards for children is true, what happened to these families?

The complicated issue involving the living standards of children and marriage promotion has become intertwined with the issues of welfare reform fund reauthorization. As welfare reform has evolved, funding for Temporary Assistance for Needy Families (TANF) has also changed. While improving living standards for children has always

been states' prominent goal, by moving families from welfare to work, states have been allowed to choose their own method of using federal dollars to accomplish this goal. The individuation of states has complicated this issue. Some states choose to provide affordable child care, education, and job training as a way to move families from welfare to work, and in so doing, they have managed to improve living standards for children. With the marriage promotion initiative, states that show higher levels of marriage rates receive more federal dollars for the welfare reform initiative. Although there is no empirical evidence that this type of programming works, states are likely to adopt programs that promote marriage, regardless of whether or not these programs are effective in improving living standards for children. Some states do this merely to increase funding levels.

The issue is not merely about living standards for children. It has evolved into the issue of making poor people get married in order to keep children from enduring a lifetime of poverty. In the following selections, the issue is debated within the context of a political climate. In the YES selection, Wade Horn presents the merits of marriage within the poor population. Horn states that the issue is simple: the government should promote marriage as a way to improve family life in general and more specifically for the children involved. Horn asserts that the U.S. government must take a stand and become pro-marriage. In doing so, the government must remove tax disincentives for marriage and revamp the welfare system so that it does not punish married couples. Horn states that government programs should include premarriage education and teach couples the skills they need to help their marriage succeed. Horn provides specific techniques to encourage marriage among welfare recipients. In the NO selection, Stephanie Coontz and Nancy Folbre describe why marriage within poor families is not always feasible or wise. They contend that this issue is more complicated than Horn suggests. They cite evidence that shows that poor families need job training, increased education, and affordable child care to work their way out of poverty and to provide a higher standard of living for their children. Coontz and Folbre site the number of single parents who have high levels of education, work at well-paying jobs, and live at a middle-class standard of living. For these parents, the lack of marriage has not caused them to live in poverty.

Coontz and Folbre also show how dangerous marriage can be for single mothers and their children. The fathers whom the mothers might marry are twice as likely to abuse alcohol or drugs and are likely to physically abuse them and their children. Marriage would not take these mothers and their children out of poverty and improve their standard of living, but might push them deeper into a desperate way of living, assert Coontz and Folbre.

Does marriage improve children's standard of living? Have we looked for complicated answers to this question and overlooked an obvious way to help children in our society by encouraging their parents to marry? Should the government promote marriage as a healthy lifestyle instead of being afraid to say the "M" word? What is wrong with promoting married parents and children? On the other hand, could this marriage promotion initiative backfire? Instead of helping children, could it actually hurt them? Will the pressure to marry in order to move from welfare to work put additional stress on the family and cause increased child abuse and neglect? Society has a commitment to help children live at a standard of living that encourages positive growth and development. How society can achieve this goal is highly debatable.

YES

Wade F. Horn

Healthy Marriages Provide Numerous Benefits to Adults, Children, and Society

The case for marriage is beyond debate. Marriage is the most stable and healthy environment for raising children. Men and women who are married have been shown to be happier and healthier. And they make more money over time than their single counterparts. Communities with more households headed by married couples are beset by fewer social ills, such as crime and welfare dependency, than communities where marriage is less prevalent.

We really can't argue—or, at least, the data say we shouldn't argue—about the benefits of marriage to children, adults and society. But I do grant that it is reasonable to debate the proper role of government in promoting marriage and that, indeed, reasonable people can disagree on whether government has a place in the marriage debate. I for one, noting that marriage is related directly to child well-being, conclude that government has no choice but to promote healthy marriages.

Let's pose the question this way: Since we know marriage can help adults be happier and healthier, and help children grow up happier and healthier, don't we have a responsibility to figure out ways to help low-income couples who want to be married enjoy a strong, supportive marriage? Of course we do.

Before I lay out my vision for how government can begin to make this happen, allow me a pre-emptive strike against the criticism that descends every time I unequivocally state that government should support and promote healthy marriages. Let me discuss four things that promoting marriage is not about.

First, it is not about government matchmaking or telling anybody to get married. Obviously, government has no business doing that. Choosing to get married is a private decision. Government should [not], and will not get into the business of telling people who, or even whether, to marry. I can state without hesitation that the Bush administration has no plans to create a federal dating service. We have no plans to add an entirely new meaning to the famous phrase, "Uncle Sam Wants You!"

Second, promoting marriage cannot, intentionally or inadvertently, result in policies that trap anyone in an abusive relationship. Seeing more Americans married is not our goal. Seeing more Americans enjoying healthy marriages is our goal. Healthy marriages are good for children and adults alike. Abusive marriages are not good for anyone.

Abuse of any sort by a spouse cannot be tolerated under any circumstances, and no marriage-promotion effort should provide comfort to spouse or child abusers. The good news is that good marriages are not a matter of luck but, rather, a matter of skill. We can teach couples the skills necessary to have good marriages. We can teach couples how to negotiate conflict and how not to allow unresolved anger to escalate. Marriages that last a lifetime and marriages that dissolve after a short while often face equal amounts of conflict. The difference is that couples who stay married have learned to manage this conflict constructively. We have proven strategies for teaching these skills to couples; standing by and not sharing these skills with low-income couples is irresponsible.

Third, when we talk about promoting marriage we are not talking about withdrawing support and services for single-parent families. As noted, we are for marriage because that's what the data say is best for kids. There is no data suggesting that taking away support from single mothers helps children in any way. Many single parents make heroic efforts to raise their children despite incredible pressures. Promoting marriage and supporting single parents is not, and must not be, mutually exclusive. Together, they are part of an integrated effort to promote child well-being.

Finally, marriage promotion is not the same as cohabitation promotion. For too long, we have treated marriage as if it were a dreaded "M" word. Too afraid to say "marriage," we have instead talked about "committed relationships." But shacking up isn't getting married. Common sense says so. So does research. There is something fundamentally different about the commitment two people make within a marriage relationship versus a cohabiting relationship. In a cohabiting relationship, the commitment of each of the partners primarily is self-serving. By contrast, the marriage commitment is about serving one's spouse. This is a fundamental difference, and one that ought to be reflected in our social policy.

I recommend the following principles for government marriage promotion:

Government must resolve that it will not merely be "neutral" about marriage. For many behaviors government is rightly neutral, for others it is not. For example, the government is not neutral about home ownership because it is good for communities when people own their homes. Furthermore, the government is not neutral about charitable giving because charitable giving is good for society. In the same way, government should not be neutral about healthy marriages because they contribute directly to the general strength of a good and sound society.

First of all, we must remove disincentives for marriage. Under current law if couples (especially low-income couples) marry, our tax code and social welfare system punish them. But striking these disincentives from our laws and policies, while a very important first step, only will bring us to the state of being neutral on marriage. We must go beyond that, into active support of marriage.

More than 90 percent of adults in the United States marry at some point during their lifetimes, and the vast majority enter marriage believing it to be a lifetime commitment. Surveys consistently document that most Americans see marriage as an important life goal. Clearly, providing active support for couples who want to marry and stay married is consistent with the values of the vast majority of Americans.

In doing so, government must not be paralyzed by the unknown. What we don't know about marriage promotion cannot be allowed to stand in the way of what we do know. Some have argued that we don't know enough about marriage promotion and, therefore, we should do nothing. They are partially correct. We have much to learn about promoting and supporting healthy marriages. But there is much we do know.

For example, thanks to a nascent marriage movement in our country, we do know that premarital-education programs work. We know that programs that assign mentoring couples to newlyweds do work. We know that good marriages are a result not of luck or chance but hard work and skill. We know that these skills can be taught. Finally, we know that programs designed to save even the most troubled marriages do work. Yes, there still is much to be learned, but we know enough about what works that standing by and doing nothing would be a tragic mistake.

New research constantly is shedding more light on our path. For example, research is debunking the myth that low-income, inner-city men and women who have children out of wedlock are not linked romantically and have no interest in marriage. A recent study by researchers at Princeton and Columbia universities revealed that 48 percent of unmarried urban couples were living together at the time their child was born. Eighty percent were involved in an exclusive romantic relationship. And half believed their chances of marrying—not at sometime to somebody, but to each other—were "certain" or "near certain." In other words, drive-by pregnancies are an especially insidious urban legend.

Now that we understand the goal for marriage promotion—helping couples who choose marriage develop the skills they need to build healthy marriages—it is time to explore specific actions the government can take. A number of proposals have been put forth. Here are five of my favorites—ideas that have the best chance of improving child well-being by strengthening the institution of marriage:

- Put marriage in the hospital. Hospitals should do more than talk about paternity establishment. They can talk about marriage as well. In most cases, hospital personnel stop at telling a young man that he must establish paternity. Doing so is extremely important. But hospital personnel should also ask the simple question, "Have you considered getting married?" If the answer is "yes," the couple can be referred to helpful services, such as premarital education. If the answer is "no," that's fine. But we can't be afraid to say the "M" word in the labor and delivery ward.
- Develop a referral system for premarital education. Schools, clinics, job-training sites and welfare offices all offer opportunities to provide referrals to premarital education.
- Provide marital-enrichment services through social programs dedicated to strengthening families. Head Start provides a perfect example. Many children in Head Start live with a married mother and father. While Head Start centers routinely provide parenting-education classes, I don't know of a single Head Start program providing marriage-education classes. Head Start represents a perfect opportunity to teach parents the skills they need to maintain a long-term, healthy marriage. We should seize this and similar opportunities.
- Create public-education campaigns highlighting the benefits of healthy marriages. The government funds numerous public-education campaigns promoting various healthy behaviors. Marriage can and should be added to this list.
- Increase support for intervention services, including mentoring programs, so that troubled marriages can be made whole and strong once again.

It no longer is a question of whether government should do this, but of how. It's time to get started right away, before another generation of children misses out on the benefits of a married mom and dad.

WADE F. HORN is an assistant secretary for children and families in the Department of Health and Human Services. He has been a clinical psychologist, president of the National Fatherhood Initiative, and a columnist for *The Washington Times*.

**Stephanie Coontz and
Nancy Folbre**

 **NO**

Marriage, Poverty, and Public Policy

One of the stated objectives of welfare legislation passed in 1996 was "to end dependence by promoting marriage." With this legislation coming up for reauthorization, many policymakers want to devote more public resources to this goal, even if it requires cutting spending on cash benefits, child care, or job training. Some states, such as West Virginia, already use their funds to provide a special bonus to couples on public assistance who get married.[1] In December 2001, more than fifty state legislators asked Congress to divert funds from existing programs into marriage education and incentive policies, earmarking dollars to encourage welfare recipients to marry and giving bonus money to states that increase marriage rates. On February 26, 2002, President Bush called for spending up to $300 million a year to promote marriage among poor people.[2]

Such proposals reflect the widespread assumption that failure to marry, rather than unemployment, poor education, and lack of affordable child care, is the primary cause of child poverty. Voices from both sides of the political spectrum urge us to get more women to the altar. Journalist Jonathan Rauch argues that "marriage is displacing both income and race as the great class divide of the new century."[3] Robert Rector of the Heritage Foundation claims that "the sole reason that welfare exists is the collapse of marriage."[4] In this briefing paper, we question both this explanation of poverty and the policy prescriptions that derive from it.

Marriage offers important social and economic benefits. Children who grow up with married parents generally enjoy a higher standard of living than those living in single-parent households. Two parents are usually better than one not only because they can bring home two paychecks, but also because they can share responsibilities for child care. Marriage often leads to higher levels of paternal involvement than divorce, non-marriage, or cohabitation. Long-term commitments to provide love and support to one another are beneficial for adults, as well as children.

Public policies toward marriage could and should be improved.[5] Taxes or benefit reductions that impose a marriage penalty on low-income couples are inappropriate and should be eliminated. Well designed public policies could play a constructive role in helping couples develop the skills they need to develop healthy and sustainable relationships with each other and their children. It does not follow, however, that marriage promotion should be

a significant component of anti-poverty policy, or that public policies should provide a "bonus" to couples who marry.

The current pro-marriage agenda in anti-poverty policy is misguided for at least [three] reasons:

- Non-marriage is often a result of poverty and economic insecurity rather than the other way around.
- The quality and stability of marriages matters. Prodding couples into matrimony without helping them solve problems that make relationships precarious could leave them worse off.
- Two-parent families are not immune from the economic stresses that put children at risk. More than one third of all impoverished young children in the U.S. today live with two parents.

Single parenthood does not inevitably lead to poverty. In countries with a more adequate social safety net than the United States, single parent families are much less likely to live in poverty. Even within the United States, single mothers with high levels of education fare relatively well.

In this briefing paper, we summarize recent empirical evidence concerning the relationship between marriage and poverty, and develop the four points above in more detail. We also emphasize the need to develop a larger anti-poverty program that provides the jobs, education, and child care that poor families need in order to move toward self-sufficiency.

The Economic Context

Children living with married parents generally fare better than others in terms of family income. In 2000, 6 percent of married couple families with children lived in poverty, compared to 33 percent of female householders with children.[6] Mothers who never marry are more vulnerable to poverty than virtually any other group, including those who have been divorced.[7]

But the low income associated with single parenthood reflects many interrelated factors. Income is distributed far more unequally in the United States than in most other developed countries, making it difficult for low-wage workers (male or female) to support a family without a second income. Women who become single mothers are especially likely to have inadequate wages, both because of pre-existing disadvantages such as low educational attainment and work experience and because the shortage of publicly subsidized child care makes it difficult for them to work full time. In 2000, only 1.2 percent of children of single mothers with a college degree who worked full-time year round lived in poverty.[8] For single mothers with some college working full-time, the poverty rate was less than 8 percent.[9]

Whether single or married, working parents face high child care costs that are seldom factored into calculations of poverty and income. Consider the situation of a single mother with two children working full-time, full year round at the minimum wage of $5.15 an hour, for an income of $10,712. If she files for and receives the maximum Earned Income Tax Credit, she can receive as much as $3,816 in public assistance. But the EITC phases out quickly if she earns much more than the minimum wage, and her child care costs are very high. Unless she is lucky enough to have a family member who can provide free child care, or to find a federally subsidized child care slot, more than 20 percent of her income will go to pay for child care.[10] Federally subsidized child care remains quite limited. Most families who made a transition from welfare to employment in the 1990s did not receive a subsidy.[11]

The high cost of child care helps explain why the economic position of single parents has improved little in recent years despite significant increases in their hours of market work.[12] It may also explain why single parents are likely to live in households with other adults who can share expenses with them. About 40 percent of births to single mothers take place among cohabitors, and much of the increase in nonmarital childbearing in recent years reflects this trend rather than an increase among women living without a partner.[13] The economic stress associated with reductions in welfare benefits over the past six years may have increased the pressure on single mothers to cohabit, often with partners who are unwilling or unlikely to marry.[14]

On both a symbolic and a practical level, marriage facilitates the income pooling and task sharing that allows parents to accommodate family needs.[15] Not surprisingly, many low-income families consider marriage the ideal arrangement for child rearing.[16] The Fragile Families and Child Welfare project currently underway in about twenty cities shows that about 50 percent of unmarried parents of newborns live together and hope to marry at some point.[17] Lower expectations among some couples were associated not with disinterest in marriage but with reports of drug or alcohol problems, physical violence, conflict and mistrust.[18]

The advantages of marriage, however, do not derive simply from having two names on a marriage certificate, and they cannot be acquired merely by going through a formality. Rather, they grow out of a long-term and economically sustainable commitment that many people feel is beyond their reach.

Causality Works Both Ways

Liking the abstract idea of marriage and being able to put together a stable marriage in real life are two very different things. Unemployment, low wages, and poverty discourage family formation and erode family stability, making it less likely that individuals will marry in the first place and more likely that their marriages will deteriorate. These economic factors have long-term as well as short-term effects, contributing to changes in social norms regarding marriage and family formation and exacerbating distrust between men and women. These long-term effects help explain why African-Americans marry at much lower rates than other groups within the U.S. population. Poverty is a cause as well as a consequence of non-marriage and of marital disruption.[19]

Dan Lichter of Ohio State University puts it this way: "Marriage can be a pathway from poverty, but only if women are 'marriageable,' stay married, and marry well."[20] Precisely because marriage offers economic advantages, individuals tend to seek potential spouses who have good earnings potential and to avoid marriage when they do not feel they or their potential mates can comfortably support a family. Ethnographic research shows that low-income women see economic stability on the part of a prospective partner as a necessary precondition for marriage.[21] Not surprisingly, men increasingly use the same calculus. Rather than looking for someone they can "rescue" from poverty, employed men are much more likely to marry women who themselves have good employment prospects.[22]

Poor mothers who lack a high school degree and any regular employment history are not likely to fare very well in the so-called "marriage market." Teenage girls who live in areas of high unemployment and inferior schools are five to seven times more likely to become unwed parents than more fortunately situated teens.[23] A study of the National Longitudinal Survey of Youth confirms that poor women, whatever their age, and regardless of whether or not they are or have ever been on welfare, are less likely to marry than women who are not poor. Among poor women, those who do not have jobs are less likely to marry than those who do.[24]

It is easy to spin a hypothetical scenario in which marrying off single mothers to an average male would raise family incomes and reduce poverty. But unmarried males, and especially unmarried males in impoverished neighborhoods, are not average. That is often the reason they are not married. Researchers from the Center for Research on Child Well-Being at Princeton University report results from the Fragile Families Survey showing that unmarried fathers were twice as likely as married ones to have a physical or psychological problem that interfered with their ability to find or keep a job, and several times more likely to abuse drugs or alcohol. More than 25 percent of unmarried fathers were not employed when their child was born, compared to fewer than 10 percent of married fathers.[25]

Poor mothers tend to live in neighborhoods in which their potential marriage partners are also likely to be poorly educated and irregularly employed. Low-earning men are less likely to get married and more likely to divorce than men with higher earnings.[26] Over the past thirty years, labor market opportunities for men with low levels of education have declined substantially.[27] Several studies suggest that the decrease in real wages for low-income men during the 1980s and early 1990s contributed significantly to lower marriage rates in those years.[28]

This trend has been exacerbated by the high incarceration rates for men convicted of non-violent crimes, such as drug use. While in jail, these men are not available for women to marry and their diminished job prospects after release permanently impair their marriageability. High rates of incarceration among black males, combined with high rates of mortality, have led to a decidedly tilted sex ratio within the African-American population, and a resulting scarcity of marriageable men.[29] One study of the marriage market in the 1980s found that at age 25 there were three unmarried black women for every black man who had adequate earnings.[30] As Ron Mincy of Columbia University emphasizes, simple pro-marriage policies are likely to offer less benefit to African-American families than policies encouraging responsible fatherhood and paternal engagement.[31]

In short, the notion that we could end child poverty by marrying off impoverished women does not take into account the realities of life among the population most likely to be poor. It is based on abstract scenarios that ignore the many ways in which poverty diminishes people's ability to build and sustain stable family relationships.

Quality Matters

Happy, healthy, stable marriages offer important benefits to adults and children. But not all marriages fit this description. Marital distress leads to harsh and inconsistent parenting, whether or not parents stay together. Studies show that a marriage marked by conflict, jealousy and anger is often worse for children's well-being than divorce or residence from birth in a stable single-parent family.[32] For instance, research shows that while children born to teenagers who were already married do better than children born to never-married teens, children born to teen parents who married *after* the birth do worse on some measures, probably because of the high conflict that accompanies marriages entered into with ambivalence or under pressure. Some research suggests that, among low-income African-American families, children from single-parent homes show higher educational achievement than their counterparts from two-parent homes.[33]

The idea that marriage can solve the problems of children in impoverished families ignores the complex realities of these families. The Fragile Families study shows that many low-income parents of newborn children already have children from previous relationships. Thus, their marriages would not create idealized biological families, but rather blended families in which child support enforcement and negotiation among stepparents would complicate relationships.[34] A recent study of families in poor neighborhoods in Boston, Chicago and San Antonio also reveals complex patterns of cohabitation and coparenting.[35]

Marriage to a stepfather may improve a mother's economic situation, but it does not necessarily improve outcomes for children and in some cases leads to more problems than continued residence in a stable single-parent family. Even if programs succeed in getting first-time parents married, there is no guarantee that the couples will stay married. Research shows that marriages contracted in the 1960s in order to "legitimate" a child were highly likely to end in divorce.[36] Multiple transitions in and out of marriage are worse for children psychologically than residence in the same kind of family, whatever its form, over long periods of time.[37]

Women and children in economically precarious situations are particularly vulnerable to domestic violence.[38] While it may be true that cohabiting couples are more prone to violence than married couples, this is probably because of what social scientists call a "selection effect": People in non-abusive relationships are more likely to get married. Encouraging women in an unstable cohabiting relationship to marry their partners would not necessarily protect them or their children. Indeed, the first serious violent episode in an unstable relationship sometimes occurs only after the couple has made a formal commitment.[39]

Even when it does not take a violent form, bad fathering can be worse than no fathering. For instance, the National Center on Addiction and Substance Abuse at Columbia University found that while teens in two-parent families are, on average, much less likely to abuse drugs or alcohol than teens in one-parent ones, teens in two-parent families who have a poor to fair relationship with their father are *more* likely to do so than teens in the average one-parent family.[40]

Furthermore, even good marriages are vulnerable to dissolution. The current risks of a marriage ending in divorce are quite high, although they have come down from their peak in 1979–81. It is now estimated that approximately 40 percent of marriages will end in divorce, and the risk of divorce is elevated among people with low income and insecure jobs. Sociologist Scott South calculates that every time the unemployment rate rises by 1 percent, approximately 10,000 extra divorces occur.[41] Comparing the income of single-parent families and married-couple families in any particular year leads to an overly optimistic assessment of the benefits of marriage, because it ignores the possibility of marital dissolution.

Marriage may provide a temporary improvement in a woman's economic prospects without conferring any secure, long-term protection for her children. Indeed, if marriage encourages mothers to withdraw time from paid employment, this can lower their future earnings and increase the wage penalty that they incur from motherhood itself.[42]

Two-Parent Families Are Also Under Stress

Poverty among children is not confined to single-parent families. In 2000, about 38 percent of all poor young children lived in two-parent homes.[43] These families have been largely overlooked in the debates over anti-poverty programs and marriage. Indeed, the campaign to increase marriage has overlooked one of the most important public policy issues facing the United States: the growing economic gap between parents, whether married or unmarried, and non-parents.

The costs of raising children have increased in recent years, partly because of the expansion of opportunities for women in the labor market and partly because of the longer time children spend in school. The lack of public support for parenting has also contributed to a worsening of the economic position of parents relative to non-parents.[44] Unlike other advanced industrial countries, the United States fails to provide paid family leaves for parents, and levels of publicly subsidized support for child care remain comparatively low. Most employment practices penalize workers who take time away from paid responsibilities to provide family care.[45] The high cost of parenting in this country helps explain many of the economic disadvantages that women face relative to men.[46] It may also help explain why many men are reluctant to embrace paternal responsibilities.

The Need for a Better Social Safety Net

The association of single parenthood with poverty is not inevitable. In Canada and France, single mothers—and children in general—are far less likely to live in poverty. Sweden and Denmark, with higher rates of out-of-wedlock births, have much lower rates of child poverty and hunger than does the United States. The reason for the difference is simple: These countries devote a greater percentage of their resources to assisting families with children than we do.[47] Similarly, dramatic differences in child poverty rates within our country reflect differences in tax, child care, and income assistance policies across states.[48]

Fans of the 1996 welfare reform law point to a dramatic decline in the welfare rolls since its enactment. Much of this decline is attributable to the economic boom and resulting low unemployment rates of the late 1990s. Despite promises that work requirements and time limits would lead to a more generous package of assistance for those who "followed the rules," cash benefits have

declined. Between 1994 and 1999, the real value of maximum benefits fell in most states, with an overall decline in inflation-adjusted value of about 11 percent.[49] Average benefits declined even more, as recipients increased their earnings. Indeed, the declining value of benefits is another reason why caseloads have fallen.[50]

Punitive attitudes, as well as time limits, have discouraged many eligible families from applying for assistance. The Census Bureau estimates that less than 30 percent of children in poverty resided in a family that received cash public assistance in 1998.[51] Take-up rates for Food Stamps and Medicaid have declined in recent years.[52] The implementation of the new Children's Health Insurance program has been quite uneven. As a result, states have saved money, but many children have gone without the food or medical care they needed. Public support for child care increased on both the federal and the state level. Still, most families who made a transition from welfare to work in the late 1990s did not receive a subsidy.[53]

During the economic boom of the late 1990s, increases in earnings among single parents helped make up for declining welfare benefits. As a result, poverty rates among children declined from a high of about 21 percent in 1996 to about 16 percent in 2000.[54] But these figures do not take into account the costs of child care and other work-related expenses, and they offer little hope for the future of children in low-income families as unemployment rates once again begin to climb.[55]

The most important federal policy promoting the welfare of low income families is currently the Earned Income Tax Credit (EITC), a fully refundable tax credit aimed at low-income families with children. Because benefits are closely tied to earnings, and phase out steeply after family income reaches $12,460, the EITC imposes a significant penalty on two-earner married couples, who are less likely to benefit from it than either single-parent families or married couples with a spouse at home. This penalty is unfair and should be eliminated.

Other problems with the EITC, however, should be addressed at the same time. Families with two children receive the maximum benefit, which means that low-income families with three or more children do not receive any additional assistance. More than a third of all children in the country live in families with three or more children. Partly as a result of limited EITC coverage, these families are prone to significantly higher poverty rates.[56] Furthermore, the EITC is phased out in ways that penalize middle income families, who currently enjoy less public support for child rearing than the affluent.[57] An expanded unified tax credit for families with children could address this problem.[58]

Given the pressing need for improvements in basic social safety net programs and the threat of rising unemployment, it is unconscionable to reallocate already inadequate Temporary Assistance to Needy Families (TANF) funds to policies designed to promote marriage or provide a "marriage bonus." There is little evidence that such policies would in fact increase marriage rates or reduce poverty among children. Indeed, the main effect of marriage bonuses would probably be to impose a "non-marriage" penalty that would have a particularly negative impact on African-American children, who are significantly less likely to live with married parents than either whites or Hispanics.[59] As Julianne Malveaux points out in her discussion of the Bush proposal, "a mere $100 million can be considered chump change. But the chump who could have been changed is the unemployed worker who misses out on job training because some folks find those programs—but not marriage-promotion programs—a waste."[60]

Well-designed programs to help individuals develop and improve family relationships may be a good idea. However, they should not be targeted to the poor, but integrated into a larger provision of public health services, or built into existing health insurance programs (mandating, for instance, that both public and private health insurance cover family counseling). Such programs also should not be limited to couples who are married or planning to marry. Fathers and step-fathers who are not living with their biological children also need guidance and encouragement to develop healthy, nurturing relationships. Gay and lesbian families—who are currently legally prohibited from marriage—also merit assistance.

Public policies should not penalize marriage. Neither should they provide an economic bonus or financial incentive to individuals to marry, especially at the cost of lowering the resources available to children living with single mothers. Such a diversion of resources from public assistance programs penalizes the children of unmarried parents without guaranteeing good outcomes for the children of people who are married. A variety of public policies could help strengthen families and reduce poverty among all children, including a broadening of the Earned Income Tax Credit, expansion of publicly subsidized child care, efforts to promote responsible fatherhood, improvements in public education and job training, and efforts to reduce income inequality and pay discrimination. Unlike some of the pro-marriage policies now under consideration, these policies would benefit couples who wish to marry but would not pressure women to enter or remain in intimate relationships they would not otherwise choose.

Notes

1. Alexandra Starr, "Shotgun Wedding by Uncle Sam?" *Business Week*, June 4, 2001.

2. Cheryl Wetzstein, "States Want Pro-Family Funds," *The Washington Times*, December 10, 2001; Robin Toner and Robert Pear, "Bush Urges Work and Marriage Programs in Welfare Plan," *New York Times*, February 27, 2002.

3. Jonathan Rauch, "The Widening Marriage Gap: America's New Class Divide," *National Journal*, Friday, May 18, 2001.

4. Cheryl Weitzstein, "Unwed Mothers Set a Record for Births," *The Washington Times*, April 18, 2001.

5. See Jared Bernstein, Irv Garfinkel, and Sara McLanahan, *A Progressive Marriage Agenda*, forthcoming from the Economic Policy Institute.

6. U.S. Bureau of the Census, "Historical Poverty Statistics—Table 4. Poverty Status of Families, by Type of Family, Presence of Related Children, Race, and Hispanic Origin: 1959–2000." . . . In 1999, 36 percent of single-mother households lived in poverty. *Poverty in the U.S. 1999.* Current Population Reports, P60–210 (Washington, D.C.: Government Printing Office, 2000).

7. Alan Guttmacher Institute, "Married Mothers Fare the Best Economically, Even if They Were Unwed at the Time They Gave Birth," *Family Planning Perspectives* 31, no. 5: pp. 258–60, September, 1999; Ariel Halpern, "Poverty Among Children Born Outside of Marriage: Preliminary Findings From the National Survey of America's Families" (Washington, D.C.: The Urban Institute, 1999).

8. Calculations by Arloc Sherman, Children's Defense Fund, based on the March 2001 Current Population Survey.

9. Ibid. See also Neil G. Bennett, Jiali Li, Younghwan Song, and Keming Yang, "Young Children in Poverty: A Statistical Update," released June 17, 1999. New York: National Center for Children in Poverty. . . .

10. Linda Giannarelli and James Barsimantov, *Child Care Expenses of America's Families*, Occasional Paper Number 40 (Washington, D.C.: Urban Institute, 2000).

11. Rachel Schumacher and Mark Greenberg, *Child Care After Leaving Welfare: Early Evidence From State Studies* (Washington, D.C.: Center for Law and Social Policy, 1999).

12. Kathryn H. Porter and Allen Dupree, "Poverty Trends for Families Headed by Working Single Mothers, 1993–1999," Center on Budget and Policy Priorities, August 16, 2001. . . .

13. Pamela Smock, "Cohabitation in the U.S.: An Appraisal of Research Themes, Findings, and Implications," *American Review of Sociology* 26, no. 1 (2000): pp. 1–20.

14. Gregory Acs and Sandi Nelson, "'Honey, I'm Home.' Changes in Living Arrangements in the Late 1990s," *New Federalism: National Survey of America's Families* (The Urban Institute), June 2001, pp. 1–7. A new study by Johns Hopkins researchers, presented on February 20, 2002 at a welfare forum in Washington D.C., however,

shows that these partnerships are unstable and may not be better for children than single-parent households. See Robin Toner, "Two Parents Not Always Best for Children, Study Finds," *New York Times,* February 20, 2002.

15. Many dual-earner families with preschool age children include a parent who works evenings and nights in order to provide care during the day while their husband or wife is at work. See Harriet Presser, "Employment Schedules Among Dual-Earner Spouses and the Division of Household Labor by Gender," *American Sociological Review* 59, no. 3 (June 1994): pp. 348–364.

16. Kristen Harknett and Sara McLanahan, "Do Perceptions of Marriage Explain Marital Behavior? How Unmarried Parents' Assessments of the Benefits of Marriage Relate to Their Subsequent Marital Decision"; and Marcia Carlson, Sara McLanahan, and Paula England, "Union Formation and Stability in Fragile Families," papers presented at the meetings of the Population Association of America, Washington D.C., April 2001.

17. More details on the Fragile Families study are available at. . . .

18. Maureen Waller, "High Hopes: Unwed Parents' Expectations About Marriage," *Children and Youth Services Review* 23 (2001): pp. 457–84.

19. Sara McLanahan, "Parent Absence or Poverty: Which Matters More?" pp. 35–48 in Greg Duncan and Jeanne Brooks-Gunn, eds., *Consequences of Growing Up Poor* (New York: Russell Sage Foundation, 1997). On the impact of poverty in creating non-marriage and marital disruption, see Aimee Dechter, "The Effect of Women's Economic Independence on Union Dissolution," Working Paper Np. 92–98 (1992). Center for Demography and Ecology, University of Wisconsin, Madison, WI; Mark Testa et al., "Employment and Marriage Among Inner-City Fathers," *Annals of the American Academy of Political and Social Science* 501 (1989), pp. 79–91; Karen Holden and Pamela Smock, "The Economic Costs of Marital Dissolution: Why Do Women Bear a Disproportionate Cost?" *Annual Review of Sociology* 17 (1991), pp. 51–58. On the association of low income with domestic violence see Kristin Anderson, "Gender, Status, and Domestic Violence," *Journal of Marriage and the Family* 59 (1997), pp. 655–670; A. M. Moore, "Intimate Violence: Does Socioeconomic Status Matter?" in A. P. Gardarelli, ed., *Violence Between Intimate Partners* (Boston: Allyn and Bacon, 1997), pp. 90–100; A. J. Sedlack and D. D. Broadhurst, *Third National Incidence*

Study of Child Abuse and Neglect: Final Report (Washington D.C.: Department of Health and Human Services, 1996).

20. Daniel T. Lichter, *Marriage as Public Policy* (Washington, D.C.: Progressive Policy Institute, September 2001).

21. Kathryn Edin, "A Few Good Men: Why Poor Mothers Don't Marry or Remarry?" *The American Prospect,* January 3, 2000, p. 28; Kathryn Edin and Laura Lein, *Making Ends Meet: How Single Mothers Survive Welfare and Low-Wage Work* (New York: Russell Sage, 1998).

22. Valerie Oppenheimer and Vivian Lew, "American Marriage Formation in the 1980s," in Karen Mason and An-Magritt Jensen, eds., *Gender and Family Change in Industrialized Countries* (Oxford: Oxford University Press, 1994), pp. 105–38; Sharon Sassler and Robert Schoen, "The Effects of Attitudes and Economic Activity on Marriage," *Journal of Marriage and the Family* 61 (1999): pp. 148–49.

23. John Billy and David Moore, "A Multilevel Analysis of Marital and Nonmarital Fertility in the U.S.," *Social Forces* 70 (1992), pp. 977–1011; Sara McLanahan and Irwin Garfinkel, "Welfare Is No Incentive," *The New York Times,* July 29, 1994, p. A13; Elaine McCrate, "Expectations of Adult Wages and Teenage Childbearing," *International Review of Applied Economics* 6 (1992), pp. 309–328; Ellen Coughlin, "Policy Researchers Shift the Terms of the Debate on Women's Issues," *The Chronicle of Higher Education,* May 31, 1989; Marian Wright Edelman, *Families in Peril: An Agenda for Social Change* (Cambridge: Harvard University Press, 1987), p. 55; Lawrence Lynn and Michael McGeary, eds., *Inner-City Poverty in the United States* (Washington, D.C.: National Academy Press, 1990), pp. 163–67; Jonathan Crane, "The Epidemic Theory of Ghetto and Neighborhood Effects on Dropping Out and Teenaged Childbearing," *American Journal of Sociology* 96 (1991), pp. 1226–59; Sara McLanahan and Lynne Casper, "Growing Diversity and Inequality in the American Family," in Reynolds Farley, *State of the Union,* vol. 2, pp. 10–11; Mike Males, "Poverty, Rape, Adult/Teen Sex: Why 'Pregnancy-Prevention' Programs Don't Work," *Phi Delta Kappan,* January 1994, p. 409; Mike Males, "In Defense of Teenaged Mothers," *The Progressive,* August 1994, p. 23.

24. Diane McLaughlin and Daniel Lichter, "Poverty and the Marital Behavior of Young Women," *Journal of Marriage and the Family* 59, no. 3 (1997): pp. 582–94.

25. Wendy Single-Rushton and Sara McLanahan, "For Richer or Poorer?" manuscript, Center for

Research on Child Well-Being, Princeton University, July 2001, p. 4; Kathryn Edin, "What Do Low-Income Single Mothers Say About Marriage?" *Social Problems* 47 (2000), pp. 112–33.

26. Robert Nakosteen and Michael Zimmer, "Man, Money, and Marriage: Are High Earners More Prone than Low Earners to Marry?" *Social Science Quarterly* 78 (1997): pp. 66–82.

27. Francine D. Blau, Lawrence W. Kahn, and Jane Waldfogel, "Understanding Young Women's Marriage Decisions: The Role of Labor and Marriage Market Conditions," *Industrial and Labor Relations Review* 53, no. 4 (July 2000): pp. 624–48.

28. Robert Nakosteen and Michael Zimmer, "Men, Money, and Marriage," *Social Science Quarterly* 78 (1997); Frank F. Furstenberg, Jr., "The Future of Marriage," *American Demographics* 18 (June 1996), pp. 39–40; Francine Blau, Lawrence Kahn, and Jane Waldfogel, "Understanding Young Women's Marriage Decisions," *Industrial and Labor Relations Review* 53 (2000): pp. 624–48.

29. William A. Darity, Jr. and Samuel L. Myers, Jr., "Family Structure and the Marginalization of Black Men: Policy Implications," in *The Decline in Marriage Among African Americans: Causes, Consequences, and Policy Implications*, ed. M. Belinda Tucker and Claudia Mitchell-Kernan (New York: Russell Sage Foundation, 1995), pp. 263–308.

30. Daniel T. Lichter, D. McLaughlin, F. LeClere, G. Kephart, and D. Landry, "Race and the Retreat From Marriage: A Shortage of Marriageable Men?" *American Sociological Review* 57 (December 1992): pp. 781–99.

31. Ron Mincy, Columbia University, personal communication, February 18, 2002.

32. Mavis Hetherington, *For Better or for Worse: Divorce Reconsidered* (New York: W. W. Norton, 2001); Paul Amato and Alan Booth, "The Legacy of Parents' Marital Discord," *Journal of Personality and Social Psychology* 81 (2001), pp. 627–638; Andrew Cherlin, "Going to Extremes: Family Structure, Children's Well-Being, and Social Science," *Demography* 36 (November 1999): pp. 421–28.

33. Elizabeth Cooksey, "Consequences of Young Mothers' Marital Histories for Children's Cognitive Development," *Journal of Marriage and the Family* 59 (May 1997), pp. 245–62; Juan Battle, "What Beats Having Two Parents? Educational Outcomes for African American Students in Single- Versus Dual-Parent Families," *Journal of Black Studies* 28 (1998), pp. 783–802.

34. Ron Mincy and Chen-Chung Huang, "'Just Get Me to the Church . . .': Assessing Policies to Promote Marriage Among Fragile Families," manuscript prepared for the MacArthur Foundation Network on the Family and the Economy Meeting, Evanston, Illinois, November 30, 2001. Contact Ron Mincy, School of Social Work, Columbia University.

35. Research by Andrew Cherlin and Paula Fomby at Johns Hopkins University, as reported in Robin Toner, "Two Parents Not Always Best for Children," *New York Times,* February 21, 2002.

36. Frank Furstenberg, Jeanne Brooks-Gunn, and S. Philip Morgan, *Adolescent Mothers in Later Life* (New York: Cambridge University Press, 1987).

37. Frank Furstenberg, "Is the Modern Family a Threat to Children's Health?" *Society* 36 (1999): p. 35.

38. Richard Gelles, "Constraints Against Family Violence," *American Behavioral Scientist* 36 (1993), pp. 575–86; A. J. Sedlack and D. D. Broadhurst, *Third National Incidence Study of Child Abuse and Neglect: Final Report* (Washington, D.C.: Department of Health and Human Services, 1996); Kristin Anderson, "Gender, Status and Domestic Violence," *Journal of Marriage and the Family* 59 (1997), pp. 655–670; Jacqueline Payne and Martha Davis, "Testimony of NOW Legal Defense and Education Fund on Child Support and Fatherhood Initiatives," submitted to the United States House Human Resources Subcommittee of the Ways and Means Committee, June 28, 2001.

39. Catherine Kenney and Sara McLanahan, "Are Cohabiting Relationships More Violent Than Marriages?" manuscript, Princeton University; E. D. Leonard, 1994, "Battered Women and Criminal Justice: A Review," doctoral dissertation cited in Todd Migliaccio, "Abused Husbands: A Narrative Analysis," *Journal of Family Issues* 23 (2002), pp. 26–52; K. D. O'Leary et al., "Prevalence and Stability of Physical Aggression Between Spouses: A Longitudinal Analysis," *Journal of Consulting and Clinical Psychology* 57 (1989), pp. 263–68.

40. National Center on Addiction and Substance Abuse at Columbia University, "Back to School 1999—National Survey of American Attitudes on Substance Abuse V: Teens and Their Parents," August 1999. See also Irvin Molotsky, "Study Links Teenage Substance Abuse and Paternal Ties," *New York Times,* Aug. 31, 1999.

41. "Census Bureau Reports Poor Two-Parent Families Are About Twice as Likely to Break Up as Two-Parent Families Not in Poverty," *New York*

Times, January 15, 1993, p. A6; Don Burroughs, "Love and Money," *U.S. News & World Report,* October 19, 1992, p. 58; Scott South, Katherine Trent, and Yang Shen, "Changing Partners: Toward a Macrostructural-Opportunity Theory of Marital Dissolution," *Journal of Marriage and Family* 63, no. 3 (2001): 743–754. Also see note 17.

42. Michelle Budig and Paula England, "The Wage Penalty for Motherhood," *American Sociological Review* 66 (2001): pp. 204–225; Heather Joshi, Pierella Paci, and Jane Waldfogel, 1999, "The Wages of Motherhood: Better or Worse," *Cambridge Journal of Economics* 23, no. 5 (1999): pp. 543–564. Jane Waldfogel, "The Effect of Children on Women's Wages," *American Sociological Review* 62: 2 (1997): pp. 209–217.

43. "Young Children in Poverty: A Statistical Update," June 1999 Edition. Released June 17, 1999, prepared by Neil G. Bennett, Jiali Li, Younghwan Song, and Keming Yang. New York: National Center for Children in Poverty. . . . Data for 2000 from CPS. . . .

44. Nancy Folbre, *Who Pays for the Kids? Gender and the Structures of Constraint* (New York: Routledge, 1994); Ann Crittenden, *The Price of Motherhood* (New York: Metropolitan Books, 2001); Sylvia Ann Hewlett and Cornell West, *The War Against Parents* (New York: Houghton Mifflin, 1998).

45. Joan Williams, *Unbending Gender: Why Family and Work Conflict and What to Do About It* (New York: Oxford University Press, 2000).

46. Ann Crittenden, *The Price of Motherhood. Why the Most Important Job in the World Is Still the Least Valued* (New York: Henry Holt, 2001).

47. Timothy Smeeding, Barbara Boyle Torrey, and Martin Rein, "Patterns of Income and Poverty: The Economic Status of Children and the Elderly in Eight Countries," in John L Palmer, Timothy Smeeding, and Barbara Boyle Torrey, eds., *The Vulnerable* (Washington, D.C.: Urban Institute Press, 1988); Susan Houseknecht and Jaya Sastry, "Family 'Decline' and Child Well-Being: A Comparative Assessment," *Journal of Marriage and the Family* 58 (1996); Sara McLanahan and Irwin Garfinkel, "Single-Mother Families and Social Policy: Lessons for the United States From Canada, France, and Sweden," pp. 367–83, in K. McFate, R. Lawson, W. J. Wilson eds., *Poverty, Inequality, and the Future of Social Policy: Western States in the New World Order* (New York: Russell Sage Foundation, 1995). Michael J. Graetz and Jerry L. Mashaw, *True Security: Rethinking American Social Insurance* (New Haven: Yale University Press, 1999).

48. Marcia K. Meyers, Janet C. Gornick, and Laura R. Peck, 2001, "Packaging Support for Low-Income Families: Policy Variation Across the U.S. States," *Journal of Policy Analysis and Management* 20, no. 3: pp. 457–483.

49. Table 7–6, *Green Book 2000.* Committee on Ways and Means, U.S. House of Representatives, 106th Congress . . .

50. President's Council of Economic Advisors, *The Effects of Welfare Policy and the Economic Expansion of Welfare Caseloads: An Update* (Washington, D.C.: Council of Economic Advisors, 1999).

51. *2000 Kids Count Data Online.* . . .

52. Jennifer Steinhauer, "States Proved Unpredictable in Aiding Uninsured Children," *New York Times,* September 28, 2000. See also Leighton Ku and Brian Bruen, "The Continuing Decline in Medicaid Coverage," Series A, no. A–37 (Washington, D.C.: Urban Institute, 1999); Sheila Zedlewski and Sarah Brauner, "Are the Steep Declines in Food Stamp Participation Linked to Falling Welfare Caseloads?" Series B, no. B–3 (Washington, D.C.: Urban Institute, 1999).

53. Rachel Schumacher and Mark Greenberg, *Child Care After Leaving Welfare: Early Evidence From State Studies* (Washington, D.C.: Center for Law and Social Policy, 1999). On the added costs of child care and care-giving activities for low-income families, see Jody Heymann, *The Widening Gap: Why America's Working Families Are in Jeopardy and What Can Be Done About It* (New York: Basic Books, 2000).

54. Bureau of the Census, Current Population Reports, *Money Income and Poverty in the U.S., 1999.* . . .

55. Patricia Ruggles, *Drawing the Line: Alternative Poverty Measures and Their Implications for Public Policy* (Washington, D.C.: The Urban Institute Press, 1990); Constance Citro and Robert Michael, eds., *Measuring Poverty: A New Approach* (Washington, D.C.: National Academy of Science, 1995); Jared Bernstein, Chauna Brocht, Maggie Spade-Aguilar, *How Much Is Enough? Basic Family Budgets for Working Families* (Washington, D.C.: Economic Policy Institute, 2000).

56. Robert Greenstein, "Should EITC Benefits Be Enlarged for Families With Three or More Children?" Washington, D.C.: Center on Budget and Policy Priorities, 2000. . . .

57. David Ellwood and Jeffrey B. Liebman, "The Middle Class Parent Penalty: Child Benefits in the U.S. Tax Code," manuscript, John F. Kennedy School of Government, Harvard University, Boston, MA, 2000.

58. Robert Cherry and Max Sawicky, "Giving Tax Credit Where Credit Is Due," Briefing Paper (Washington, D.C.: Economic Policy Institute, April 2000). . . .

59. Ronald B. Mincy, "Marriage, Child Poverty, and Public Policy," *American Experiment Quarterly,* 4: 2 (Summer 2001): pp. 68–71. See also Wendy Sigle-Rushton and Sara McLanahan, "For Richer or Poorer?" manuscript, Center for Research on Child Well-Being, Princeton University.

60. Julianne Malveaux, "More Jobs, Not More Marriages, Lift Poor," *U.S.A. Today,* February 22, 2002, p. 15A.

STEPHANIE COONTZ is cochair of the Council on Contemporary Families and teaches history and family studies at Evergreen State College in Olympia, Washington. She has written several books, including *The Way We Never Were: American Families and the Nostalgia Trap* (Basic Books, 1992).

NANCY FOLBRE is cochair of the National Network on the Family and the Economy and is professor of economics at the University of Massachusetts. Her interests include the interface between economics and feminist theory. She has written numerous books and papers.

EXPLORING THE ISSUE

Does Marriage Improve Living Standards for Children?

Critical Thinking and Reflection

1. According to Coontz and Folbre, how can marriage be a short-term fix for single moms living in poverty but fail in the long term?
2. Discuss two of the realities of the poor population that make marriage difficult to attain. Can you identify any ways that these difficulties could be overcome or even eradicated from society?
3. The research shows conflicting information in regard to the effect of teens marrying before versus after the birth of their children. What is the contradictory information and what do you make of it?

Is There Common Ground?

Horn states that government programs should include premarriage education and teach couples the skills they need to help their marriage succeed. Most people would agree that strengthening marriages would be considered a positive thing. However, it is also understood that the issue is complicated and having a good marriage is not the only important thing necessary for raising living standards. It would seem that a multifaceted approach in dealing with marriage standards but also other components of family living would be the ideal one to take in order to work toward raising the living standards of children in America.

Additional Resources

American College of Pediatricians. Marriage and the Family. Retrieved on April 11, 2011, from www .acpeds.org/Marriage-and-the-Family.html

This website discusses some of the benefits of married families on children.

For Your Marriage. Why Married Parents Are Important for Children. Retrieved on April 11, 2011, from http://foryourmarriage.org/married-parents-are-important-for-children/

This website, put out by the Conference of Catholic Bishops, discusses information about how marriage can be important for children.

Create Central

www.mhhe.com/createcentral

Internet References . . .

KidsHealth—Living with a Single Parent. Retrieved on April 11, 2011

This website is written for kids who live with single parents. It contains advice and suggestions for this type of living arrangement.

http://kidshealth.org/kid/feeling/home_family/single_parents.html

Single Parent Families—The Effects on Children. Retrieved on April 11, 2011

This website discusses some of the effects that children can experience when living in a single parent home.

http://family.jrank.org/pages/1577/Single-Parent-Families-Effects-on-Children.html

Selected, Edited, and with Issue Framing Material by:
Kourtney Vaillancourt, *New Mexico State University*

ISSUE

Do Children Who Are Homeschooled Have a Limited View of Society?

YES: Rob Reich, from "The Civic Perils of Homeschooling," *Educational Leadership* (April 2002)

NO: Thomas W. Washburne, J.D., from "The Boundaries of Parental Authority: A Response to Rob Reich of Stanford University," *National Center for Home Education Special Report* (Home School Legal Defense Association, April 22, 2002), http://nche.hslda.org/docs/nche/000010/200204230.asp

Learning Outcomes

After reading this issue, you should be able to:

- Describe some of the reasons that parents may choose homeschooling for their children.
- Identify challenges that homeschooled children face as a result of their educational situation.
- Identify some of the benefits that children who are homeschooled can experience.

ISSUE SUMMARY

YES: Rob Reich, assistant professor of political science, at Stanford University, states that children who are homeschooled are limited by their teachers, who are usually their parents.

NO: Thomas Washburne, director of the National Center for Home Education, disagrees with Reich and believes his opposition to homeschooling denies parents their unalienable right to educate their children as they choose.

Homeschooling was the accepted method of education in the United States until the 1850s. At that time, it was replaced by public schooling, but home schools made a comeback in the 1970s. Home schools are now legal in every state in the nation and more than two million children are homeschooled every year. There has been a steady rise in homeschooling since 1999. In 2007, students who were reported to be homeschooled totaled 1.5 million. The percentage of homeschooled children increased from 1.7 percent in 1999 to 2.9 percent in 2007. As such, the advantages and disadvantages of homeschooling are becoming an increasingly controversial subject in America. Advocates argue that homeschooling offers an alternative to the growing violence, bullying, and poor academic performance prevalent in schools. Opponents argue that homeschooling eliminates essential social interaction and contact.

According to the National Center for Education Statistics (NCES), students are considered homeschooled if their parents report them as being schooled at home instead of at a public or private school for at least part of their education and if their part-time enrollment in public or private schools does not exceed 25 hours a week. Homeschooling advocates feel that this definition does not accurately account for the true number of homeschooled children. Currently, parents can choose to educate their children at home or send them to public or private school depending on their particular situation. Although one type of setting may look more attractive, parents who look at each child as an individual will choose the type of educational environment that considers the child's unique needs. For example, a child who learns well on his own might do better in a home school, while a child who needs to interact with others in order to learn would perform best in a public or private school setting.

Parents choose to homeschool their children for many reasons. Some parents disagree with the values presented in public as well as private schools. They also site disagreements with specific curricula or teaching methods used by schools. Parents who favor homeschooling believe public schools do not promote self-discipline and self-motivation or provide an environment in which each child's particular talents might flourish.

According to the NCES, in 2003 the most frequently cited factor for homeschooling was parents' concern about the environment of other schools including safety, drugs, or negative peer pressure. Eighty-five percent of home-schooled students were being homeschooled, in part, because of this concern. The other two most often cited reasons for homeschooling were to provide religious or moral instruction (72 percent) and a general dissatisfaction with academic instruction at other schools (68 percent). When asked about the most important reason for the decision to homeschool, parents cited providing moral or religious instruction (33 percent) and concern about the environment of traditional schools (30 percent).

Homeschooling advocates defend their cause by pointing at the better test scores of children schooled at home. They also point to the growing problems of violence, bullying, and drug abuse in the public and private school systems. Opponents argue that homeschooled children lose vital social support and contact by being removed from the school environment. They feel that this loss of social interaction outweighs any positive academic effects. Some educators even fear that homeschooling may be harmful to a child's overall development. Children schooled at home may not have the opportunity to develop and interact with their peer group and miss learning social skills. Another common concern is that homeschool teachers may not have the appropriate skills, training, education, and knowledge to teach children effectively.

Parents who do not want their children shaped by hours of rigid institutional learning may opt for the more flexible home school setting. However, it should be noted that home schooling is challenging and sometimes difficult to implement. Parents must be willing to take the time to learn to teach their children effectively. Homeschooling can be a full time job and may necessitate a separate income source for the parent educator.

Another issue that must be considered in home-schooling is college recognition of high school credits earned via home schools. Although increasing numbers of colleges and universities accept homeschooled students with adequate scores on college entrance tests, parents who are teachers must be mindful of meeting state requirements for certification. Appropriate authorities must sanction class-meeting times and course content so that local boards of education recognize and accept home school credits.

There is a possibility that homeschooling will promote parental enmeshment with children in some families. Abuse and neglect, which are often reported by school personnel, could go unnoticed and unreported if children remain in the home for school. Home educators need to provide their children with social outlets and activities to ensure that their children are able to function effectively in social situations with peers. On the other hand, children who attend public and private schools may model themselves after their peers. They may adopt unacceptable or inappropriate behaviors.

Unfortunately, reliable research on this matter is hard to obtain. Homeschooling advocates point out that those who school their children at home are often resentful of their taxes being used on a school system they do not use. Advocates theorize that homeschooling parents are likely to underreport information about homeschooling.

States have differing definitions and standards of accountability for homeschoolers resulting in a lack of consistent nationwide statistics. In Florida, families can homeschool but must directly report to their school district on an annual basis. One very popular method of avoiding these responsibilities is to enroll the student in a specially established "Cover School." The family has now legally enrolled their child in a private school and has no reporting requirements to the state. In California, there are "homeschool charter schools," which get funds from the state to take responsibility for the children's education. They enroll students and provide distance education that is usually done at home. These are just two examples of different types of homeschooling. With these complexities, it is difficult to gather reliable and accurate data on children schooled at home.

The two selections in this issue question whether the ultimate interest in children's education is the state or the parents. Rob Reich feels that the state needs its citizens to have a certain tolerance in order to make informed judgments. As such, he argues that children need to experience the hassles and rewards of social contact with others of differing viewpoints. On the other hand, Thomas Washburne feels that parents have the ultimate choice in their children's education. He points out that many parents do not feel that increased tolerance is necessarily a good thing and that the Constitution guarantees them the right to make educational decisions for their children.

As you read the following selections, think about the following questions: Do you agree with Reich's argument that children learn important civic lessons in school? Do you believe Washburne's claim that parents have the right to educate their children in whatever way they choose? Who has the greater interest, the state or the parents? Read the following selections and decide for yourself if children who are homeschooled have a limited view of society.

YES

Rob Reich

The Civic Perils of Homeschooling

Just 10 years ago, educating a child at home was illegal in several states. Today, not only is homeschooling legal everywhere, it's booming. Homeschooling is probably the fastest-growing segment of the education market, expanding at a rate of 15 to 20 percent a year (Lines, 2000a). More children are homeschooled than attend charter schools. More children are homeschooled than attend conservative Christian academies.

And it's not just left-wing unschoolers and right-wing religious fundamentalists who are keeping their children at home. Taking advantage of the Internet and other new technologies, more middle-of-the-road suburbanites are homeschooling, too. *Time* and *Newsweek* have featured homeschooling on their covers. The U.S. Congress passed a resolution in 1999 declaring the week of September 19 to be National Home Education Week. Homeschooling has gone mainstream.

In response to the rise of homeschooling, policymakers and public school administrators and teachers need to consider what makes homeschooling so popular. Chief among the many reasons to homeschool is the ability to customize a child's education at home.

Customizing Education at Home

The ability to custom-tailor an education for their children is often the motivation for parents to homeschool. No other education arrangement offers the same freedom to arrange an education designed for an individual student; in homeschools, parents are responsible not only for selecting what their children will learn, but when, how, and with whom they will learn. In this sense, homeschooling represents the apex of customization in education.

But is this customization always a good thing? From the standpoint of the parents who choose to homeschool, it surely is; they wouldn't be doing it otherwise, especially in light of the considerable energy and time it requires of them. But considered from the standpoint of democratic citizenship, the opportunity to customize education through homeschooling isn't an unadulterated good. Customizing education may permit schooling to be tailored for each individual student, but total customization also threatens to insulate students from exposure to diverse ideas and people and thereby to shield them from

the vibrancy of a pluralistic democracy. These risks are perhaps greatest for homeschoolers. To understand why we need first to understand more about the current practice of homeschooling.

Homeschooling Today

Homeschooling is more than an education alternative. It is also a social movement (Stevens, 2001; Talbot, 2001). In 1985, approximately 50,000 children were being educated at home. In 2002, at least 1 million children are being homeschooled, with some estimates pegging the number at 2 million, an increase of 20- or 40-fold. (It's symptomatic of the unregulated environment of homeschooling that precise figures on the number of homeschoolers are impossible to establish.) Depending on the estimate you choose (Bielick, Chandler, & Broughman, 2001; Lines, 2000a), homeschoolers account for 2–4 percent of the school-going population.

Homeschooling parents are politically active. Former Pennsylvania Representative Bill Goodling, the former chair of the House Committee on Education and the Workforce, has called homeschoolers "the most effective education lobby on Capitol Hill" (as cited in Golden, 2000). Homeschoolers have established both local and national networks for lobbying purposes and for offering curricular support to one another. Several national organizations, led by the Home School Legal Defense Association, promote homeschooling. Even the former Secretary of Education, William Bennett, is a fan—he has created a for-profit company called K12, the purpose of which is to supply curricular and testing materials to homeschoolers.

But who homeschools, and why? Two main groups of homeschoolers have emerged, both of which raise difficult questions about customization.

The larger of the groups is the Christian right. Although homeschooling has become a much more diverse enterprise in the past 10 years, its strength as a social movement and the majority of its practitioners are conservative Christians. Precise data are scarce, but researchers tend to agree that whereas homeschools of the 1970s "reflected a liberal, humanistic, pedagogical orientation," the majority of homeschools in the 1980s and 1990s "became grounds of and for ideological, conservative, religious expressions of educational matters" (Carper,

2000, p. 16). Today, most parents choose to educate their children at home because they believe that their children's moral and spiritual needs will not be met in campus-based schools.

Those who educate their children at home for religious reasons often object to the secular bias of public schools. By keeping their children at home, they seek to provide a proper religious education free from the damning influences of secularism and pop culture. These homeschoolers wish to avoid the public school at all costs.

The second group practices a different kind of homeschooling. They seek partnerships with public schools to avail themselves of resources, support, guidance, and extracurricular activities that they could not otherwise obtain or provide at home. For these parents, some participation in public schools is desirable.

Various mechanisms have emerged to allow homeschooled students to connect on a partial basis with the public school system. In California, for example, approximately 10 percent of the charter schools serve students whose primary learning is at home (Lines, 2000b). Other districts have set up "virtual" academies online to aid in the enrollment of homeschoolers. Still other school districts permit students to attend some classes but not others and to participate in extracurricular activities (Rothstein, 2002). Finally, a few public school districts have set up homeschooling resource centers, staffed by public school teachers and professional curriculum developers, that homeschooling parents can use at their convenience.

Democratic Citizenship and Customization

Each kind of homeschooler—the family who teaches the child solely at home and the family who seeks some interaction with the public school system—is practicing customization in education. For the first, parents can tailor the education environment to their own convictions and to their beliefs about what their child's needs and interests are. For the second, parents can select the aspects of the public system they and their child want, creating an overall program designed for their child.

What's to worry about either kind of customization? Let me put the matter quite simply. Customizing a child's education through homeschooling represents the victory of a consumer mentality within education, suggesting that the only purpose that education should serve is to please and satisfy the preferences of the consumer. Education, in my view, is not a consumption item in the same sense as the food we select from the grocery store.

Many homeschoolers would surely protest here that their energetic efforts to overcome numerous obstacles to educate their children at home are motivated by a desire to shield their children from rampant consumerism and to offer their children a moral environment in which they learn deeper and more important values. No doubt this is true.

But my point is not that homeschooling parents are inculcating in their children a consumer mentality. My point is that many homeschooling parents view the education of their children as a matter properly under their control and no one else's. They feel entitled to "purchase" the education environment of their children from the marketplace of learning materials, with no intermediary between them and their child. The first kind of homeschooler actually does purchase learning materials for the home. The second kind of homeschooler treats the public school system as a provider of services and activities from which parents choose what they want, as if it were a restaurant with an extensive menu.

And this attitude is the crucial point. Homeschooling is the apogee of parental control over a child's education, where no other institution has a claim to influence the schooling of the child. Parents serve as the only filter for a child's education, the final arbiters of what gets included and what gets excluded.

This potentially compromises citizenship in the following ways:

- In a diverse, democratic society, part of able citizenship is to come to respect the fact that other people will have beliefs and convictions, religious and otherwise, that conflict with one's own. Yet from the standpoint of citizenship, these other people are equals. And students must learn not only that such people exist, but how to engage and deliberate with them in the public arena. Thus, students should encounter materials, ideas, and people that they or their parents have not chosen or selected in advance.
- Citizenship is the social glue that binds a diverse people together. To be a citizen is to share something in common with one's fellow citizens. As the legal scholar Sunstein (2001) has argued, a heterogeneous society without some shared experiences and common values has a difficult time addressing common problems and risks social fragmentation. Schooling is one of the few remaining social institutions—or civic intermediaries—in which people from all walks of life have a common interest and in which children might come to learn such common values as decency, civility, and respect.
- Part of being a citizen is exercising one's freedom. Indeed, the freedoms that U.S. citizens enjoy are a democratic inheritance that we too often take for granted. But to be free is not simply to be free from coercion or constraint. Democratic freedom requires the free construction and possible revision of beliefs and preferences. To become free, students must be exposed to the vibrant diversity of a democratic society so that they possess the liberty to live a life of their own design.

Because homeschooled students receive highly customized educations, designed usually to accord with the preferences of parents, they are least likely in principle to be exposed to materials, ideas, and people that have not been chosen in advance; they are least likely to share common education experiences with other children; and they are most likely to have a narrow horizon of experiences, which can curtail their freedom. Although highly customized education for students may produce satisfied parents as consumers, and even offer excellent academic training to the student, it is a loss from a civic perspective.

Civic Perils

I do not argue that homeschooling undermines citizenship in all cases. On the contrary, I have elsewhere defended the practice of homeschooling, when properly regulated (Reich, 2002). Many homeschooling parents are deeply committed to providing their children with an education that introduces them to a great diversity of ideas and people. And for those homeschoolers who seek partnerships with public schools, their children do participate in common institutions with other children. I do not intend to condemn homeschooling wholesale, for I have met many homeschooled students who are better prepared for democratic citizenship than the average public school student.

My claim is about the potential civic perils of a homeschooled education, where schooling is customizable down to the tiniest degree. Customization, and, therefore, homeschooling, seem wonderful if we think about education as a consumption item. But schooling, from the time that public schools were founded until today, has served to cultivate democratic citizenship. And though this may be a largely forgotten aim, as many have argued, we should not allow a new consumer mentality to become the driving metaphor for the education of children.

References

Bielick, S., Chandler, K., & Broughman, S. (2001, July 31). *Home schooling in the United States: 1999* (NCES 2001-033). Washington, DC: U.S. Department of Education.

Carper, J. C. (2000, April). Pluralism to establishment to dissent: The religious and educational context of home schooling. *Peabody Journal of Education, 75*(1,2), 8–19.

Golden, D. (2000, April 24). Homeschoolers learn how to gain clout inside the beltway. *Wall Street Journal*, p. Al.

Lines, P. (2000a, Summer). Home schooling comes of age. *Public Interest, 140,* 74–85.

Lines, P. (2000b, April). When homeschoolers go to school: A partnership between families and schools. *Peabody Journal of Education, 75*(1, 2), 159–186.

Reich, R. (2002). *Bridging liberalism and multiculturalism in American education.* Chicago: University of Chicago Press.

Rothstein, R. (2002, January 2). Augmenting a homeschool education. *New York Times*, p. B11.

Stevens, M. (2001). *Kingdom of children: Culture and controversy in the homeschooling movement.* Princeton, NJ: Princeton University Press.

Sunstein, C. (2001). *Republic.com.* Princeton, NJ: Princeton University Press.

Talbot, M. (2001, November). The new counterculture. *Atlantic Monthly, 288*(4), 136–143.

Rob Reich is an assistant professor of political science and ethics in society at Stanford University and senior research associate for the Aspen Institute Program on Education in a Changing Society.

Thomas W. Washburne, J.D.

The Boundaries of Parental Authority: A Response to Rob Reich of Stanford University

From August 30 to September 2, 2001, the American Political Science Association held its annual meeting in San Francisco, California. Rob Reich, of the Department of Political Science at Stanford University, presented a paper at this meeting which has captured the attention of many home schooling families, including members of the Home School Legal Defense Association (HSLDA). Several members of HSLDA have asked for our opinion of this paper. This report has been prepared to satisfy these inquiries. It is not intended to be a point by point refutation of the paper, but is rather a brief examination of the major themes explored, and some of HSLDA's major criticisms and concerns. Reich's position should not be taken lightly. It is illustrative of many of the challenges home educators are facing as their numbers increase. Moreover, if Reich's views were adopted by the courts, home education as we know it today would simply cease to legally exist.

Mr. Reich's paper was entitled *Testing the Boundaries of Parental Authority Over Education: The Case of Homeschooling*. The paper is a precursor to a book by Reich to be entitled *Bridging Liberalism and Multiculturalism in Education*, which the University of Chicago Press is anticipated to publish in 2002. In his paper, Reich traces the rise of home education, the interests in education held by the government, the parent, and the child, and sets forth his suggestions for balancing these interests. These suggestions lead Reich to conclude that "while the state should not ban homeschooling it must nevertheless regulate its practice with vigilance." He then briefly offers a few suggestions for how a state should regulate home education, and some of the difficulties the state may encounter.

Reich's proposed regulations include "periodic assessments that would measure their success in examining and reflecting upon diverse worldviews." These regulations are in furtherance of Reich's view that:

> Children are owed as a matter of justice the capacity to choose to lead lives—adopt values and beliefs, pursue an occupation, endorse new traditions—that are different from those of their parents. Because the child cannot him or herself ensure the acquisition of such capacities and the parents

may be opposed to such acquisition, the state must ensure it for them. The state must guarantee that children are educated for minimal autonomy.

A brief review of the constitutional basis for home education will lead one to quickly understand the serious implications of Reich's theories. It has long been recognized by Americans, legal scholars, and the Supreme Court that the original intent of the drafters of the Constitution of the United States was to protect many rights which are not expressly set forth in the founding documents. It has also long been held by Americans and the Supreme Court, and rightfully so, that the right of parents to direct the upbringing of their children is a fundamental right. In fact, this basic understanding of the role of parents long predates the founding of the United States.

Nevertheless, no right is absolute. In that regard, the American legal system has created a method by which the limits of fundamental rights are tested. It is said by the Courts examining constitutional challenges to government law and regulation that the fundamental right at issue may not be infringed upon unless the government can show a compelling interest in doing so, and, if there is such an interest, it then infringes in the least restrictive manner. In such cases, the court must balance the "interests" of the state against the "interests" of the individual asserting a right. For example, in the case of the First Amendment right to free speech, the government has a compelling interest to maintain public safety and order and can therefore prohibit the wrongful shouting of "fire" in a crowded theatre, even though this infringes a person's right to free speech.

As noted before, the regulation of home education by the government is limited by the fact that parents have a fundamental right to direct the upbringing of their children which is protected by the Constitution. Accordingly, unless the state can show some compelling interest in regulating the parent's involvement in education, the parent's views are heeded. So, it becomes critical to understand what the state's interest in education is.

Fortunately for home schoolers, this issue was addressed decades ago, and reaffirmed on occasion since. It is well understood from a legal perspective that the government's *compelling* interest in education is limited. It has been held numerous times that the government's interest in education is basically only of two varieties: civic and economic. The first involves the government's interest in seeing that a child is prepared for citizenship. In other words, will he have capability to vote? The economic interest addresses the state's desire to see that citizens will be able to provide for themselves and not become a burden. So, for example, when a state attempts to impose a requirement that all home educators have teaching degrees, the state must show that this requirement is essential in achieving its interest in education—that is, good citizenship, economic success, etc. To rebut the government, the home educator merely needs to show that home educators without teaching degrees are raising children who are competent, functional. Such a showing renders the government's proposed regulation as unnecessary to achieve the government's compelling interest.

There has been considerable debate about whether the government's interest in education should be extended. So far, thankfully, the courts have been reluctant to do so. Not even the most liberal of judges have taken the initiative to override centuries of respect for the institution of the family and the parental interest in raising children.

It is at this point that we can begin to see the implications, indeed danger, of Reich's ideas for home education. For Reich, while recognizing that there can be debate on the topic, essentially concedes that the state's interest in education does not lend itself to regulating home education. It is not Reich's contention that parental rights should be overridden because the state's compelling interest in education is not being fulfilled. Reich rather sets forth the argument that children have their own interests in education, which are different from both the parent's and the state's. It is this interest, the child's, which in Reich's view justifies limiting parental rights.

Reich sees the interest of the child as being twofold. First, "a child has an interest in education because education is necessary to developing into an adult capable of independent functioning." While setting forth this interest, it appears that Reich sees it as largely duplicating what are already addressed by the state and parental interests in education. Reich does "not mean to imply anything potentially controversial about independent functioning." It is in the second interest of children in education, as seen by Reich, that the controversy is made clear.

For Reich, children have a fundamental interest in "becoming autonomous." This refers "to the capacity of the child to develop into an independent adult who can seek and promote his or her own interests, as he or she understands them, and who can participate, if he or she chooses, in political dialog with others." This interest comes from his perception that children should be shielded from "an unquestioning subordination of one's own will to the ethical ideals of another person or persons." In Reich's view, "Neither parents nor the state can justly attempt to imprint indelibly upon a child a set of values and beliefs, as if it were an inheritance one should never be able to question, as if the child must always defer and be obedient. To do so would in effect render the child servile."

The insertion of the supposed interest of children to be autonomous into the balancing of parental and state interests leads to interesting conclusions. Reich provides the following:

> I submit that even in a minimal construal of autonomy, it must be the function of the school setting to expose children to and engage children with values and beliefs other than those of their parents. [citation omitted] To achieve minimal autonomy requires that a child know that there are ways of life other than that into which he or she has been born. Minimal autonomy requires, especially for its civic importance, that a child be able to examine his or her own political values and beliefs, and those of others, with a critical eye. It requires that the child be able to think independently. If this is all true, then, at a bare minimum, the structure of schooling cannot simply replicate in every particularity the values and beliefs of a child's home.

To ensure the children's interest, "[t]he state must therefore ensure that all children, regardless of the environment in which they are schooled, receive an education that exposes them to and engages them with values and beliefs other than those they find at home." Moreover, "[b]ecause children are a politically inert group, regulations in their interest must be defended by other organizations, such as the Children's Defense Fund, which typically have less at stake in home schooling, or by state officials, who are of course responsible for a much broader children's agenda than guarding against home schooling abuses."

At first glance, Reich's arguments appear persuasive. We cannot deny that children have significant rights which the state protects. For instance, children may not be abused, neglected, or abandoned. In fact, the entire juvenile justice system is predicated on the fact that children have unique interests, that children have special concerns. All of this begs the question, "why don't children have an interest in education?" And if they do, could Reich be right? As Reich points out, children are not the property of their parents to do with whatever they desire.

But the subject is more complex than what Reich is setting forth. First and foremost, children are not adults. Children are people, yet children, by their very nature, are in a class of their own. When children are involved, society, and the law, duly note their special status. Accordingly, some human rights are afforded children, and some are not. Generally, this reflects the fact that children cannot fend for themselves and lack the capacity to form certain judgments. In examining what rights children enjoy, and what rights they do not, a helpful distinction may be drawn between rights of children to protection and rights of children to choice.

Rights of protection involve the right to life, freedom from bodily harm, etc. All people, by being people, are entitled to some liberty in their person. Children are no exception. In children, rights of protection take the form of protection from abuse, abandonment, etc.

Rights of choice are legal rights that permit persons to make "affirmative choices of binding consequence. Rights of choice includes such rights as voting, marrying, exercising religious preference, and choosing whether to seek education." These rights, however, are not extended to all. Our law has always recognized that to exercise these rights, a person must have capacity. This is why contracts with children are unenforceable. This is why children may not vote, or marry without permission. These are adult rights and children are not adults. It is in the consideration of rights of choice that Reich's arguments begin to lose their persuasion.

Consider a child's right to autonomy as posited by Reich. Can it really be said that children are owed, "as a matter of justice," the capacity to lead lives different than their parents? Most parents would quickly concur that children do not have, nor should they have, the right to dictate when they go to bed, what they watch on television, what magazines they read, whether they do their chores, or whether they obey their parents. To recognize a child's right to choice would lead to the child's doom. Yes, the law protects children. But the law cannot change children into adults simply by giving them the choices of adults. The law cannot give them something which, being children, they do not have by nature the ability to exercise.

The right to autonomy, to view the world as you want to, is only properly enjoyed by adults. While prudent parenting includes efforts to inform and help children understand the world about them, responsible parenting also demands that children be taught right from wrong, in a word—truth.

A major problem Reich's theory does not directly address is that all teaching has at its base a worldview, a philosophy of life. Even so-called neutrality betrays an underlying worldview of relativism. Accordingly, by definition, reality, or whatever label one puts on it, every child is being taught a worldview by someone. There really is no such thing as neutrality in education. Putting it in Reich's language, even if a child had a right to autonomy in education, it could never be exercised. The state, in enforcing the child's interest, will by necessity become an advocate of some worldview. While there might be some danger in allowing parents to convey worldviews to children, history will attest that having the state indoctrinate children has much larger consequences.

Granting choice rights to children, and having the state enforce them, is especially problematic for worldviews arising out of religion. Many religions, and especially Christianity, necessitate the teaching of truth. Not,

"This is my truth," but "True truth." There is no room for relativism. There is no way that the child can be merely exposed to all worldviews. While Christian parenting can involve exposure to other worldviews, Christian parenting cannot allow for a neutral presentation. Christian parents cannot say to the child: "This is true for me, it may not be true for you." The best Christian parents can do is say, "This is true, and you must come to terms with your response to this truth."

In at least one way, Reich anticipates this objection. He notes that:

> [T]he problem arises when the secular state authority is exercised over the rearing of children. Conflict between the state and religious parents on this score may be endemic and inevitable. On my view, even given the deep importance of religious freedom, the state cannot relinquish its regulatory role in education in cases where parents invoke their religious beliefs as a bulwark against secular authority.

One of the reasons why home education has exploded as a movement is that the public schools no longer teach truth as truth. The court has so hemmed in the role of public education that secular humanism and relativism have become the only underlying philosophies that survive constitutional scrutiny. To a certain degree, Reich's ideas have met with success, as evidenced by the number of children in public education. While this is acceptable to many Americans, and in particular the so-called intellectual elite, it is simply unacceptable to many others.

We must ask ourselves at this point, "why is Reich so afraid of home education?" We are a small segment of society. If we are really afraid that children are suffering from a lack of autonomy in education, why not focus upon the much larger populations of children who really will suffer a lack of autonomy, even as adults. By any definition, children who grow up illiterate, unable to do basic math, and lack even the capacity as adults to exercise choice rights are far less autonomous than home educated children who have received an education based on the world view of their parents. Home schoolers represent little more than 2% of school aged students. Why focus on them? If it is children we care about, we should focus on those kids who are not being given even the most rudimentary of education in America's failing public schools. If Reich really cares, perhaps he should initially focus on those children trapped in educational failure.

The real root of the problem home education presents to Reich is that home educators have removed themselves from America's educational system and its underlying values. Their children are beyond the reach of the elite and the predominate worldview of relativism or secular humanism. As home schooling continues to grow and prosper, this will become increasingly troublesome to the educational establishment. But more than being beyond the intellectual elite, the children of home educators are largely beyond the reach of the state. It will take novel legal theories to break this constitutional protection. And it is here that Reich's theories are most concerning, indeed dangerous.

What Reich is doing, intentional or not, is setting an academic framework by which an activist judge might rule in favor of heavy restrictions on home education, while at the same time avoiding the obvious assault on precedent and the Constitution. By extending what are in essence adult rights of choice to children, and declaring

children to have an interest in education separate from the state's and separate from their parent's, Reich provides the opportunity to take away freedoms which Americans, indeed humans in general, have deemed fundamental for thousands of years.

THOMAS W. WASHBURNE, J.D. is the director of the National Center for Home Education. He directs the Home School Legal Defense Association's federal policy staff and its legislative activities in Washington, DC.

EXPLORING THE ISSUE

Do Children Who Are Homeschooled Have a Limited View of Society?

Critical Thinking and Reflection

1. What does Reich claim are the potential civic perils of education? Do you believe these are as great a threat as he proposes? Why or why not?
2. Do you believe homeschooling is a good idea or a bad one? Give three reasons for your answer from the readings.
3. What are the limits on regulation of education by the government? Do you think these are a good thing? Why or why not?
4. Explain the difference between the government's civic and economic interests in education.

Is There Common Ground?

Do children who are homeschooled have a limited view of society? Who has the greater claim on education, the state or the parents? Is a tolerant population the best thing for the state? Do you agree that it is a good thing for children to be exposed to a range of ideas? Do you agree that parents have the right and the duty to educate their children as they see fit? With an ever-increasing homeschooling population, society will continue to face this issue. The challenge is answering these questions while taking the best interest of students into consideration. It is obvious that a one-size-fits-all approach to education is not the best way to go; therefore, finding some middle ground is very important in this debate.

Create Central

www.mhhe.com/createcentral

Additional Resources

About.com Homeschooling. Retrieved on April 13, 2011, from http://homeschooling.about.com/cs/supportgroups/a/hsingusa.htm

This website provides legal information, organizations, support groups, community events, and online resources about homeschooling for each state.

A to Z Homeschool Curriculum, Laws, Programs, Social Networks. Retrieved on April 13, 2011, from http://homeschooling.gomilpitas.com/

This website is a comprehensive guide to curriculum, laws, and so forth for homeschooling.

Internet References . . .

Homeschool Central. Retrieved on April 13, 2011

This website provides resources for families who homeschool their children.

www.homeschoolcentral.com/

Public Schools vs. Home Schools. Retrieved on April 13, 2011

This website discusses the pros and cons of homeschooling versus public school.

www.allaboutparenting.org/public-schools-vs-home-school-faq.htm

Selected, Edited, and with Issue Framing Material by:
Kourtney Vaillancourt, *New Mexico State University*

ISSUE

Is the Media Responsible for the Rise in Childhood Obesity?

YES: The Henry J. Kaiser Family Foundation, from "The Role of Media in Childhood Obesity," *Issue Brief* (February 2004)

NO: Center for Science in the Public Interest, from "Dispensing Junk: How School Vending Undermines Efforts to Feed Children Well," *Report from Center for Science in the Public Interest* (May 2004)

Learning Outcomes

After reading this issue, you should be able to:

- Summarize each author's stance on the reasons for the increase in childhood obesity.
- Decide which of the author's positions you feel is the largest contributor to the increase in childhood obesity and give supporting reasons for your answer.
- Demonstrate an understanding of food items that are identified as unhealthy and contributing to obesity in children as well as the types of ads that are believed to influence unhealthy eating habits.

ISSUE SUMMARY

YES: The Henry J. Kaiser Family Foundation, a private nonprofit foundation focusing on major health care issues facing the nation, cites research studies that show that the more children watch television, the more likely they will be overweight. They also contend that the rise in childhood obesity can be traced to the increased use of media.

NO: The Center for Science in the Public Interest, a consumer advocacy organization on nutrition and health, views the high-calorie, non-nutritious foods found in school vending machines as the culprit in the rise in childhood obesity rates.

The rise in childhood obesity is considered an epidemic because the rates of childhood overweight have grown so rapidly in such a short amount of time. According to the Centers for Disease Control and Prevention, National Center for Health Statistics, since 1980 the proportion of overweight children has more than doubled. The rate for teens has tripled since 1980. Currently, 10 percent of 2- to 5-year-olds are overweight, and 15 percent of 6- to 19-year-olds are overweight. The numbers go up to 20 percent for 2- to 5-year-old children, and 30 percent for 6- to 19-year-old children when you add in those at risk for being overweight. Children of color are at greater risk with 4 out of 10 Mexican-American and African-American children being overweight. Recently, the problem has gained renewed interest as Michelle Obama has become an advocate for prevention strategies to curb the rates of obesity in children.

Childhood obesity is the term used to describe the problem in the population while individual children are generally referred to as being overweight. Overweight and at risk for being overweight are terms used to define children whose height and weight fall within a certain range on a chart referred to as the BMI (body mass index). The BMI measures the ratio of weight to height. BMI measures for children are age- and gender-specific because children's body fat varies with age and gender. A child's BMI is plotted on a growth curve that reflects that child's age and gender. This plotting yields a value, BMI for age, that provides a consistent measure across age groups. Percentile scores indicate how a particular child compares with other children of the same age and gender. The Centers for Disease Control classifies children above the 95th percentile for their age and gender as overweight. Children are considered at risk for being overweight if they fall between the 85th and 95th percentile for age and gender. Healthy children have a BMI of 6 to 85 percent, and underweight children have a BMI of less than 5 percent.

Why is the rise in childhood obesity considered such a problem? Along with being overweight comes a host of physical and mental health problems such as diabetes, high blood pressure, depression, and poor body image. The health care costs for these medical conditions are exorbitant, not to mention the reduced quality of life for the children. The probability that overweight children will become overweight adults is 50 percent; thus, these health care issues may follow the child into adulthood. The subsequent reduced productivity levels of adults, whose overweight condition follows them into adulthood, have economic and social implications. Instead of contributing to society and the economy, individuals may be relying on these institutions to take care of them.

A review of the extensive literature that has been emerging on childhood obesity shows there are a multitude of reasons cited for the epidemic. Almost every American institution has been blamed as being responsible for the increase in children's weight. Grocery stores, schools, communities, families, restaurants, fast food, media, and the economy have had a role in making children overweight. Specifically, grocery stores are accused of stocking high-fat, high-calorie foods; the cost of healthy foods such as fruits and milk are more than processed snack foods and sodas. Schools house vending machines full of foods with little nutritive value and loads of calories; often school officials hesitate to get rid of the offending machines because they depend on them for revenue to purchase needed school supplies. There has been a reduction in the amount of hours and level of intensity of physical education classes in the schools, thus children do not get a chance to burn off calories in school the way they have in the past.

Other institutions have encouraged overeating while discouraging physical activity. Communities and neighborhoods do not lend themselves to exercise with few sidewalks for walking and few parks in which to play. Children do not feel safe enough in their neighborhoods to go out and play after school. Full-service restaurants and fast food venues have super sized their portions and encourage people to overeat. Buffets lure people to overeat by offering "all you can eat" for a lower price than a nutritious meal with vegetables and reasonable portions.

The work/family dilemma of too little time shows up in family schedules that are hectic and leave little time for family meals together. Eating together as a family has been associated with reducing child weight. Parents may be contributing to childhood obesity by providing too much and the wrong type of food as well as not encouraging more physical activity of their children or themselves.

There is an overwhelming amount of media available to encourage sedentary behavior. Watching television, surfing the Web, and playing video games create an environment that discourages physical activity. Interestingly enough, research studies show that when children reduce time watching TV, physical exercise time does not necessarily increase; the children may replace this TV time with other sedentary activities like reading, talking on the phone, or playing board games.

Although there are many factors that contribute to childhood obesity, will the concern for reducing childhood weight turn into an obsession with weight and lead to other types of problems? Already, there is a concern among educators that more eating disorders such as anorexia or bulimia will emerge. In addition, there may be more of a tendency for overweight children to be discriminated against and develop a poor body image, which can ultimately lead to mental illness and depression. In the YES selection, personnel from The Henry J. Kaiser Family Foundation propose that the rise in childhood obesity is due to the influence of the media, specifically the huge numbers of hours of television that children watch. In the NO selection, personnel from the Center for Science in the Public Interest assert that the high-calorie, low-nutrient food found in school vending machines encourages children to develop poor eating habits and leads to their being overweight.

YES

The Henry J. Kaiser
Family Foundation

The Role of Media in Childhood Obesity

Introduction

In recent years, health officials have become increasingly alarmed by the rapid increase in obesity among American children. According to the Centers for Disease Control and Prevention (CDC), since 1980 the proportion of overweight children ages 6–11 has more than doubled, and the rate for adolescents has tripled. Today about 10% of 2- to 5-year-olds and 15% of 6- to 19-year-olds are overweight. Taking into consideration the proportion who are "at risk" of being overweight, the current percentages double to 20% for children ages 2–5 and 30% for kids ages 6–19. Among children of color, the rates are even higher: 4 in 10 Mexican American and African American youth ages 6–19 are considered overweight or at risk of being overweight.

According to the American Academy of Pediatrics, the increase in childhood obesity represents an "unprecedented burden" on children's health. Medical complications common in overweight children include hypertension, type 2 diabetes, respiratory ailments, orthopedic problems, trouble sleeping, and depression. The Surgeon General has predicted that preventable morbidity and mortality associated with obesity may exceed those associated with cigarette smoking. Given that an estimated 80% of overweight adolescents continue to be obese in adulthood, the implications of childhood obesity on the nation's health—and on health care costs—are huge. Indeed, the American Academy of Pediatrics has called the potential costs associated with childhood obesity "staggering."

In an effort to seek the causes of this disturbing trend, experts have pointed to a range of important potential contributors to the rise in childhood obesity that are unrelated to media: a reduction in physical education classes and after-school athletic programs, an increase in the availability of sodas and snacks in public schools, the growth in the number of fast-food outlets across the country, the trend toward "super-sizing" food portions in restaurants, and the increasing number of highly processed high-calorie and high-fat grocery products.

The purpose of this issue brief is to explore one other potential contributor to the rising rates of childhood obesity: children's use of media.

During the same period in which childhood obesity has increased so dramatically, there has also been an explosion in media targeted to children: TV shows and videos, specialized cable networks, video games, computer activities and Internet Web sites. Children today spend an average of five-and-a-half hours a day using media, the equivalent of a full time job, and more time than they spend doing anything else besides sleeping. Even the very youngest children, preschoolers ages six and under, spend as much time with screen media (TV, videos, video games and computers) as they do playing outside. Much of the media targeted to children is laden with elaborate advertising campaigns, many of which promote foods such as candy, soda, and snacks. Indeed, it is estimated that the typical child sees about 40,000 ads a year on TV alone.

For the first time, this report pulls together the best available research, going behind the headlines to explore the realities of what researchers do and do not know about the role media plays in childhood obesity. In addition, the report lays out media-related policy options that have been proposed to help address childhood obesity, and outlines ways media could play a positive role in helping to address this important public health problem.

Pediatricians, child development experts, and media researchers have theorized that media may contribute to childhood obesity in one or more of the following ways:

- The time children spend using media displaces time they could spend in physical activities;
- The food advertisements children are exposed to on TV influence them to make unhealthy food choices;
- The cross-promotions between food products and popular TV and movie characters are encouraging children to buy and eat more high-calorie foods;
- Children snack excessively while using media, and they eat less healthy meals when eating in front of the TV;
- Watching TV and videos lowers children's metabolic rates below what they would be even if they were sleeping;
- Depictions of nutrition and body weight in entertainment media encourage children to develop less healthy diets.

The research to date has examined these issues from a variety of perspectives ranging from health sciences and public health, to child development and family relations, to advertising and mass communications. These investigations have been methodologically diverse, and the results have often been mixed. As with any research, caution must be used when comparing the outcomes of studies because of variations in the methods and measures used. For example, some studies are regional, while others use large, nationally representative samples. Some focus on specific demographic subsets, such as 6th-grade girls, while others are broader. Some studies rely on detailed data sets, others on fairly simplistic measures. For example, television use may be measured through self-reports, parental reports, or detailed diaries. Likewise, body fat may be assessed through multiple clinical measures or by self-reports of height and weight.

DEFINING CHILDHOOD OBESITY

The phrases "obese," "overweight," and "at risk for being overweight" are commonly used in the public health community. With regard to children, the terms "obese" and "overweight" are generally used interchangeably in the medical literature. The Body Mass Index (BMI), which measures the ratio of weight to height, is a standard tool used to define these terms. BMI definitions for children and adolescents are age- and gender-specific in order to accommodate growth patterns. The Centers for Disease Control and Prevention (CDC) classify children as "overweight" if they are above the 95th percentile for their age and sex, and "at risk of being overweight" if they are between the 85th and 95th percentile.

The following section of this report reviews the major research that has been conducted on the key issues concerning media and childhood obesity, and summarizes the major findings.

Research on Media and Childhood Obesity

Do major studies find a relationship between childhood obesity and the time children spend using media? The first major evidence that children's media consumption may be related to their body weight came in a 1985 article by William Dietz and Stephen Gortmaker in the journal *Pediatrics*, and it was dramatic. An analysis of data from a large national study of more than 13,000 children, the National Health Examination Survey (NHES), found significant associations between the amount of time children spent watching television and the prevalence of obesity. The authors concluded that, among 12- to 17-year-olds, the prevalence of obesity increased by 2% for each additional hour of television viewed, even after controlling for other variables such as prior obesity, race, and socio-economic status. Indeed, according to the authors, "only prior obesity had a larger independent effect than television on the prevalence of obesity." In a commentary published in 1993, the authors went on to note that another interpretation of their findings is that "29% of the cases of obesity could be prevented by reducing television viewing to 0 to 1 hours per week."

Since then, several more studies have found a statistically significant relationship between media use and rates of obesity, while others have found either a weak relationship or no relationship at all. In addition to the Dietz and Gortmaker study, other large-scale national studies have found a correlation between media use and body weight:

- Analysis of data from a nationally representative survey of more than 700 kids ages 10–15, conducted in the late 1980s, concluded that "the odds of being overweight were 4.6 times greater for youth watching more than 5 hours of television per day compared with those watching for 0–1 hours," even when controlling for prior overweight, maternal overweight, race, and socio-economic status. The authors concluded, "Estimates of attributable risk indicate that more [than] 60% of overweight incidence in this population can be linked to excess television viewing time."
- Data from the 1988–1994 waves of the National Health and Nutrition Examination Surveys (NHANES) were analyzed to explore the relationship between TV watching and obesity among 8- to 16-year-olds. The study concluded that "television watching was positively associated with obesity among girls, even after controlling for age, race/ethnicity, family income, weekly physical activity, and energy intake." The study did not find a correlation for boys.
- Another analysis of the 1988–1994 NHANES data found that among 8- to 16-year-olds, both boys and girls "who watched the most television had more body fat and greater BMIs than those who watched less than 2 hours a day."
- A study based on the CDC's 1999 Youth Risk Behavior Survey which sampled more than 12,000 high school students nationwide, found that watching television more than 2 hours a day was related to being overweight; these findings were consistent for the entire student population, controlling for race, ethnicity, and gender.
- A later study found a link between television viewing and obesity using a different methodology. The Framingham Children's Study was a longitudinal study in which slightly more than 100 children were enrolled as preschoolers and followed into early adolescence. In this study, published in 2003, the authors found that "television watching was an independent predictor of the change in the child's BMI" and other measures of body fatness. They noted that the effect of TV viewing was "only slightly attenuated" by controlling for factors such as the child's body-fat measures at the time they

were enrolled in the study, and their parents' BMI or education. The authors concluded that "television watching is a risk factor for change in body fat, not simply reflective of more obese children tending to watch more television as a consequence of their obesity making it difficult to exercise."

Other studies—one from a nationally representative cross-sectional sample and the others from specific regions or communities—have not found a relationship between television viewing and childhood obesity:

- A recent analysis of data from a national study of more than 2,800 children ages 12 and under, which relied on detailed time-use diaries, found a "striking" lack of relationship between time spent watching television and children's weight status. On the other hand, this study did find a relationship between obesity and time spent playing video games, although that relationship was not linear: Children with higher weight played moderate amounts of games, while those with low weight played electronic games either very little or a lot.
- A 1993 study of 6th- and 7th-grade girls in Northern California found that over a two-year period "baseline hours of after-school television viewing was not significantly associated with either baseline or longitudinal change in BMI." The authors argued that their study "refutes previous suggestions that . . . television viewing is causally related to obesity."
- A study of nearly 200 preschoolers in Texas observed the children for several hours on each of four different days a year, over the course of three years, recording the amount of TV the children watched and their physical activities. This study found that although television watching was weakly negatively correlated with physical activity levels, it was not associated with body composition.

In evaluating this research, it is important to note that some of these studies are cross-sectional rather than longitudinal—that is, they take a specific point in time and look at whether TV viewing is associated with obesity. One problem with this approach is that while a study may indicate a relationship between TV viewing and being overweight, it does not prove that the TV viewing *caused* the increased weight. Controlling for other risk factors such as socio-economic status and parental body weight (as many studies do) can help clarify the results. Another problem with the cross-sectional approach is that the causal relationship could run in the opposite direction: that is, being obese may cause children to engage in more sedentary (and isolated) activities, including watching more television.

Longitudinal studies can help address the causality issue; however, the results of these studies have varied. As noted above, the two-year longitudinal study of adolescent girls in Northern California did not find a causal relationship between children's weight and the time they spent with media. On the other hand, the Framingham Children's Study, which tracked preschoolers through early adolescence, did find such a relationship. The authors of the latter study have theorized that the effects of media use on body weight may emerge slowly over time, and hence were not revealed in the two-year study in Northern California. It has also been argued that the lack of effect in that study may be due to factors specific to the sample of 6th- and 7th-grade girls in Northern California. Additionally, the study of 700 10- to 15-year-olds referenced above used height and weight data from 1986 and compared it to TV viewing and BMI measures in 1990. These authors concluded that "no evidence was found for a selective effect of overweight; i.e., children who were overweight in 1986 were unlikely to watch more television in 1990 than were children who were not overweight."

Others argue that the only way to truly demonstrate a causal relationship is through an experimental trial; for example, reduce TV viewing and see whether that affects children's weight when compared to a control group. Several interventions of this nature have been found to have a positive impact in reducing children's body weight.

Do experimental interventions that reduce children's media time result in weight loss? Experimental trials are considered the best way of determining whether there is a causal relationship between television viewing and childhood obesity. Some experiments have incorporated reductions in media time as part of a more comprehensive program involving diet and increased physical activity as well. Another experiment used reduced media time as the only intervention, yet still found an impact on children's weight and body fatness.

- During the 1996–97 school year, Stanford University researchers conducted a randomized controlled trial in which they reduced the amount of time a group of about 100 3rd- and 4th-graders in Northern California spent with TV, videos, and video games. Two matched elementary schools were selected to participate, one of which served as the control group. The intervention involved a "turnoff" period of no screen time for 10 days followed by limiting TV time to 7 hours per week, as well as learning media literacy skills to teach selective viewing. At the end of a 6-month, 18-lesson classroom curriculum, students who received the intervention achieved statistically significant reductions in their television viewing and meals eaten in front of the TV set, as well as decreases in BMI, triceps skinfold thickness, waist circumference, and waist-to-hip ratio. While these changes were not accompanied by reduced high-fat food intake or increased physical activity, the findings do appear to demonstrate the feasibility of decreasing body weight by reducing time spent with screen media.
- Another school based intervention found improved diet, increased physical activity, and decreased television time to be effective. The study, which measured prevalence, incidence, and remission of

obesity among ethnically diverse middle-school boys and girls, involved a randomized controlled field trial with five intervention and five control schools. Classroom teachers in math, science, language arts, social studies, and physical education incorporated lessons within the existing curricula over two years. The lessons focused on decreasing television viewing to 2 hours per day, increasing physical activity, reducing consumption of high-fat food, and increasing servings of fruits and vegetables. For each hour television viewing was reduced, the prevalence of obesity was reduced among girls in the intervention schools compared with the control schools; no similar effect was found for boys. The program also resulted in an increase in girls' consumption of fruits and vegetables.

- A family-based weight-control program found that decreasing sedentary behaviors (such as screen media use) is a viable alternative to increasing physical activity in treating childhood obesity. Families with obese children ages 8–12 were randomly assigned to one of four groups that included dietary and behavior-change information, but differed in whether they tried to decrease sedentary activities or increase physical activity. Results indicated that significant decreases in percent of overweight and body fat were associated with decreasing sedentary behaviors such as watching TV or videos, or playing video or computer games.

These interventions indicate that reducing the time children spend with media may indeed be an effective way to address childhood obesity. Researchers, health professionals, and advocates have theorized several ways media may contribute to childhood obesity. The following sections summarize some of the major scientific studies in order to provide an understanding of media's potential influence on the incidence of overweight among children and adolescents in the United States.

Does the time children spend using media displace time spent in more physical activities? From toddlers to teens, American youth are spending a substantial part of every day of their lives using media. But the time children spend using media does not necessarily mean a decrease in time spent in physical activities. Surprisingly, few studies have examined this relationship, and results have been mixed. Some studies have found a weak but statistically significant relationship between hours of television viewing and levels of physical activity, while others have found no relationship between the two.

- A study of 6th- and 7th-grade adolescent girls in four Northern California middle schools found that the number of hours they spent watching TV after school was negatively associated with their level of physical activity; however, the relationship accounted for less than 1% of the variance and there was no connection with body weight.

- A study of a small sample of preschool children in Texas, conducted in a naturalistic setting, found a weak but statistically significant relationship between TV viewing and physical activity, although it did not find a relationship between viewing and body weight.

- A recent national telephone survey of parents of children ages 4–6 found that children who spent more than two hours watching TV the previous day spent an average of a half-hour less playing outside that day than did other children their age.

- A review of data from the 1999 National Youth Risk Behavior Study, which includes a nationally representative sample of more than 15,000 high school students, found that among white female students only, time spent watching TV was associated with being sedentary.

- A survey of close to 2,000 9th-graders in Northern California found a weak but statistically significant relationship between TV viewing and physical activity for white males only.

- A study of national data from the 1988–1994 NHANES found no relationship between TV viewing and the number of bouts of vigorous physical activity, although it did find a statistically significant relationship between TV viewing and body weight.

While logic suggests that extensive television viewing is part of a more sedentary lifestyle, the evidence for this relationship has been surprisingly weak to date. In order for this relationship to be true, as one study noted, children who watch less TV would have to be choosing physically vigorous activities instead of TV, rather than some other relatively sedentary pastime such as reading books, talking on the phone, or playing board games.

Another possibility is that the act of watching TV itself actually reduces children's metabolic rate, contributing to weight gain. One study of 8- to 12-year-olds found that TV viewing decreased metabolic rates even more than resting or sleeping, but several other studies found no such effect.

The fact that most studies have failed to find a substantial relationship between the time children spend watching TV and the time they spend in physical activity may suggest that the *nature* of television viewing—that is, how children watch and what they watch—may be as or more important than the number of hours they watch.

Do the food ads children are exposed to on TV influence them to make unhealthy food choices? Many researchers suspect that the food advertising children are exposed to through the media may contribute to unhealthy food choices and weight gain. Over the same period in which childhood obesity has increased so dramatically, research indicates that the number of ads children view has increased as well. In the late 1970s, researchers estimated that children viewed an average of about 20,000 TV commercials a year; in the late 80s, that estimate grew to more than 30,000 a year. As the number of cable channels exploded in the 1990s, opportunities to advertise directly to children expanded as well. The most recent estimates are that children now see an average of more than 40,000 TV ads a year.

The majority of ads targeted to children are for food: primarily candy (32% of all children's ads), cereal (31%), and fast food (9%). One study documented approximately 11 food commercials per hour during children's Saturday morning television programming, estimating that the average child viewer may be exposed to one food commercial every 5 minutes. According to another study, even the two minutes of daily advertising targeted to students in their classrooms through Channel One expose them to fast foods, candy, soft drinks, and snack chips in 7 out of 10 commercial breaks.

A review of the foods targeted to children in commercials on Saturday morning television indicates that the nutritional value has remained consistently low over the past quarter-century. Over the years, the most prevalent foods advertised have been breakfast cereals. Up until the 1990s, the next most-advertised products were foods high in sugar, such as cookies, candy, and other snacks. By the mid-1990s, canned desserts, frozen dinners, and fast foods overtook ads for snack foods. The data indicate that ads for these high-fat and high-sodium convenience foods have more than doubled since the 1980s. While studies vary as to the exact percentages, the same pattern emerges: a predominance of ads for high-sugar cereals, fast food restaurants, and candy, and an absence of ads for fruit or vegetables.

The effect of food advertising on children The vast majority of the studies about children's consumer behavior have been conducted by marketing research firms and have not been made publicly available. Clearly, the conclusion advertisers have drawn is that TV ads can influence children's purchases—and those of their families. Fast food outlets alone spend $3 billion in television ads targeted to children. Recent years have seen the development of marketing firms, newsletters, and ad agencies specializing in the children's market. The New York Times has noted that "the courtship of children is no surprise, since increasingly that is where the money is," and added that marketing executives anticipate that children under 12 will spend $35 billion of their own money and influence $200 billion in household spending in 2004. The enthusiasm of marketers can be felt in the Februray 2004 edition of Harris Interactive's "Trends and Tudes" newsletter, which notes that "This generation has become a huge consumer group that is worthy of attention from many businesses seeking to maximize their potential. Kids, teens and young adults spend significant amounts of their own money, and they influence the shopping behavior of their parents, their siblings, their relatives, and other adults in their lives."

Scientific studies that are available in the public realm back up these marketing industry assessments of the effectiveness of advertising directed at children. Studies have demonstrated that from a very young age, children influence their parents' consumer behavior. As many parents can attest after a trip down the grocery aisle with their children, television viewing has also been found to impact children's attempts to influence their parents' purchases at the supermarket. For example, several studies have found that the amount of time children had spent watching TV was a significant predictor of how often they requested products at the grocery store, and that as many as three out of four requests were for products seen in TV ads. These studies have also found that children's supermarket requests do indeed have a fairly high rate of success.

One study found that among children as young as 3, the amount of weekly television viewing was significantly related to their caloric intake as well as their requests and parent purchases of specific foods they saw advertised on television. Another study manipulated advertising shown to 5- to 8-year-olds at summer camp, with some viewing ads for fruit and juice, and others ads for candy and Kool-Aid. This study found that children's food choices were significantly impacted by which ads they saw.

Experimental studies have demonstrated that even a brief exposure to food commercials can influence children's preferences. In one study, researchers designed a randomized controlled trial in which one group of 2- to 6-year-olds from a Head Start program saw a popular children's cartoon with embedded commercials, and the other group saw the same cartoon without commercials. Asked to identify their preferences from pairs of similar products, children who saw the commercials were significantly more likely to choose the advertised products. Preference differences between the treatment and control group were greatest for products that were advertised twice during the cartoon rather than only once.

Researchers are beginning to document a link between viewing television and children's consumption of fast foods and soda, a possible result of exposure to food advertising. A recent study found that students in grades 7–12 who frequently ate fast food tended to watch more television than other students. Another study found that middle-school children who watched more television tended to consume more soft drinks.

Other evidence of television's potential impact on children's dietary habits indicates a negative relationship between viewing television and consuming fruits and vegetables. The USDA's Dietary Guidelines recommend that youth eat three to five daily servings of fruits and vegetables, yet only 1 in 5 children meet the guideline, and one-quarter of the vegetables consumed reportedly are french fries. In a recent study, more than 500 middle school students from ethnically diverse backgrounds were studied over a 19-month period to determine whether daily television and video viewing predicted fruit and vegetable consumption. Using a linear regression analysis, researchers found that for each additional hour of television viewed per day, daily servings of fruits and vegetables decreased among adolescents. The researchers who conducted the study conclude that this relationship may be a result of television advertising.

Some researchers believe that TV ads may also contribute to children's misconceptions about the relative health benefits of certain foods. One of the earlier studies found that 70% of 6- to 8-year-olds believed that fast foods were more nutritious than home-cooked foods. Another study showed a group of 4th- and 5th-graders a series of paired food items and asked them to choose the healthier item from each pair (for example, corn flakes or frosted flakes). Children who watched more television were more likely to indicate that the less healthy food choice was the healthier one. These results replicated the results of an earlier study conducted with children of the same age.

Do cross-promotions between food products and popular TV and movie characters encourage children to buy and eat more high-calorie foods? Recent years have seen what appears to be a tremendous increase in the number of food products being marketed to children through cross-promotions with popular TV and movie characters. From SpongeBob Cheez-Its to Hulk pizzas and Scooby-Doo marshmallow cereals, today's grocery aisles are filled with scores of products using kids' favorite characters to sell them food. Fast food outlets also make frequent use of cross-promotions with children's media characters.

A recent article in the New York Times business section noted that "aiming at children through licensing is hardly new. What has changed is the scope and intensity of the blitz as today's youth become unwitting marketing targets at ever younger ages through more exposure to television, movies, videos and the Internet." One food industry executive was quoted as saying that licensing "is a way to . . . infuse the emotion and popularity of a current kids' hit into a product."

Some promotions involve toys based on media characters that are included in the food packages or offered in conjunction with fast food meals. McDonald's and Disney have an exclusive agreement under which Happy Meals include toys from top Disney movies. In the past, Happy Meals have reportedly also included toys based on the Teletubbies TV series, which is aimed at pre-verbal babies. Burger King has also featured Teletubbies tie-ins, along with Rugrats, Shrek, Pokemon and SpongeBob. More than a decade ago, researchers were finding that the typical "kid's meal" advertised to children consisted of a cheeseburger, french fries, soda, and a toy. One study found that about 1 in 6 (16.9%) food commercials aimed at children promise a free toy. In addition to the use of toys as an incentive in marketing food to children, many commercials use cartoon characters to sell products, which research has shown to be particularly effective in aiding children's slogan recall and ability to identify the product.

A recent example of the effectiveness of this technique is the growth in the dried fruit snack market. Almost half (45%) of fruit snacks had licensing agreements in 2003 compared to 10% in 1996. Sales have increased substantially every year since 1999: 5.6% in 2000, 8.7% in 2001, 3.2% in 2002, and 5.5% in 2003. Marketing experts attribute the sales growth to children's influence on their parents' purchasing decisions and parental beliefs that dried fruit snacks are healthier than other sweets.

Do depictions of nutrition and body type in entertainment media encourage children to develop less healthy diets and eating habits? Over the years, some critics have argued that TV, movies, and magazines have promoted unrealistically thin body types as the ideal, possibly encouraging teen girls to engage in unhealthy dieting or eating disorders. But after years of an imbalance toward depictions of thin characters, the true weight-related health emergency among young people is, paradoxically, obesity. This paradox has yet to be explained.

Some advocates note that television gives children and teens contradictory messages about dietary habits and ideal body type: be thin but eat fatty foods, sugary sweets, and salty snacks. They point out that on the one hand, the stories media tell are about thin people who are popular and successful, while on the other hand, thin and average-size people on TV can eat whatever they want and almost never gain weight.

Some advocates and researchers also have criticized TV producers for not including more depictions of obese characters, and for negatively portraying the obese characters that do make it onto the screen. On the other hand, it could be argued that portraying obesity as an unhealthy and undesirable characteristic—and associating it with overeating—sends an *appropriate* message to youth. And while some critics fault the media for leaving obese characters off the screen, adding to stigmatization and isolation, other critics complain that too many minority characters are overweight.

THE HENRY J. KAISER FAMILY FOUNDATION is a nonprofit, private operating foundation that focuses on providing unbiased information on major health care issues.

Center for Science in
the Public Interest

 **NO**

Dispensing Junk: How School Vending Undermines Efforts to Feed Children Well

Executive Summary

In September and October 2003, 120 volunteers in 24 states (including the District of Columbia) surveyed the contents of 1,420 vending machines in 251 schools, including 105 middle and junior high schools, 121 high schools, and 25 schools with other combinations of these grade levels (e.g., 7th–12th grades).

The results suggest that the overwhelming majority of options available to children in school vending machines are high in calories and/or low in nutrition. **In both middle and high schools, 75% of beverage options and 85% of snacks were of poor nutritional quality.** The most prevalent options are soda, imitation fruit juices, candy, chips, cookies, and snack cakes. The high prevalence of junk food in school vending machines does not support students' ability to make healthy food choices or parents' ability to feed their children well.

This is of concern because 1) 74% of middle/junior high schools and 98% of senior high schools have vending machines, school stores, or snack bars, 2) children are in school for a substantial portion of the week, and 3) obesity rates are rising rapidly in children and teens.

Given the rising obesity rates and children's poor eating habits, the time has come to ensure that school environments support healthy eating and parents' efforts to feed their children well. A number of policies and programs should be put in place or strengthened to address childhood obesity. **One important strategy is for federal, state, and/or local governments, schools, and school districts to enact policies to ensure that foods sold out of vending machines, school stores, fundraisers, a la carte, and other venues outside of the school meal programs are healthful and make a positive contribution to children's diets.**

At the federal level, Congress should give the U.S Department of Agriculture (USDA) authority to establish and enforce regulations for all food sales anywhere on school campuses throughout the school day as a condition for participating in the National School Lunch Program or School Breakfast Program. USDA has strong nutrition policies for school meals. It also should set nutrition standards for foods and beverages sold outside those meals.

States, cities, school districts, and schools also could implement strong nutrition standards for foods and beverages sold out of vending machines, school stores, a la carte (snack lines), fundraisers, and other venues outside of the school meal programs. We recognize that school budgets are tight and that the sale of foods in schools provides much-needed revenue. However, a number of schools around the country have replaced soda in school vending machines with healthier beverages and have not lost money.

Introduction

Vending machines are prevalent in schools, yet quantitative data regarding their contents are lacking. Such data would be important to have because most children eat diets of poor nutritional quality, with too much saturated fat, sodium, and refined sugars and too few nutrient-rich fruits, vegetables, and whole grains. Those nutrient imbalances can lead to heart disease, high blood pressure, cancer, dental cavities, and other health problems. In addition, children's calorie intake has increased (and they are insufficiently active) and, as a result, rates of overweight in children have increased. While obesity is a complex, multi-factorial problem, over-consumption of soft drinks and snack foods plays a key role.

Junk food in school vending machines undermines parents' efforts to feed their children well. (This is especially problematic when children have diet-related health problems, such as high cholesterol or diabetes.) When parents send their child to school with lunch money, they do not know whether the child will buy a balanced school lunch or a candy bar and a soda. Long cafeteria lines, short lunch periods, and activities during the lunch period mean that some students rely on foods from vending machines rather than buy lunch from the cafeteria line.

The food industry is taking advantage of schools' financial problems by offering them incentives to sell low-nutrition foods in schools. But bridging school budget gaps by selling junk food to students is a shortsighted approach. In the long run, society is sure to spend more money treating the resulting obesity and diet-related diseases, such as diabetes, heart disease, cancer, and osteoporosis, than schools can raise by selling soda and snack foods to students.

There are ways schools can raise money without jeopardizing children's health. A number of schools in Maine, California, Minnesota, Pennsylvania, and elsewhere have replaced soda with healthy beverages and not lost revenue. In addition to selling healthy foods, schools can sell gift wrap or candles, sponsor fun runs, host car washes, or conduct other profitable fundraisers that do not undermine children's health.

Methods

In late September and early October 2003, 120 individuals in 24 states (including Arkansas, California, Connecticut, the District of Columbia, Illinois, Iowa, Maine, Maryland, Michigan, Mississippi, Missouri, Montana, New Mexico, New York, North Carolina, North Dakota, Ohio, Oregon, Pennsylvania, South Carolina, South Dakota, Vermont, Washington, and Wisconsin) surveyed the contents of vending machines in their local middle and high schools. The individuals collecting the data were primarily health professionals, employees of health organizations, and school employees. Volunteers surveyed a total of 1,420 vending machines in 251 schools, including 105 middle and junior high schools, 121 high schools, and 25 schools with other combinations of these grade levels.

School sites included both urban and rural schools, schools in a range of socioeconomic areas, and schools ranging in size from 110 to 2,600 students. Vending machines in areas accessible only to teachers and staff were not included.

The average number of vending machines per high school was eight. Some high schools had only one vending machine, while others had as many as 22 vending machines. The average number of vending machines per middle or junior high school was four. Some middle and junior high schools had only one vending machine, while others had up to 10 vending machines.

Vending machines were assessed by counting the number of slots per machine for each beverage or snack category and totaling the number of slots in all machines. Study participants were given a standardized survey form . . . and protocol. Participants had the opportunity to participate in a pre-survey conference call to discuss the protocol and methods for the survey. Participants sent their completed surveys to the Center for Science in the Public Interest (CSPI) for data aggregation and analysis.

The categorization of foods and beverages as "healthier" and "less healthful" was based on and generally in accordance with the nutrition standards for school foods developed by a national panel of experts convened by the California Center for Public Health Advocacy. The following types of beverages were categorized as "healthier" options: water, fruit juice containing at least 50% real juice, low-fat (1%) or fat-free milk (regular or flavored),

and diet drinks. The following types of beverages were categorized as "less healthful" options: soda pop (regular), fruit drinks containing less than 50% real juice, whole or 2% milk, sports drinks, iced tea, and lemonade. Only 1% of the options in beverage vending machines ended up being categorized into the "other" category.

The following types of snacks were categorized as "healthier" options (which includes healthy foods and nutritionally-improved versions of unhealthy vending snacks): low-fat chips, pretzels, crackers, Chex Mix, fruits, vegetables, granola bars, cereal bars, nuts, trail mix, low-fat cookies, and other low-fat baked goods. While some of the options are not the healthiest products—high in sodium or made with refined flour—they are considered healthier alternatives to common vending options. The following types of snacks were categorized as being of "poor nutritional quality": regular chips, crackers with cheese, candy, cookies, snack cakes, and pastries. Foods that did not fit into these categories were categorized as "other." Just 2% of the options in snack vending machines ended up being categorized into the "other" category.

Results

The vending machine options in middle and high schools were markedly similar. In middle-school vending machines, 73% of beverage options and 83% of snack options were of poor nutritional quality. In high-school vending machines, 74% of beverage options and 85% of snack options were nutritionally-poor options.

The types of beverages available in middle and high school vending machines are listed in Table 1. **Seventy percent of those beverages were sugary drinks such as soda pop, juice drinks, iced tea, and sports drinks.** Of the sodas available in vending machines for both high schools and middle schools, 86% of soda slots were regular sugary sodas and 14% were diet. 12% of the beverages available were water. Of the "juices" offered, two-thirds (67%) were juice drinks that contained less than 50% juice. Only 5% of beverage options were milk. The majority (57%) of milks offered in school vending machines were the fattier types (either whole or 2%), with 43% of the milk either low-fat (1%) or fat-free.

The types of snacks available in middle and high school vending machines are listed in Table 2. The snack items most commonly available were: candy (42%), chips (25%), and sweet baked goods (13%), which together accounted for 80% of snacks available in school vending machines.

Children need fruits and vegetables to provide key nutrients and reduce future risk of heart disease and cancer. Yet of 9,723 total snack slots, only 26 slots contained a fruit or vegetable. Only 7% of the beverage options were fruit juice (i.e., contained greater than 50% real juice). This finding highlights the potential value of increasing the number of refrigerated snack vending machines in schools to provide more fruits and vegetables to children.

Table 1

Beverages Available in Middle and High School Vending Machines

Beverage Type	Middle Schools Percent of Total (Number of Slots)	High Schools Percent of Total (Number of Slots)	Middle Schools, High Schools, & Other Secondary Schools Combined Percent of Total (Number of Slots)
Soda (regular)	28 (1110)	39 (3489)	36 (4860)
Fruit drinks (less than 50% real juice)	17 (664)	12 (1079)	13 (1801)
Sports drinks	17 (671)	11 (994)	13 (1826)
Iced tea, lemonade, or other sweetened drink	9 (362)	8 (752)	9 (1167)
Whole or 2% milk (including flavored)	1 (46)	3 (268)	3 (367)
Water	13 (515)	11 (1001)	12 (1611)
Fruit juices (at least 50% real juice)	8 (295)	6 (563)	7 (896)
Diet soda	4 (149)	6 (555)	6 (769)
Low-fat/1% or fat-free milk (including flavored)	1 (47)	2 (177)	2 (276)
Other drinks	2 (64)	< 0.5 (13)	1 (77)
TOTAL	100 (3,923)	98 (8,891)	102 (13,650)

Table 2

Snacks Available in Middle and High School Vending Machines

Snack Type	Middle Schools Percent of Total (Number of Slots)	High Schools Percent of Total (Number of Slots)	Middle Schools, High Schools, & Other Secondary Schools Combined Percent of Total (Number of Slots)
Candy	38 (882)	43 (3028)	42 (4062)
Chips (regular)	24 (555)	25 (1787)	25 (2391)
Cookies, snack cakes, and pastries	14 (310)	13 (928)	13 (1270)
Crackers with cheese or peanut butter	7 (154)	4 (306)	5 (484)
Chips (low-fat) or pretzels	7 (152)	5 (332)	5 (489)
Crackers or Chex Mix	2 (52)	3 (235)	3 (303)
Granola/cereal bars	2 (56)	1 (103)	2 (171)
Low-fat cookies and baked goods	2 (44)	1 (106)	2 (155)
Nuts/trail mix	2 (41)	1 (89)	1 (141)
Fruit or vegetable	< 0.5 (8)	< 0.5 (18)	< 0.5 (26)
Other snacks	2 (39)	3 (178)	2 (231)
TOTAL	100 (2,293)	100 (7,110)	100 (9,723)

Rationale for Improving School Foods

I. Schools Should Practice What They Teach

This study found that most choices available in school vending machines are of poor nutritional quality. Current school vending practices are not supportive of healthy eating.

Schools should practice what they teach. Selling low-nutrition foods in schools contradicts nutrition education and sends children the message that good nutrition is not important. The school environment should reinforce nutrition education in the classroom to support and model healthy behaviors.

II. The Sale of Low-Nutrition Foods in Schools Undermines Parents' Ability to Feed Their Children Well

Parents entrust schools with the care of their children during the school day. The sale of low-nutrition foods in schools makes it difficult for parents to ensure that their children are eating well. This is especially problematic when children have diet-related conditions, such as diabetes, high cholesterol, or overweight.

Without their parents' knowledge, some children spend their lunch money on the low-nutrition foods from vending machines rather than on balanced school meals. Long cafeteria lines, short lunch periods, or activities during the lunch period lead some students to purchase foods from a vending machine rather than a lunch from the cafeteria line.

III. Children's Eating Habits and Health

Obesity rates have doubled in children and tripled in adolescents over the last two decades. As a result, diabetes rates among children also have increased and type 2 diabetes can no longer be called "adult onset" diabetes. Also, 60% of obese children have high cholesterol, high blood pressure, or other risk factors for cardiovascular disease. While obesity is a complex, multi-factorial problem, over-consumption of soft drinks and snack foods plays a key role.

While low levels of physical activity are an important part of the problem, children are clearly eating more calories now than in the past. Between 1989 and 1996, children's calorie intake increased by approximately 80 to 230 extra calories per day (depending on the child's age and activity level). Soft drinks and low-nutrition snack foods are key contributors to those extra calories. Children who consume more soft drinks consume more calories and are more likely to be overweight than kids who drink fewer soft drinks. A recent study found that a school-based nutrition education program that encouraged children to limit their soda consumption reduced obesity among the children.

Consumption of soft drinks also can displace from children's diets healthier foods like low-fat milk, which can help prevent osteoporosis, and juice, which can help prevent cancer. In the late 1970s, teens drank almost twice as much milk as soda pop. Twenty years later, they are drinking twice as much soda pop as milk. The number of calories children consume from snacks increased by 30% (from 460 to 610 calories) between 1977 and 1996.

The health benefits of eating fruits and vegetables are well-documented; eating enough fruits and vegetables is important for preventing cancer, heart disease, high blood pressure, and other diseases. People who eat five or more servings of fruits and vegetables each day have half the cancer risk of those who eat fewer than two servings per day. However, children are not consuming enough fruits and vegetables to receive maximum health benefits. The average 6 to 11 year old eats only 3.5 servings of fruits and vegetables a day, achieving only half the recommended seven servings per day for this age group. Fewer than 15% of elementary-school-aged children eat the recommended five or more servings of fruits and vegetables daily. While fruit juices can have as many calories as soda, they provide important nutrients and health benefits that soda does not.

Milk is an important source in children's diets of essential vitamins and minerals, such as calcium and vitamins A and D. Since 98% of maximum bone density is reached by age 20, it is especially important that children get enough calcium. However, milk is also the largest source of saturated fat in children's diets. While low-fat and fat-free milk make important contributions to children's diets, whole and 2% milk contribute to children's risk of heart disease.

IV. Short-Term Profits from Selling Junk Food in Schools Pale in Comparison with the Long-Term Costs for Diet-Related Diseases

While schools are facing serious budget gaps, it is short-sighted to fund schools at the expense of our children's health. Diet- and obesity-related diseases, such as diabetes, heart disease, and cancer, cause disabilities and affect quality of life. The financial costs also are staggering. Annual medical spending attributed to obesity is estimated to be $75 billion per year, and half of that amount is financed by federal taxpayers through Medicare and Medicaid. From 1979 to 1999, annual hospital costs for treating obesity-related diseases in children rose threefold (from $35 million to $127 million).

The federal government also spends large amounts of money treating other diet-related diseases such as heart disease, cancer, diabetes, stroke, and osteoporosis through the Medicaid and Medicare programs and federal employee health insurance. Those diseases have their roots in childhood. According to the USDA, healthier diets could save at least $71 billion per year in medical and related costs.

V. Schools That Stop Selling Soda and Junk Food Are Not Losing Money

Even in the short-term, schools are finding that they can raise funds without undermining children's diets and health. A number of schools and school districts including Aptos Middle School (CA), Folsom Cardova Unified School District (CA), Monroe High School (CA), Venice High School (CA), Vista High School (CA), Fayette County Public Schools (KY), Old Orchard Beach Schools (ME), School Union 106 (ME), Shrewsbury School District (MA), North Community High School (MN), McComb School District (MS), Whitefish Middle School (MT), Sayre Middle School (PA), and South Philadelphia High School (PA) have improved the nutritional quality of school foods and beverages and not lost money.

Venice High School in Los Angeles eliminated unhealthy snack and beverage sales on campus. The school vending machines now offer a variety of waters, 100% juices and soy milk as well as a variety of healthy snacks including granola and cereal bars. After one year, snack sales in the student store were up by over $1,000 per month compared to the same time the previous year. Two years after the changes, snack sales per month had roughly doubled ($6,100 in May 2002 compared with $12,000 in March 2004). The students also raise significant funds with fundraisers that do not undermine children's health, such as a celebrity basketball game, car washes, and holiday gift wrapping.

Old Orchard Beach Schools in Maine wrote school vending policies that led to the removal of sodas and junk foods, and replaced them with water, 100% fruit juices, and healthier snack options. The vending machine signage was changed to advertise water instead of soda pop. Vending revenues have remained the same as they were prior to the changes.

North Community High School in Minneapolis replaced most of its soda vending machines with machines stocked with 100% fruit and vegetable juices and water and slightly reduced the prices of those healthier options. As a result, the sale of healthier items increased and the school has not lost money.

Though school vending is lucrative, it often represents only a small percentage of total school budgets. Soft drink contracts generate between $3 and $30 per student **per year;** even the most profitable contracts provide less than 0.5% of a school district's annual budget. In addition, the money raised from vending machines in schools is not a donation from the soft drink and snack food industries—it comes from the pockets of children and their parents.

VI. School Foods Can Be Improved at the Federal, State, or Local Level

States and localities have historically left the development of nutritional guidance to the federal government. The federal government has developed the [Food Guide Pyramid], *Dietary Guidelines for Americans*, and nutrition facts labeling standards for packaged foods.

In addition, unlike other aspects of education that are primarily regulated at the state and local level, school foods have historically been regulated at the federal level—by Congress and the U.S. Department of Agriculture (USDA). The National School Lunch Program was created in 1946 under the Truman administration, "as a measure of national security, to safeguard the heath and well-being of the Nation's children and to encourage the domestic consumption of nutritious agricultural commodities and other food."

The federal government invests enormous resources in the school meal programs ($8.8 billion in FY 2003, including cash payments and commodities) and has strong nutrition standards for those meals, as well as provides technical assistance and support for states and local food service authorities to meet those standards. Selling junk foods in school vending machines undermines that investment.

USDA sets detailed standards and requirements for the foods provided through the school meal programs, including which foods are served, the portion sizes of those foods, and the amounts of specific nutrients that school meals must provide over the course of a week. In contrast, foods sold in vending machines, a la carte lines, fund-raisers, and other venues outside the school meal programs are not required by the USDA to meet comparable nutrition standards. The USDA currently has limited authority to regulate those foods.

For foods sold outside of school meals, USDA restricts only the sale of "Foods of Minimal Nutritional Value" (FMNV). A FMNV provides less than 5% of the Reference Daily Intake (RDI) for eight specified nutrients per serving. During meal periods, the sale of FMNV is prohibited by federal regulations in areas of the school where USDA school meals are sold or eaten. However, FMNV can be sold anywhere else on-campus—including just outside the cafeteria—at any time. In addition, many nutritionally poor foods are not considered FMNV despite their high contents of saturated or trans fat, salt, or refined sugars, including chocolate candy bars, chips, and fruitades (containing little fruit juice), and thus can be sold anywhere on school campus anytime during the school day.

In order for USDA to set nutrition standards for all foods sold on school campuses throughout the school day, Congress needs to grant USDA additional authority. Implementation of those nutrition standards could be required as a condition for participating in the school meal programs.

States and cities have express authority to set nutrition standards in addition to the federal standards for foods sold out of school vending machines, a la carte lines, and other venues outside of the meal programs. A number of states have set or are working to set stronger nutrition standards for such foods (for examples, see http://cspinet .org/schoolfood/school_foods_kit_part3.pdf). Such state and local actions are needed given the limitations of current federal regulations.

Modest improvements in vending machine offerings can significantly reduce the calorie content of items purchased by students. . . .

Conclusions

This study found that the overwhelming majority of beverage and snack options in school vending machines are of poor nutritional quality. While foods and beverages sold in school vending machines are not the sole cause of childhood obesity, improving school nutrition environments is a key step toward ensuring that children have access to foods that promote their health and well-being. (For more information and model policies regarding other approaches to addressing nutrition, physical activity, and obesity, visit www.cspinet.org/nutritionpolicy.)

With skyrocketing childhood obesity rates, it is urgent that schools, school districts, and local, state, and federal governments enact policies to ensure that all foods and beverages available in schools make a positive contribution to children's diets and health. . . .

Center for Science in the Public Interest is a consumer advocacy organization that conducts research in order to represent citizens' interests and provides information to consumers about health.

EXPLORING THE ISSUE

Is the Media Responsible for the Rise in Childhood Obesity?

Critical Thinking and Reflection

1. Briefly describe each side of the issue of childhood obesity according to the authors. Give examples of supporting research provided in the readings for each perspective.
2. What is your opinion of each side of the childhood obesity issue? Do you think television viewing is the primary contributing factor or is it the vending machines in schools? Or, do you think it is another factor altogether? Why?
3. What types of foods do the authors identify as contributors to childhood obesity?
4. In the introduction to this issue, it is stated that Mexican American and African American children are at a higher risk of being overweight. However, the two papers addressing the topic of childhood obesity focus on television viewing and vending machines in schools. Is it possible that these two ethnic groups engage in viewing more television and eating more unhealthy snacks from vending machines more than other ethnic groups? If so, what might be a reason for this? What else might explain the higher risk that these ethic groups have for childhood obesity?

Is There Common Ground?

The Henry J. Kaiser Family Foundation points out that since 1980 the rates of childhood obesity doubled in 6- to 11-year-olds and tripled in adolescents. It later pointed out that kids are not choosing to play outside but instead turn to video games, reading, board games, and so forth, when television was not available in the studies they examined. Television viewing and technology are probably not the only contributors to r educed physical activity outside. Other factors, such as safety concerns for the outside environment/neighborhood must be considered. Researcher and practitioners need to take a comprehensive approach to address the issue of childhood obesity.

Authors of numerous research reports and surveys, which have appeared in the popular press as well as professional journal articles, agree that there is an increase in the rate of childhood obesity in the United States, where the debate begins is over the reasons for this obesity epidemic. The Kaiser Foundation believes media is the culprit, while the Center for Science in the Public Interest feels vending machines in the schools are the cause of the problem. A balanced perspective would include both of these variables in explaining childhood overweight in addition to other factors such as parental influence, community access to exercise and nutritious food, economic cost of nutritious food, neighborhood safety, and education.

The Center for Science in the public interest argues that vending machines contribute to childhood obesity. One of their arguments is that due to kids not wanting to stand in long lines and other factors such as short lunch periods, kids use their lunch money to purchase snacks from vending machines rather than the healthy lunch provided by the school, thus undermining the parents' attempt to feed their child a well-balanced diet. Would removing the vending machines solve the other problems related to why the adolescents do not purchase their lunches? Would not having the vending machine option mean that they would buy their lunch from the school? If the parents are sending their children to school with lunch money, how many snacks are they able to purchase given the high cost of vending machines? Is this enough to significantly impact the child's weight?

Create Central

www.mhhe.com/createcentral

Additional Resources

Kids Health: How TV Affects Your Child. (2008). Retrieved on May 27, 2011, from http://kidshealth .org/parent/positive/family/tv_affects_child.html#

This website provides information regarding television viewing and how it affects children. It addresses different factors associated with television viewing such as the amount of time spent watching television, negative exposures such as violence, sexual content, and drugs that may be viewed, the effects of commercials and how too much television is associated with obesity in children. The website also provides pointers for encouraging healthy television viewing with your child.

Medical Advices: The Greatest Wealth Is Health. (2010). Retrieved on May 24, 2011, from www .medicaladvices.net/Child_Health/rising-childhood-obesity-and-vending-machines-a14.html

This Web page addresses nutritional factors regarding vending machine food choices and how it is difficult for the schools to turn down the unhealthy food and drink choices with the financial gains they are offered from the companies. The Web page also addresses encouraging healthy eating at home.

National Center for Chronic Disease Prevention and Health: Promotion Division of Adolescent

and School Health. (2010). Retrieved on May 24, 2011, from www.cdc.gov/heatlhyyouth/obesity/

This website provides some basic facts regarding childhood obesity and addresses school involvement. An article on the website explains body mass index (BMI) and national and local school-based programs that are intended to monitor BMI.

Internet Reference . . .

Pros and Cons of In-School Vending Machines. (2010). Retrieved on May 24, 2011

This website addresses pros and cons of having vending machines in schools. It also provides a list of articles and references for more information on this topic.

www.ehow.com/list_6778100_pros-cons-in_school
-vending-machines.html

Selected, Edited, and with Issue Framing Material by:
Kourtney Vaillancourt, *New Mexico State University*

ISSUE

Do Bilingual Education Programs Help Non-English-Speaking Children Succeed?

YES: Jill Wu, from "A View from the Classroom," *Educational Leadership* (December 2004/January 2005)

NO: Christine Rossell, from "Teaching English Through English," *Educational Leadership* (December 2004/January 2005)

Learning Outcomes

After reading this issue, you should be able to:

- Understand and describe different bilingual education programs that are offered in the public school system.
- Describe each author's perspective and justification for the issue of bilingual education.
- Decide where you stand on the issue of whether to teach non-English-speaking students in English or first teach them in their native language and transition them into English instruction.

ISSUE SUMMARY

YES: Jill Wu, a former graduate student at the University of Colorado, shares her experiences in helping students develop literacy skills in their native languages first, as a more effective means of transferring those skills to learning English.

NO: Christine Rossell, a professor of political science at Boston University, suggests that English immersion programs tend to be more effective for students learning English because they actually learn in the second language (i.e., English).

Since bilingual education first became a political issue in the 1960s, it has been hotly debated. A child who does not speak English has as much of a right to an education as a child who does speak English. However, parents, politicians, researchers, and educators cannot seem to agree on the best way to educate non-English-speaking children. When children are taught in their native language only, opponents argue that they may lack sufficient immersion into the culture and appropriate fluency in the dominant language (i.e, English), which are necessary to succeed in our society. When children are taught in an English-only classroom, opponents argue, this leads to the students (especially ones who are of middle-school age or older) disliking school. These students do not understand what is being said. This, in turn, leads to disenchantment with the educational system and an alarmingly high number of non-English-speaking students becoming dropouts.

There is little consistency among bilingual programs throughout schools in the United States. Numerous types of bilingual programs are being implemented. Each program is different, and each comes with its own set of advocates and opponents. For example, one school may have a program in which every subject is taught in the child's native tongue, with a small amount of class time reserved for English instruction. In another school, the child may start out being taught in Spanish, for example, and within 3–5 years be transitioned into an English-only classroom. In yet another school, a child may be immersed into English-only classes with a small amount of time reserved for tutoring in his or her native language.

Even in more successful bilingual education programs, in which students are oriented to the language before being immersed in English, there are problems. These types of programs may take much longer in integrating the students into English-only classrooms. This, in turn, leaves the non-English-speaking students in danger of falling behind the other students academically, which could require them to be in school for more years than their English-speaking counterparts. If research were consistent enough to determine the best way to provide services to English-as-a-second-language learners, we would still be left with the dilemma of dealing with bilingual education when more languages need to be taught.

Although the majority of children in bilingual classrooms speak Spanish as their native tongue, there are students who speak Portuguese, Korean, Chinese, and any number of other languages. Is it possible to implement bilingual programs in every school for every language needed?

In the selections that follow, you will read two points of view about the argument over what types of bilingual education programs best help non-English-speaking children to succeed. In the YES selection, Jill Wu details what her experiences were in successfully teaching students in their native language first and then in English. In the NO selection, Christine Rossell believes that immersion is the most efficient and effective way to teach English as a second language. The controversy over the efficacy of bilingual education continues in states, provinces, counties, school districts, and even in individual schools

and homes. Arguments ensue over the statistics and how to interpret the existing body or research literature in the field. However, one must not lose sight of the most important thing in this battle—the children. What approaches provide the best possible education for the non-English-speaking students involved? As debates spiral round and round, we need to be mindful of why we are debating in the first place. Both sides want the same thing—an education for these students.

As you read the following sections, put yourself in the positions of decision makers—teachers, school administrators, politicians, parents. Which approach do you believe is most effective? Which teaching methods are most feasible in terms of time and money? Which methods lead to integration into English-speaking society and guard best against school drop-out?

YES

Jill Wu

A View from the Classroom

As the number of English language learners in U.S. schools increases, experts continue to seek ways to effectively educate these students. Those who argue for English immersion and for other practices emphasizing English-only instruction believe that this approach avoids segregating language learners, promotes assimilation of immigrants, and helps students learn English as quickly as possible. Bilingual education, they feel, divides society and limits Latinos' opportunities. These supporters cite evidence of ineffective bilingual programs and stories of immigrant children who have succeeded in immersion programs (Chavez, 2000; Duignan, n.d.).

Many second-language acquisition experts and others counter that immersion programs have not been proven effective. They believe that bilingual education programs, which provide initial instruction in students' first language, are more successful in helping students acquire English (Krashen, 2000; Mora, 2002; Slavin & Cheung, 2004). For example, Crawford (1998) found that students in programs that stressed native language instruction had much larger increases in English reading and math skills than did students in English immersion programs or programs that stressed early transition to English.

My experiences teaching English language learners in three different settings help to explain why bilingual education programs sometimes work and sometimes do not. These experiences demonstrate what advocates on both sides of the issue often fail to realize: that not all bilingual programs are the same; that no program will guarantee success for all students in all settings; and that English language learners often receive confusing and inconsistent instruction whether their program is called bilingual or immersion.

A Dual Language Classroom

My first experience with bilingual education was in a dual language immersion school in Wisconsin. In this setting, native English speakers and native Spanish speakers learned together in the same classroom. Instruction began in Spanish for both English and Spanish speakers. As students acquired a good reading base in Spanish, we gradually incorporated English. By 5th grade, students received half of their instruction in each language.

Unlike transitional bilingual education, which views native language instruction as a means to learn English, dual language programs aim to produce students who are fluent in both languages. According to speech-language experts Roseberry-McKibbin and Brice (2004), studies have shown that English language learners in dual immersion programs have higher academic achievement than do those taught in English immersion programs. By taking an enrichment approach rather than a remedial approach, dual language immersion produces bilingual and biliterate students who can switch effortlessly from one language to the other.

As I worked in this school, I realized why the dual language immersion approach was successful. No one group had the dominant language—the language of power. The native Spanish speakers felt empowered, not only because they acquired literacy and found success in their own language, but also because they were models for the English-speaking students. The English-speaking students also benefited by acquiring a second language at an early age.

In 1st grade, these students were exciting to teach. They spurred one another on. Classroom discourse naturally alternated between English and Spanish, unlike the conversation in many bilingual classrooms where students never speak English except when talking to the teacher.

Socially, this approach had powerful implications. At the beginning of the year, I saw many shy Spanish speakers who congregated together. As I taught these students to read in Spanish, they became more confident in their Spanish literacy skills, but they were still reluctant to use English. Slowly, however, the native Spanish speakers and the native English speakers began to communicate with one another. As students interacted, they learned English and Spanish in meaningful ways, communicating with their peers on the playground and in the classroom. When one of the English speakers had a birthday party at her house, I had the opportunity to see the children interact outside the classroom. I was surprised when Leah, a native Spanish speaker whom I had never heard use English, spoke in fluent English as she communicated with her English-speaking friends at the party.

Bilingual Education Inconsistently Applied

When I left Wisconsin, I was enthusiastic about dual immersion bilingual education and all that it could accomplish. My next school district, in Colorado, had recently adopted a transitional bilingual model in which Spanish-speaking students would acquire literacy in their primary language and then gradually achieve literacy in English.

I took a job as a 1st grade bilingual teacher. Most of my students were Spanish speakers who did not know any English. I was surprised to discover that they had no letter-recognition skills—in fact, no literacy skills at all. I soon figured out that the problem stemmed from their kindergarten experience the year before.

The district-adopted transitional bilingual policy had not yet filtered down from the central office to the school level, so my 1st grade students had not received reading readiness instruction in their primary language. Instead, the school had placed all of the native Spanish speakers in one kindergarten class with an English-speaking teacher who made little effort to make English comprehensible to them. These students spoke Spanish in almost all settings of their lives. But for a few hours each day, they came to school and listened to a lady speak English. The input they received was similar to what we might hear from Charlie Brown's teacher—"wa, wa, wa, wa." Although some of my students had learned their colors and how to say words like *bathroom,* they had no phonemic awareness or letter-recognition skills in either language.

When I tested the students' knowledge of letter-sound correlation, I got another shock. I asked students which words started with the *A* sound and gave them some examples of Spanish words from alphabet posters with corresponding pictures. The students insisted that *manzana* started with an *A* sound, *abeja* started with a *B* sound, *belado* started with an *I* sound, and so on. I was confused. Why couldn't the students hear the beginning sounds of these words?

Then I realized what had happened. *Manzana* means *apple* in English; *abeja* means *bee*; and *belado* means *ice cream*. In kindergarten, the students had memorized the pictures that go with the letters in the English alphabet. They had never learned how to say *apple, bee,* or *ice cream* in English; they had translated the words into Spanish. They had never learned to hear the sounds; they had merely learned that the picture of a *manzana* somehow matches the symbol *A*.

Although the students' kindergarten instruction had given them almost no prereading skills, I was eager to teach them to read in Spanish, as directed by the district's new bilingual policy. We spent hours every day working on letter sounds. Simultaneously, I taught other core subjects (math, social studies, and science) in Spanish, gradually incorporating more English and developing the students' oral English skills as we discussed concepts from these subjects.

As the students and I struggled through the first four months, I began to wonder when they would make progress learning to read in any language. Many of them still struggled with blending letters. Eventually, however, it all seemed to click. A few students started to read, and the rest soon followed.

Because Spanish is a completely phonetic language, when students know how to decipher syllables they can decode almost anything. Learning how to read in Spanish empowered my students. After their Spanish literacy skills became more solid and their oral English skills improved, many of them began to read in English. This time, the goal seemed easily attainable because all their reading skills from Spanish transferred to English. This experience confirmed the views of language experts who have found that once we can read in one language, we do not need to learn how to read all over again (August, Calderon, & Carlo, 2001; Krashen, 2000). In addition, my students had the English vocabulary to comprehend what they read; they were delighted when they could sound out *C-O-W* and know what the word meant.

Although this method of teaching was not quite as natural or easy as teaching in the dual language school in Wisconsin, it still worked and gave me many reasons to support transitional bilingual education. If I had taught the students to read in English initially, it would have taken much longer for them to acquire literacy. Because I taught core subjects in Spanish, students could keep up with grade-level content because they could understand what they were learning. Their success learning in one language motivated them to succeed in the second.

Another 1st grade class of English language learners in the school that year had a different experience. After their bilingual teacher left early in the year, they received instruction from a full-time substitute who spoke no Spanish. When my students went on to 2nd grade, their teachers told me that they were much better prepared and spoke and wrote better English than the students who had been taught in an English-only class. My students had acquired English in a natural way, and they had transferred their Spanish reading skills smoothly to English.

Incoherent Programs

Later, I moved to 4th grade at a different school in the same district. I was excited by the change; I wanted to see firsthand how older students were gaining English literacy skills.

To meet the needs of the bilingual students, the school had decided to group the 4th and 5th grade English language learners for reading. Two teachers would teach a group of 4th and 5th graders who were performing on or near grade level, which included many native Spanish speakers who had transitioned to English. Another teacher would teach a group of Spanish-speaking students who had just moved to the United States and were not ready to transition. I would teach the group of students who were just beginning to transition to English literacy. I was excited about teaching these students, assuming that like my 1st graders, they would just need a little push to master learning and reading in English.

Unfortunately, the reality soon became clear. All the students in my reading group were performing far below grade level and lacked many reading skills. They did not have the same motivation that the 1st graders had displayed. How had the bilingual program failed them? Why, by the time they reached 4th grade, were these 30 kids still reading at the 1st grade level or below?

Ineffective Grouping

At first, I thought that the practice of grouping our students by language level for reading instruction sounded wonderful; the students' needs would be similar and I would be able to teach them more effectively. Unfortunately, my group included not just the bilingual students, but all students who came into 4th or 5th grade reading at the 1st grade level or below. This meant that the class contained struggling English readers who spoke Spanish, the school's few Vietnamese and Cambodian students, and many of the special education and emotionally disturbed students.

A class that could have helped students transition into reading in English became the class to dump all the students with "needs." But just because these students struggled to read did not mean that they struggled to read for the same reasons. Effective instruction for the class's English language learners would not necessarily address the needs of other struggling students with different needs.

Even the English language learners in the group had experienced many different instructional environments. Some had attended the same school since kindergarten and had received Spanish language reading instruction through 1st grade, with a transition to English in 2nd grade. Others were new immigrants to the United States. Some had recently moved from other districts or from other schools in the same district that were unable to staff bilingual classes. Because of high mobility rates, some students had switched several times between Spanish language and English language instruction.

Reading Skills and Background Knowledge

Reading involves many complex processes, and learning to read presents extra challenges for second-language learners. August and colleagues (2001, 2003) discovered that English language learners acquire decoding skills easily, but they struggle more than native English speakers in their reading comprehension. By the time these students read to the end of a sentence or a book, they may have no idea what either means. They have a hard time monitoring their comprehension.

My 4th and 5th graders' struggles confirmed August's observations. My students' biggest challenge was their lack of background knowledge and vocabulary. They had no frame of reference to understand the books we studied. I often heard such questions as "What is the ocean?", "What is a zoo?", and "Do we really have mountains near here?" Because many of the students had never left their neighborhoods, a book about life under the sea posed difficulties for them. They not only had to work on their decoding, fluency, and vocabulary, but they also had to comprehend content that was outside their realm of experience.

Second-language acquisition experts say that developing students' first language gives them subject-matter knowledge that enables them to comprehend what they read and hear in English (Krashen, 2000). I found that many of my students had not been given the opportunity to develop skills in any language. Perhaps the students had been transitioned too quickly, before they developed solid reading skills and background knowledge in Spanish, and thus they did not have fully formed skills to transfer over to English. Consequently, they had not experienced success that would motivate them. Instead of creating bilingual students, we had created students who could speak two languages to some degree but who could not read or comprehend academic material in either.

Success in Spite of Frustration

In spite of the barriers that the system had put in their way, many of my students learned and progressed. Hard work and belief in students can accomplish a lot. And a few students far exceeded expectations. What accounted for their success?

Maria and Marcos, two 5th graders in my reading class, had only been in the United States a little more than a year, but they were ready to transition to reading in English. Both progressed to near grade-level proficiency in one year, surpassing other students who had been in the country longer.

One of the reasons Maria and Marcos succeeded was that they had a solid education in their native language. They were fluent readers in Spanish and had strong background knowledge. Researchers have found that the amount of formal schooling a student receives in the first language is the strongest predictor of how that student will perform academically in the second (Thomas & Collier, 2002) and that the most successful English language learners are those who have maintained bilingualism and a strong connection with their family's culture (Rumbaut & Portes, 2001). Marcos and Maria could connect whatever they read about in English with knowledge and concepts that they had learned in Spanish. Thus, they felt successful and motivated.

Experience Supports Research

For English language learners, becoming fluent in English is a challenging process that cannot be accomplished in a single year. Because of accountability pressures, the debate that surrounds bilingual education, and the panic to get students on grade level, schools often push students rapidly into English-only instruction, where they flounder or get labeled as needing special education.

My experience suggests that students acquire a second language most easily when they develop literacy skills and content knowledge in their native language, have opportunities to interact with English-speaking peers, and learn with students of different ability levels. We need to remember that the fastest way is not necessarily the most

effective way. When advocates push for English fluency at any cost, they fail to realize that the cost may be students' literacy and academic development.

JILL WU received her master's degree in applied linguistics from the University of Colorado, Denver. She has taught in several different styles of bilingual education programs throughout the United States.

Christine Rossell

Teaching English Through English

During the last 25 years, U.S. public schools have developed six different instructional approaches to support students learning English as a second language:

- *Structured immersion—or sheltered English immersion*—provides instruction almost entirely in English, but in a self-contained classroom consisting only of English language learners (ELLs).
- *ESL pullout* programs supplement regular, mainstream classroom instruction with instruction in a small-group setting outside the mainstream classroom aimed at developing English language skills.
- The *sink-or-swim* approach provides mainstream classroom instruction with no special help or scaffolding.
- *Transitional bilingual education* initially delivers instruction and develops students' literacy in the students' native language but puts a priority on developing students' English language skills.
- *Two-way bilingual education* (also known as *two-way immersion*) is designed to develop fluency in both the students' first language and a second language; teachers deliver instruction in both languages to classes consisting of both native English speakers and speakers of another language (most commonly Spanish).
- *Bilingual maintenance* programs generally consist of non-English speakers and, like two-way bilingual education programs, place equal emphasis on maintaining students' primary language and developing their English proficiency.

Notice the order in which I have listed these programs. According to my own research and my reading of others' research, this list proceeds from the most effective to the least effective approaches in terms of helping students become proficient at speaking, writing, and learning in English. This research indicates that in general, the most effective way for students to learn a second language and to learn subject matter in that second language is to learn *in* the second language—as in the first three programs—rather than learn in the students' native language, as in the last three programs (see Baker & de Kanter, 1981, 1983; Genesee, 1976, 1987; Gersten, Baker, & Otterstedt, 1998; Lambert & Tucker, 1972; Rossell, 2002, 2003, 2004; Rossell & Baker, 1996a, 1996b).

I am aware that this conclusion is highly controversial. In the past, bilingual education has enjoyed enormous support among many researchers and educators. But the apparently successful implementation of sheltered English immersion in California, Arizona, and Massachusetts may change the common perception.

When Is "Bilingual" Not Bilingual?

Despite the common belief in the effectiveness of bilingual education, my observations and my analyses of data from state department of education Web sites indicate that only a minority of immigrant children in the United States are enrolled in bilingual programs in any form. In California, only about 29 percent of English language learners were enrolled in bilingual education in 1998, the year in which this approach was voted out as the default assignment for such students. Approximately 71 percent of California's English language learners participated in programs that used English as the dominant language of instruction—most of them in sink-or-swim or near-sink-or-swim situations (Rossell, 2002). Similarly, in Arizona in 2000 and in Massachusetts in 2002—the years in which these states mandated a switch to structured immersion—only 40 percent of English language learners at most were enrolled in bilingual education (Arizona Department of Education, 2004; Massachusetts Department of Education, personal communications, 2004).

Indeed, despite the lack of intellectual support for the sink-or-swim method, it seems to be the dominant approach to educating English language learners throughout the United States—perhaps because educators believe that the benefits of integration and language role modeling by fluent English speakers outweigh the disadvantages of students' initial noncomprehension of the curriculum, or perhaps because it is simply easier.

Another approach, sheltered English immersion (also called structured immersion), similarly predominates in more schools than one would assume from looking at statistical reports. A sheltered English immersion classroom differs from a mainstream, sink-or-swim classroom because the class is composed entirely of English language learners and is taught by a teacher trained in second-language acquisition techniques. The teacher conducts instruction almost exclusively in English, but at a pace students can keep up with.

Many programs throughout the United States identified as "bilingual education" can be more accurately described as sheltered English immersion because they are actually taught completely or almost completely in English. For example, during the two decades I have spent observing bilingual classrooms across the country, I have observed many Chinese "bilingual education" programs—but have never seen one taught in Chinese. Teachers in these classes believe that Chinese reading and writing skills are not transferable to English because the two written languages are so different. Teachers seldom even teach orally in Chinese because spoken Chinese encompasses many dialects, and it is rare that all students in a classroom speak the same one.

In fact, after observing numerous Russian, Vietnamese, Chinese, Khmer, Haitian, Cape Verdean, Spanish, Japanese, Hebrew, and Portuguese "bilingual education" classrooms and talking with their teachers, I have concluded that schools almost never offer bilingual education that fits the theoretical model, in which students learn to read and write initially as well as learn subject matter in their native language. The sole exception is in languages that use a Roman alphabet. If the primary language doesn't use the Roman alphabet, teachers perceive the transferability of reading skills as too small to justify the effort.

These practical reasons—ignored in the theoretical literature—account for the fact that in the United States, non-Spanish "bilingual education" programs are actually sheltered English immersion programs. This also means that statistics on bilingual education enrollment consistently overestimate the number of students who actually receive native language instruction.

Sheltered English immersion also travels under other labels, such as *content ESL* and, at the secondary level, *sheltered subjects*. I once visited a school in New York City that, according to the board of education Web site, had a Bengali bilingual program. When I arrived at the classroom door, however, I found a sign that said *Content ESL*. In this classroom, Bengali-speaking English language learners were taught by a teacher who was fluent in Bengali. Students who had little English fluency spent most of the day in this class learning English and learning subjects through English. The teacher taught no Bengali at all; he claimed that he did not even use it orally to clarify or explain. These students were actually in a sheltered English immersion class that tailored instruction to their needs.

At the secondary level, many students receive sheltered English immersion in the form of sheltered subject classes (such as sheltered algebra and sheltered U.S. history). *Sheltered subject* classes have been around for decades, but they often go unnoticed because the language of instruction is English and the curriculum is similar to that of a mainstream classroom. In a sheltered algebra class, for example, the teacher would teach algebra in English to a class composed solely of English language learners.

Although the literature specifies a number of ways in which sheltered English immersion classes differ from mainstream classes (Echevarria & Graves, 2002; Haver, 2002), I have observed many of these classrooms and have seen little difference between the two. Teachers in sheltered English immersion classes seem to speak no more slowly than those in mainstream classes do, and they do not use more visual props. The teachers tell me that the major difference is that they cover less material and use more repetition. Some of these sheltered classes are called "bilingual" if all the students have the same country of origin, but only Spanish speakers in secondary bilingual classes ever hear more than a minimal amount of their native language used in instruction.

Lessons from California

Although sheltered English immersion has been around for decades under various labels, it became the default assignment for English language learners by state mandate in California in 1998, in Arizona in 2000, and in Massachusetts in 2002. Research and observation in California yield some valuable insights about the ways in which teachers implement instruction for their English language learners and the relative effects of the bilingual education and sheltered immersion approaches.

Responding to the Research

In response to the California law (Proposition 227), schools developed two structured immersion models that differ by the ethnic composition of the classrooms and by the amount of sheltering provided. Programs serving English language learners from a variety of linguistic backgrounds provide instruction and conversation in English only. Programs serving exclusively Spanish-speaking students, however, often use Spanish to explain or clarify concepts.

Because the school districts do not reliably distinguish between these different models, evaluating the academic impact of sheltered English immersion is difficult, if not impossible. We can, however, compare with some confidence the academic outcomes of keeping or dismantling transitional bilingual education because the California, Arizona, and Massachusetts laws all allow a school to offer bilingual education to students if the students' parents sign a waiver and if the school can justify using this approach on pedagogical or psychological grounds.

Approximately 10 percent of English language learners in California are still enrolled in bilingual education. My analyses (Rossell, 2002, 2003) show that after controlling for student and school characteristics, the average score increased by six points in reading and by three points in mathematics in schools that eliminated bilingual education. This is a .56 standard deviation gain in reading (a large effect) and a .21 standard deviation gain in math (a small effect). Bali (2001) found that taking Pasadena students out of bilingual education increased their reading scores by two points (.18 standard deviation) and their math scores by one-half point (.03 standard deviation) compared with ELLs who had always been in English immersion classes.

Testing rates are another measure of the effectiveness of alternative programs because a lower testing rate means that the school considers more students unready to take the test. My research (Rossell, 2002) found that schools with more than 240 ELLs enrolled in bilingual education had lower testing rates in reading and math than did those with no ELLs enrolled in bilingual education, after controlling for student and school characteristics. Bali (2000) found that prior to 1998, the rate of testing for English language learners enrolled in bilingual education was 50 percent, compared with 89 percent for those enrolled in English language classrooms. Los Angeles Unified School District found that after five years of participating in the program, only 61 percent of ELLs enrolled in bilingual education were tested, compared with 97 percent of those in English language classrooms (1998).

Unfortunately, there is no scientific research that directly compares the success rates of English language learners in a sheltered English immersion classroom with the success rates of ELLs in a mainstream classroom with ESL pullout. Nevertheless, I believe that at least for the first year, a sheltered classroom is a better environment for most English language learners than a mainstream classroom. My interviews in California indicated that teachers who formerly taught bilingual education but who now teach in sheltered English immersion programs believe the same.

After the first year, however, most English language learners are probably better off in a mainstream classroom with some extra help. Most of them will know English well enough that a sheltered English immersion classroom would slow them down unnecessarily, particularly when new students without any English skills enter the class. The one-year time limit ("not normally intended to exceed one year") is part of the sheltered English immersion laws in California, Arizona, and Massachusetts and is a provision my fellow researcher and I recommended in our writing (Rossell & Baker, 1996a, 1996b).

Teacher Implementation

My observations of almost 200 classrooms in California from spring 1999 through fall 2004 identified several themes that provide insight into the effectiveness of sheltered English immersion in the state.

Former Spanish bilingual education teachers were impressed by how quickly and eagerly their Spanish-speaking English language learners in kindergarten and 1st grade learned to speak and read in English and how proud the students were of this accomplishment. The teachers were also surprised at how much they themselves liked teaching in sheltered English immersion classrooms, although they had never worked harder (see Haager, Gersten, Baker, & Graves, 2001).

When I asked the teachers in 2001 whether they would ever want to return to teaching in a bilingual education classroom, all of them said no (Rossell, 2002). Bilingual education was a good theory, they claimed, but in practice it had too many problems. They attributed these problems to a lack of materials, teachers, and support.

Interestingly, Chinese bilingual teachers saw Proposition 227 as a non-event. Because they had already been teaching in English, nothing had changed for them except that Proposition 227 justified their practices.

Besides moving most English language learners into sheltered immersion programs, Proposition 227 also changed the way Spanish bilingual education programs operated. The teachers with whom I spoke in the remaining Spanish bilingual education classes in spring 1999 said that they were using more English for instruction than they had in the past. They gave two reasons. First, the Proposition 227 vote expressed California's citizens' preference for a greater emphasis on English, and teachers believed that they should respond to the wishes of the people they served. Second, because the law greatly reduced the demand for bilingual classes, there was no guarantee in any specific school that a bilingual class could be assembled for the next grade in the following year. Accordingly, teachers felt the need to prepare their students for the possibility that they could soon be in an English language classroom. Thus, the task of comparing the effectiveness of bilingual education with that of sheltered immersion is further complicated by the fact that the former is less bilingual than it has been in the past.

Instruction in the Target Language Is Key

Despite the strong support for sheltered English immersion that now exists among educators, policymakers, and the public in California, only about half of all English language learners are actually enrolled in such programs. Most of the other half are in mainstream classrooms, and about 10 percent are still in bilingual education, albeit with more use of English than before.

My classroom observations in California indicate that most educators base decisions about how to teach not just on state mandates but also on their assessment of what their English language learners need, the numbers of English language learners in their classes, and their own philosophy. Most teachers with whom I have talked believe that teaching students in English is more important than ensuring that the students are in a sheltered environment (although the state law requires both).

In general, a mainstream classroom that provides extra help seems to be more practical for many schools, and any academic harm caused by such classrooms is apparently not significant enough to be noticeable to most educators or to offset the relative ease with which schools can form such classrooms. After all, most immigrant children in the United States and throughout the world are in mainstream classrooms, and most of them seem to swim, not sink.

CHRISTINE ROSSELL is a professor of political science at Boston University. She holds the Maxwell Chair in United States Citizenship and is the author of five books and many other scholarly articles and reports in the areas of school desegregation and bilingual education policy.

EXPLORING THE ISSUE

Do Bilingual Education Programs Help Non-English-Speaking Children Succeed?

Critical Thinking and Reflection

1. What bilingual education programs were identified by the authors? In your opinion, which program is best and why?
2. What does each author say about bilingual education programs? Do you see any problems with either author's perspective regarding how non-English speaking children should be integrated into the education system?
3. After reading both articles, what is your opinion of bilingual education programs? What about the children who speak languages that are not offered in schools?

Is There Common Ground?

Christine Rossell argues that in order for students to learn English they must be taught in English. She gives an example of a teacher who only spoke English to his students in spite of the fact that he was fluent in the students' native language of Bengali. Rossell did not go on to clarify whether this method was effective with the students in this class; however, if it were, is it possible that it was effective because the teacher could effectively communicate with the parents versus a teacher who only speaks English? What role do the parents play in the education of their child and how important do you feel it is for parents to feel a sense of empowerment with regard to their child's education and assisting them in succeeding?

Jill Wu discusses how inconsistent bilingual instruction is and Christine Rossell makes the same point in her paper. Rossell goes on to address scores of students in California who switched into mainstream classrooms actually scoring a few points higher on reading and math tests. Does this evidence point to mainstream classrooms being more effective? Is it possible that the California programs are not providing consistent instruction and/or poor instruction due to grouping many students with different needs together such as in the example that Jill Wu gave? Does this example of higher scores justify the need to do away with bilingual education programs or does this mean that the programs need to be reevaluated and restructured?

Create Central

www.mhhe.com/createcentral

Additional Resources

National Association for Bilingual Education. (2009). Retrieved on April 3, 2011, from www.nabe.org/

The NABE website, which provides information on becoming a member, NABE's mission statement, and information on their work to better bilingual education.

Rethinking Schools: Bilingual Education Resources. (2011). Retrieved on April 3, 2011, from www.rethinkingschools.org/special_reports/bilingual/resources.shtml

This website provides a list of articles on bilingual education that have been published by Rethinking Schools.

Teaching Indigenous Languages: Bilingual Education Links. (2011). Retrieved on April 3, 2011, from www2.nau.edu/~jar/BME.html

This site provides a list of general resources, articles, organizations, and government offices that can be utilized as resources regarding bilingual education.

Internet References . . .

PBS

www.pbs.org/kcet/publicschool/roots_in_history/bilingual.html

Education Week

www.edweek.org/topics/bilingualeducation/

Selected, Edited, and with Issue Framing Material by:
Kourtney Vaillancourt, *New Mexico State University*

ISSUE

Is Gay Adoption and Foster Parenting Healthy for Children?

YES: National Adoption Information Clearinghouse, from "Gay and Lesbian Adoptive Parents: Resources for Professionals and Parents," *Child Welfare Information Gateway* (April 2000)

NO: Paul Cameron, from "Gay Foster Parents More Apt to Molest," *Journal of the Family Research Institute* (November 2002)

Learning Outcomes

After reading this issue, you should be able to:

- Describe the issues that surround homosexual adoption and foster parenting.
- Identify and discuss the main points addressed by each article concerning this issue.
- Decide where you stand on the issue of homosexual adoption and foster parenting.

ISSUE SUMMARY

YES: The National Adoption Information Clearinghouse (NAIC) presents facts regarding gay and lesbian adoptive parents. The NAIC gives current information on the background and laws regarding homosexual parenting, and confronts the issues and concerns many people have regarding homosexual adoption, including the idea that children are molested by homosexual parents.

NO: Dr. Paul Cameron, of the Family Research Institute, presents his case against allowing homosexuals to become parents—foster parents in particular. He mainly discusses case study information regarding the proclivity for homosexual parents to molest foster children.

A current topic being hotly debated in our society is gay and lesbian marriage. On the heels of this topic comes a closely related one regarding the fitness of homosexuals to raise children. Does sexual orientation affect parenting skills? Are gay and lesbian parents likely to promote homosexual behavior in their children? Will children "learn" to become homosexual from their gay parents? Are children at greater risk of molestation if they are raised in a homosexual household? These are just a sampling of the multitude of questions that some segments of our society have raised as we embrace this highly controversial and volatile issue. Although there are segments of the heterosexual population that do not disfavor homosexual parenting, there are many concerns and fears that others have about homosexual parents. The question is whether or not any of those concerns have merit.

Those opposed to homosexual parenting, foster parenting, and adoption fear for the effects it may have on the children. Will children in these homes experience ridicule by their peers when a child tells a friend that they have two moms and no dad? Are young boys who are being raised by gay men being exposed to a lifestyle that is morally wrong? Will this exposure cause these boys to "turn gay"? Those opposed also worry about the safety of the children. In particular, they fear that children living in these environments could be molested by a parent or family friend. Furthermore, some groups have claimed that the children themselves will become gay because they are learning the lifestyle from their parents. The teasing children may endure from their friends because of having homosexual parents is a haunting concern. Those opposed to homosexual parenting also point to the need for children to have both a father and mother figure in order to grow up "normally." Some also contend that the vast majority of religions are vehemently against children being raised in a homosexual family because this is an "unnatural lifestyle."

There are not only homosexual, but heterosexual, segments of society that support the right of gays and lesbians to bear or adopt children and parent them. These groups contend that most of the concerns mentioned above are founded in the deep-seated homophobia that exists throughout the world. They point to research on homosexuality, which suggests that while homosexual parenting is challenging, especially with respect to children's relations with peers, most of the concerns of the opposition group are not based upon any scientific evidence and therefore are unfounded and without merit. They contend that homosexual parents face the same challenges as any other parent in raising their children. Gays and lesbians can be just as appropriately loving and nurturing as anyone else, and have the right to raise children and experience family life to the same degree that heterosexuals enjoy this right.

In the YES article, which supports gay and lesbian parenting, the National Adoption Information Clearinghouse presents information about adoption in general and how gays and lesbians can initiate the adoption process as well. The article addresses many of the concerns that segments of society have regarding homosexual parenting. Current laws regarding adoption, by homosexual parents, are also presented. Dr. Paul Cameron, from the Family Research Institute, in the NO article, which opposes homosexual parenting, argues that one of the most worrisome concerns that people have regarding homosexual parenting—children being molested—is occurring, yet social workers and placement agencies are choosing to overlook it.

There are increasing types of unique family forms that are coming to light as we move more deeply into the twenty-first century. Gay- and lesbian-headed families are perhaps the most prominent of these forms. As a consequence, these new family forms challenge the traditional notions of who should be a parent and how families should look. Gay and lesbian families force us as a society to examine the relation between gender and parenting, the role of society in family life, and biological relations as prerequisite to the formation of a family. Is, for example, a lesbian mother, who is the biological parent of her seven-year-old daughter, and the mother's partner, who is committed to loving and caring for the seven-year-old, a family in the legal sense? Is it necessary for a family to be a "legal" family for the children within the family to develop into well-adjusted adults? Are these nontraditional homosexual families significantly different than common law–type heterosexual families?

The intensity of the beliefs and feelings behind the arguments for each side of the issue of homosexual parenting is immense. This is, however, but one issue in the ongoing dialogue of what is moral and what is immoral in our society. Some factions believe that it is immoral to raise a child without exposing that child to a religion. Atheists, however, are allowed to adopt and raise children and be foster parents. Others feel that adulterers, chronic gamblers, and those who abuse drugs and alcohol are immoral. Clearly, there are countless families where children are raised as parents grapple with these issues. Who decides where we draw the line as to who is moral and who is not when it comes to raising children? With such powerful feelings and emotions coming from the adults involved in this argument, it is most important to remember that we, as a community, should be working toward what is best for the children, rather than satisfying the urge to be right in our beliefs.

As you read the following articles, realize that your personal beliefs and value system will heavily influence how you respond to each article. The issue of homosexuality and homosexual rights is one of the more divisive controversies in our society. As a personal challenge, read each article with the intent of not supporting one side or the other. Instead, try your best to understand the points made in the article that is more opposite of your views on homosexual parenting. Remember, to understand a point of view different than yours does not necessarily mean that you condone such a view. It merely aids you in seeing things from a different perspective.

YES

**National Adoption
Information Clearinghouse**

Gay and Lesbian Adoptive Parents: Resources for Professionals and Parents

Introduction

Gay men and lesbians have always adopted, though in the past they usually hid their sexual orientation. Today, just as they are becoming visible in all other aspects of U.S. society, they are being considered more seriously as potential adoptive parents. This change has been aided by the increase in the number of gay and lesbian biological parents in the United States.

In 1976, there were an estimated 300,000 to 500,000 gay and lesbian biological parents; as of 1990, an estimated 6 to 14 million children *have* a gay or lesbian parent.[1] And, between 8 and 10 million children are being *raised* in gay and lesbian households.[2] The US Department of Health and Human Services, Adoption and Foster Care Analysis Reporting System (AFCARS), estimated in 1999 there were approximately 547,000 children in foster care in the United States, of which 117,000 are legally free and therefore eligible for adoption. But, in 1997, there were qualified adoptive families (including single parents) available for only twenty percent of these children. It is also estimated that approximately ten percent of the U.S. population—or 25 million individuals—are homosexual.[3]

Based on these increasing numbers, can gay and lesbian individuals be realistically and automatically excluded from consideration as potential adoptive parents?

Despite this increase in gay and lesbian parenting, social workers may have reservations when considering gay adoptive parents for a child. They might wonder how the children will be raised and how they will feel about themselves and their parents. Will they be embarrassed because they have two mothers or two fathers, or because their single mother dates women or their unmarried father has a boyfriend? Will their friends tease them? Will they be more likely to be homosexual than will children raised by heterosexual parents? And most important, how will having been raised by gay or lesbian parents affect them as they grow into adulthood?

This fact sheet addresses the issues faced both by social workers evaluating prospective gay or lesbian adoptive parents and by gays and lesbians considering adoption. An extensive list of sources of support and information that may be helpful to gay and lesbian adoptive parents and adoption professionals is available online . . . , or by contacting the Clearinghouse at . . . (888) 251–0075.

The Status of Gay and Lesbian Parenting

Defining the family structure of gay and lesbian parents can be a challenging task. The most common type of homosexual household is step or blended families. These are gay and lesbian parents who had their biological children in a former heterosexual relationship, then "came out," and created a new family with another partner. Other types of family structures include single gay or lesbian parents and couples having children together. Both of these family types may be created through adoption, but more frequently reproductive technology is being utilized.[4]

There has been some research on biological families with gay and lesbian parents. This research focuses mainly on children born to donor-inseminated lesbians or those raised by a parent, once married, who is now living a gay lifestyle. While research on these situations has not addressed all the issues relevant to adoptive parenting, this information is invaluable for social workers struggling with difficult decisions, for gay men and lesbians who want to be parents, for their families and friends, and for anyone seeking information on this nontraditional type of family.

Unfortunately, the effects on children of being raised by lesbian and gay adoptive parents cannot be predicted. The number of homosexuals who have adopted is unknown, and because of the controversial nature of the issue, their children are often reluctant to speak out. Testimony of children who have grown up in gay households may turn out to provide the best information about the results of gay parenting.

Research studies, often conducted by individuals or organizations with a vested interest in the outcome, are contradictory. Studies linked to conservative political and religious groups show negative effects on children of gay and lesbian parents; while studies which support homosexual parenting are said to reflect the bias of those who are themselves gay or who support gay rights. Clearly, what are needed are definitive studies that would follow larger numbers of children over a long period of time. That research, when completed, will provide more definitive information for the debate.

Child Welfare Information Gateway, April 2000.

In the meantime, it is critical to address the issues and concerns so that social workers can examine their own personal biases to make informed decisions and gay and lesbian adoptive families can receive the support they need to thrive.

Issues and Concerns

"What Is Sexual Orientation?"

The American Psychological Association defines sexual orientation as "one of four components of sexuality and is distinguished by an enduring emotional, romantic, sexual or affectionate attraction to individuals of a particular gender. The three other components of sexuality are biological sex, gender identity (the psychological sense of being male or female) and social sex role (the adherence to cultural norms for feminine or masculine behaviors)."[5]

For most people sexual orientation emerges in early adolescence without any prior sexual experience. Sexual orientation is different from sexual behavior because it refers to innate feelings and self-concept and may not be expressed in behavior. Understanding the source of sexual orientation depends on which side of the nature versus nurture debate you fall. Some theories point to genetic or inborn hormonal factors; others to early childhood life experiences. Many believe sexual orientation is shaped at an early age through a combination of biological, psychological and social factors.[6]

"Children Will Be Molested by Homosexual Parents"

There is no legitimate scientific research connecting homosexuality and pedophilia. Sexual orientation (homosexual or heterosexual) is defined as an adult attraction to other adults. Pedophilia is defined as an adult sexual attraction or perversion to children.[7] In a study of 269 cases of child sex abuse, only two offenders where found to be gay or lesbian. More relevant was the finding that of the cases involving molestation of a boy by a man, seventy-four percent of the men were or had been in a heterosexual relationship with the boy's mother or another female relative. The conclusion was found that "a child's risk of being molested by his or her relative's heterosexual partner is over one hundred times greater than by someone who might be identifiable as being homosexual."[8]

"Children Will Be Teased and Harassed"

Children of gay men and lesbians are vulnerable to teasing and harassment, particularly as they approach adolescence, when any sign of difference is grounds for exclusion. How much of a problem is it? Is it likely to cause lasting psychological damage?

Gay and lesbian parents are well aware of the difficulties that a child may face—many have dealt with prejudice

all of their lives. Most see it as an opportunity for ongoing discussion that will help their children grow as people.

Abby Ruder, a therapist, lesbian, and adoptive mother, acknowledges that children will be teased, and takes great pains to prepare her gay and lesbian clients for some of the problems that their children will face. She feels that families should have a plan for dealing with society's attitude toward them. "Children with gay or lesbian parents need to be taught when it's okay to tell people and when not to. A family doesn't have to be 'out' all of the time. My 9-year-old . . . has become very adept at knowing when to tell people that she has two mommies."

Wendell Ricketts and Roberta Achtenberg, in the article "Adoption and Foster Parenting for Lesbians and Gay Men: Creating New Traditions in Family" from *Homosexuality and Family Relations*, address social workers grappling with the issue by asking, ". . . should children be sheltered from every experience in which their difference might challenge prejudice, ignorance, or the status quo (or in which they would be 'exposed' to the difference of others)? Agencies conforming to such a standard must ask themselves whether it is their function to honor the system that generates stigma by upholding its constraints." They continue, "Teasing is what children do. Does this mean that child welfare policy must be set at a level no higher than the social interactions of children?"

In custody cases involving a gay or lesbian parent, courts have considered the fact that a child might be teased as contrary to the best interests of the child. They argue that the stigma attached to having a gay or lesbian parent will damage a child's self-esteem. This has been refuted in many studies. Research has found that although children of gays and lesbians do report experiencing teasing because of their parent(s), their self-esteem levels are no lower than those of children of heterosexual parents.[9]

In 1984 the Supreme Court heard a case, *Palmore v Sidoti*, in which a Florida man sought custody of his daughter on the grounds that his white ex-wife was now married to a black man and that this would expose his daughter to the stigma of living in an interracial family. The Court ruled that the girl should stay with her mother, saying that under the Equal Protection Clause of the Fourteenth Amendment, "private biases may be outside the reach of the law, but the law cannot, directly or indirectly, give them effect." Although the Court's ruling dealt specifically with racial prejudices, several researchers have mentioned the case as a rebuttal to the argument that placing a child in a family subject to social stigma is automatically contrary to the child's best interests.[10]

Nonetheless, social workers and even some gay men and lesbians considering adoption wonder if it is in the best interest of a child to be raised by homosexual parents. "It can be too hard a transition for some children, especially those who are older and have already formed preconceived notions about homosexuality," explains therapist Ruder. "Younger children usually have an easier time adjusting to a gay and lesbian parented home. They haven't learned the societal biases against gays and lesbians yet." When a gay person is being considered as a potential adoptive parent for an older child, the child should be told about the person's sexual orientation and asked his feelings about it. If the child is comfortable with the information, the caseworker can proceed to the next step.

Gay and lesbian adoptive parents must also think about how they will explain to younger children, in age-appropriate language, not only how and why the child was adopted but also about the parents' sexual orientation. Both are complex subjects that should be addressed a number of times as the child grows and matures, each time adding new information as the child asks and is able to absorb and understand more. Then both topics become accepted facts of family life.

"Children Raised in Homosexual Households Will Become Gay"

The bulk of evidence to date indicates that children raised by gay and lesbian parents are no more likely to become homosexual than children raised by heterosexuals. As one researcher put it, "If heterosexual parenting is insufficient to ensure that children will also be heterosexual, then there is no reason to conclude that children of homosexuals also will be gay."[11]

Studies asking the children of gay fathers to express their sexual orientation showed the majority of children to be heterosexual, with the proportion of gay offspring similar to that of a random sample of the population. An assessment of more than 300 children born to gay or lesbian parents in 12 different samples shows no evidence of "significant disturbances of any kind in the development of sexual identity among these individuals."[12]

"Children Will Develop Problems Growing Up in an 'Unnatural' Lifestyle"

Courts have expressed concern that children raised by gay and lesbian parents may have difficulties with their personal and psychological development, self-esteem, and social and peer relationships. Because of this concern, researchers have focused on children's development in gay and lesbian families.

The studies conclude that children of gay or lesbian parents are no different than their counterparts raised by heterosexual parents. In "Children of Lesbian and Gay Parents," a 1992 article in *Child Development*, Charlotte Patterson states, "Despite dire predictions about children based on well-known theories of psychosocial development, and despite the accumulation of a substantial body of research investigating these issues, not a single study has found children of gay or lesbian parents to be disadvantaged in any significant respect relative to children of heterosexual parents."

Psychiatrist Laurintine Fromm, of the Institute of Pennsylvania Hospital, agrees with that finding. "[The] literature . . . does not indicate that these children fare any worse [than those of heterosexual parents] in any area of psychological development or sexual identity formation. A parent's capacity to be respectful and supportive of the child's autonomy and to maintain her own intimate attachments, far outweighs the influence of the parent's sexual orientation alone."

What the Law Says

Only one state, Florida, specifically bars the adoption of children by gay and lesbian adults. Similar legislation was introduced in Utah prohibiting unmarried couples, including same-sex couples, from adopting children. The bill claims it is not in a child's best interest to be adopted by persons "cohabiting in a relationship that is not a legally valid (binding) marriage." The bill passed the State of Utah's House and Senate in February 2000 and is waiting the Governor's signature. The Governor has pledged to sign it. [Editorial note: The Governor signed the bill in 2000. In 2011, a Utah Senate Committee voted to table a bill that would have allowed second-parent adoptions for unmarried couples, including gay and lesbian couples. The Salt Lake Tribune reports [www.sltrib.com/sltrib /home/51205267-76/bill-committee-couples-lake.html.csp]: By a 5-1 vote, the Senate Health and Human Services committee voted to table SB62, which would have allowed a legal parent of a child to designate a second, adoptive co-parent. Utah law prohibits anyone who is living in an unmarried, cohabiting relationship from adopting or fostering children. Married couples and single individuals may adopt.

www.connexion.org/gay-news/news?id=966175
Utah Rejects Second-Parent Adoption Bill That Included Gay Couples

Gay News From Towleroad News
2/7/2011 11:49 AM - 302 views

Yet, in April 2000, Vermont lawmakers approved legislation that makes the State the first in the nation to recognize same-sex couples' right to form "civil unions." Partners in a civil union would be given the same benefits of married couples—the ability to transfer property, to make medical decisions for each other, to be eligible for inheritance, and the necessity to dissolve the union in Family Court (equivalent to a divorce). More than 30 other states have tried to avoid such unions through the passage of the Defense of Marriage Act. The act defines marriage as a union between a man and a woman and denies recognition of same-sex marriages performed elsewhere.

Legislation has also been introduced in Mississippi that would ban gay and lesbian couples from adoption and forbid the State of Mississippi from recognizing gay and lesbian adoptions that have previously been granted by other state courts—an unprecedented provision. Anti-sodomy statutes in 19 states and the lack of legal recognition of homosexual couples complicate adoption in the states that don't specifically prohibit gay and lesbian adoption.

Professor William Adams Jr., co-counsel in a case challenging Florida's ban on adoptions by gays and lesbians, has noted courts are increasingly turning to expert testimony to resolve questions in gay rights cases. He theorizes that there are several factors contributing to this trend, among them the courts' desire to justify their decisions in light of the controversy surrounding the issue and the efforts of gay litigants and civil rights organizations to provide the court with information. Although Adams sees this as a positive step, he comments, "citation to social science data should not be mistaken for a court's full understanding of it, however, because courts sometimes struggle to make sense of the research, or strain to ignore it."[13]

Nine states—California, Massachusetts, New Jersey, New Mexico, New York, Ohio, Vermont, Washington and Wisconsin—and the District of Columbia have allowed openly gay or lesbian individuals or couples to adopt. Although some joint adoptions have been successful, the most common practice is for a single person to apply as the legal adoptive parent of the child. Couples who both want custody then apply for a second parent, or coparent, adoption.

Second parent adoption or the adoption by nonmarital partners, leaves the parental rights of one legally recognized parent intact and creates a second legally recognized parent for the adoptive children. Second parent adoption, which has become routine for children of heterosexual stepparents, is the only way for gay couples to both become legal parents of their children.[14] Although state statutes generally provide a "stepparent exception," these exceptions emphasize the existence of a legal marriage between the biological parent and the stepparent.[15]

This growing practice was tested in a landmark case in Vermont in 1993. Jane Van Buren had given birth to two boys through anonymous donor insemination. According to the law, only Ms. Van Buren was considered their parent—her partner, Deborah Lashman, had no legal standing. The couple filed a petition for a second parent adoption, asking the probate court to allow Ms. Lashman to adopt the children while leaving Ms. Van Buren's parental rights intact. The court denied the adoptions because Ms. Lashman was not married to the biological parent. On June 18, 1993, the Vermont Supreme Court unanimously reversed the decision of the lower court and awarded joint custody to the couple.[16] With this decision, the Vermont Supreme Court became the first State Supreme Court to recognize lesbian co-parent adoptions. As a result of this finding, other couples are likely to find second parent adoptions easier to accomplish in Vermont and other areas of the country.

Second parent adoptions (by unmarried couples) have been granted by the courts (the approvals were generally from the lower level courts) in 21 states and the District of Columbia: Alabama, Alaska, California, Illinois, Indiana, Iowa, Maryland, Massachusetts, Michigan, Minnesota, Nevada, New Jersey, New Mexico, New York, Ohio, Oregon, Pennsylvania, Rhode Island, Texas, Vermont and Washington.[17]

Types of Adoption

Depending on the type of adoption gay and lesbian parents are interested in—public, private, independent, open or international—there may be different considerations involved in disclosing sexual orientation. How open prospective adoptive parents are about their homosexuality depends upon the couples' personal feelings on disclosure, whether direct questions are asked and what the laws in the State of residency are.

One important point for all prospective adoptive parents to be aware of is the difference between not sharing private information and deliberately lying at any time in the adoption process. Although it is completely legal to omit information regarding homosexuality, it is illegal to lie about it when confronted directly.[18] Let it be clear that failing to tell the truth is considered fraud and raises the opportunity for either an adoption not being finalized or a possible disruption.

Public Agency Adoption

Success in adopting from the public child welfare system depends on the State adoption law and the attitude of the agency. For example, in New York and California, gay and lesbian prospective adoptive parents are protected against discrimination. It is illegal for public agencies in those states to reject adoptive parents on the basis of sexual orientation. However, that is not a guarantee that prejudices don't exist. Social workers who are uncomfortable with homosexuality may find the prospective adoptive parents unsuitable for other reasons.[19]

Each state decides independently who can adopt. Since the final decision is made by judges at the county level, the availability of adoption as an option to openly gay and lesbian couples is influenced by the political and social community in which the family lives. The court's decision hinges on the "best interest" of the child, a concept interpreted differently by different judges.

Private Agency Placements

Private agencies establish their own criteria for the prospective adoptive parents. Age, religion, fertility status, marital status and sexual orientation all may be agency considerations. Some private agencies may disregard sexual orientation, and present the prospective parent as a single adopter who lives with another adult who will share the responsibilities of raising the child. This omission of sexual orientation is based on the agency's judgement and relevancy to the applicant's parenting qualifications.

Independent and Open Adoption

An independent adoption is an adoption facilitated by those other than caseworkers associated with an agency. They may be a physician, an attorney, or an intermediary and are illegal in some states. In an independent adoption the placement decision (within the provisions of the state statute) is completely up to the families involved. However, independent adoption does not necessarily mean an open adoption. An open adoption involves some amount of initial and/or ongoing contact of birth and adoptive families. The adoptive and birth parents agree upon the birth parents' role, future communication and the degree of openness prior to adoption. Being honest with the birth parents from the first contact allows gay and lesbian adoptive parents the opportunity to have a relationship without the possibility of a disrupting secret.

International Adoption

Adopting a child from a foreign country may involve finding an agency willing to accept the adoptive parents' sexual orientation, disclosing the information to the contacts in the sending country, and presenting the information to the foreign government. However, conservative, or religious and often developing countries may not be as receptive to gay and lesbian couples. Adoptive parents need to be aware that foreign governments and courts are making placement decisions based on their cultural standards and what they feel is in the best interest of the child.

The Social Worker's Dilemma

Placement Decisions

The debate goes on and will continue as long as there are conflicting views about homosexuality. Considering these different views, should social workers place children with gay men or lesbians? To make the best placement decision for children, social workers need to answer the following questions:

- Is this person or couple caring, nurturing, and sensitive to others?
- Do they have the qualities needed to parent a child?
- What are their individual strengths and weaknesses?
- How do their strengths/weaknesses complement the needs of the child?
- Do they have the capacity to nurture a child not born to them?

In addition, for prospective homosexual adoptive parents, Denise Goodman, Ph.D., a consultant and trainer in Ohio, firmly believes that workers need to have a holistic understanding that includes finding out answers to questions about their homosexuality:

"I counsel workers to ask homosexual applicants where they are in their individual development. Have they recently come out? Are they comfortable with their self-image and with being gay?

Having a positive self-image will provide a model for an adopted child. I want to know about family support and how those who are important in their lives view them and their idea of adopting. I ask questions about the stability of their relationship and try to see how committed they are to each other. Do they have wills? Have they bought a home? Do they share finances? Once you know more about their situation, you can help them access appropriate resources and connect them with other gay or lesbian adoptive parents."

Goodman, who has trained thousands of social workers in Ohio, sees the opportunity for change, but has a few concerns:

"While it is gratifying to see social workers become more open, if agency administrators are not fully behind the workers, little will change. Families will be approved and never hear about an available child; those who aren't open about their sexuality will receive a child, while "honest" applicants will wait, or other issues will surface so that a family is not accepted."

If a sense of trust and openness is established between a social worker and applicant, the worker can help to decide when privacy is the best route or when an applicant can be more outspoken. It ultimately depends on state laws and the views of presiding judges.

Professional Prejudices and Policy Decisions

Adoption professionals need to be aware of their own personal prejudices and prejudgments when working with gay and lesbian prospective adoptive parents. Experiences and beliefs come from family background and values, religious beliefs, and community views on homosexuality and will affect social workers' and agency staff's ability to assess the couple.[20] Ann Sullivan, of the Child Welfare League of America, suggests in her article "Policy Issues in Gay and Lesbian Adoption," that professionals consider several key issues:

- The client is the child in need of an adoptive family. All families should be given equal consideration and the potential resources available weighed for the placement of the child.
- No single factor should be the determining factor in assessing suitability for adoption.
- In considering gay and lesbian prospective adoptive parents, sexual orientation and the capacity to nurture a child are separate issues and should not be confused in the decision making process.
- Each placement decision should be based on the strengths and needs of the individual child and the perceived ability of the prospective adoptive family to meet those needs and develop additional strengths.

Coping with the Agency Preference Hierarchy

Many gay and lesbian prospective adoptive parents are troubled by the feeling that adoption agencies offer them the children who are the most difficult to place: those with physical, mental, or emotional disabilities; those who are older; children of color; and members of sibling groups.

"Often gay parents will get harder children because it's the last resort," Bob Diamond, the former Executive Director of AASK Northern California in Oakland, admits. "A lot of social workers will say, 'Well, no one is going to take this kid except gay people.' Being homosexual is not usually seen as a positive factor," he adds, noting that single people in general are usually treated as "second-class citizens" by most adoption agencies.[21]

Roberta Achtenberg, Executive Director of the National Center for Lesbian Rights in San Francisco, bluntly confirms that there is an unspoken ranking within the adoption network. "The hierarchy prefers white, married, middle or upper middle class couples, and these couples don't want the special needs kids. The less preferred children then go to unmarried couples of all kinds, single individuals, and gay people. The children are less preferred, and the recipients are less preferred."

What strikes psychologist April Martin, author of *The Lesbian and Gay Parenting Handbook*, as ironic is that the same bureaucracies that believe that lesbians and gay men are not suitable parents will place children who require the most highly skilled parenting with them. She and others have pointed out that nontraditional families have unique strengths that make them excellent, and in some cases, the best homes for certain children. Among them is an ability to accept differences, to understand what it is like to be in the minority, to demonstrate flexible gender roles, to be open about sexuality with children who have been sexually abused, and to understand the special needs of homosexual children.

April Martin suggests that gays and lesbians who want to adopt younger, healthier children can find them by working with private agencies or by working directly with birthparents. Some birthparents have specifically chosen openly gay households for their children.

Life after Adoption

Explaining Sexuality to Children

All families at one time or another will have "the" discussion on sexuality. For gay and lesbian families this can be an even more sensitive subject. However, a healthy family, regardless of sexual orientation, shares the same core values—love and respect, commitment and understanding. It is especially important when talking with children to stress what these values mean to the family and to

recognize that there are many different cultures, communities and families around the world.

The Family Pride Coalition, a national advocacy and support organization, offers several suggestions for parents discussing sexuality with their children:[22]

- Be honest about your own identity and comfort level.
- If you are uncomfortable, let your children know you find this hard to talk about, but that you feel it is important for families to talk about difficult things.
- Listen closely to your child and when possible, let your children take the lead. Let them ask questions. Take cues about their level of understanding from the questions they ask and interact at that level.
- Be as clear as you can be about your own feelings connected to sexuality, coming out, privacy, and family values.
- Consider your child's age and how much information they need.

Getting Support

Once an adoption is completed, the business of family life begins. Like all adoptive parents, gay men and lesbians are seeking ways to incorporate their children into their lives and to help them make a smooth transition. They also want to meet other homosexuals who have taken on the challenge of parenting. There are a growing number of support groups to meet these needs.

Len and Fernando, a multiethnic gay couple who adopted 3-year-old Isabel as a toddler, are members of an active group in the Philadelphia area. "Speaking to the parents of older children gives us ideas of how to cope with issues as they come up. Most of the members are women. We could use a few more men!"

Isabel, who is African-American, has the chance to meet other African-American adopted children and enjoys the many activities planned for families. Their group is part of a larger support network, Philadelphia Family Pride, that serves more than 250 gay and lesbian families in the Delaware Valley. In addition to giving its members a chance to socialize, the group's advocacy and educational projects encourage parents to work with teachers on adoption, race, and alternative family issues that affect their children. Members participate in conferences, receive local and national newsletters, and learn about books and articles for themselves and their children. Older children of gay parents have formed their own network, Colage— Children of Lesbians and Gays Everywhere.

A vital support network of family and friends is important for any family—adoptive, biological, one with heterosexual parents, or one with homosexual parents. Some gay and lesbian adoptive parents have found that even if their parents had a difficult time accepting their homosexuality, the parents readily accept their new role as grandparents. It is almost as if having children makes them more like mainstream families. "Our parents reacted to our desire to parent pretty much the same way they reacted to our coming out," says Tim Fisher, father of two and former Executive Director of the Family Pride Coalition (formerly Gay and Lesbian Parents Coalition International). "They said, 'We love you . . . but let's not talk about it.' With the kids, they have softened their tone a little. They are grandparents who adore their grandchildren."

Conclusion

The increasing number of gay men and lesbians choosing to adopt has brought the issue of gay and lesbian parenting to the forefront. Social workers are being asked to look carefully at their own feelings and to make reasonable judgments about what is in the best interest of children who need families. And, the increasing number of children needing adoptive families puts pressure on workers to find appropriate families.

The questions linger—should stable, nurturing, mature applicants be turned away on the basis of sexual orientation? What if a substantial number of children face the possibility of never achieving permanency, when they could have been adopted by a gay or lesbian family?

Endnotes

1. Sullivan, A., (1995). Issues In *Gay and Lesbian Adoption: Proceedings of the Fourth Annual Peirce-Warwick Adoption Symposium*, Washington, DC: Child Welfare League of America.
2. Editors of the *Harvard Law Review*. (1990). *Sexual Orientation and the Law*. Cambridge, MA: Harvard University Press.
3. Sullivan, A.
4. Rohrbaugh, J.B. Lesbian Families: Clinical Issues and Theoretical Implications. (1992). *Professional Psychology: Research and Practice*, 23: 467–473.
5. Blommer, S.J. (undated). Answers to Your Questions About Sexual Orientation and Homosexuality: A Fact Sheet. Washington, DC. American Psychological Association.
6. Blommer, S.J.
7. Lesbian and Gay Rights Project—ACLU. (1999). ACLU Fact Sheet—Overview of Lesbian and Gay Parenting, Adoption and Foster Care. New York, NY: American Civil Liberties Union.
8. Carole, J. Are Children at Risk for Sexual Abuse by Homosexuals? (1994). *Pediatrics*, 94 (1)
9. Huggins, S.L. A Comparative Study of Self-Esteem of Adolescent Children of Divorced Lesbian Mothers and Divorced Heterosexual Mothers. (1989). *Journal of Homosexuality*, 18 (1/2): 123–135.
10. Adams, W. E. Whose Family Is It Anyway? The Continuing Struggle for Lesbians and Gay Men Seeking to Adopt Children. (1996). *New England Law Review*, 30 (3): 579–621.
11. Bigner, J. J., Bozett, F. W. 1990. Parenting by Gay Fathers. In: *Homosexuality and Family Relations*. Bozett, F. W., Sussman, M. B. New York, NY: Haworth Press, Inc.
12. Patterson, C. J. Children of Lesbian and Gay Parents. (1992). *Child Development:* 1025–1039.
13. Adams, W. E.
14. Lambda Legal Defense and Education Fund. (1997). Lesbian and Gay Parenting: A Fact Sheet. New York: NY: Lambda Legal Defense and Education Fund.
15. Mishra, D. The Road to Concord: Resolving the Conflict of Law Over Adoption by Gays and Lesbians. (1996). *Columbia Journal of Law and Social Problems*, 30 (1): 91–136.
16. Patterson, C. J.
17. Lambda Legal Defense and Education Fund.
18. Martin, A. (1993). *The Lesbian and Gay Parenting Handbook*. New York, NY: HarperCollins Publishers, Inc.
19. Martin, A.
20. Sullivan, A. Policy Issues in Gay and Lesbian Adoption. (1995). *Adoption and Fostering*, 19 (4): 21–25.
21. Perry, D. Homes of Last Resort. (1993). *The Advocate*: 46.
22. Cronin, M. E. (1999). Guide to Talking with Your Child About California's Knight Initiative. San Diego, CA: Family Pride Coalition.

NATIONAL ADOPTION INFORMATION CLEARINGHOUSE provides accurate information related to adoption and is a federal service of the Children's Bureau, Administration for Children Youth and Families, U.S. Department of Health and Human Services.

Paul Cameron

Gay Foster Parents More Apt to Molest

No matter how professionals in our society extol the virtues of 'science,' if empirical evidence goes against their beliefs, they often ignore it or avoid it. The employment of homosexuals as foster parents is a perfect case in point.

When a 16-year-old foster son was molested and raped by two gay foster parents in Vermont, Tom Moore, Deputy of the State's Social and Rehabilitation Services, told me on June 25, 2002 that neither he nor the Commissioner knew of any evidence about the molestation rates of children by homosexual foster parents. He was apparently echoing his boss, Commissioner William Young, who the papers quoted as saying "I don't know of any screening instrument for [sexual molestation]. Certainly, sexual preference doesn't have anything to do with it, or religious beliefs or socioeconomic status. It's so frustrating because there isn't a predictor." (*Rutland Herald* 6/21/02)

Really? Traditional common sense holds that married parents are likely to be the best foster placement, and homosexuals among the worst, in part because of the risks of sexual molestation. But tradition holds almost no weight for these bureaucrats. How can this be? Can the traditions that worked to build arguably the world's most successful culture be ignored without injuring society? What kind of belief-system is so much better that it should be followed instead?

When I interviewed the reporter who wrote the story for the *Rutland Herald*, he refused to specify whether what he had called the "male couple" in the newspaper story was in fact a homosexual couple. He said that the *Rutland Herald* never released the sexual orientations of those accused of crimes. When I spoke with his editor, she repeated the policy. The "male couple" certainly acted as though they were gay, but the newspaper staff wasn't about to say or print it.

Fortunately, those at the District Court of Vermont were not so protective of 'sexual orientation privacy.' They provided the entire record. The rest of the story about the 16-year-old fit traditional common sense perfectly.

It turns out that the natural parents of the boy who was victimized strenuously objected to the placement of their hard-to-control son with these two gays. Yet, following a policy laid down 15 years ago, their objections were ignored. Additionally, when the boy complained to the Department that his new foster parents had asked him whether he had engaged in anal intercourse with his brother, the Department, through David Stanley, its Case Worker, concluded that the boy had been 'coached' to say this by his natural parents. Stanley said the gay foster parents denied saying such a thing and he believed them. So as far as the case worker was concerned, the boy had lied, so he was forced to stay with the 'male couple.'

Soon thereafter, the men gave the boy a magazine containing depictions of scantily clad men. They told the boy to 'masturbate to these pictures.' The boy complied, and hid the magazine under his bed.

Here, another factor of the case supported traditional common sense. Traditional thought holds that homosexuals have difficulty containing their sexual desires for youth. And sure enough, even in the face of all this investigation and conflict about possible molestation, the boy was with these homosexuals only two more weeks before they began to rape him!

Think of it. The investigation had already put these two gays 'on notice,' and yet this warning kept them from acting upon their temptation for only two weeks. Then, both men, who were in a 'committed relationship' with one another, had their way sexually with the boy. Sometimes, just one of them raped the boy alone, sometimes it happened when they were together. The boy managed to escape only by pretending that the sex was OK, and then fleeing to a hospital when the 'family' went to town to shop.

As it turned out, the men's magazine was the 'clincher' when the boy fingered his foster 'parents.' Because the magazine was where the boy said it was, the police were able to get the men to confess.

Notice what happened here. Vermont's child protective agency, without evidence of any sort, adopted a new policy 15 years ago that discarded tradition. Why? Because traditional common sense relegated homosexuals as 'not suitable for foster-placement' status. The child protective agency thought it had a 'better way.'

What was this 'better way?' What is this belief system that is so much better than traditional thought?

I filed a Freedom of Information request regarding this case and the policy changes that had been instituted by the agency, asking 17 specific questions. Some of these included: how many foster parents or foster parent pairs who have been involved in foster parenting a child or children were homosexual? Did your department conclude that the 16-year-old boy's claim was false that his foster parents had asked him whether he performed anal intercourse with his brother?

Less than a month later, Jody Racht, the Assistant Attorney General for Vermont, informed me that asking specific questions rather than "access to identified public records" fell outside of "any provision of state law."

So while certain policies had apparently been established to protect homosexuals—both in the child protective agency and at the *Rutland Herald*—neither institution would explain their basis. They just followed 'the policy.'

So what was this 'better way'?

Deputy Commissioner Moore said that, because of privacy and confidentiality concerns, no follow-up of placements with homosexuals had been conducted, nor were any contemplated. This strategy of 'deliberate ignorance' is not unique to Vermont. Over the past 10 years, I have talked with representatives of the District of Columbia, El Paso County (Colorado Springs, CO), and Seattle, WA—jurisdictions which place foster children with homosexuals—and gotten the same replies. In Colorado Springs, the wishes of the family regarding the placement of a 6-year-old boy—whose lesbian mother was judged unsuitable to parent—were overridden by child protective services in favor of the 'right of homosexuals to keep their children.' The little boy was given to a lesbian couple instead of his married aunt—an aunt who had been chosen by the extended family as the 'best fit' for the boy.

The social work representatives in the other three jurisdictions with whom I had contact said that since the National Association of Social Workers (NASW) declared homosexuals to be foster parents 'as fit' as heterosexuals, they believed that they were as unlikely to sexually abuse their charges as non-homosexuals. Indeed, the 1987 NASW resolution decrying "resistance to using single parents, . . . including lesbian and gay parents, as potential foster care and adoption resources" was passed, in substantial part, to counter the traditional belief that children placed with homosexual foster parents would be at higher risk of sexual exploitation.

NASW Influence

This NASW resolution and the new 'theory' behind it has informed social workers for the past 15 years. In one high profile case in 1992, the faculty of the Saint Cloud State University Social Work Department told potential students that this new 'theory' trumped not only traditional common sense, but also any religious beliefs. These faculty decreed that 'social homophobia' is a form of "human oppression." And citing the NASW code of ethics (Sec. 2.3), they noted that "accepting gay and lesbian people does not mean accepting them as individuals while simultaneously abhorring their behavior. . . . The only legitimate position of the social work profession is to abhor the oppression that is perpetrated in gay and lesbian people and to act personally and professionally to end the degradation in its many forms." That is, this 'new faith statement' must trump any other belief—including traditional religious beliefs like Christianity.

Is the NASW claim that homosexual and unmarried foster parents are 'as fit' as married heterosexuals warranted? No empirical literature concerning the issue appears to exist—although the evidence regarding the general parenting of homosexuals suggests that it is inferior to that of the married. Under the current system for placing foster children, putting the NASW claim to an empirical test cannot be done. The bureaucrats who could track the success of homosexual foster parents refuse to do so, and—citing privacy and confidentiality concerns—also prevent outsiders from doing it.

The 'faith' of the social worker profession, consisting of resolutions passed by a tiny committee within the NASW, is sufficient. No evidence is required! What a maddening mess! Fortunately, I found a way to bypass the current bureaucratic strategy of 'deliberate ignorance' regarding foster placements with homosexuals. My strategy exploited recent changes in the technology of newspaper publishing.

Here Is What I Did

While a successful foster-parenting outcome does not make the news, a highly unsuccessful outcome does. If homosexual foster parents do not differ from non-homosexuals, gross failure at foster parenting—such as the sexual molestation of foster kids—ought to occur at rates approximately proportionate to the frequencies of homosexual and heterosexual foster parents. Lexis-Nexis Academic Universe, an internet search service, scans the whole text of over 50 regional and national newspapers, largely in the U.S., but also including major papers in Australia, England, Canada, and New Zealand (e.g., *Baltimore Sun, Boston Globe, Independent* [England], *Ottawa Citizen* [Canada]).

This past summer, I examined every news story from 1989 through 2001 that included "child molestation"—a total of 5,492 stories. The findings were double-checked by also running "foster" against this database in early September, 2002. Only news stories or first-person accounts were tallied, not editorials nor opinion pieces, so the stories basically covered recent events, not reflections on older items.

This technique is obviously different from a comparison study where matched parents—homosexual and heterosexual—are randomly drawn from the total set of foster parents to see how they stack up. News stories are limited in the content they cover, nor are they necessarily consistent from reporter to reporter or paper to paper. Nonetheless, this method has its advantages. News stories are reports about 'the real world,' and not just responses to questionnaires from people who know they are being questioned or scrutinized.

Only a few of the news stories listed the sexual preferences of the perpetrators. Nevertheless, following the classification of method of infection for AIDS by the U.S. Centers for Disease Control, I was able to classify the perpetrators by the kinds of sex they engaged in (e.g., 'male with male' was considered homosexual, 'male with female' heterosexual). Since marital status is generally provided in stories about child molestation, where it was not reported, the perpetrator was assumed to be unmarried.

What I Found

Thirty stories about molestation of foster kids were located. They were numbered by date of the first newspaper story about the molestation, from 1 to 30. The location and date are given below. In 22 stories foster children were sexually abused. Five stories bore upon the character of the foster parent or guardian, though no foster child was reported as having been sexually molested. In three stories, foster caregivers molested their charges as they were held in group quarters.

Result #1. In 22 stories, the perpetrator(s) molested foster children:

1. Arlington, VA (3/2/89): An unmarried man, who had had boys placed in his home for 10 years, was charged with having sex with one of the foster boys (this was counted as one homosexual male perpetrator, one victim).

2. San Diego (3/1/89): A mother (who was married to an oft-absent husband in the military) and son lost their foster day care license when charges of possible molestation of two children were filed against her (counted as a female perpetrator and two victims of unknown sex).

4. Los Angeles (6/6/90): A man and wife lost their license when the man was accused of molesting two foster daughters (counted as a heterosexual male perpetrator and two girl victims).

7. St. Louis (10/21/90): An unmarried man, both a foster parent to one boy and the supervisor of a unit at a children's home, was convicted of molesting his foster son as well as 4 other boys at the home (counted as a homosexual male perpetrator and one boy victim).

8. British Columbia, Canada (3/26/92): A man (marital status not provided) was released from prison for molesting a 14-year-old foster daughter (counted as a male heterosexual perpetrator and one girl victim).

10. Los Angeles (7/8/93): A man and wife lost their foster care license when the man was charged with molesting 2 of his foster daughters (counted as a male heterosexual perpetrator and 2 girl victims).

11. St. Petersburg, FL (1/11/94): An unmarried man was convicted of molesting his 12-year-old foster son (counted as a homosexual male perpetrator and one boy victim).

12. Maryland (4/16/94): An unmarried judge was charged with molesting his 17-year-old foster son (counted as a homosexual male perpetrator and one boy victim).

13. San Francisco (12/13/94): A married man was convicted of molesting boys and girls, including 3 foster children (counted as one homosexual male perpetrator and 3 victims of unknown sex).

15. Atlanta (1/30/97): A married man molested his 12-year-old foster son (counted as a homosexual male perpetrator and one boy victim).

17. Connecticut (3/22/97): A man and wife lost their foster-care license when he was accused of molesting his foster son (counted as a homosexual male perpetrator and a boy victim).

18. New York (6/29/97): An apparently unmarried foster mother sexually molested her foster daughter from the time she was age 5 until she was 17 (counted as a homosexual female perpetrator and a female victim).

19. Seattle (12/3/97): An unmarried couple molested an 8-year-old foster daughter (counted as a homosexual female perpetrator and a male heterosexual perpetrator and a female victim).

21. England (12/5/98): An unmarried foster parent was convicted of molesting his 12-year-old foster son (counted as a homosexual male perpetrator and a boy victim).

22. Atlanta (2/27/99): An unmarried foster parent was convicted of molesting his 3 foster children, a girl and two boys (counted as a homosexual male perpetrator and a girl and two boy victims).

23. Boston (11/3/99): A married foster parent was convicted of molesting "foster children" (counted as a male perpetrator with 2 victims of unknown sex).

24. Toronto (4/3/00): A married foster parent was convicted of molesting a foster daughter (counted as a heterosexual male perpetrator and a girl victim).

25. San Diego (4/25/00): A married foster parent was convicted of molesting two twin 9-year-old foster daughters (counted as a heterosexual male perpetrator and two girl victims).

26. San Diego (6/23/00): An unmarried foster father was charged with sexual improprieties with his foster son, 11, and hiring him out for sex with other men (counted as a homosexual male perpetrator and a boy victim).

28. San Diego (9/24/00): An unmarried openly homosexual male, living with a partner who was a convicted homosexual child molester (the partner had sexually abused his own son and daughter), was given custody of an 11-year-old foster son. He then raped him. Over the years the foster father also offered his foster son to others who were sexually interested in the boy. At least three individuals accepted the foster-father's offer (counted as a homosexual male perpetrator and a boy victim).

29. Los Angeles (7/10/01): An unmarried woman pled no contest to the accusation of sexually abusing her 12-year-old foster daughter, and then lost her foster-care license (counted as a homosexual female perpetrator and a female victim).

30. St. Louis (12/31/01): An unmarried foster father was charged with molesting 2 foster sons, both 13 years old (counted as a homosexual male perpetrator and two boy victims).

Comment: It is noteworthy that in two of the 12 stories involving gays, the homosexual not only molested his foster son, but prostituted him as well. Something seems to be morally 'wrong' with homosexuals.

Result #2. Five stories concerned the character of the foster parent:

3. Boston (5/18/89): An unmarried man had illicit pictures of boys. Although he had been convicted of child molestation on a boy in 1967 (and given a suspended sentence), starting in 1977 the Massachusetts Probation Department used him as a placement for "24 adolescent males during the past 12 years."
5. Seattle (8/28/90): An unmarried man, with whom 5 foster children were currently living, admitted to molesting two boys, 14 and 15, in his Scout troop. He had been dishonorably discharged from the Navy for "similar incidents involving young boys."
6. St. Louis (8/31/90): An unmarried child molester had a 14-year-old boy placed in his home by the Missouri Division of Family Services. The boy's older brother also lived with the man. The child molester had been convicted of attempted rape of and then stabbing a 12-year-old boy. It is not clear whether he had had sex with the foster boys.
9. Los Angeles (12/29/92): A man and wife lost their foster care license when the man was charged with molesting 2 of his daughters from a previous marriage.
20. Seattle (11/3/98): An unmarried foster parent of a boy was accused of molesting 5 boys. The boys were apparently from a church youth group he assisted.

Comment: Is it a statistical fluke that 3 of the 4 gay foster parents above already had 'a record of child molestation' and yet were given boys to foster parent? Perhaps. But the bias that child protective services seem to exhibit in favor of homosexuals offers a more chilling possibility. While the 'fox' is not running the henhouse, there appear to be a considerable number of 'foxes' in these agencies—and in the current climate of ceding victimhood status to gays, even the non-foxes are inclined to 'give homosexuals a second chance.'

Result #3. In three stories, children in a group home were molested:

14. Los Angeles (5/2/96): For the second time in the year, the state initiated action to revoke the foster home license of Gay and Lesbian Adolescent Social Services because an additional number of boys reported having been molested by male staff members (counted as 3 homosexual male perpetrators and 6 boy victims).
16. Wales, Great Britain (2/4/97): Dozens of staff members at 30 children's homes sexually abused 180 victims, "most . . . were boys, some as young as 8."
27. Los Angeles (8/30/00): At least 3 male counselors raped at least 3 boys and a girl at group homes. One of the perpetrators was single, and at least one boy he raped obtained a judgment against him. There were no follow-up stories about the other perpetrators.

Comment: These stories suggest character flaws inherent to the homosexual lifestyle—flaws that put children under the care of homosexuals at considerable hazard. Note that although there are a lot of girls in children's homes, the boys appear to be at special risk. And why was a homosexual social service allowed to run group homes?

What Do These Stories Suggest?

A pattern of disproportionate molestation of foster children by those who engage in homosexuality is evident in each of the three sets of stories above. The 22 stories involving molestation of foster children, in particular, bear directly upon whether homosexual or unmarried foster parents commit more sexual offenses against their charges. Of the 22 stories, 15 (68%) involved homosexual molestation. Of the 23 perpetrators, 19 (83%) were men, and 4 (17%) were women. Of the 19 men, 12 (63%) engaged in homosexuality. Three (25%) of these 12 were married, while 9 were single. Seven (37%) of the 19 male perpetrators practiced heterosexuality. Of these 7, at least 5 (71%) were married and at least one was single.

Of the 4 women, 3 engaged in homosexuality and were unmarried. The other was married but her sexual proclivities were not revealed. Overall, of the 22 perpetrators whose marital status was known, 13 (59%) were single.

In the 22 stories, among the 32 foster children who were victimized, at least 12 (38%) were girls and at least 13 (41%) were boys. Since 2.5 of the girls were victimized by females (counting the girl who was victimized by the unmarried man and woman as being 0.5 homosexually and 0.5 heterosexually victimized), altogether, out of the 28 victims of perpetrators where a sexual preference could be determined, 8.5 (30%) were victimized by heterosexuals and 19.5 (70%) by homosexuals. Also, of the 32 children, at least 15 (43%) were victimized by the unmarried.

So What Does This Evidence Indicate about Gay Foster Parents?

Undoubtedly, only a fraction of child molestation by foster parents over the 13 years I examined was included in any news stories. If they did 'make the paper,' many—like the molestation of the boy in Vermont in 2002 that led me to conduct this study—only made the local newspaper, not the newspapers covered by Academic Universe. But there is no reason to believe that this sample was biased against those who engage in homosexuality.

Indeed, a number of the newspapers included in Academic Universe have editorialized in favor of special social protections for those who engage in homosexuality (e.g., *Los Angeles Times*, *New York Times*, *Boston Globe*). And these same newspapers have also expressed support for 'marital status nondiscrimination.' So they would have seemingly little reason to 'pick on' gay foster parents.

That at least 15 of the 22 instances of molestation of a foster child by a foster parent involved those who engaged in homosexuality is sharply at odds with the National Association of Social Workers' (NASW) 1987 resolution decrying "resistance to using single parents, . . . including lesbian and gay parents, as potential foster care and adoption resources." It also flies in the face of the NASW's appeal to its members to 'correct' this 'injustice.'

The empirical evidence is lined up against the NASW—of the 21 stories where the sexual proclivities of the perpetrator could be determined, 71% implicated homosexuals! Likewise, at least 57% of the 22 perpetrators were unmarried, and they accounted for at least 47% of the 32 child victims.

Homosexuality was also a disproportionate problem in the other 8 stories. When they are around or 'in charge' of kids, homosexuals are far more apt to seek to have sex with them. Nevertheless, we hear a lot from talk show hosts that homosexuals are no more apt to molest kids—tell that to the children who were victimized in these stories!

These news stories suggest that homosexuals and unmarried individuals are more apt to molest their foster charges. Because of this, they would not seem to be 'as fit' foster parents as married heterosexuals. The boy in story number 28, despite being raped, desired to return to live with the perpetrator. So he was apparently willing to 'live with molestations,' perhaps because there were other compensatory benefits in the arrangement. However, no matter how 'great' a parent they might be otherwise, there is no way someone can be a 'fit' foster parent if they sexually abuse their placements.

In a study FRI published earlier this year, interviews with 57 children with gay parents revealed that living in a homosexual home was a trying experience for children. In addition, the largest comparison study done to date—58 kids with married parents, 58 kids with cohabiting heterosexual parents, and 58 kids with homosexual parents—reported that the children with homosexual parents did less well at school, less well socially, and often gave evidence of personal distress. Thus, there is no particular reason to believe that either homosexuals or the unmarried generally compensate for their sexual weaknesses by offering exceptional foster-service in 'other areas.'

If the welfare of children is regarded as the most important consideration in foster-placement, these findings that the unmarried and those who engage in homosexuality are more likely to sexually molest their foster children suggest that the traditional aversion to their use as foster parents is rational and reasonable. Our society makes a lot of noise about 'protecting the children' and 'for the sake of the children.' But our foster system—which may process almost half a million kids every year—is being run throughout the country according to an alien, anti-child social philosophy.

Organizations like the NASW and many child protective service agencies across the land should lose their federal and state funding, until and unless they quit using kids' lives as bricks to reinforce unproven assertions that 'homosexuals are just as good' or that 'the unmarried are just as good.' Kids who need foster care are usually already under considerable stress—they don't need social revolutionaries putting them in highly sexually-charged environments.

Paul Cameron is the publisher of the Family Research Report, Colorado Springs, Colorado, which examines data on families, sexual social policy, drug addiction, and homosexuality.

EXPLORING THE ISSUE

Is Gay Adoption and Foster Parenting Healthy for Children?

Critical Thinking and Reflection

1. What are some of the main concerns that social workers tend to have with regard to allowing a child to be adopted or fostered by a homosexual person or couple?
2. With the issue of molestation, what does each article say about the likelihood that a homosexual person will molest? Do you agree with Paul Cameron's perspective that homosexuals are more likely to molest? Why or why not?
3. What is your perspective of gay adoption or fostering? Did any of the information in the articles help you see valid arguments for the opposite perspective and if so, which information?

Is There Common Ground?

The National Adoption Information Clearinghouse includes a statement given by Abby Ruder, a therapist and lesbian adoptive mother, where she stated that children with homosexual parents may need to be taught when it is okay to tell people about their parents and when it is not. What is your opinion of this statement? Should a child be put into a situation where they feel that they have to conceal their home/family life? Is this sending the child mixed messages about whether their family is immoral or not?

Paul Cameron argues that homosexuals are more apt to molest their foster and adoptive children. However, the basis for his argument comes from 22 news stories where he assumes that the perpetrators were homosexual because they molested a child of the same gender. Do you agree with Cameron's assumption or is it possible that the adults were in fact heterosexual? Cameron only found 22 articles of the total 5492 stories listed that possibly implicated homosexual perpetrators as the molesters to their foster or adoptive children. What about the rest? Is this small number evidence enough to prove that homosexuals are at a higher risk of molesting? What could be some problems with basing your evidence for something simply off of news stories?

Cameron ends his article by stating the findings in a study, which he fails to reference, that compared 58 kids from married homes, cohabiting heterosexual homes, and homes where there were homosexual parents. He then goes on to state that the study found that the children with homosexual parents did less well in school, less well socially, and often gave evidence of personal distress. What is your opinion of these findings and this study? Do you feel that this is a credible source?

With the need for qualified foster parents and adoptive parents for older children rising, should society automatically disqualify foster and adoptive parents because of their sexual orientation? It is true that there are many heterosexual married couples ready and waiting to adopt newborns in this country, but the need for reliable foster parents and adoptive parents for older children is great.

Would it be better for a child to be raised in a loving home, rather than moved from placement to placement, regardless of the sexual orientation of the parents? Some advocates for homosexual parenting rights suggest that children raised in gay and lesbian families will develop a greater capacity for empathy, tolerance for others, and a healthy respect for differences among people than those children raised in traditional, heterosexual families because these children are forced to embrace these issues more overtly. Is teaching tolerance and respect for differences not a significant goal for *all* parents in the twenty-first century?

Create Central

www.mhhe.com/createcentral

Additional Resources

Gates, G., Badgett, L., Macomber, J., & Chambers, K. (2010). Adoption and Foster Care by Lesbian and Gay Parents in the United States. Retrieved on April 4, 2011, from www.urban.org/publications/411437.html

This website lists an article with full text available regarding information provided by government data sources regarding gay, lesbian, and bisexual parents who are fostering or adopting children.

Jones, E. (2009). Adoption of Children by Same Sex Couples. Retrieved on April 4, 2011, from www.idebate.org/debatabase/topic_details.php?topicID=51

This article lists the pros and cons associated with the debate of allowing gays and lesbians to adopt and foster children.

Soulforce Inc.: Relentless Nonviolent Resistance. (2011). Discrimination in Adoption and Foster Care for Children. Retrieved on April 4, 2011, from www.soulforce.org.article/647

This site lists current policies and issues surrounding the gay/lesbian foster and adopted parenting debate in five states where the policies may discriminate against gays and lesbians.

Internet References . . .

Huffington Post

www.huffingtonpost.com/tag/gay-adoption

NOLO: Law for All

www.nolo.com/legal-encyclopedia
/gay-lesbian-adoption-parenting-29790.html

Selected, Edited, and with Issue Framing Material by:
Kourtney Vaillancourt, *New Mexico State University*

ISSUE

Should the HPV Vaccination Be Mandatory for Girls in Later Childhood?

YES: Cynthia Dailard, from "Achieving Universal Vaccination Against Cervical Cancer in the United States: The Need and the Means," *Guttmacher Policy Review* (Fall 2006)

NO: Roni Rabin, from "A New Vaccine for Girls, but Should It Be Compulsory?" *The New York Times* (July 18, 2006)

Learning Outcomes
After reading this issue, you should be able to: • Describe what the HPV vaccine is and what purpose vaccinating all young girls would serve.   • Understand each perspective regarding this issue.   • Decide where you stand on this issue and give supporting evidence.

ISSUE SUMMARY

YES: Cynthia Dailard, a senior public policy associate for the Alan Guttmacher Institute, suggests that the HPV vaccine be administered to females as a school entry requirement. She believes the vaccine is safe and effective and therefore should be universally administered to young girls. The best way to ensure the vaccine is available to these girls is by enacting state laws or policies requiring children to be vaccinated before school or day care enrollment.

NO: Roni Rabin, a columnist for *The New York Times*, objects to making the HPV vaccine mandatory for girls. She agrees that the vaccine is a significant development for the health and safety of our children. However, she does not believe every girl should be required to be vaccinated because the vaccine is costly and HPV can be managed through current, less costly procedures such as Pap smears.

Human papillomavirus (HPV) is a common sexually transmitted disease that most infected individuals do not realize they have. It usually clears up within a few years on its own. The problem with HPV is that some strains (e.g., HPV-16 and HPV-18) cause most of the genital warts and the vast majority of cancers of the cervix, anus, and even the throat. People who contract the various strains of HPV do not always develop cancer or genital warts, but the risk of contracting the strains that cause these problems is ever present. Gardasil is the brand name for an HPV vaccine that was approved by the Food and Drug Administration in 2006 to prevent cervical cancer and genital warts.

The HPV vaccination may be one of the greatest health advances for women in the past several decades. In two studies by the Centers for Disease Control and Prevention (CDC), the vaccine was 100 percent effective in preventing precancerous lesions and genital warts. In the second study, it was 98 percent effective in protecting against precancerous cervical lesions. Because Gardasil prevents the human papillomavirus from infecting sexually active women, the CDC recommends that females obtain the vaccination prior to becoming sexually active. They suggest being inoculated at ages 11 to 12. However, girls as young as 9 can get the vaccination, and those aged 13 to 26 are still advised to receive the vaccine even though it is not as effective if sexual activity has already begun. Since the CDC has added Gardasil to the recommended childhood vaccination schedule, several states are currently considering whether to make the vaccine mandatory for public school attendance.

Advocates for the vaccine promote universal vaccination and support laws to mandate vaccination as a prerequisite to attending school. A recent CDC study found that nearly 25 percent of women aged 14 to 59 and 49 percent of women aged 20 to 24 currently have HPV.

HPV is very prevalent not only in the United States but in less industrialized countries as well. In places where Pap tests are not as readily available, there is greater prevalence of cervical cancer. In order to minimize the spread of HPV, advocates for the vaccination believe young girls across the globe should be inoculated prior to any sexual activity. To prevent deaths from measles and Polio, vaccinations for these diseases had to reach the universal level. Advocates for the HPV vaccine hope the same should happen for Gardasil.

Opponents believe vaccination should be a personal choice for parents to make for their children. Mandating inoculation would further erode parents' rights to raise their children as they see fit. Other opponents are fearful that having the vaccination may actually encourage girls to engage in premarital sex because they would not be fearful of contracting HPV. Still others prefer having regular Pap screenings, which they believe are preferable in detecting HPV, because the long-term effects of the vaccine are still unknown. They argue that the virus is not transmitted through casual contact. Consequently, the vaccination should not be universally mandated. They do not believe all girls need to be vaccinated that young. Another argument states most cases of cervical cancer in the United States come from women who do not regularly receive Pap tests. Opponents also say the vaccine is expensive and contend that the women who can afford the HPV vaccine are not the women who need it because they are annually getting Pap tests, which detect the HPV virus.

The following selections convey points for and against universal use of the HPV vaccine. Are viruses that are transmitted through casual contact more easily approved and subsequently mandated by federal law? Is sexual contact such a controversial issue that it affects the judgment of policymakers and parents? Think about these questions as you read the next two articles arguing for and against making the vaccination for HPV mandatory for young girls.

YES

Cynthia Dailard

Achieving Universal Vaccination Against Cervical Cancer in the United States: The Need and the Means

The advent of a vaccine against the types of human papillomavirus (HPV) linked to most cases of cervical cancer is widely considered one of the greatest health care advances for women in recent years. Experts believe that vaccination against HPV has the potential to dramatically reduce cervical cancer incidence and mortality, particularly in resource-poor developing countries where cervical cancer is most common and deadly. In the United States, the vaccine's potential is likely to be felt most acutely within low-income communities and communities of color, which disproportionately bear the burden of cervical cancer.

Because HPV is easily transmitted through sexual contact, the vaccine's full promise may only be realized through near-universal vaccination of girls and young women prior to sexual activity—a notion reflected in recently proposed federal guidelines. And history, as supported by a large body of scientific evidence, suggests that the most effective way to achieve universal vaccination is by requiring children to be inoculated prior to attending school. Yet the link between HPV and sexual activity—and the notion that HPV is different than other infectious diseases targeted by vaccine school entry requirements—tests the prevailing justification for such efforts. Meanwhile, any serious effort to achieve universal vaccination among young people with this relatively expensive vaccine will expose holes in the public health safety net that, if left unaddressed, have the potential to exacerbate long-standing disparities in cervical cancer rates among American women.

The Case for Universal Vaccination

Virtually all cases of cervical cancer are linked to HPV, an extremely common sexually transmitted infection (STI) that is typically asymptomatic and harmless; most people never know they are infected, and most cases resolve on their own. It is estimated that approximately three in four Americans contract HPV at some point in their lives, with most cases acquired relatively soon after individuals have sex for the first time. Of the approximately 30 known types of HPV that are sexually transmitted, more than 13 are associated with cervical cancer. Yet despite the prevalence

of HPV, cervical cancer is relatively rare in the United States; it generally occurs only in the small proportion of cases where a persistent HPV infection goes undetected over many years. This is largely due to the widespread availability of Pap tests, which can detect precancerous changes of the cervix that can be treated before cancer sets in, as well as cervical cancer in its earliest stage, when it is easily treatable.

Still, the American Cancer Society estimates that in 2006, almost 10,000 cases of invasive cervical cancer will occur to American women, resulting in 3,700 deaths. Significantly, more than half of all U.S. women diagnosed with cervical cancer have not had a Pap test in the last three years. These women are disproportionately low income and women of color who lack access to affordable and culturally competent health services. As a result, the incidence of cervical cancer is approximately 1.5 times higher among African American and Latina women than among white women; women of color are considerably more likely than whites to die of the disease as well. Two new HPV vaccines—Gardasil, manufactured by Merck & Company, and Cervarix, manufactured by GlaxoSmithKline—promise to transform this landscape. Both are virtually 100% effective in preventing the two types of HPV responsible for 70% of all cases of cervical cancer; Gardasil also protects against two other HPV types associated with 90% of all cases of genital warts. Gardasil was approved by the federal Food and Drug Administration (FDA) in June; GlaxoSmithKline is expected to apply for FDA approval of Cervarix by year's end.

Following FDA approval, Gardasil was endorsed by the Centers for Disease Control and Prevention's Advisory Committee on Immunization Practices (ACIP), which is responsible for maintaining the nation's schedule of recommended vaccines. ACIP recommended that the vaccine be routinely administered to all girls ages 11–12, and as early as age nine at a doctor's discretion. Also, it recommended vaccination of all adolescents and young women ages 13–26 as part of a national "catch-up" campaign for those who have not already been vaccinated.

The ACIP recommendations, which are closely followed by health care professionals, reflect the notion that to eradicate cervical cancer, it will be necessary to achieve near-universal vaccination of girls and young women prior to sexual activity, when the vaccine is most effective. Experts believe that such an approach has the potential to significantly reduce cervical cancer deaths in this country and around the world. Also, high vaccination rates will significantly reduce the approximately 3.5 million abnormal Pap results experienced by American women each year, many of which are caused by transient or persistent HPV infections. These abnormal Pap results require millions of women to seek follow-up care, ranging from additional Pap tests to more invasive procedures such as colposcopies and biopsies. This additional care exacts a substantial emotional and even physical toll on women, and costs an estimated $6 billion in annual health care expenditures. Finally, widespread vaccination fosters "herd immunity," which is achieved when a sufficiently high proportion of individuals within a population are vaccinated that those who go unvaccinated—because the vaccine is contraindicated for them or because they are medically underserved, for example—are essentially protected.

The Role of School Entry Requirements

Achieving high vaccination levels among adolescents, however, can be a difficult proposition. Unlike infants and toddlers, who have frequent contact with health care providers in the context of well-child visits, adolescents often go for long stretches without contact with a health care professional. In addition, the HPV vaccine is likely to pose particular challenges, given that it must be administered three times over a six-month period to achieve maximum effectiveness.

A large body of evidence suggests that the most effective means to ensure rapid and widespread use of childhood or adolescent vaccines is through state laws or policies that require children to be vaccinated prior to enrollment in day care or school. These school-based immunization requirements, which exist in some form in all 50 states, are widely credited for the success of immunization programs in the United States. They have also played a key role in helping to close racial, ethnic and socioeconomic gaps in immunization rates, and have proven to be far more effective than guidelines recommending the vaccine for certain age-groups or high-risk populations. Although each state decides for itself whether a particular vaccine will be required for children to enroll in school, they typically rely on ACIP recommendations in making their decision.

In recent months, some commentators have noted that as a sexually transmitted infection, HPV is "different" from other infectious diseases such as measles, mumps or whooping cough, which are easily transmitted in a school setting or threaten school attendance when an outbreak occurs. Some socially conservative advocacy groups accordingly argue that the HPV vaccine does not meet the historical criteria necessary for it to be required for children attending school; many of them also contend that abstinence outside

of marriage is the real answer to HPV. They welcome the advent of the vaccine, they say, but will oppose strenuously any effort to require it for school enrollment.

This position reflects only a limited understanding of school-based vaccination requirements. These requirements do not exist solely to prevent the transmission of disease in school or during childhood. Instead, they further society's strong interest in ensuring that people are protected from disease throughout their lives and are a highly efficient means of eradicating disease in the larger community. For example, states routinely require school-age children to be vaccinated against rubella (commonly known as German measles), a typically mild illness in children, to protect pregnant women in the community from the devastating effects the disease can have on a developing fetus. Similarly, states currently require vaccination against certain diseases, such as tetanus, that are not "contagious" at all, but have very serious consequences for those affected. And almost all states require vaccination against Hepatitis B, a blood born disease which can be sexually transmitted.

Moreover, according to the National Conference of State Legislatures (NCSL), all 50 states allow parents to refuse to vaccinate their children on medical grounds, such as when a vaccine is contraindicated for a particular child due to allergy, compromised immunity or significant illness. All states except Mississippi and West Virginia allow parents to refuse to vaccinate their children on religious grounds. Additionally, 20 states go so far as to allow parents to refuse to vaccinate their children because of a personal, moral or other belief. Unlike a medical exemption, which requires a parent to provide documentation from a physician, the process for obtaining nonmedical exemptions can vary widely by state.

NCSL notes that, in recent years, almost a dozen states considered expanding their exemption policy. Even absent any significant policy change, the rate of parents seeking exemptions for nonmedical reasons is on the rise. This concerns public health experts. Research shows that in states where exemptions are easier to obtain, a higher proportion of parents refuse to vaccinate their children; research further shows that these states, in turn, are more likely to experience outbreaks of vaccine-preventable diseases, such as measles and whooping cough. Some vaccine program administrators fear that because of the social sensitivities surrounding the HPV vaccine, any effort to require the vaccine for school entry may prompt legislators to amend their laws to create nonmedical exemptions where they do not currently exist or to make existing exemptions easier to obtain. This has the potential not only to thwart the effort to stem the tide of cervical cancer, but to foster the spread of other vaccine-preventable diseases as well.

Financing Challenges Laid Bare

Another barrier to achieving universal vaccination of girls and young women will be the high price of the vaccine. Gardasil is expensive by vaccine standards, costing

THE POTENTIAL ROLE OF FAMILY PLANNING CLINICS IN AN HPV VACCINE 'CATCH-UP' CAMPAIGN

Family planning clinics, including those funded under Title X of the Public Health Service Act, have an important role to play in a national "catch-up" campaign to vaccinate young women against HPV. This is particularly true for women ages 19–26, who are too old to receive free vaccines through the federal Vaccines for Children program but still fall within the ACIP-recommended age range for the HPV vaccine.

Almost 4,600 Title X—funded family planning clinics provide subsidized family planning and related preventive health care to just over five million women nationwide. In theory, Title X clinics are well poised to offer the HPV vaccine, because they already are a major provider of STI services and cervical cancer screening, providing approximately six million STI (including HIV) tests and 2.7 million Pap tests in 2004 alone. Because Title X clients are disproportionately low income and women of color, they are at particular risk of developing cervical cancer later in life. Moreover, most Title X clients fall within the ACIP age recommendations of 26 and under for the HPV vaccine (59% are age 24 or younger, and 18% are ages 25–29); many of these women are uninsured and may not have an alternative source of health care.

Title X funds may be used to pay for vaccines linked to improved reproductive health outcomes, and some Title X clinics offer the Hepatitis B vaccine (which can be sexually transmitted). Although many family planning providers are expressing interest in incorporating the HPV vaccine into their package of services, its high cost—even at a discounted government purchase price—is likely to stand in the way. Clinics that receive Title X funds are required by law to charge women based on their ability to pay, with women under 100% of the federal poverty level (representing 68% of Title X clients) receiving services completely free of charge and those with incomes between 100–250% of poverty charged on a sliding scale. While Merck has expressed an interest in extending its patient assistance program to publicly funded family planning clinics, it makes no promises. In fact, a statement on the company's Web site says that "Due to the complexities associated with vaccine funding and distribution in the public sector, as well as the resource constraints that typically exist in public health settings, Merck is currently evaluating whether and how a vaccine assistance program could be implemented in the public sector."

approximately $360 for the three-part series of injections. Despite this high cost, ACIP's endorsement means that Gardasil will be covered by most private insurers; in fact, a number of large insurers have already announced they will cover the vaccine for girls and young women within the ACIP-recommended age range. Still, the Institute of Medicine estimates that approximately 11% of all American children have private insurance that does not cover immunization, and even those with insurance coverage may have to pay deductibles and copayments that create a barrier to care.

Those who do not have private insurance or who cannot afford the out-of-pocket costs associated with Gardasil will need to rely on a patchwork system of programs that exist to support the delivery of subsidized vaccines to low-income and uninsured individuals. In June, ACIP voted to include Gardasil in the federal Vaccines for Children program (VFC), which provides free vaccines largely to children and teenagers through age 18 who are uninsured or receive Medicaid. The program's reach is significant: In 2003, 43% of all childhood vaccine doses were distributed by the VFC program.

The HPV vaccine, however, is not just recommended for children and teenagers; it is also recommended for young adult women up through age 26. Vaccines are considered an "optional" benefit for adults under Medicaid, meaning that it is up to each individual state to decide whether or not to cover a given vaccine. Also, states can use their own funds and federal grants to support the delivery of subsidized vaccines to low-income or unin-

sured adults. Many states, however, have opted instead to channel these funds toward childhood-vaccination efforts, particularly as vaccine prices have grown in recent years. As a result, adult vaccination rates remain low and disparities exist across racial, ethnic and socioeconomic groups—mirroring the disparities that exist for cervical cancer.

In response to all this, Merck in May announced it would create a new "patient assistance program," designed to provide all its vaccines free to adults who are uninsured, unable to afford the vaccines and have an annual household income below 200% of the federal poverty level ($19,600 for individuals and $26,400 for couples). To receive free vaccines, patients will need to complete and fax forms from participating doctors' offices for processing by Merck during the patients' visits. Many young uninsured women, however, do not seek their care in private doctors' offices, but instead rely on publicly funded family planning clinics for their care, suggesting the impact of this program may be limited. . . .

Thinking Ahead

Solutions to the various challenges presented by the HPV vaccine are likely to have relevance far beyond cervical cancer. In the coming years, scientific breakthroughs in the areas of immunology, molecular biology and genetics will eventually permit vaccination against a broader range of acute illnesses as well as chronic diseases. Currently, vaccines for other STIs such as chlamydia, herpes and HIV are in various stages of development. Also under study are vaccines for Alzheimer's disease, diabetes and a range of cancers. Vaccines for use among adolescents will also be increasingly common. A key question is, in the future, will individuals across the economic spectrum have access to these breakthrough medical advances or will disadvantaged individuals be left behind?

When viewed in this broader context, the debate over whether the HPV vaccine should be required for school enrollment may prove to be a healthy one. If the HPV vaccine is indeed "the first of its kind," as some have characterized it, it has the potential to prompt communities across the nation to reconsider and perhaps reconceive the philosophical justification for school entry requirements. Because the U.S. health care system is fragmented, people have no guarantee of health insurance coverage or access to affordable care. School entry requirements might therefore provide an important opportunity to deliver public health interventions that, like the HPV vaccine, offer protections to individuals who have the potential to become disconnected from health care services later in life. Similar to the HPV vaccine's promise of cervical cancer prevention, these benefits may not be felt for many years, but nonetheless may be compelling from a societal standpoint. And bearing in mind that school dropout rates begin to climb as early as age 13, middle school might be appropriately viewed as the last public health gate that an entire age-group of individuals pass through—regardless of race, ethnicity or socioeconomic status.

Meanwhile, the cost and affordability issues raised by the HPV vaccine may help draw attention to the need to reform the vaccine-financing system in this country. In 2003, the Institute of Medicine proposed a series of reforms designed to improve the way vaccines are financed and distributed. They included a national insurance benefit mandate that would apply to all public and private health care plans and vouchers for uninsured children and adults to receive immunizations through the provider of their choice. Legislation introduced by Rep. Henry Waxman (D-CA) and Sen. Edward Kennedy (D-MA), called the Vaccine Access and Supply Act, adopts a different approach. The bill would expand the Vaccines for Children program, create a comparable Vaccines for Adults program, strengthen the vaccine grant program to the states and prohibit Medicaid cost-sharing requirements for ACIP-recommended vaccines for adults.

Whether the HPV vaccine will in fact hasten reforms of any kind remains to be seen. But one thing is clear: If the benefits of this groundbreaking vaccine cannot be enjoyed by girls and women who are disadvantaged by poverty or insurance status, then it will only serve to perpetuate the disparities in cervical cancer rates that have persisted in this country for far too long.

CYNTHIA DAILARD was a senior public policy associate for the Alan Guttmacher Institute, a nonprofit research and advocacy group on women's sexual and reproductive health issues. She wrote numerous articles and spoke prolifically on matters such as family planning and adolescent sexual behavior. She passed away on December 24, 2006, at the age of 38.

Roni Rabin

A New Vaccine for Girls, but Should It Be Compulsory?

Around the time report cards came home this spring, federal health officials approved another new vaccine to add to the ever-growing list of recommended childhood shots—this one for girls and women only, from 9 to 26, to protect them from genital warts and cervical cancer.

One of my own daughters, who just turned 9, would be a candidate for this vaccine, so I've been mulling this over. A shot that protects against cancer sounds like a great idea, at first. States may choose to make it mandatory, though the cost for them to do so would be prohibitive.

But let's think carefully before requiring young girls to get this vaccine, which protects against a sexually transmitted virus, in order to go to school. This isn't polio or measles, diseases that are easily transmitted through casual contact. Infection with this virus requires intimate contact, of the kind that doesn't occur in classrooms.

Besides, we already know how to prevent cervical cancer in this country, and we've done a darn good job of it. In the war against cancer, the battle against cervical cancer has been a success story.

Why, then, did federal health officials recommend the inoculation of about 30 million American girls and young women against the human papillomavirus, a sexually transmitted disease that in rare cases leads to cervical cancer?

Vaccine supporters say that some 3,700 American women die of cervical cancer each year, and close to 10,000 cases are diagnosed. Cervical cancer has a relatively high survival rate, but every death is tragic and treatment can rob women of their fertility.

Still, you have to see the numbers in context. Cervical cancer deaths have been dropping consistently in the United States—and have been for decades.

Cervical cancer has gone from being one of the top killers of American women to not even being on the top 10 list. This year cervical cancer will represent just 1 percent of the 679,510 new cancer cases and 1 percent of the 273,560 anticipated cancer deaths among American women. By contrast, some 40,970 women will die of breast cancer and 72,130 will die of lung cancer.

According to the American Cancer Society Web site, "Between 1955 and 1992, the number of cervical cancer deaths in the United States dropped by 74 percent." Think about it: 74 percent.

The number of cases diagnosed each year and the number of deaths per year have continued to drop, even though the population is growing.

From 1997 to 2003, the number of cervical cancers in the United States dropped by 4.5 percent each year, while the number of deaths dropped by 3.8 percent each year, according to a government Web site that tracks cancer trends, called SEER or Surveillance, Epidemiology and End Results. . . . This, while many other cancers are on the rise.

If current trends continue, by the time my 9-year-old daughter is 48, the median age when cervical cancer is diagnosed, there will be only a few thousand cases of the cancer in women, and about 1,000 deaths or fewer each year, even without the vaccine.

The secret weapon? Not so secret. It's the Pap smear. A simple, quick, relatively noninvasive test that's part and parcel of routine preventive health care for women. It provides early warnings of cellular changes in the cervix that are precursors for cancer and can be treated.

An American Cancer Society spokeswoman said that most American women who get cervical cancer these days are women who either had never had a Pap smear or had not followed the follow-up and frequency guidelines. So perhaps we could redirect the public money that would be spent on this vaccine—one of the most expensive ever, priced at $360 for the series of three shots—to make sure all women in the United States get preventive health care.

Because even if you have the new vaccine, which protects against only some of the viral strains that may bring on cervical cancer, you still need to continue getting Pap smears.

To be clear, I'm talking only about American women. Sadly, hundreds of thousands of women worldwide die of cervical cancer each year because they don't have access to Pap smears and the follow-up care required. For them, and for American women at high risk, the vaccine should be an option.

Black, Hispanic and some foreign-born women are at higher risk, though rates have dropped precipitously among blacks. Certain behavior—smoking, eating poorly, having multiple sexual partners and long-term use of the pill, for example—are also associated with an increased risk. But most people infected with the human papilloma-virus clear it on their own.

Vaccine supporters, including the American Cancer Society, say the immunization will reduce abnormal Pap test results, and the stress, discomfort and cost of follow-up procedures and painful treatments. That's a strong argument for the vaccine.

But vaccines carry risks. In recent years, children have been bombarded with new immunizations, and we still don't know the full long-term implications. One vaccine, RotaShield, was removed from the market in 1999, just a year after being approved for infants.

Merck has tested the cervical cancer vaccine in clinical trials of more than 20,000 women (about half of them got the shot). The health of the subjects was followed for about three and a half years on average. But fewer than 1,200 girls under 16 got the shots,

among them only about 100 9-year-olds, Merck officials said, and the younger girls have been followed for only 18 months.

Public health officials want to vaccinate girls early, before they become sexually active, even though it is not known how long the immunity will last.

But girls can also protect themselves from the human papillomavirus by using condoms; a recent study found that condoms cut infections by more than half. Condoms also protect against a far more insidious sexually transmitted virus, H.I.V.

So yes, by all means, let's keep stamping out cervical cancer. Let's make sure women and girls get Pap smears.

Roni Rabin is a columnist for *The New York Times* who writes extensively on women's health issues.

EXPLORING THE ISSUE

Should the HPV Vaccination Be Mandatory for Girls in Later Childhood?

Critical Thinking and Reflection

1. What population receives the HPV vaccine? What is the purpose of this vaccine and what does it protect against?
2. Briefly describe each author's perspective about making the HPV vaccine mandatory for young and adolescent girls.
3. What is your opinion about this issue? Should the government be able to make a vaccination that is so relatively new mandatory without knowing the long-term effects?

Is There Common Ground?

Roni Rabin makes a point in her article that cervical cancer has dramatically decreased over the years due to Pap testing. However, Dailard points out that cervical cancer is not the only consequence of HPV. Dailard argues that females who contract HPV must still seek follow-up care due to genital warts and abnormal Pap results leading to a physical and emotional toll as well as possible infertility. Although the Pap test detects the HPV virus, women still go through biopsies and colposcopies, which can be invasive. Given this information, would you want to vaccinate your daughter?

Rabin argues that Pap tests are effective in preventing cervical cancer. However, she makes the point that women of color are less likely to receive routine Pap tests, which she attributes to cost. She then makes the suggestion that instead of government funding going to provide vaccines, they should offer free Pap tests to women who otherwise could not receive one due to no insurance. Can you think of any other reasons why women of color may not be receiving regular Pap tests? Would offering free Pap tests ensure that all women would receive annual Pap tests?

Dailard points out that some who oppose the HPV vaccine for young girls fear that they would be sending the wrong message encouraging premarital sex. What is your opinion of this fear? Do you think it is good cause not to vaccinate?

Neither of the articles mentioned males getting vaccinated for HPV although males can be vaccinated. How might the opinions change if we were talking about making it mandatory for males and females to be vaccinated or just males? Why do you think this is not mentioned?

Create Central

www.mhhe.com/createcentral

Additional Resources

Centers for Disease Control and Prevention. (2011). Human Papillomavirus. Retrieved on April 24, 2011, from www.cdc.gov/hpv/

This website provides information about HPV regarding prevention, treatment, signs and symptoms, and so forth. The website also gives information regarding being vaccinated.

Health Information and Education. (2011). Helping Parents Understand the HPV Vaccine. Retrieved on April 24, 2011, from www.healthed.org/consulting /Articles/20081216ParentsUnderstandHPVVaccine.htm

This website addresses questions that parents may have regarding the HPV vaccine. It provides information about the safety of the vaccine as well as other issues that parents may have with deciding whether or not to have their daughters vaccinated.

The American Congress of Obstetricians and Gynecologists. (2010). Ob-Gyns Recommend HPV Vaccination for Young Girls: Adolescents and Young Women May Also Benefit. Retrieved April 24, 2011, from www.acog.org/from_home/publications/press_releases /nr08-23-10-3.cfm.

This article gives supporting evidence for vaccinating girls as young as 11 or 12 for HPV as well as some guidelines that parents should know with regard to the vaccine.

Internet References . . .

Centers for Disease Control and Prevention

www.cdc.gov/vaccines/vpd-vac/hpv/vac-faqs.htm

PBS

www.pbs.org/newshour/bb/health/jan-june13/hpv
_06-20.html

Unit 4

Adolescence

UNIT

Adolescence

*M*any people use the term teenage years to describe adolescence. This is the period of time from ages 13 through 19. During this period of development the child typically begins puberty, and there are dramatic physical changes that occur as the child becomes a young adult. Much less obvious than the physical changes are the cognitive and emotional changes in children at this stage of development. In early adolescence the child is increasingly able to think on an abstract level. Adolescents also undertake the daunting process of identity development, defining who they are. This final section considers some of the key issues related to decisions about values and sexuality that teens make as they move through adolescence.

Selected, Edited, and with Issue Framing Material by:
Kourtney Vaillancourt, *New Mexico State University*

ISSUE

Are Male Teens More Aggressive Than Female Teens?

YES: **Lori Rose Centi,** from "Teenage Boys: From Sweet Sons to Narcissistic Teens," *The Washington Times* (January 2012)

NO: **Frances McClelland Institute,** from "Aggression Among Teens: Dispelling Myths About Boys and Girls," *Research Link* (2009)

Learning Outcomes

After reading this issue, you should be able to:

- Describe the overall findings from each article that either support or do not support gender differences with regard to aggression in teens.
- Decide for yourself if the research presented is compelling enough to help you decide which side of the issue you are on.

ISSUE SUMMARY

YES: Lori Rose Centi addresses the differences in male and female brain development, and how gray and white matter in the brain can impact adolescent behaviors. She also discusses other brain changes that may contribute to males being more impulsive and less careful than their female peers.

NO: The Frances McClelland Institute shares a fact sheet which dispels "myths" about the differences in male and female teens. It reports on a meta-analysis of 148 studies and the resulting major findings. Different types of aggression are defined and discussed.

Research on aggression and adolescents suggests that aggressive acts are neither uncommon nor restricted to a certain demographic. School bullying and aggression cut across all economic, cultural, ethnic, and gender boundaries. The reported rates of bullying and aggression for the United States suggest that a significant number of adolescents have either been a victim of school aggression or have bullied others themselves. This is a concern because aggression is associated with a host of behavioral, social, and emotional adjustment difficulties.

In order to answer the question "Are male teens more aggressive than female teens?" it is important to understand what we mean by "aggression." Social scientists define aggression as behavior intended to hurt, harm, or injure another person. However, research has demonstrated that children engage in a variety of forms of aggressive behavior. The most important distinction for classification purposes is whether aggression is physical or relational in form.

Physical, or direct, aggression consists of behaviors that harm another through damage to one's physical well-being.

Physical aggression among adolescents has received considerable attention from researchers. Some have argued that there is a general tendency for physical violence to worsen over time, with behaviors like minor aggression giving way to more serious behaviors, including assault and robbery. Other research has shown that, among boys, early physical aggression predicts an elevated risk of physical violence in adolescence as well as nonviolent forms of delinquency.

Relational, or indirect, aggression includes behaviors that harm others through damage to relationships or feelings of friendship, acceptance, or social inclusion. Existing evidence suggests that relational aggression, like physical aggression, can result in emotional harm to victims. Outcomes include a range of psychosocial problems including lower social and emotional adjustment, poorer relationships with peers, and more loneliness. An added concern among some researchers who study relational aggression is the potential for retaliatory violence by those who have been victimized. Research has shown that a majority of females use relational aggression to secure their social status and maintain social harmony.

In general, convention states that males tend to employ more physical aggression, while females are more likely to use relational aggression. However, recent research suggests that it is not always appropriate to categorize aggression types by gender. Several studies have found that male and female teens appear to use a complex combination of both physical and relational aggression.

In addition to the aggression issue, be mindful of the age group on which these selections focus. Adolescence is a time of physical, developmental, social, and emotional change. Adolescents often feel out of control and overwhelmed by daily living. Remember when you were a teenager? Were you ever a victim or perpetrator of physical or relational aggression? Who were more aggressive, males or females? Which one of these views best reflects your experiences?

The question remains: Are male teens more aggressive than female teens? As you read the following two selections, keep in mind the different types of aggression.

YES

Lori Rose Centi

Teenage Boys: From Sweet Sons to Narcissistic Teens

HUNTINGDON, PA—January 8, 2012—Teenage boys can be an enigma to their mothers, who are often perplexed by the way their sweet young boys have seemingly morphed overnight into moody, narcissistic young teenagers.

A plethora of images fill a mother's mind when considering her teenage son and his behaviors. Some of the images may be of laughing and talking together, enjoying time outdoors, or pleasant family time playing cards or board games. Other images may not be as positive.

These less than positive experiences, involving some recalcitrant behaviors, uncharacteristic outbursts, demands for more freedom and fewer rules, may not completely be the teen's fault. In other words, his growing, developing brain may be at "fault," but he as a person is not completely to blame. Recent research conducted on the development of the male and female brains, beginning in infancy and often continuing to age 20, have corroborated many psychiatrists' (and parents') previous assertions with physiological findings.

These findings may help parents to not only understand their teenage sons better, but also to advocate for the enhancement of education geared toward reaching both sexes more effectively. It may also make parents of teens feel less frustration and more empathy for their growing, often misunderstood, sons.

Many friends and colleagues have expressed confusion about the differences between their male and female children, especially during the teen years. Comments, such as "He is so immature compared to her," and "He seems to be unable to control his anger at times, while she just cries," are commonly heard in the parenting realm. Now, at least, the research has revealed valid, solid reasons for the sometimes churlish, impulsive behavior exhibited by our male offspring.

"Adolescence is a period of rapid changes. Between the ages of 12 and 17, for example, a parent ages as much as 20 years." Author unknown.

The National Institute of Health released a report on "Male/Female Difference Offers Insight into Brain Development" stating "there are gender differences in the trajectory of gray matter maturation in adolescent girls and boys that may have lasting effects on the brain." Male adolescent brains have more gray matter than female brains. Gray matter is sometimes called "thinking matter."

However, developing female brains have more white matter, responsible for connecting various parts of the brain than their male counterparts. So, in spite of this seeming "advantage," boys are actually at a disadvantage because the information acquired usually cannot be fully processed due to the inability of their brains to make adequate connections.

Perhaps the actual physiology of male and female teens' brains is the most revealing aspect of the studies. The cortex, which contains both gray and white matter, is the part of the brain responsible for thinking, perceiving, and processing language. More specifically, the prefrontal cortex, a portion of the brain right behind the forehead, is one of the last areas of the brain to mature in males. This part of the brain is necessary for "good judgment, controlling impulses, solving problems, setting goals, organizing and planning, and other skills that are essential to adults," according to "The Amazing Adolescent Brain," compiled by Dr. Linda Burgess Chamberlain, Ph.D., MPH.

In addition to the physiology of the brain, a teen's gender and hormones affect his or her developing brain in myriad ways. It may also help you to understand why your son spends hours on video games that involve more violence than you and your husband have allowed him to see in his short lifetime. In addition, you may now understand why your son grunts or mutters incomprehensible words while his fingers rapidly press buttons on his game controller.

Hormones contribute greatly to the differences in male and female brain development. The hippocampus, which helps to move newly acquired information into long-term storage in the brain, responds to the primary female hormone, estrogen. As a result, the hippocampus grows and matures much faster in teenage girls than in teenage boys. This cerebral advantage allows girls to do better in social settings and causes them to show emotions more freely than boys.

Conversely, the amygdala and the hypothalamus are affected by male sex hormones and, consequently, grow larger in teenage males. Both of these parts of the brain are involved in responding to frightening and/or dangerous situations. These brain functions are exhibited by boys' greater enjoyment of physically challenging sports and being more aggressive in some settings than females.

It also may, in part, explain their need for excitement, whether literal or virtual. (Hence, those video games.) Researchers also contend that this aspect of brain development makes males less able to sit still for long periods of time. For that reason, males often learn better while moving around in a learning environment.

The greatest difference between the male and female adolescent brains, however, appears to be the delayed development of the prefrontal cortex.

Mark Weist, Ph.D., professor of psychology at the University of South Carolina and the father of three boys and two girls, concurs that male brains take longer to mature.

"Compared to teenage girls, teenage males have less developed brain functions in the frontal lobe region, associated with more impulsive behavior and less careful processing of information."

Unfortunately for males, brain development often continues into the early to mid-20s. This puts them at a higher risk for engaging in dangerous, superfluous behaviors that could cause them to make poor decisions. If drug or alcohol use is involved, brain development may also be adversely affected.

So how can parents and/or family members assist teenage boys though this difficult time? One thing that experts recommend is encouraging your son, family member, etc., to become actively involved in athletic endeavors, artistic activities (such as theatrical productions), and outdoor recreation. Being physically and mentally involved in activities that allow teens to move around while learning is especially beneficial to males. These kinds of activities are also both mentally and physically stimulating, so they aid in the development of the brain as well.

In addition, parents should also remember that because the prefrontal cortex is still developing in male teens, it is wise to give them simple instructions, rather than overwhelming them with information. Also, the information should be given in a step-by-step fashion.

It is helpful to give your teenager a planner to help him organize his homework and extra-curricular activities. Ask him to be responsible and listen to the teacher or coach's instructions, then write the instructions in the planner. This will help to reinforce the information that has been conveyed to him.

Neuroscientists stress that both male and female teenagers are often sleep-deprived due to a biological tendency to become drowsy later at night than adults. Sleep deprivation can exacerbate teenagers' tendencies to make poor decisions or to act impulsively. Parents should encourage their teenagers to get a minimum of nine hours of sleep per night. Getting extra sleep on weekends is also beneficial.

During the teen years of rapid growth and change, teenagers need family togetherness and ties that only you can give him or her. Family dinners and discussions are as important to his development into a person of good character and responsibility as any facet of his educational process.

"Even as kids reach adolescence, they need more than ever for us to watch over them. Adolescence is not about letting go. It's about hanging on during a very bumpy ride," according to Ron Taffel, renowned child development expert.

LORI ROSE CENTI is a writer and a teacher on the postsecondary level.

Frances McClelland Institute

 **NO**

Aggression Among Teens: Dispelling Myths About Boys and Girls

A new study dispels the popular belief that girls are more likely than boys to hurt other children through gossip, rumor, and social rejection. While boys do tend to hit, push, and call their peers names more than girls do, they are just as likely as girls to hurt other kids socially.

Background

Why study aggression in children and adolescents? Such behaviors are associated with maladjustment—that is, difficulties coping with problems and social relationships. For over 100 years, scientists have studied children who physically and verbally attack other kids, what we now call "direct" aggression. Since most people previously thought that physical attacks were typical of boys, researchers often left girls out of their studies. In addition, in the last 20 years, girls have been linked with social or "indirect" aggression—that is, they hurt other girls through talking badly about them and keeping them out of their social group. Over time, a belief has grown that social aggression is a female form of aggression. But new evidence shows that boys hurt their peers socially, too. . . .

The study also dispelled another myth, that girls tend not to be physically aggressive. This myth may exist because public opinion is more likely to approve the use of direct aggression by boys than by girls. But even though boys use direct aggression more than girls, girls are directly aggressive, too.

Implications

- We need to study direct and social aggression, but not because one is a male form and the other female. Both forms of aggression affect both genders, and boys and girls who engage in aggression are equally likely to experience maladjustment.
- To understand whether aggression causes poor adjustment, or vice versa, we need to do longitudinal studies. We must look at aggressive kids over time to see which condition—aggression or maladjustment—comes before the other.
- People who work with aggressive children can look for signs of delinquent behavior, attention problems, depression, or anxiety. Indirectly aggressive

children are as much at risk for problems as directly aggressive children.
- Researchers can look at the source of perceptions of aggression. Do they arise in adult or children's minds?

THIS RESEARCH BRIEF SUMMARIZES THE FOLLOWING REPORT:

Card, N. A., Stucky, B. D., Sawalani, G. M., & Little, T. D. (2008). Direct and indirect aggression during childhood and adolescence: A meta-analytic review of gender differences, intercorrelations, and relations to maladjustment. *Child Development, 79,* 1185–1229.

SUGGESTED CITATION FOR THIS RESEARCH LINK:

Van Campen, K. S., & Card, N. A. (2009). Aggression Among Teens: Dispelling Myths About Boys and Girls (Frances McClelland Institute for Children, Youth, and Families Research Link Vol. 1, No. 2). Tucson, AZ: The University of Arizona.

About the Study

A recent meta-analysis examined 148 studies that consisted of almost 74,000 children. The goal of the meta-analysis, which examined direct and social forms of aggression, was to understand three things:

1. Are direct and social aggression more common among boys or among girls, and how large are these gender differences?
2. To what extent are children who are directly aggressive also socially aggressive, and vice versa?
3. How much does aggressive behavior explain the likelihood that a child will suffer from problems such as depression or delinquency? . . .

Finding 1

Boys tend to engage in hitting and punching more than girls, but girls do physically hurt others to a moderate degree. For example:

- Imagine a school with 100 boys and 100 girls, and 100 children are directly aggressive and 100 are not.
- Of these 100 aggressive children, about 65 would be boys and 35 would be girls.
- So even though direct aggression is nearly twice as common among boys than girls, there are still a lot of girls who use direct aggression.

Boys and girls are equally likely to use social aggression. For example:

- Imagine again a school with 100 boys and 100 girls, and 100 children are indirectly aggressive and 100 are not.
- Of these 100 indirectly aggressive children, about 51 would be girls and 49 would be boys.
- The amount of difference in social aggression between boys and girls is so small that it is not meaningful.

Finding 2

Physically and socially aggressive behaviors tend to be used together. For example:

- Imagine again a school of 200 children and that 100 of them are directly aggressive and 100 are indirectly aggressive.
- Because there is overlap between the two forms, about 85 or 90 children use both direct and social aggression.
- But because the two forms are not perfectly overlapping, there is a large number—about 20 to 30—who use only one form or the other.
- So, although most aggressive children will use both types, some will only use one form or the other.

Finding 3

Both direct and social aggression are related to behavioral problems, but to different types. For example:

- There is a *strong* link between direct aggression and problems we can see in a child. That is, children who hit and punch tend to misbehave and act impulsively more so than children who gossip and hurt others socially.
- Directly aggressive children are also more likely to have poor relations with their peers than other children.
- There is a *moderate* link between social aggression and problems that are harder to see. That is, children who are indirectly aggressive are more likely to suffer from depression and anxiety than other children.
- Children who use direct aggression show low prosocial behavior (e.g., helping, sharing, cooperating), while children who use social aggression show high rates of acting prosocially toward others.
- No matter which type of aggression they use, girls and boys experience poor adjustment in the same ways. This finding contradicts previous beliefs that boys who gossip and spread rumors and girls who hit and punch are especially likely to have poor adjustment.

Misperceptions of Aggression in Girls

The myth that girls tend to be more socially aggressive than boys is strong among teachers, parents, and even some researchers. These adults may set social expectations for girls early in life that are hard to shake. Recent movies and books that depict girls as mean and hurtful maintain these stereotypes. According to the meta-analysis, teachers and parents were more likely to say that girls were more socially aggressive than boys. Meanwhile, peers and research observers were likely to view boys and girls as equally socially aggressive.

> "These findings challenge the popular belief that social aggression is a female form of aggression," says Noel A. Card, assistant professor of Family Studies and Human Development at The University of Arizona and the study's lead author.

FRANCES MCCLELLAND INSTITUTE for Children, Youth, and Families serves as a catalyst for cross-disciplinary research on children, youth, and families at the University of Arizona.

EXPLORING THE ISSUE

Are Male Teens More Aggressive Than Female Teens?

Critical Thinking and Reflection

1. What evidence did each article present for whether the authors believe there are gender differences in aggressive behavior among teens?
2. Identify some limitations in each article regarding the participants, methods, and overall generalizability to the entire teen population. Given these limitations, can you think of ways to improve these studies and build on the research?

Is There Common Ground?

Both articles examined gender differences in aggression among teenage males and females. However, neither of the articles mentioned the ethnic or cultural background. Whether this was omitted for the purposes of condensing the articles or it was just left out, could this information explain some of the findings? How might ethnic or cultural background influence aggression in each gender? What about teens in rural versus urban areas?

Both sets of researchers utilized children from elementary school as part of their study, partly to examine patterns of aggression based on earlier experiences and behavior patterns at a younger age into adolescence. How might the results of their findings be different if only adolescents had been used? Although information regarding the behaviors from childhood to adolescents is important, is it possible that these behaviors may change as the adolescents move further away from their preadolescent years?

Can you think of ways in which the research presented and other research like it will contribute to school-age children (elementary through high school)? What is the significance of knowing whether gender differences exist with regards to these possible contributions of the research?

Create Central

www.mhhe.com/createcentral

Additional Resources

Karriker-Jaffe, K. J., Foshee, V. A., Ennett, S. T., & Suchindran, C. (2008). The Development of Aggression During Adolescence: Sex Differences in Trajectories of Physical and Social Aggression Among Youth in Rural Areas. *Journal of Abnormal Child Psychology*, 36(8), pp. 1227–1236. doi: 10.1007/s10802-008-9245-5. Retrieved on April 24, 2011, from www.ncbi.nlm.nih.gov/pmc /articles/PMC2773662/.

The authors report findings in the study that support that male teens tend to be more physically aggressive than female teens.

National Youth Violence Prevention Resource Center. (2002). Facts for Teens: Aggression. Retrieved on April 24, 2011, from http://herkimercounty.org/content /departments/View/11:field=services;/content /DepartmentServices/View/68:field=documents; /content/Documents/File/123.PDF

This website offers information about different types of aggression and explains some of the contributing factors to aggression in adolescents and how this might relate to earlier childhood.

Nichols, T. R., Graber, J. A., Brooks-Gunn, J., & Botvin, G. J. (2006). Sex Differences in Overt Aggression and Delinquency Among Urban Minority Middle School Students. *Applied Developmental Psychology*, 27, pp. 78–91. doi: 10.1016/j.appdev.2005.12.006. Retrieved on April 24, 2011, from www.med.cornell.edu/ipr/PDF/ Nichols-et-al-2006-JADP.pdf

This article describes a longitudinal study that examined minority male and female adolescents' aggressive behavior with relation to precursors such as family disruption, anger, and self-control.

Internet Reference . . .

Global Post

http://everydaylife.globalpost.com/aggressive
-behavior-teenagers-2848.html

Scientific American

www.scientificamerican.com/article.cfm?id=bitch
-evolved-girls-cruel

Selected, Edited, and with Issue Framing Material by:
Kourtney Vaillancourt, *New Mexico State University*

ISSUE

Is Abstinence-Only Sex Education the Best Way to Teach About Sex?

YES: Robert E. Rector, Melissa G. Pardue, and Shannan Martin, from "What Do Parents Want Taught in Sex Education Programs?" *The Heritage Foundation Backgrounder* (January 28, 2004)

NO: Debra Hauser, from Five Years of Abstinence-Only-Until-Marriage Education: Assessing the Impact (*Advocates for Youth*, 2004)

Learning Outcomes

After reading this issue, you should be able to:

- Define both abstinence-only and comprehensive sex education.
- Discuss the major tenets of the abstinence-only sex education movement.
- Discuss the major tenets of a comprehensive sex education program.
- Describe the arguments for and against abstinence-only and comprehensive sex education programs.

ISSUE SUMMARY

YES: Robert Rector, who is a research fellow for the Heritage Foundation, and Melissa Pardue and Shannan Martin, policy analysts for the Heritage Foundation, argue that comprehensive sex education approaches are misleading because they do little to promote abstinence. Under the auspices of the Heritage Foundation, a conservative organization based in Washington, D.C., they present the results of a poll they conducted that sought to measure parental support for ideas taught in "abstinence-only" and "comprehensive sex education" programs.

NO: Debra Hauser, vice president of Advocates for Youth, argues that the assertions made by proponents of *abstinence-only sex education* are unfounded. In reviewing the efficacy of abstinence-only programs, she found that although these programs may show changes in attitudes about abstinence, they also discourage safe sexual practices and actually increase the risks of premarital pregnancy and the spread of sexually transmitted infections.

In our culture, it is impossible to avoid the constant presence of sexual references. Sex is the number one marketing tool to sell a product in our society. Sex is pervasive on television, on the Internet, and in the movies. The media oftentimes gives a false image of what sex really is, so that teens may see sex in unrealistic contexts, with no responsibility associated with sex-related decisions. Sex education in schools may be the only sound information sources available to adolescents. Most people agree about the need for some type of sex education for our children in our schools. There is little argument that abstinence is the safest choice an adolescent can make regarding sexual activity. It is the only 100 percent effective way to avoid pregnancy and the hundreds of

sexually transmitted diseases that are epidemic in our society. However, the reality is that adolescents do engage in premarital sexual behaviors. The problem is that parents and educators cannot agree on the best way to teach children and adolescents about the implications of premarital sex. One group believes that the best approach is comprehensive sex education, which encourages abstinence but also provides information on birth control, protection against sexually transmitted diseases, and the emotional aspects of engaging in sex. Other groups promote abstinence-only sex education, which provides information on the hazards of sex (i.e., pregnancy, STDs, broken hearts, etc.) and sometimes includes information on self-esteem and dealing with peer pressure to have premarital sex.

Advocates for comprehensive sex education argue that many adolescents will have premarital sex; as a consequence, adolescents need to be taught about birth control methods and STD prevention techniques. Those supporting abstinence-only sex education believe that teaching about birth control methods and STD prevention sends mixed messages about premarital sex. It could give teens the impression that teachers and parents accept that adolescents cannot help themselves from having sex, which is contrary to the pro-abstinence movement's goals.

To intensify the debate, the government has established a federal entitlement program for "abstinence-only-until-marriage" education. When schools and other agencies accept these grants, they must adhere to the program's rules, which include requiring schools to teach little about sexuality but instead to send a strong message that sexual activity outside of marriage is psychologically and physiologically harmful. Therefore, teaching about or discussing premarital sex should be avoided. This is worrisome for comprehensive sex education advocates because they believe that education about sexuality is the best way to empower adolescents to make sound decisions regarding premarital sex.

In the YES selection, Robert Rector, Melissa Pardue, and Shannan Martin argue against comprehensive sex education on the grounds that this approach does not do enough to promote abstinence and that according to their poll, parents overwhelmingly prefer their children to be taught abstinence-only programs in sex education. In the NO selection, Debra Hauser counters with the argument that abstinence-only programs, when closely examined, do not show much evidence of having a long-term impact on attitudes and behaviors regarding premarital sex. She goes on to say that these programs discourage the use of contraception, such as condoms, to prevent premarital pregnancy and sexually transmitted infections among adolescents.

Many questions should be considered when deciding on a sex education curriculum. Should parents or professionals have the sole decision-making power to decide what type of sex education a student receives? Should students have a voice in this decision? Should religion and moral values be a factor when deciding which type of sex education is best? Will comprehensive sex education encourage teens to have more casual sex as long as they use protection? Will comprehensive sex education encourage teens to start having sex sooner? Is abstinence-only sex education very realistic? Are we as a society being realistic if we believe that most teens will abstain from premarital sex? As you read both selections, think back to your days in high school and the sources and types of education about sexuality you received. Was the education sufficient? Should it have been different? If so, in what ways? Also, put yourself in the place of a parent of an adolescent. Consider what approach to sex education this parent would support and why.

YES

**Robert E. Rector, Melissa G. Pardue,
and Shannan Martin**

What Do Parents Want Taught
in Sex Education Programs?

Debates about sex education have focused on two different approaches: "safe sex" courses, which encourage teens to use contraceptives, especially condoms, when having sex, and abstinence education, which encourages teens to delay sexual activity.

In recent years, advocacy groups such as SIECUS (the Sex Information and Education Council of the United States) and Advocates for Youth have promoted another apparent alternative, entitled "comprehensive sexuality education" or "abstinence plus." These curricula allegedly take a middle position, providing a strong abstinence message while also teaching about contraception. In reality, this claim is misleading. Comprehensive sexuality education curricula contain little or no meaningful abstinence material; they are simply safe-sex programs repackaged under a new, deceptive label.

Abstinence programs teach that:

- Human sexuality is primarily emotional and psychological, not physical, in nature;
- In proper circumstances, sexual activity leads to long term emotional bonding between two individuals; and
- Sexual happiness is inherently linked to intimacy, love, and commitment—qualities found primarily within marriage.

Abstinence programs strongly encourage abstinence during the teen years, and preferably until marriage. They teach that casual sex at an early age not only poses serious threats of pregnancy and infection by sexually transmitted diseases, but also can undermine an individual's capacity to build loving, intimate relationships as an adult. These programs therefore encourage teen abstinence as a preparation and pathway to healthy adult marriage.

By contrast, comprehensive sex-ed curricula focus almost exclusively on teaching about contraception and encouraging teens to use it. These curricula neither discourage nor criticize teen sexual activity as long as "protection" is used. In general, they exhibit an acceptance of casual teen sex and do not encourage teens to wait until they are older to initiate sexual activity. For example, the curricula do not encourage teens to abstain until they have

finished high school. "Protected" sex at an early age and sex with many different partners are not treated as problems. Sexuality is treated primarily as a physical phenomenon; the main message is to use condoms to prevent the physical problems of sexually transmitted diseases and pregnancy. Comprehensive sex-ed curricula ignore the vital linkages between sexuality, love, intimacy, and commitment. There is no discussion of the idea that sex is best within marriage.

Determining Parental Attitudes toward Sex-ed Curricula

This paper presents the results of a recent poll on basic issues concerning sex education. The poll questions seek to measure parental support for the themes and values contained in abstinence curricula as well as support for the values embodied in comprehensive sex education.

The data presented are drawn from a survey of parents conducted by Zogby International in December 2003. Zogby conducted telephone interviews with a nationally representative sample of 1,004 parents with children under age 18. Parents were asked 14 questions concerning messages and priorities in sex education; the questions used were designed by Focus on the Family. The margin of error on each question is plus or minus 3.2 percent points. The responses to the questions showed only modest variation based on region, gender of the parent, or race.[1] The poll questions were designed to reflect the major themes of abstinence education. The descriptions of the messages contained in abstinence and comprehensive sex-ed curricula in the following text are based on a forthcoming content analysis of major sex-ed curricula conducted by The Heritage Foundation. . . .

"Sex Should Be Linked to Marriage; Delaying Sex until Marriage Is Best"

Abstinence education curricula stress a strong linkage between sex, love, and marriage. The Zogby poll shows strong parental support for this message.

Parents want teens to be taught that sexual activity should be linked to marriage.

Parents Want Teens to Be Taught to Delay Sexual Activity until They Are Married or Close to Marriage

Some 47 percent of parents want teens to be taught that "young people should not engage in sexual activity until they are married." Another 32 percent of parents want teens to be taught that "young people should not engage in sexual intercourse until they have, at least, finished high school and are in a relationship with someone they feel they would like to marry."

When these two categories are combined, we see that 79 percent of parents want young people taught that sex should be reserved for marriage or for an adult relationship leading to marriage. Another 12 percent of parents believe that teens should be taught to delay sexual activity until "they have, at least, finished high school." Only 7 percent of parents want teens to be taught that sexual activity in high school is okay as long as teens use contraception.

These parental values are strongly reinforced by abstinence education programs, which teach that sex should be linked to marriage and that it is best to delay sexual activity until marriage. By contrast, comprehensive sex-ed programs send the message that teen sex is okay as long as contraception is used; the underlying permissive values of these programs have virtually no support among parents.

Parents Want Teens to Be Taught That Sex Should Be Linked to Love, Intimacy, and Commitment and That These Qualities Are Most Likely to Occur in Marriage

Some 91 percent of parents want teens to be taught this message about sexuality.

This is a predominant theme of all abstinence curricula. By contrast, comprehensive sex-ed programs do not discuss love, intimacy, or commitment and seldom mention marriage. Casual sex is not criticized; sex is presented largely as a physical process; and the main lesson is to avoid the physical threats of pregnancy and disease through proper use of contraception. Comprehensive sex-ed programs do not present sexuality in a way that is acceptable to most parents.

Parents Want Teens to Be Taught That It Is Best to Delay Sex until Marriage

Some 68 percent of parents want schools to teach teens that "individuals who are not sexually active until marriage have the best chances of marital stability and happiness."

This theme is strongly supported by abstinence programs, all of which urge teens to delay sexual activity until marriage. It is ignored completely by comprehensive sex-ed courses, which do not criticize casual sex and seldom mention marriage.

General Support for Abstinence

The poll shows overwhelming parental support for other abstinence themes as well.

Parents Want Teens to Be Taught to Abstain from Sexual Activity during High School Years

Some 91 percent of parents support this message. However, for most parents, this is a minimum standard; 79 percent want a higher standard taught: abstinence until you are married or near marriage.

All abstinence curricula strongly encourage abstinence at least through high school, and preferably until marriage. By contrast, comprehensive sex-ed curricula do not encourage teens to delay sex until they have finished high school; most do not even encourage young people to wait until they are older.

Parents Want Teens to Be Taught That Abstinence Is Best

Some 96 percent of parents support this message.

Abstinence curricula obviously support this theme. Comprehensive sex-ed programs may claim to support this message, but in reality they do not. They teach mainly that abstinence is the "safest" choice, but that teen sex with protection is safe. Their overall message is that abstinence is marginally safer than safe sex. Beyond this, they have little positive to say about abstinence.

"Sex at an Early Age, Sex with Many Partners, and Casual Sex Have Harmful Consequences"

Parents believe that sex at an early age, casual sex, and sex with many partners are likely to have harmful consequences. They want teens to be taught to avoid these behaviors.

Parents Want Teens to Be Taught That the Younger the Age an Individual Begins Sexual Activity, the Greater the Probability of Harm

Some 93 percent of parents want teens taught that "the younger the age an individual begins sexual activity, the more likely he or she is to be infected by sexually transmitted diseases, to have an abortion, and to give birth out-of-wedlock."

Abstinence programs strongly support this message; they teach teens to delay sex until they are older, preferably until they are married. Comprehensive sex-ed programs teach about the threat of unprotected sex, not about the harm caused by sex at an early age. They do not urge young people to delay sex until they are older; voluntary sex at any age is depicted as okay as long as "protection" is used.

Parents Want Teens Taught That Teen Sexual Activity Is Likely to Have Psychological and Physical Effects

Some 79 percent of parents want teens to be taught this message.

Abstinence curricula clearly teach this message; comprehensive sex-ed curricula do not. Comprehensive sex-ed curricula focus on encouraging condom use; they do not criticize or discourage teen sex as long as "protection" is used.

Parents Want Schools to Teach That Teens Who Are Sexually Active Are More Likely to Be Depressed

Some 67 percent of teens who have had sexual intercourse regret it and say they wish that they had waited until they were older. (The figure for teen girls is 77 percent.)[2] Sexually active teens are far more likely to be depressed and to attempt suicide than are teens who are not sexually active.[3] Nearly two-thirds of parents support the message that sexually active teens are more likely to be depressed; a quarter of parents oppose it.

Abstinence curricula inform teens about the basic facts of regret and depression; comprehensive sex-ed curricula ignore this topic.

Parents Want Sex Education to Teach That the More Sexual Partners a Teen Has, the Greater the Likelihood of Physical and Psychological Harm

Some 90 percent of parents want this message taught to teens.

Abstinence curricula emphasize the harmful effects of casual teen sex; comprehensive sex-ed curricula do not.

Parents Want Teens Taught That Having Many Sexual Partners at an Early Age May Undermine One's Ability to Develop and Sustain Loving and Committed Relationships as an Adult

Some 85 percent of parents want teens to be taught that "having many sexual partners at an early age may undermine an individual's ability to develop love, intimacy and commitment." Another 78 percent of parents want teens to be taught that "having many different sexual partners at an early age may undermine an individual's ability to form a healthy marriage as an adult."

These are major themes of abstinence programs. They teach that teen sexual relationships are inherently short-term and unstable and that repeated fractured relationships can lead to difficulties in bonding and commitment in later years. This perspective is accurate; women who begin sexual activity at an early age will have far more sexual partners and

are less likely to have stable marriages as adults.[4] Comprehensive sex-ed curricula ignore this topic completely.

"What's More Important, Abstinence or Contraception?"

Parents believe that abstinence should be given emphasis that is more than, or equal to, that given to contraception. Some 44 percent of parents believe that teaching about abstinence is more important than teaching about contraception; another large group (41 percent) believe that abstinence and contraception should be given equal emphasis. Only 8 percent believe that teaching about contraception is more important than teaching about abstinence.

Regrettably, government spending priorities directly contradict parental priorities. Currently, the government spends at least $4.50 promoting teen contraceptive use for every $1.00 spent to promote teen abstinence.[5]

Parents Overwhelmingly Reject Main Values and Messages of Comprehensive Sex Education

Despite the claims of advocacy groups such as SIECUS and Advocates for Youth, comprehensive sex education curricula contain weak to non-existent messages about abstinence. These programs focus almost exclusively on (1) explaining the threat of teen pregnancy and sexually transmitted diseases and (2) encouraging young people to use contraception, especially condoms, to combat these threats. Many of these curricula appear to be written from a limited health perspective. Sexuality is treated as a physical process (like nutrition), and the goal is to reduce immediate health risks.

While comprehensive sex-ed curricula do not explicitly and directly encourage teen sexual activity, they do not discourage it either. As long as "protection" is used, teen sexual activity is represented as being rewarding, normal, healthy, and nearly ubiquitous. While "unprotected" sex is strongly criticized and discouraged, "protected" teen sex is presented as being fully acceptable. There is little or no effort to encourage young people to wait until they are older before becoming sexually active. By presenting "protected" teen sex activity as commonplace, fulfilling, healthy, and unproblematic, comprehensive sex-ed courses send a strong implicit anti-abstinence message to teens.

The new poll of parental attitudes shows that less than 10 percent of parents support the main values and messages of comprehensive sex education programs. Specifically:

Parents Oppose Teaching That Teen Sex Is Okay If Condoms Are Used

In comprehensive sex-ed curricula, "protected" teen sex is neither criticized nor discouraged. These courses explicitly or implicitly send the strong message that "it's okay for teens in school to engage in sexual intercourse as long as they use condoms." Only 7 percent of parents support this message; 91 percent reject it.

At a Minimum, Parents Want Teens to Be Taught to Abstain from Sexual Activity until They Have Finished High School

Some 91 percent of parents want teens to be taught this minimum standard; most want a far higher standard. But comprehensive sex-ed curricula do not teach that teens should abstain until they have finished high school; in fact, these courses do not provide any clear standards concerning when sexual activity should begin. For the most part, they do not even encourage young people to wait until they are vaguely "older"; they are simply silent on the issue.

Comprehensive Sex-Ed Courses Are Silent on Vital Issues Such as Casual Sex, Intimacy, Commitment, Love, and Marriage

. . . Parents overwhelmingly support the main themes of abstinence education and want these topics to be taught to their children. These themes are conspicuously absent from comprehensive sex-ed. These courses therefore fail to meet the needs and desires of most parents.

Should Abstinence Programs Teach about "Safe Sex" or Contraception?

The poll shows an apparent divergence between abstinence education and parental attitudes on only one issue: Some 75 percent of parents want teens to be taught about both abstinence and contraception. Except for describing the likely failure rates of various types of birth control, abstinence curricula do not teach about contraception.

However, the fact that abstinence programs, per se, do not include contraceptive information does not mean that teens will not be taught this material. Abstinence and sex education are seldom taught as stand-alone subjects in school; they are usually offered as a brief part of a larger course, most typically a health course.[6]

In addition, sex education is usually taught not once, but in multiple doses at different grade levels as the student matures. When students are taught about abstinence, in most cases, they will also receive biological information about reproduction and contraception in another part of their course work. By 11th or 12th grade, some 91 percent of students have been taught about birth control in school.[7]

There is no logical reason why contraceptive information should be presented as part of an abstinence curriculum. Not only would this reduce the limited time allocated to the abstinence message, but nearly all abstinence educators assert that it would substantially undermine the effectiveness of the abstinence message.

In general, parents tend to agree that abstinence and contraceptive instruction should not be directly mixed. . . . Some 56 percent of parents believe either that contraception should not be taught at all or that, if both abstinence and contraception are taught, they should be taught separately. (Some 22 percent believe that contraception should not be taught, while 35 percent want the two subjects taught separately.)

Although most parents want teens to be taught about both abstinence and contraception, there is no strong sentiment that these topics must be combined into one curriculum. The stronger a parent's support for abstinence, the less likely he or she is to want abstinence and contraception merged into a single curriculum.

The fact that 75 percent of parents want both abstinence and contraception taught to teens should not, in any way, be interpreted to mean support for comprehensive sex-education. Comprehensive sex-ed curricula are focused almost exclusively on promoting contraceptive use and contain little or no mention of abstinence, yet only 8 percent of parents believe that schools should give greater emphasis to contraception than to abstinence.

Moreover, parents have reservations concerning the type of contraceptive education these curricula contain. While 52 percent of parents want schools to provide "basic biological and health information about contraception," only 23 percent want schools "to encourage teens to use condoms when having sex, teach teens where to obtain condoms, and have teens practice how to put on condoms." The latter aggressive type of contraceptive promotion is typical of comprehensive sex-ed curricula, though it lacks wide support among parents.

In general, parents want teens to be taught a strong abstinence message as well as being given basic biological information about contraception. The polls suggest that most parents would be satisfied if young people were given a vigorous abstinence course and were taught about the basics of contraception separately. This is probably the typical situation in most schools where authentic abstinence is taught. On the other hand, extremely few parents (7 percent to 8 percent) would be happy if abstinence education were to be replaced by comprehensive sex-ed.

Conclusion

The newly released poll shows strong (in many cases, nearly unanimous) support for the major themes of abstinence education. Abstinence programs provide young people with the strong, uplifting moral messages desired by nearly all parents.

Multiple evaluations show that abstinence programs are effective in encouraging young people to delay sexual activity.[8] The effectiveness of these programs is quite remarkable, given that they typically provide no more than a few hours of instruction per year. In those few hours, abstinence instructors seek to counteract thousands of hours of annual exposure to sex-saturated teen media, which strongly push teens in the opposite direction.

Most parents not only want vigorous instruction in abstinence, but also want teens to be taught basic biological information about contraception. Such information is not contained in abstinence curricula themselves but is frequently provided in a separate setting such as a health class. Overall, the values and objectives of the overwhelming majority of parents can be met by providing teens with a strong abstinence program while teaching basic biological information about contraception in a separate health or biology class. This arrangement appears common in schools where abstinence is taught.

In recent years, groups such as Advocates for Youth and SIECUS have sought to eliminate funding for abstinence or to replace abstinence education with comprehensive sex-ed. This is always done under the pretext that comprehensive sex-ed contains a strong abstinence message and, thereby, renders traditional abstinence superfluous. In reality, comprehensive sex-ed curricula have weak to nonexistent abstinence content. Replacing abstinence education with these programs would mean eliminating the abstinence message in most U.S. schools; nearly all parents would object to this change.

Only a tiny minority (less than 10 percent) of parents support the values and messages taught in comprehensive sex education curricula. Since the themes of these courses (such as "It's okay for teens to have sex as long as they use condoms") contradict and undermine the basic values parents want their children to be taught, these courses would be unacceptable even if combined with other materials.

The popular culture bombards teens with messages encouraging casual sexual activity at an early age. To counteract this, parents want teens to be taught a strong abstinence message. Parents overwhelmingly support abstinence curricula that link sexuality to love, intimacy, and commitment and that urge teens to delay sexual activity until maturity and marriage.

Regrettably, this sort of clear abstinence education is not taught in most schools. As a result, the sexual messages that parents deem to be most important are not getting through to today's teens.

Notes

1. Responses to individual questions categorized by region, gender, and race are available upon request.
2. National Campaign to Prevent Teen Pregnancy, America's Adults and Teens Sound Off About Teen Pregnancy, December 2003, p. 17.
3. Robert E. Rector, Kirk A. Johnson, Ph.D., and Lauren R. Noyes, "Sexually Active Teenagers Are More Likely to Be Depressed and to Attempt Suicide," Heritage Foundation Center for Data Analysis Report No. 03–04, June 3, 2003.
4. Robert E. Rector, Kirk A. Johnson, Lauren Noyes, and Shannan Martin, The Harmful Effects of Sexual Activity and Multiple Sexual Partners Among Women: A Book of Charts, The Heritage Foundation, June 23, 2003, pp. 4, 10.
5. Melissa G. Pardue, Robert E. Rector, and Shannan Martin, "Government Spends $12 on Safe Sex and Contraceptives for Every $1 Spent on Abstinence," Heritage Foundation Backgrounder No. 1718, January 14, 2004.
6. Some 85 percent of the sex education taught in the United States is part of a larger course on a broader subject, most typically a health or biology class. See Sex Education in America (Menlo Park, Cal.: Kaiser Family Foundation, 2000), p. 90.
7. Ibid., p. 18.
8. Robert E. Rector, "The Effectiveness of Abstinence Education Programs in Reducing Sexual Activity Among Youth," Heritage Foundation Backgrounder No. 1533, April 8, 2002.

ROBERT E. RECTOR is a senior research fellow for the Heritage Foundation. He is an authority on poverty, marriage, and the U.S. welfare system.

MELISSA G. PARDUE is a former policy analyst for the Heritage Foundation.

SHANNAN MARTIN is a research assistant in welfare policy at the Heritage Foundation.

Debra Hauser

 **NO**

Five Years of Abstinence-Only-Until-Marriage Education: Assessing the Impact

Introduction

Since 1991, rates of teenage pregnancy and birth have declined significantly in the United States. These are welcome trends. Yet, teens in the United States continue to suffer from the highest birth rate and one of the highest rates of sexually transmitted infections (STIs) in the industrialized world. Debate over the best way to help teens avoid, or reduce, their sexual risk-taking behavior has polarized many youth-serving professionals. On one side are those that support comprehensive sex education—education that promotes abstinence but includes information about contraception and condoms to build young people's knowledge, attitudes, and skills for when they do become sexually active. On the other side are those that favor abstinence-only-until-marriage—programs that promote "abstinence from sexual activity outside marriage as the expected standard" of behavior. Proponents of abstinence-only programs believe that providing information about the health benefits of condoms or contraception contradicts their message of abstinence-only and undermines its impact. As such, abstinence-only programs provide no information about contraception beyond failure rates.

In 1996, Congress signed into law the Personal Responsibility & Work Opportunities Reconciliation Act, or "welfare reform." Attached was the provision, later set out in Section 510(b) of Title V of the Social Security Act, appropriating $250 million dollars over five years for state initiatives promoting sexual abstinence outside of marriage as the only acceptable standard of behavior for young people.

For the first five years of the initiative, every state but California participated in the program. (California had experimented with its own abstinence-only initiative in the early 1990s. The program was terminated in February 1996, when evaluation results found the program to be ineffective.) From 1998 to 2003, almost a half a billion dollars in state and federal funds were appropriated to support the Title V initiative. A report,

detailing the results from the federally funded evaluation of select Title V programs, was due to be released more than a year ago. Last year, Congress extended "welfare reform" and, with it, the Title V abstinence-only-until-marriage funding without benefit of this, as yet unreleased, report.

As the first five-year funding cycle of Title V came to a close, a few state-funded evaluations became public. Others were completed with little or no fanfare. This document reviews the findings from the 10 evaluations that Advocates for Youth was able to identify. Advocates for Youth also includes evaluation results from California's earlier attempt at a statewide abstinence-only initiative.

Available Evaluations

Ten states made some form of evaluation results available for review. For Arizona, Florida, Iowa, Maryland, Minnesota, Oregon, Pennsylvania, and Washington, Advocates was able to locate evaluation results from state Title V programs. For Missouri and Nebraska, Advocates located evaluation findings from at least one program among those funded through the state's Title V initiative. Finally, the evaluation of California's abstinence-only program was published in a peer-reviewed journal and readily available.

Funding*

During the first five years of abstinence-only-until-marriage Title V programming, the 10 states received about $45.5 million in federal funds. To further support the initiatives and to cover their required funding match, these states appropriated about $34 million in additional funds over the five years. In addition, California spent $15 million in state funds between 1991 and 1994 to support its abstinence-only initiative. In sum, the program efforts discussed in this paper cost an estimated $94.5 million in federal and state dollars.

---

* In federal fiscal year 2003, the 10 states discussed here with evaluations of Title V programs received $8,810,281 in federal funds. Under the law, states are required to provide matching funds of three state-raised dollars for every four federal dollars received. Thus in 2003, the 10 states supplied $7,268,060 in state dollars, bringing the total of public monies to Title V funded abstinence-only-until-marriage programs to $16,078,341.

Program Components

For the most part, Title V funds were administered through states' departments of health and then sub-granted to abstinence-only contractors within each state. Program components varied from state to state and from contractor to contractor within each state. However, all programs discussed in this document included an abstinence-only curriculum, delivered to young people in schools or through community-based agencies. Popular curricula included: *Education Now Babies Later (ENABL), Why Am I Tempted? (WAIT), Family Accountability Communicating Teen Sexuality (FACTS), Choosing the Best Life, Managing Pressures before Marriage,* and AC Green's *Game Plan,* among others. Some programs included peer education, health fairs, parent outreach, and/or *Baby Think it Over* simulators. Some states supplemented their educational programs with media campaigns, also funded through Title V.

Evaluation Designs

The 11 evaluations summarized in this document represent those Advocates for Youth could uncover through extensive research. The quality of the evaluation designs varied greatly. Most evaluations employed a simple pretest/posttest survey design. Slightly fewer than half (five) assessed the significance of changes from pre- to posttest, using a comparison group. Additionally, seven evaluations included some form of follow-up to assess the program's impact over time, although results are not yet available for two. Three of these seven also included a comparison group. For those programs that included follow-up, surveys were administered at three to 17 months after students completed their abstinence-only-until-marriage program.

Because the quality of the evaluation designs varied from state to state, Advocates relied heavily on the evaluators' own analyses and words to describe each program's impact.

Summary of Results

Evaluation of these 11 programs showed few short-term benefits and no lasting, positive impact. A few programs showed mild success at improving attitudes and intentions to abstain. No program was able to demonstrate a positive impact on sexual behavior over time. A description follows of short- and long-term impacts, by indicator.

Short-Term Impacts of State Abstinence-Only Programs

In 10 programs, evaluation measured the short-term impact of the program on at least one indicator, including attitudes favoring abstinence, intentions to abstain, and/or sexual behavior. Overall, programs were most successful at improving participants' attitudes towards abstinence and were least likely to positively affect participants' sexual behaviors.

Attitudes Endorsing Abstinence—10 evaluations tested for short-term changes in attitudes.

- Three of 10 programs had no significant impact on attitudes (Maryland, Missouri, and Nebraska).
- Four of 10 showed increases in attitudes favorable to abstinence (Arizona, Florida, Oregon, and Washington).
- Three of 10 showed mixed results (California, Iowa, and Pennsylvania).**

Intentions to Abstain—Nine evaluations measured short-term changes in intentions.

- Four of nine programs showed no significant impact on participants' intentions to abstain (California, Maryland, Nebraska, and Oregon).
- Three of nine programs showed a favorable impact on intentions to abstain (Arizona, Florida, and Washington).
- Two of nine programs showed mixed results (Iowa and Pennsylvania).**

Sexual Behaviors—Six evaluations measured short-term changes in sexual behavior.

- Three of six programs had no impact on sexual behavior (California, Maryland, and Missouri).
- Two of six programs reported increases in sexual behavior from pre- to posttest (Florida and Iowa). It was unclear whether the increases were due to youth's maturation or to a program's effect, as none of these evaluations included a comparison group.
- One of the six programs showed mixed results (Pennsylvania).**

Long-Term Impacts of State Abstinence-Only Programs

Seven evaluations included some form of follow-up survey to assess the impact of the abstinence-only programs over time. Results from two of these are not yet available (Nebraska and Oregon). Of the remaining five, three were of statewide initiatives (Arizona, California, and Minnesota). Two were evaluations of programs within statewide initiatives (Missouri's *Life Walk* Program and Pennsylvania's LaSalle Program). All five evaluations included questions to assess changes in participants' attitudes and behaviors between pretest/posttest and follow-up. Four also measured changes in intentions to abstain. Three evaluations included a comparison group.

** Mixed results indicated that attitudes changed in both desired and undesired directions, either by survey questions within one initiative, or by individual programs within an initiative.

- **Attitudes Endorsing Abstinence**—Five evaluations included assessment of changes in attitudes. Four of five evaluations showed no long-term positive impact on participants' attitudes. That is, participants' attitudes towards abstinence either declined at follow-up, or there was no evidence that participating in the abstinence-only program improved teens' attitudes about abstinence relative to the comparison groups, at three to 17 months after taking the abstinence-only program (Arizona, California, Missouri, and Pennsylvania's LaSalle Program). Follow-up surveys in Minnesota showed mixed results.
- **Intentions to Abstain**—Four evaluations measured long-term intentions to abstain. Three of four evaluations showed no long-term positive impact on participants' intentions to abstain from sexual intercourse. That is, participants' intentions either declined significantly at follow-up or there was no statistically significant difference in participants' attitudes relative to controls at follow-up (Arizona, California, and Minnesota). In one of the four (Pennsylvania's LaSalle Program), evaluation showed a positive impact at follow-up on program participants' intentions to abstain relative to comparison youth.
- **Sexual Behavior**—Five programs measured long-term impacts on sexual behavior. No evaluation demonstrated any impact on reducing teens' sexual behavior at follow-up, three to 17 months after the program ended (Arizona, California, Minnesota, Missouri, or Pennsylvania's LaSalle Program).

Comparisons of Abstinence-Only-Until-Marriage versus Comprehensive Sex Education

Two evaluations—Iowa's and the Pennsylvania's Fulton County program—compared the impact of comprehensive sex education with that of abstinence-only-until-marriage programs.

In Iowa, abstinence-only students were slightly more likely than comprehensive sex education participants to feel strongly about wanting to postpone sex but less likely to feel that their goals should not include teen pregnancy. There was little to no difference between the abstinence-only students and those in the comprehensive sex education program in understanding why they should wait to have sex. Evaluation did not include comparison of data on the sexual behavior of participants in the two types of programs.

In Fulton County, Pennsylvania, results found few to no differences between the abstinence-only and comprehensive approaches in attitudes towards sexual behavior. Evaluators found that, regardless of which program was implemented in the seventh and eighth grades, sexual attitudes, intentions, and behaviors were similar by the end of the 10th grade.

Discussion

These evaluation results—from the first five-year cycle of funding for abstinence-only-until-marriage under Section 510(b) of Title V of the Social Security Act—reflect the results of other studies. In a 1994 review of sex education programs, all the studies available at the time of school-based, abstinence-only programs [were assessed] that had received peer review and that measured attitudes, intentions, *and* behavior. [It was] found that none of the three abstinence-only programs was effective in producing a statistically significant impact on sexual behaviors in program participants relative to comparisons. In a 1997 report for the National Campaign to Prevent Teen Pregnancy, Doug Kirby reviewed evaluations from six abstinence-only programs, again finding no program that produced a statistically significant change in sexual behavior. This was again confirmed in 2000, when another review by Kirby found no abstinence-only program that produced statistically significant changes in sexual behaviors among program youth relative to comparisons. This failure of abstinence-only programs to produce behavior change was among the central concerns expressed by some authors of the evaluations included in this document. . . . It is important to note that a great deal of research contradicts the belief that changes in knowledge and attitudes alone will necessarily result in behavior change.

A few evaluators also noted the failure of abstinence-only programs to address the needs of sexually active youth. Survey data from many of the programs indicated that sexually experienced teens were enrolled in most of the abstinence-only programs studied. For example:

In Erie County, Pennsylvania, researchers found that 42 percent of the female participants were sexually active by the second year of the program.

In Clinton County, Pennsylvania, data collected from program participants in the seventh, eighth, and ninth grades showed a dramatic increase in the proportion of program females who experienced first sexual intercourse over time (six, nine, and 30 percent, respectively, by grade).

In Minnesota, 12 percent of the eighth grade program participants were sexually active at posttest.

In Arizona, 19 percent of program participants were sexually active at follow-up. Concurrently, Arizona's evaluators found that youth's intent to pursue abstinence declined significantly at follow-up, regardless of whether the student took another abstinence-only class. Eighty percent of teens reported that they were likely to become sexually active by the time they were 20 years old.

Abstinence-only programs provide these youth with no information, other than abstinence, regarding how to protect themselves from pregnancy, HIV, and other STIs.

A third, related concern of evaluators was abstinence-only programs' failure to provide positive information about contraception and condoms. Evaluators noted more than once that programs' emphasis on the failure rates of contraception, including condoms, left youth ambivalent, at best, about using them.

In Clinton County, Pennsylvania, researchers noted that, of those participants that reported experiencing first sexual intercourse during ninth grade, only about half used any form of contraception.

Arizona's evaluation team found that program participants' attitudes about birth control became less favorable from pre- to posttest. They noted that this was probably a result of the "program's focus on the failure rates of contraceptives as opposed to their availability, use and access." . . .

Conclusion

Abstinence-only programs show little evidence of sustained (long-term) impact on attitudes and intentions. Worse, they show some negative impacts on youth's willingness to use contraception, including condoms, to prevent negative sexual health outcomes related to sexual intercourse. Importantly, only in one state did any program demonstrate short-term success in delaying the initiation of sex; none of these programs demonstrates evidence of long-term success in delaying sexual initiation among youth exposed to the programs or any evidence of success in reducing other sexual risk-taking behaviors among participants.

DEBRA HAUSER is executive vice president for Advocates for Youth and previously served as director of Community Health Services for the City of Atlantic City where she designed, implemented, and evaluated sexuality education, health promotion, teen pregnancy prevention, and teen parenting programs for an urban population.

EXPLORING THE ISSUE

Is Abstinence-Only Sex Education the Best Way to Teach About Sex?

Critical Thinking and Reflection

1. Do you believe sex education should be abstinence based or comprehensive? For elementary school students? For high school students? Defend your answer.
2. Do you think region of the country, culture, and religion should be factors in deciding what type of sex education should be taught in schools? Why or why not?
3. Do you think abstinence-only programs will help decrease or impede the teen pregnancy and sexually transmitted disease problem?
4. If you were the parent of an adolescent, what type of sex education program would you feel most comfortable with your child being exposed to, abstinence-only education or comprehensive? Why?

Is There Common Ground?

As a society, we need to be cognizant of the fact that schools are not the only place where children receive sex education. All one has to do is listen to students during lunchtime at an elementary school, middle school, or high school to hear that they are receiving information about sex from peers. The Internet and other mass media are full of information about sex as well. Also, our own behaviors that we model to our children send strong messages about sexuality. It seems that the true mission of schools is to empower our children with accurate, developmentally appropriate information about their sexuality as a way to counterbalance the sometimes erroneous messages they receive from other aspects of their lives. Which approach most effectively addresses this goal? Or, is there a middle ground that has not been presented?

Additional Resources

Advocates for Youth. Retrieved on April 6, 2011, from www.advocatesforyouth.org/%20%09%20index.php?option=com_content&task=view&id=46&Itemid=75

This website, established in 1980 as the Center for Population Options, works to help young people make informed and responsible decisions about their reproductive and sexual health, fostering a positive and realistic approach to adolescent sexual health.

Go Ask Alice! Retrieved on April 6, 2011, from www.goaskalice.columbia.edu/

Go Ask Alice! is a health question-and-answer site sponsored by Columbia University's health education program. The mission of this site is to provide in-depth, factual, and nonjudgmental information to assist individuals' decision making about their physical, sexual, emotional, and spiritual health. Questions about sexuality, sexual health, and relationships are frequent. This site includes hundreds of relevant links.

Create Central

www.mhhe.com/createcentral

Internet References . . .

Information for Health. Retrieved on April 6, 2011

www.infoforhealth.org/

The INFO Project (Information and Knowledge for Optimal Health Project), based at the Johns Hopkins University Bloomberg School of Public Health's Center for Communication Programs, is focused on understanding how knowledge and information can improve the quality of reproductive health programs, practice, and policies.

WebMD Sexual Health Center. Retrieved on April 6, 2011

www.webmd.com/sex/gender-identity-disorder

This website provides information from a medical perspective on gender identity disorder.

Selected, Edited, and with Issue Framing Material by:
Kourtney Vaillancourt, *New Mexico State University*

ISSUE

Is the Internet a Safe Place
for Teens to Explore?

YES: Michele Fleming and Debra Rickwood, from "Teens in Cyberspace: Do They Encounter Friend or Foe?" *Youth Studies Australia* (vol. 23, no. 3, 2004)

NO: Chang-Hoan Cho and Hongsik John Cheon, from "Children's Exposure to Negative Internet Content: Effects of Family Content," *Journal of Broadcasting and Electronic Media* (December 2005)

Learning Outcomes

After reading this issue, you should be able to:

- Summarize the main concerns associated with children/teens' Internet use.
- Identify some ways in which parents can help their child/teen avoid exposure to harmful Internet material.
- Explain the significance of the findings of Chang-Hoan Cho and Hongsik John Cheon's research.
- Decide how safe you think teens are on the Internet.

ISSUE SUMMARY

YES: Michele Fleming and Debra Rickwood, professors at the University of Canberra in Australia, contend that parents need to be vigilant about their teens surfing the Web, but that it is generally a safe place and that the prevalence of cyber predators is overstated.

NO: Chang-Hoan Cho, assistant professor at the University of Florida, and Hongsik John Cheon, assistant professor at Frostburg State University, believe that the Web can be a dangerous place for teens to explore. They conducted a study that found that children are exposed to more negative Internet content than parents expect. Factors that reduced children's exposure to negative Internet content included parental interaction and family cohesion.

Parents naturally want to protect their children from all harm. When children are young, they are under parental control and easier to protect because they are physically in parents' sight. They are dependent on parents for physical needs such as food and shelter. As children get older, they are more mobile, particularly when they learn to drive. Parents of teens are usually sleep deprived because they cannot sleep until they know their teens are home safely from a night activity with their friends. But how can parents protect their children from the dangers of the Internet? Teens can be right in front of them in the house working on the computer and still be in possible danger. They don't even have to be out of the house to be exposed to dangers on the Internet such as sexual predators.

Is this true or is it an exaggeration? Although media reports suggest that children and teens are being sexually solicited on the Internet at an alarming rate, some researchers state that the incidence of sexual predators on the Internet is grossly overstated. Media reports often quote the statistic that one in five children, aged 10 to 17, per year, are sexually solicited online. What they don't tell you is that this statistic comes from a report that defines sexual solicitation as anything from a classmate asking his girlfriend if she is a virgin to something more serious like adults asking children to meet for a sexual encounter. One is a simple question, while the other is an example of the serious problem of online predators.

Studies on Internet use and its effects report conflicting and varied results. Some studies on children's use of the Internet show that it has positive effects on academic achievement and no negative effects on social or psychological development. Other studies report children experience lasting psychological damage as a result of surfing the Web. For example, one study stated that 42 percent of Internet users aged 10 to 17 had seen online pornography in the past year, with the majority saying that they did not seek it out and were very disturbed by it. Of the more than 450 million porn websites, 3 percent ask for proof of age and are more than willing to show scenes that are sexually explicit.

Not only is there confusion over how much real danger the Internet poses, but parents must also contend with the new language that children and teens use when surfing the Web. For example, "lol" means laughing out loud; "pos" means parents over shoulder. In order to protect and guide children in the new world of the Internet, parents must learn about hardware, software, and a new language!

Common Sense Media and Media Wise from the National Institute on Media and the Family list Internet safety by age and stage as well as rules on Internet safety. For children aged 2 to 6, they suggest keeping children away from the Internet, even the games. For ages 7 to 9,

e-mailing is OK, but not instant messaging (IM) as it is too difficult to control. Web surfing can be done if a filter is installed. No chat rooms, online games, or downloading should be allowed for this age group. For ages 10 to 12, children begin exploring the Web much more at school, at home, and at their friends' homes. They insist on IMing and surfing the Web for games and need to be supervised closely. MySpace, which is a website for social networking for young people, is inappropriate at this age. Children aged 13 to 16 can e-mail, IM, surf the Web, download, and play games as long as they follow the rules of Internet safety.

In the following selections, Internet safety for children and teens is debated. Michele Fleming and Debra Rickwood recognize that dangers on the Internet exist, but that children use the Web mostly to interact with friends from their existing social networks, for homework, and for entertainment. From their study of 178 families, Chang-Hoan Cho and Hongsik John Cheon found that children are exposed to more negative Internet content than most parents had previously thought.

YES ←

**Michele Fleming and
Debra Rickwood**

Teens in Cyberspace: Do They Encounter Friend or Foe?

Recent media reports of relationships developed "online" have fuelled parents' concerns about the safety of their children using the Internet ('Runaway schoolgirl contacts family after Internet liaison', The Canberra Times, 17 July 2003, p. 15). Many parents hold ambivalent views about the Internet, being aware of its positive educational value but fearful of its "influence" on their children. In particular, parents are concerned that their children might become socially isolated due to excessive Internet use, might view sexually explicit images, and might divulge sensitive information to strangers.

The effects of "excessive" use of the Internet have not yet been clearly established. Some studies have looked at "computer" addiction and some at time spent playing video games. Both these activities have been linked to negative outcomes when done to excess. Excessive video game play, even when not of a violent nature, has been linked to aggression in numerous studies. Teens who use computers to excess have been found to report psychiatric symptoms, such as anxiety, hostility and obsessive-compulsivity. However, studies on the effects of excessive use of computers have not clearly shown the direction of the relationship and the negative outcomes reported may themselves be the cause of overuse.

Many teens are logging onto the Net both at school and at home but it is not yet known how many of them are using it to excess. Different criteria for Internet "addiction" are used by different researchers, making any valid assessment of how many individuals might be classified as addicted very difficult. Nonetheless, young people who spend inordinate amounts of time online, to the detriment of other activities, might be classified as "at-risk." Griffiths, in examining the impact of electronic technology on children and adolescents, suggested that when any activity is engaged in for such large amounts of time and other activities are displaced, it is likely that educational and social relationships will suffer.

The association between Internet use and psychological well-being in adults has been studied by Robert Kraut of the Carnegie Mellon University over the past few years. Kraut and colleagues have found greater Internet use to be associated with reduced psychological well-being, and reduced social support and increased depression. In a 1998 longitudinal study, undertaken with a relatively small but diverse US sample of 169 participants, including teenagers, greater Internet use was found to be associated with less family communication, greater loneliness and greater depression. In partial support of Kraut et al.'s findings, a study of high school seniors in the USA found that level of Internet use was not related to depression but was found to be related to poorer relationships with mothers and friends. However, it has also been suggested that it is people who are already lonely who spend time on the Internet.

In contrast, some research suggests that the Internet increases social connectedness and results in many positive face-to-face relationships. The anonymity of online relationships can increase intimate self-disclosure. For those who have difficulty with face-to-face relationships, the Internet may allow them to more easily express themselves and thereby experience social connectedness. Some people seem to feel that they are more their real selves on the Internet, which in turn leads to the formation of strong online attachments. For many teens, online communication may be just another way of keeping in touch with existing friends. Instead of being on the phone after school, teens are "talking" to their friends online.

Parents are also concerned about the amount of pornography children are exposed to online. Although some young people may deliberately seek out pornographic sites, others may be subjected to it unwittingly. Parents fears are not entirely unfounded, with 25% of youth aged 10 to 17 years indicating they had been exposed to unwanted pornography in a national survey conducted in the USA.

However, the biggest concern for parents is "stranger-danger." Parents have long been concerned about stranger-danger in the real world and this has now extended to the virtual world. Parents are fearful that children might divulge information that makes them vulnerable to potential predators who might be able to trace them through information disclosed on the Internet. Parents also fear that children might form a relationship with someone unsuitable online, possibly even a paedophile. Certainly, young people are the most vulnerable section of society when it comes to sexual assault and abduction. Crime statistics for Australia show that children aged 10 to 14 years and adolescents aged 15 to 19 years are three times more likely than the general population to have been recorded as a victim of sexual assault. Adolescents are also three times more likely to be the victims of robbery and kidnapping than the general population. Thus fears about safety in the real world are based in fact. To date, there is little but growing evidence that fears about safety as a result of contacts made online are also well-founded.

How Often Are Youth Online?

Children and young people are using the Internet in ever-increasing numbers. Research done in the USA has found that teenagers are much heavier users of the Internet than are adults. In one US study of 754 teens aged 12 to 17 years, it was found that 73% used the Internet and of these 42% went online daily.

In a national survey conducted by the Australian Broadcasting Authority in 2000, 58% of Australian children aged 5 to 12 years and 86% of teens aged 13 to 18 years were reported to have Internet access either at home or at school. The latest Australian Bureau of Statistics figures, using 2001 data, found that 28% of Australian children aged 0 to 17 years had accessed the Internet from home in the previous week. Given that this figure includes very young children and babies, the likelihood is that use by teens is substantially higher than indicated by these figures. Furthermore, many young people use the Internet at school and some of this use is undoubtedly for reasons other than schoolwork.

Why Do Young People Use the Internet?

Research into reasons for young people's use of the Internet is relatively scarce. However, research with adults suggests that the Internet is used for entertainment, education, information gathering and communication. In a sample of 236 American college students with a mean age of 20 years, the main reasons for using the World Wide Web were entertainment, passing time, social information, relaxation and information. In a survey of 684 adults, the main reasons reported for using the Internet were to find information, to relieve boredom, to get to know others and for entertainment.

Recently, some studies have begun to investigate the reasons for teens' use of the Internet. An American survey conducted by America Online of 6,700 teens aged 12 to 17 years, found that 81% used their computers for email; 70% for instant messaging; 70% to play online games; 58% for homework research; and 55% for listening to and downloading music. In a study of 625 American youth aged 10 to 17 years, 71% used the Internet to get news or information about current events; 68% used their computers to send and receive emails; 56% to get information about sports, entertainment and hobbies; 54% to talk in chat rooms; 17% to get health or medical information; and 17% to shop.

Younger children's reasons for using the Internet were examined in a study of 194 Dutch children aged 8 to 13 years. Children reported using the Internet because they had an affinity with computers; in order to gather information; for entertainment; to avoid boredom; for online social interaction; and for off-line social action, in that order. The last mentioned reason "off-line social interaction" referred to children's desire to talk about the Internet with friends because their friends were also using it.

Results of the Pew Internet and American Life Project showed that teens go online for entertainment and information. Some of the things teens specifically reported going online for were to send or receive email; to use instant messaging (IM); to visit web sites about movies, television shows, music groups and sports stars; to look for news; to look for hobby information; to play and download games; to research information on items they might like to buy; and to play and download music. Teens reported that IM messaging is very important to them, with 74% of online teens using IM. One-fifth of teenagers in the study reported using IM as the main means of contacting friends.

Cyberspace: Consequences for Children and Adolescents

The overwhelming concern of parents and the public alike is that young people will form cyber-relationships with predatory strangers, which in turn may lead to them being lured into a meeting with a paedophile. A growing body of evidence suggests that both adults and teens are forming relationships online, and in some cases turning online relationships into offline ones. However, American studies report that most teens and adults are taking appropriate precautions when meeting with online "friends." The news from Japan, however, is rather more worrying, with reports of a number of sexual assaults on teens as a result of meetings arranged via online dating sites. On the positive side, American research also suggests that most young people tend to form relationships with similar age peers rather than with older people, and that many of these online relationships are initiated through existing social networks. Similarly, there appears no evidence as yet that spending time online results in social isolation; on the contrary, research to date with adolescents suggests that Internet use increases social interaction.

Psychological Well-Being and Social Connectedness

Most of the time, young people online are interacting with friends from their existing social networks. In an American study of 130 children aged 11 to 13 years, participants' IM partners were usually friends from school. However, 12% of IM partners in this study had been met online. Most of the online communication was devoted to the usual topics discussed offline, such as friends and gossip, and was motivated by a desire of companionship. Of concern, however, is the finding that those young people who felt lonely and/or anxious were more likely to have online relationships with people with whom they did not have a close affiliation. This is consistent with research which suggests that not all teens are equally likely to form new online relationships. In one US study, boys who had poor communication with their parents or were highly troubled were more likely to form close online relationships than were other boys. Similarly, girls who had high levels of conflict with their parents or were highly troubled, were more likely to form close online relationships than were other girls.

Some teens, however, have reported that use of the Internet improves their relationships with friends. Results of the Pew Internet and American Life Project, in which 754 young people aged 12 to 17 and 754 of their parents were interviewed, showed that 73% of teens were online. Of these online youths, 48% said that use of the Internet improved their relationships with friends; and 32% reported that the Internet had helped them make new friends. Girls aged 12 to 14 years were the most enthusiastic about the Internet's ability to help them make new friends online. Teens in this study reported that the Internet allowed them to be more their true self, which is in line with research with adults.

Frequent Internet users have reported engaging in more social activities than less frequent users. In a study with 927 Israeli teenagers aged 13 to 18 years from a representative sample of Israeli households, it was reported that more than a third of the respondents were frequent Internet users, although the authors classified frequent use as anything more than once per week. Only 10% of respondents reported using the Internet daily. Importantly, however, frequent users reported having fewer friends and feeling more socially isolated than did light users.

Pornography and Sexual Harassment

Parents' concerns that their children will be subjected to online pornography are valid. Young people may visit pornographic sites by choice but also they may be subjected to pornographic material unwittingly. In a national survey of American youth aged 10 to 17 years who were regular Internet users, 25% had been exposed to unwanted sexual pictures in the previous year. Of these, the majority reported no negative effect of their exposure but 25% reported distress at being exposed. More boys than girls reported exposure and older youths reported substantially more exposure than did younger children.

With a younger sample of Dutch children aged 8 to 13 years, 4% reported experiencing violence on the net, 4% reported experiencing pornography, and 1.5% reported experiencing sexual harassment. Although these figures are small, they are nonetheless of concern.

As part of the Australia Broadcasting Authority's survey of Internet use in the home, a cyber-panel of Australian families was questioned regarding exposure to offensive material on the Net. A total of 192 of the cyber-panel members were teens aged 11 to 17 years and almost half (47%) of them reported having been exposed to offensive content such as violence, pornography and nudity. The overwhelming majority of offensive content cited by these teens was pornography.

Even more disturbing than viewing unwanted pornography is being sexually solicited online. A survey of American youth found that 19% of Internet users aged 10 to 17 years had received an unwanted sexual solicitation in the previous 12 months. Thankfully, none of these solicitations resulted in any sexual contact or assault.

Safety

Young people, for the most part, spend their time online with people they already know but nonetheless many do appear to form friendships with strangers. In a large US survey of 1,501 adolescents aged 10 to 17 years who regularly used the Internet, 55% had used chat rooms, IM and other forms of online communication in the previous year, to communicate with people they did not know face-to-face. For some of these youths, the online strangers were in fact friends-of-friends. Twenty-five percent of the participants reported forming a casual online friendship, while 14% reported forming a close online friendship, 7% had a face-to-face meeting, and 2% had established an online romantic relationship. In all, 17% of young people reported establishing some form of close online relationship. The majority of participants stated that mutual interests and activities were what initially drew them together. Of the 101 young people who had face-to-face encounters, 77% were accompanied to the meeting by a friend or relative, 1% were made to feel afraid at the meeting, and none of the youths were physically or sexually assaulted at the meeting.

Reassuringly, the majority of teens in the Wolak, Mitchell and Finkelhor study who met their online friends face-to-face, were accompanied to the meeting. This caution in face-to-face encounters is consistent with research conducted with a group of 30 undergraduates who regularly used the Internet. In this study, 80% of the undergraduates had formed online friendships and 33% met their online friends face-to-face. Most of the participants reported that they were careful to protect their anonymity and took precautions before meeting face-to-face. Nonetheless, not all teens are cautious, which raises serious concerns for parents.

In contrast to the relatively small number of face-to-face encounters reported in the Wolak, Mitchell & Finkelhor study, are findings from a survey conducted in Japan and reported by Yasumasa Kioka of the Japanese National Policy Agency at a conference earlier this year. Japan adopted the latest third- generation (3G) technologies early on, thus Japanese children were some of the first to use mobile-Internet services. In 2002, Japan had 3,401 "dating sites" available from Internet-mobiles and Kioka reported that a survey completed in 2002 showed that 22% of female high school students and 18% of male high school students had used one of these dating sites.

Of these, 43% of females and 28% of males had met their date face-to-face. The arrest statistics for dating sites in Japan showed that 84% of a total of 1,517 crime victims were children under the age of 18 and that the majority of dating site crimes were related to mobile-Internet use.

Fears that children and teens may be tracked on the Internet to their home addresses are also not entirely without foundation. Although many web sites have privacy policies, they do not cover the advertising banners that pop up seemingly endlessly when accessing many web sites. Young people may be lulled into a false sense of security when on the Internet and may disclose sensitive information. In research conducted in the US with 304 youth aged 10 to 17 years, one-third of younger teens or "tweens" aged 10 to 12 years reported visiting chat rooms while half of those aged 13 to 17 years reported doing so. Of those going online, 73% said they "look to see if a web site has a privacy policy before answering any questions" and 79% agreed that teenagers should get consent from their parents before they give out information online. However, many of the youngsters in this study were prepared to give out sensitive information when a free gift was offered. Interestingly, gender differences were found, with girls less prepared than boys to provide information to web sites in return for a free gift; girls were also less prepared than boys to trust web sites not to share information with others. Girls were also significantly more likely than were boys to have talked to their parents about how to deal with giving out information on the web. While this study suggests that many teens are conscious of cyber-safety, a sizeable minority are not. Lack of caution was also shown by teens surveyed in the Pew Internet and American Life Project, with 22% of online teens who used IM reporting that they had shared their password with a friend.

Although many parents report closely supervising children's Internet use, there appears to be a gap between children's reporting of parental supervision and parents' reporting, with parents saying they keep a closer eye on children's Internet use than their children report. This inconsistency might be due to teens being unaware of their parents' supervision; alternatively, parents may be over-reporting their level of supervision.

For parents who are particularly concerned that their children may be accessing inappropriate material on the Net, there are various tools which can be used to block access, such as filters, labels and safe zones. A good Internet site, which provides information about these tools and other tips on safety for both children and parents, is the Australian Broadcasting Authority Cybersmart Kids site. . . .

Teens in Cyberspace: Finding Friend or Foe?

There appears to be strong agreement between parents and teens that the Internet is a valuable tool that helps young people with their schoolwork. For many young people the Internet is also useful for entertainment, information and social communication. Although no definite figures exist for the numbers of teenagers that use the Internet to "excess," it is likely that those who are neglecting their schoolwork, their sports and their leisure activities in order to surf the Net, are in danger of becoming addicted.

It is likely that children and teens will be subject to occasional violent and pornographic images and parents need to be aware of this and discuss it with their children. Older teens are more vulnerable than younger teens to this type of exposure, probably because of the amount of time they spend on the Net and perhaps because they are more likely than younger children to explore more and varied sites. The consequences of young people's exposure to pornography are not yet known; however, research with adults suggests negative consequences. In particular, exposure to violent pornography has been found to be associated with violence against women and repeated exposure to non-violent pornography has been found to be associated with the promotion of more permissive sexual attitudes.

To date, research suggests that online relationships of some kind, whether casual or close, are formed by large numbers of teens. Reassuringly for parents, most of these relationships seem to be extensions of the young person's social circle. The early evidence from American studies suggests that cyber-safety is not a big problem as yet; however, evidence from Japan suggests otherwise. Japan is perhaps a few years ahead of most other countries in terms of ease of Internet accessibility. Nonetheless, it remains to be seen whether the problems with "dating sites" is one that is peculiar to Japanese culture, or whether the type of problem currently seen in Japan will emerge in Australia and other Western cultures in the near future.

For some children and young people, the anonymity of online relationships may be helpful as they go about practising their social communications. Teens with healthy, happy offline relationships are likely to continue to explore and expand those relationships further via online chat. Young people who are geographically remote, disabled or housebound due to illness, may find online chat an important form of communication. However, of concern, is the fact that a small minority of young people who are socially anxious or lonely may deliberately seek out relationships online.

Parents need to be aware that some children and teens will form close, intimate relationships online. Existing relationships that are extended and consolidated on the Internet, appear to be healthy ones although the jury is still out on the quality of relationships that are newly formed online. It is important that parents discuss issues of Internet safety with children and teens and try to discourage face-to-face meetings; however, if these do take place, children and even older teens should be accompanied to the meeting by a friend or family member and it should occur in a very public place. Girls appear to have taken the messages of privacy and safety to heart more than boys have. This may be due to parents talking more to their daughters about Internet safety than to their sons.

The Internet is a juggernaut which parents cannot stop. Even without home access, many teens have access to the Internet at school, at friends' houses or at Internet cafés. Rather than banning online communication, parents need to be aware of what children and adolescents are doing online by talking to them about their Internet use and showing an interest in what they are doing. Imposing some restrictions on the information that young people are allowed to disclose online and imposing restrictions on the amount of time spent online are first steps towards keeping kids safe. Even though many teens appear Net-savvy, they still need to be reminded of the potential dangers lurking online. There may be many friends in cyberspace but there are undoubtedly a number of foes.

MICHELE FLEMING is a lecturer in the Center for Applied Psychology at the University of Canberra, Australia. Her current research focuses on the effects of new media, such as video games and the Internet, on children's well-being.

DEBRA RICKWOOD is an associate professor in psychology at the University of Canberra, Australia. Her research interests include adolescent help-seeking behavior and the use of new media with regard to enhancing the well-being of young people in Australia.

Chang-Hoan Cho and
Hongsik John Cheon

Children's Exposure to Negative Internet Content: Effects of Family Content

The Internet has become an indispensable element of life for most people in the contemporary world, and children are not excluded. Because of the ubiquitous availability of Internet access, in schools and libraries, children are increasingly becoming involved in this new technology. As of December 2003, 23 million children in the United States ages 6 to 17 have Internet access at home, which is a threefold increase since 2000. According to a survey conducted by the Corporation for Public Broadcasting in July 2002, 78% of family households with children have Internet access at home. A survey by Yahoo and Carat showed that children ages 12 to 17 used the Internet an average of 16.7 hours per week in 2003. Given this extensive usage, the Internet has the potential to be a very powerful socialization agent.

The Internet has a double-edged sword characteristic for children: providing many opportunities for learning while exposing children to potentially negative content. The Internet not only provides significant benefits for children, such as research access, socialization, entertainment, and a communication tool with families, but it also connotes negative aspects such as violence, pornography, hate sites, isolation, predators, and commercialism. The Web sites considered detrimental include those dedicated to negative content such as pornography, violent online games, online gambling, and so forth. For example, many children can easily access pornographic content on the Internet. They can also be accidentally exposed to numerous obscene pop-up banner ads and extensive pornographic content when they type seemingly innocent key words into a search engine, for example, the name of a singer such as Britney Spears, Christina Aguilera, or Madonna. According to Finkelhor et al., 25% of the respondents ($n = 1,501$, ages 10–17) reported receiving unwanted exposure to sexual materials while online, and 19% received a sexual solicitation online.

Despite the potential negative effects on children using the Internet, more than 30% of surveyed parents had not discussed the downside of Internet use with their children, and 62% of parents of teenagers did not realize that their children had visited inappropriate Web sites. Recognizing the ever-serious negative aspects of children using the Internet and parents' possible underestimation of, or ignorance about, their children's Internet usage and its effects, this study explores the degree of children's exposure to negative Internet content and detects the possible discrepancy between what parents think their children are doing online and their children's actual activities. In doing so, this study carefully dissects the possible causes and consequences of perceived parental control over children's Internet usage. Concerned that inappropriate Internet content may jeopardize the health or safety of children, the present study is a crucial attempt that aims to address the following research inquires with regard to children's Internet usage: (a) to understand the degree to which children are exposed to negative Internet content, (b) to detect a possible discrepancy between parents' perception and children's actual exposure to negative Internet content, (c) to examine various antecedents explaining perceived parental control over children's Internet usage, and (d) to suggest various ways to decrease children's exposure to negative Internet content.

Literature Review

In fall 2002, 99% of public schools in the United States had access to the Internet and 64% of children ages 5 to 17 had Internet access at home (National Center for Education Statistics, 2002). Children ages 13 to 17 spent more time online than watching television—3.5 hours versus 3.1 hours per day, and used the Internet mostly for exploration (surfing and searching), followed by education (learning and homework), multimedia (music, video, etc.), communications (e-mail, chat, and instant messages), games, and e-commerce. The place children were most likely to use the Internet was in the home, rather than at a library or school: 20% of children ages 8 to 16 had a computer in their bedroom, of which 54% had Internet access.

Negative Effects of Using the Internet

There is an increasing concern from educators, psychologists, and parents about the negative effects of using the Internet on the physical (e.g., information fatigue syndrome), cognitive (e.g., inability to discriminate between the real and cyber world), and social development (e.g., identity confusion) of children, among which, detriment to social development (hurting children's skills and patience to conduct necessary social relations in the real world) is a paramount problem. One of the most serious concerns regarding children's social development involves the proliferation and easy accessibility of negative content on the Internet, such as pornography, violence, hate speech, gambling, sexual solicitation, and so forth. It is easy to see how these types of negative content harm children and destroy their development. Extant literature shows that children's exposure to inappropriate media content yields many negative outcomes such as increased aggression, fear, desensitization, poor school performance, prevalence of symptoms of psychological trauma, antisocial behavior, negative self-perception, low self-esteem, lack of reality, identity confusion, and more.

In particular, sexually explicit materials on the Internet can desensitize children to deviant sexual stimuli and encourage them to enact antisocial aggressive sexual behaviors. Furthermore, the anonymity of the Internet makes it easier for pedophiles to approach children through online chatting. Children who spend hours in chat rooms looking for friends or just passing time can be easily targeted and abused by unknown adult sexual offenders. Violent online games are another serious concern. It is known that violent computer games increase children's physical, verbal, relational, and antisocial aggressions. These negative effects of violent games on children are even more serious regarding the Internet because access to such violent games has become easier for unsupervised children due to free or fee-based online games. Online gambling has also been cited as a serious Internet problem affecting children. It can seriously disrupt children's social and psychological development, for example, addiction, being unable to repay debts, missing school, and so forth.

However, little is known about children's actual amount of exposure to such inappropriate content and activities on the Internet. Extant literature shows that a discrepancy exists between the reports of parents and children on children's media usage; for example, parents tend to underestimate time spent on television viewing and the amount of violence to which children are exposed. This discrepancy leads parents to underrate the impact of media messages on their children and to not exert much control over their children's media use. Surprisingly, 38% of surveyed children ages 8 to 18 said that their parents do not enforce any rules on watching television, 95% of older children watch television without their parents, and 81% of children ages 2 to 7 watch television unsupervised. This may be true for children's Internet usage, but we know little about the possible discrepancy between parental estimates and children's actual Internet usage. In this vein, the present study tries to detect the degree to which children are exposed to these sources of negative content and whether parents overestimate or underestimate their children's exposure to such content. In doing so, this study strives to examine how children's exposure to such negative Internet content relates to the social context of Internet usage, that is, the role of family

communication and relationship on children's exposure to such content.

Social Context of Children's Internet Use

People use media within a social realm, and children are no exception. Social context of media usage, especially parental influence, is crucial in children's social development. However, many social aspects of children's Internet usage are still unknown. Therefore, this study focuses on the social context of children's Internet use, especially relative to family environment such as parental guidance, influence, and relationship with children.

Children live within a family boundary; therefore, parental influence on children's media usage and effect is very important. Extant research shows that family communication exerts the greatest influence on children's socialization and development. Stemming from political socialization research, family communication patterns have been widely applied to various socialization contexts such as consumption, political process, media usage, and so forth. In particular, in mass media research, it was found that family communication patterns mediate the extent and type of children's mass media use and effects, for example, watching public affairs television programs, interest in and knowledge about politics, imitating their parents' television usage, interpreting televised violence, attitude towards nontraditional sex roles, child consumer learning, and so forth.

More specifically, concerning children's Internet usage, Wartella et al. found that parental attitude and guidance significantly influence children's judgment of quality Internet materials. Recognizing the importance of family context on children's Internet usage, the present study tries to examine the role of family context (parent–child communication, relationship, and activity) on children's exposure to Internet content and parents' control over children's Internet use. In short, the research contributes to this area in the following three aspects: (a) understanding children's actual Internet usage in terms of content, not by Web sites or general activities; (b) examining the role of family environment on children's negative Internet exposure; and (c) providing a theoretical framework to explain children's exposure to negative Internet content and parents' perceived control over their children's Internet usage. . . .

Discussion

This study was an exploratory study to understand children's exposure to negative Internet content. The objective was to provide insight into family context factors that influence children's exposure to negative Internet content and to test their proposed interrelationships. In pursuing that goal, a theoretical model of children's negative Internet exposure was synthesized from the theoretical traditions of a representative body of diverse referent disciplines. Possible contributions of this study are threefold.

First, it is the first attempt toward understanding children's negative Internet exposure in terms of content, rather than by Web sites or general activities. Second, this study builds a theoretical model explaining children's exposure to negative Internet content. Third, the study identifies the importance of family environment on children's negative Internet exposure and suggests two important family context variables that reduce children's exposure to negative content.

This study found that parents generally underestimate their children's exposure to negative Internet content. This finding suggests that children are more exposed to negative Internet content than what parents expect. It implies that the effect of negative Internet content on children can be more serious than what most parents estimate. Moreover, among various demographic variables such as family income, parents' education level, and age and gender of children, only the gender of children is related to children's exposure to negative content (male children are exposed to negative content more than female children). This finding suggests that demographic variables do little to explain children's negative Internet exposure, which amplifies the importance of identifying other significant factors that explain children's Internet exposure. This study proposed family relationship, interaction, and control as important antecedents of children's exposure to negative Internet content and built a theoretical model on the effect of family context on children's negative exposure.

The acceptable fit of the final model generally supports the stated hypotheses: Parents' perceived control is explained by shared Web activity and family cohesion, and perceived control results in more appropriate use of the Internet by their children (less exposure to negative Internet content). . . . There was a significant effect of family cohesion/intimacy on parents' perceived control over children's Internet usage. The result suggests that parents who perceive high family cohesion/intimacy tend to have high perceived control over their children's Internet usage. This finding implies that parents need to maintain intimate emotional bonding with their children to have better understanding of, and control over, their children's behaviors (negative Internet exposure). The result is consistent with previous studies on the role of family cohesion on the parent–child relationship, and this study substantiates the importance of family cohesion in the context of children's negative Internet exposure.

. . . Findings demonstrate a significant effect of shared Web activities on parents' perceived control over children's Internet usage. The result implies that parents who spend more time online with their children are more likely to have high perceived control over their children's Internet usage. The result is consistent with previous studies on the role of shared family activities on parent–child mutual understanding and children's media usage and learning. This study further confirms the importance of shared family activities in the context of children's negative Internet exposure. Although not initially hypothesized, a new causal relationship (family cohesion → shared Web activity) was discovered. This relationship seems conceptually sound because high emotional bonding among parents and children may lead to more shared activities and interactions between them. Actually, previous studies have demonstrated the positive relationship between family bonding and family interaction.

Unexpectedly, however, the effect of parents' Internet skill on perceived control over children's Internet usage was not confirmed. The hypothesized relationship was derived from "flow" research (more skill, higher cognitive control), but the result failed to show the importance of parents' Internet skill on the perceived control over their children's Internet usage. The finding suggests that parents' Internet knowledge and skill do not necessarily give high competency and control to parents; instead, emotional bonding and shared Web activities contribute to increase parents' perceived control over children's Internet usage. In terms of relative importance, shared Web activity exhibited the strongest predicting power of parents' perceived control ($\gamma = .43$), followed by family cohesion ($\gamma = .39$). The result suggests that the most important contributor of parents' perceived control over children's Internet usage is shared Web activities between parents and children. In addition, parents' perceived control led to decreased children's exposure to negative Internet content. This suggests that parents' perceived control through shared Web activities and family cohesion actually reduces children's exposure to negative Internet content.

The findings of the present research provide substantial implications for child education in school and at home. This study suggests possible home education strategies to parents, for example, locating the computer in a common area and having regular shared Internet sessions, encouraging children to evaluate Web sites and Internet ads and commenting on and explaining the subjects, teaching quality Web browsing and clicking choices, building and maintaining family love, affirmation and intimate relationship with children, and so forth. Parental oversight and interaction through these home education strategies can help reduce the temptation for children to use the computer to explore inappropriate content. The results of the study also can help educational organizations and governmental agencies develop various workshops or educational programs for children and parents to teach quality Internet use and importance of family context in children's negative Internet exposure. The study also provides implications for government regulations regarding Web sites that are potentially negative to children, for example, the need for developing a universal rating system for inappropriate Internet content (such as early childhood, everyone, teen, mature, and adults only) and requiring the Web sites to post the rating to better inform children and parents about the content of the Web sites before they observe the content.

Limitations and Future Research

This study has several noted limitations. The first concern relates to sampling issues. First, the sample was relatively more upscale in terms of reported family income and parent education level than reflected in the sample school's general student population. Second, the sample size of 178 was relatively small and was not a national sample. Third, the sample was limited to children ages 11 to 16. Therefore, it would be valuable to replicate the present study with a larger and more representative national sample including younger, more vulnerable children. Another concern is that the study employed self-reported measurement of children's Internet exposure without any actual observation of the children's behavior. Even though this study tried to address social desirability effects by assuring the anonymity of participants and employing accidental exposure, as well as intentional exposure, there is still a chance that social desirability may have factored into the responses. Hence, it would be fruitful to conduct an experiment that directly measures actual children's Internet exposure (e.g., log file analysis, surveillance software, etc.) by controlling social desirability effects. Similarly, for the measure of parents' control, it might be more valid to assess actual behavioral control, instead of perceived control, for example, how often parents intervene, monitor, filter, and/or supervise. In addition, the list of inappropriate Internet content could have been more exhaustive; for example, hate Web sites were not included. Hence, it would be useful to include a more exhaustive list of inappropriate content for future research. Last, family communications patterns inventory could be another important indicator of parents' perceived control of their children's use of the Internet. Therefore, the relationship would be worthwhile for future study.

In conclusion, this study has provided a theoretical framework for understanding the role of family environment on children's negative Internet exposure, such as family cohesion, shared Web activity, and parents' perceived control. The proposed model is an initial step in understanding the relationship between family context and children's exposure to negative Internet content. Theoretical approaches to understanding children's Internet exposure have rarely been conducted in previous literature, and this study was undertaken to guide future empirical research and theoretical work. For example, the focus was on the family environment from the parents' perspective. It would be worthwhile to examine children's perspectives of family context, such as the role of children's Internet skill, children's perceived intimacy with their parents, children's perceived shared Web activities with their parents, and children's perceived control over Internet content. Second, this study only examined the role of family environment on children's negative Internet exposure. It should be noted that other social contexts might also be crucial in children's media usage. For example, children interact with other peer students outside family boundaries in school or other places. Children's exposure to negative content may be influenced by their interactions with other peer children. In addition, education in school on quality Internet usage may also significantly reduce children's negative Internet exposure. Therefore, as future research, it would be fruitful to examine the effects of peer interaction and school education on children's exposure to negative Internet content.

CHANG-HOAN CHO is an assistant professor of advertising, College of Journalism and Communications, University of Florida. His research interests include Internet advertising, new media technology, product placement, interactive television, multicultural advertising, and international advertising.

HONGSIK JOHN CHEON is an assistant professor in the department of marketing and finance, College of Business, at Frostburg State University. His research interests include interactive marketing, international marketing, and consumer information processing.

EXPLORING THE ISSUE

Is the Internet a Safe Place for Teens to Explore?

Critical Thinking and Reflection

1. What are some of the concerns with children and teens being on the Internet that were mentioned in both articles?
2. What did the authors identify as some ways in which parents can help decrease their child/teen's exposure to negative Internet material? Can you think of any other ways parents can help ensure their teen's safety?
3. Cho and Cheon conducted a study examining how parental guidance, influence, and relationship with their children affect children's Internet use. What were their findings and how are they significant to families?
4. The YES article argues that although there are dangers on the Internet, with proper monitoring and teaching from parents, teens can be safe while utilizing this resource. The NO article points out that parents many times underestimate the dangers that their children/teens are exposed to, although their study points out that high parental involvement tends to decrease this as well. What is your opinion of teens' safety and the Internet?

Is There Common Ground?

The articles presented in this issue cited information as early as 1998; 13 years ago. What technologies have been developed with Internet browsers and antivirus protection to help combat inappropriate pop-up material that might be viewed by children?

Another Internet problem that has become prevalent since these articles were published, and was not addressed, is Internet bullying (cyberbullying) among children and teens. What are some of the negative consequences that can result from this problem and what ideas do you have for helping parents prevent this from occurring?

In Cho and Cheon's study, they found that parents' knowledge and skill with regard to the Internet was not directly related to perceived control over their child's Internet use. However, does this mean that parents do not need to have general knowledge of their computer and the Internet to ensure their child's safety? How can parent's level of knowledge affect their ability to monitor their child's Internet use?

Create Central

www.mhhe.com/createcentral

Additional Resources

National Center for Missing and Exploited Children. (2010). Net Smartz Workshop. Retrieved on April 29, 2011, from www.netsmartz.org/Teens

This website provides information about remaining safe online and also has videos of teens telling their own stories of becoming victims of online predators and other situations.

Teens Health. (2011). Internet Safety: Safe Surfing Tips for Teens. Retrieved on April 29, 2011, from http://kidshealth.org/teen/safety/safebasics/internet_safety.html

This website provides information for teens to help them identify information that should always be kept private as well as how to deal with encountering uncomfortable situations in chat rooms or handling cyberbullying.

Washington State Office of the Attorney General. (2008). Internet Safety. Retrieved on April 29, 2011, from www.atg.wa.gov/InternetSafety/Teens.aspx

This site provides information and tips on how to remain safe on the Internet and social networking sites. It provides some scenarios and points out common mistakes that teens make while using the Internet that can put them at risk.

Internet References . . .

Palo Alto Medical Foundation

www.pamf.org/teen/life/risktaking/internet.html

Huffington Post

www.huffingtonpost.com/news/internet-safety

Microsoft Safer Online Facebook page

www.facebook.com/saferonline

Selected, Edited, and with Issue Framing Material by:
Kourtney Vaillancourt, *New Mexico State University*

ISSUE

Do Video Games Increase Aggression in Teenagers?

YES: **Brad Bushman**, from "Video Games Can Spark Aggression," *Daily News* (March 2013)

NO: **Benedict Carey**, from "Shooting in the Dark," *NY Times* (February 2013)

Learning Outcomes

After reading this issue, you should be able to:

- Describe some of the evidence that indicates that video games can contribute to increased violence.
- Discuss some of the reasons that it may not be possible to definitively prove that video games cause violence.
- Describe the difficulty in ascertaining a cause and effect relationship for video games and violence.

ISSUE SUMMARY

YES: Brad Bushman recognizes that there is no definitive way to prove that violent video games cause violence. However, he describes evidence that they do contribute to an increase in aggressive behaviors. He concludes with the recommendation that we as a society should limit access to violent video games for children and teens.

NO: Benedict Carey highlights the debate about how much video games contribute to increased societal violence. He shares findings from three types of studies: short-term lab experiments, long-term studies, and correlational studies. Included are recommendations for parents about how to manage their child's exposure to video games.

In a time when violence is seemingly becoming commonplace, it is natural that society begins to look for ways to prevent mass shootings, bombings, and other senseless acts of violence toward others. Each time a tragedy occurs, the media turns to discussions about what caused the perpetrators to become violent and to act out in extreme ways. If it would be possible to pinpoint where someone received the influence to become violent, the hope would be that preventative strategies could then be employed. One commonly accused culprit, especially for violence among males, is the video game.

In the United States, video games represent a $13.6 billion industry. According to a *Harvard Mental Health Newsletter,* the Pew Research Center provides statistics from 2008 that indicate 97 percent of 12- to 17-year olds play some type of video game, two thirds of which played action and adventure games with violent content.

Another study found that over half of all video games that are rated by the Entertainment Software Ratings Board (ESRB) included violence, even 90 percent which were rated for children as young as 10.

And, while video games used to be accessed only through computers and gaming systems, they are now mobile with the increased use of smart phones and tablet devices. So, it is understandable that parents and researchers would like to know if these games are exerting a negative influence on their players, and if so, can that influence be mitigated by other factors.

As you read the following selections, think about the people in your life who play video games. Consider the information presented and think about how it relates to your own experiences. And, try to identify strategies that you believe might be important for parents to employ when making decisions about their child(ren)'s video game habits.

Brad Bushman

Video Games Can Spark Aggression

Maybe not the cause of violence, but certainly a contributing factor

When terrible shooting sprees occur, people start looking for easy answers to the problem of violence in our society. They want to identify "the" cause: guns, psychosis, the culture, etc.

In the wake of Newtown, much scrutiny has fallen on violent video games. Recent reports suggest that Adam Lanza may have been obsessed with other shooting rampages and was following a script, as if he were a shooter in a violent video game.

It is crucial to understand there is no single cause of a crime like Lanza's, and no responsible scholar could claim that violent video games cause murder.

But as one who has spent years researching these products and their effects, I'm here to tell you that it's also fair to say that playing violent video games again and again does, in fact, make young people more aggressive.

Significant and repeated exposure to violent video games is not healthy for young people, especially young people who are otherwise maladjusted.

Those who believe otherwise constantly pose this question to me: "I've played violent video games for years. Why am I not a killer?"

My answer is usually pretty simple. You come from a good, stable home. You have friends. You weren't bullied in school. You have a healthy brain.

People want to believe that if millions of people play violent video games and they don't all become killers, then those games must be harmless.

Unfortunately, that's not true. We haven't "proven" video games directly cause violence because it can't be proven. There is no way to ethically run experiments that see if some threshold of playing a violent game like Call of Duty may push a person into violence.

But that doesn't mean we are left without evidence. We know that video game violence is certainly correlated with violence—just like smoking is correlated with lung cancer. We know from many experimental studies that playing violent video games causes less serious forms of aggressive behavior.

In one recent experiment, for example, I and several colleagues found that typical college students who played video games for 20 minutes at a time for three consecutive days showed increasingly higher levels of aggressive behavior each day they played. How might weeks and months and years of playing such games affect a person who has other risk factors for violent behavior?

Of course, one can always find a few studies that say video game violence is harmless. But in one analysis I co-authored, we found that scientists who believe video game violence is harmful have published over 48 times more studies in top-tier scientific journals than did those who believe it is not harmful.

In other words, scientists who have done the best work on the subject are more likely to believe the media violence is harmful.

I am not blaming real-life violence solely on video games. Violent criminal behavior is complex. It is caused by many factors, many of which are outside our control. But if you list all the factors that we know are associated with violent behavior, the use of violent video games is one of tho easiest for society—and for parents—to control.

Being a male is associated with violence. That's not something we can change. Peer rejection is a strong risk factor for violence. That's not something that most parents can control, either.

But we as a society can make it more difficult for children and teens to get access to violent video games. Parents can ban them from their homes and talk to their children about avoiding them at friends' houses.

Will this eliminate violence? Of course not. But that's not an excuse to avoid doing what we can to protect our children.

BRAD BUSHMAN is a professor of communication and psychology at Ohio State University.

Benedict Carey

Shooting in the Dark

The young men who opened fire at Columbine High School, at the movie theater in Aurora, Colo., and in other massacres had this in common: they were video gamers who seemed to be acting out some dark digital fantasy. It was as if all that exposure to computerized violence gave them the idea to go on a rampage—or at least fueled their urges.

But did it really?

Social scientists have been studying and debating the effects of media violence on behavior since the 1950s, and video games in particular since the 1980s. The issue is especially relevant today, because the games are more realistic and bloodier than ever, and because most American boys play them at some point. Girls play at lower rates and are significantly less likely to play violent games.

A burst of new research has begun to clarify what can and cannot be said about the effects of violent gaming. Playing the games can and does stir hostile urges and mildly aggressive behavior in the short term. Moreover, youngsters who develop a gaming habit can become slightly more aggressive—as measured by clashes with peers, for instance—at least over a period of a year or two.

Yet it is not at all clear whether, over longer periods, such a habit increases the likelihood that a person will commit a violent crime, like murder, rape, or assault, much less a Newtown-like massacre. (Such calculated rampages are too rare to study in any rigorous way, researchers agree.)

"I don't know that a psychological study can ever answer that question definitively," said Michael R. Ward, an economist at the University of Texas, Arlington. "We are left to glean what we can from the data and research on video game use that we have."

The research falls into three categories: short-term laboratory experiments; longer-term studies, often based in schools; and correlation studies—between playing time and aggression, for instance, or between video game sales and trends in violent crimes.

Lab experiments confirm what any gamer knows in his gut: playing games like, "Killzone 3" or "Battlefield 3" stirs the blood. In one recent study, Christophe, a psychologist at Iowa State University, led a research team that had 47 undergraduates play "Mortal Kombat: Deadly Alliance" for 15 minutes. Afterward, the team took various measures of arousal, both physical and psychological. It also tested whether the students would behave more aggressively, by having them dole out hot sauce to a fellow student who, they were told, did not like spicy food but had to swallow the sauce.

Sure enough, compared with a group who had played a nonviolent video game, those who had been engaged in "Mortal Kombat" were more aggressive across the board. They gave their fellow students significantly bigger portions of the hot sauce.

Many similar studies have found the same thing: A dose of violent gaming makes people act a little more rudely than they would otherwise, at least for a few minutes after playing.

It is far harder to determine whether cumulative exposure leads to real-world hostility over the long term. Some studies in schools have found that over time digital warriors get into increasing numbers of scrapes with peers—fights in the schoolyard, for example. In a report published last summer, psychologists at Brock University in Ontario found that longer periods of violent video game playing among high school students predicted a slightly higher number of such incidents over time.

"None of these extreme acts, like a school shooting, occurs because of only one risk factor; there are many factors, including feeling socially isolated, being bullied, and so on," said Craig A. Anderson, a psychologist at Iowa State University. "But if you look at the literature, I think it's clear that violent media is one factor; it's not the largest factor, but it's also not the smallest."

Most researchers in the field agree with Dr. Anderson, but not all of them. Some studies done in schools or elsewhere have found that it is aggressive children who are the most likely to be drawn to violent video games in the first place; they are self-selected to be in more schoolyard conflicts. And some studies are not able to control for outside factors, like family situation or mood problems.

"This is a pool of research that, so far, has not been very well done," said Christopher J. Ferguson, associate professor of psychology and criminal justice at Texas A &M International University and a critic of the field whose own research has found no link. "I look at it and I can't say what it means."

Neither Dr. Ferguson, nor others interviewed in this article, receive money from the gaming industry.

Many psychologists argue that violent video games "socialize" children over time, prompting them to imitate the behavior of the game's characters, the cartoonish machismo, the hair-trigger rage, the dismissive brutality. Children also imitate flesh and blood people in their lives, of course—parents, friends, teachers, siblings—and one question that researchers have not yet answered is when, exactly, a habit is so consuming that its influence trumps the socializing effects of other major figures in a child's life.

That is, what constitutes a bad habit? In surveys about 80 percent of high school-age boys say they play video games, most of which are thought to be violent, and perhaps a third to a half of those players have had a habit of 10 hours a week or more.

The proliferation of violent video games has not coincided with spikes in youth violent crime. The number of violent youth offenders fell by more than half between 1994 and 2010, to 224 per 100,000 population, according to government statistics, while video game sales have more than doubled since 1996.

In a working paper now available online, Dr. Ward and two colleagues examined week-by-week sales data for violent video games, across a wide range of communities. Violence rates are seasonal, generally higher in summer than in winter; so are video game sales, which peak during the holidays. The researchers controlled for those trends and analyzed crime rates in the month or so after surges in sales, in communities with a high concentrations of young people, like college towns.

"We found that higher rates of violent video game sales related to a decrease in crimes, and especially violent crimes," said Dr. Ward, whose co-authors were A. Scott Cunningham of Baylor University and Benjamin Engelstätter of the Center for European Economic Research in Mannheim, Germany.

No one knows for sure what these findings mean. It may be that playing video games for hours every day keeps people off the streets who would otherwise be getting into trouble. It could be that the games provide "an outlet" that satisfies violent urges in some players—a theory that many psychologists dismiss but that many players believe.

Or the two trends may be entirely unrelated.

"At the very least, parents should be aware of what's in the games their kids are playing," Dr. Anderson said, "and think of it from a socialization point of view: what kind of values, behavioral skills, and social scripts is the child learning?"

Benedict Carey is an American journalist and reporter on medical and science topics for *The New York Times*.

EXPLORING THE ISSUE

Do Video Games Increase Aggression in Teenagers?

Critical Thinking and Reflection

1. Explain how video games and violent behaviors have been connected to one another.
2. What can parents do when making decisions about their child(ren)'s video game habits to mitigate any effects that video games might have on their child(ren)?
3. Do you believe that society would be supportive of a change in video games' accessibility for children as a way to attempt violence prevention? Why or why not?

Is There Common Ground?

Probably everyone can agree that too much of any activity is not optimal for development. In the case of video games, no one is purporting that children should be allowed unlimited access to games of any type. However, the argument lies in the notion of whether we can attribute violent outburst that are harmful to others to someone's use of video games. The mitigating factors become important, and are acknowledged by both sides. For example, should parents make their own decisions about the appropriateness of a particular games' content for their child, or should the ratings system be beefed up and an unquestionable guide for parents to follow? And, as smart phones are increasing the availability and immediacy of games, how should society respond and react? Finally, it is important that, no matter anyone's opinion about video games

specifically, society continues to work on preventing violence and aggressive behaviors.

Create Central

www.mhhe.com/createcentral

Additional Resources

Entertainment Software Ratings Board, ESRB Ratings Guide. Retrieved on May 21, 2013, from www.esrb.org/ratings/ratings_guide.jsp

Fact Monster, Video Games Rating System. Retrieved on May 21, 2013, from www.factmonster.com/science/computers/video-game-rating-system.html

Internet Reference . . .

Office of Justice Programs, Youth Violence Prevention. Retrieved on May 21, 2013

www.ojp.gov/programs/youthviolenceprevention.htm

Selected, Edited, and with Issue Framing Material by:
Kourtney Vaillancourt, *New Mexico State University*

ISSUE

Is Cyberbullying Really a Problem?

YES: stopbullying.gov, from "What Is Cyberbullying?" (U.S. Department of Health and Human Services)

NO: Nick Gillespie, from "Stop Panicking About Bullies," *The Wall Street Journal* (April 2012)

Learning Outcomes

After reading this issue, you should be able to:

- Describe some of the effects that bullying may have on a child or adolescent.
- Discuss the reasons why bullying has gained so much media attention in recent years.
- List some ways in which parents can intervene if their child is the victim of a bully.

ISSUE SUMMARY

YES: stopbullying.gov defines cyberbullying and the potential effects it can have on victims. It also discusses the frequency of cyberbullying, according to recent studies.

NO: Nick Gillespie acknowledges that bullying occurs, but argues that there are other issues that parents should be more concerned about. He discusses some of the reasons he believes that people have become so sensitive to bullying, and how it may be impacting parenting strategies.

No one would deny that being bullied is a problem. For decades studies have focused on how bullying impacts both the victim and the perpetrator. Programs worldwide have worked on preventative programs to keep bullying out of schools. The I-SAFE Foundation reports that over half of all teens have been bullied online, and also over half of all teens have engaged in cyberbullying of someone else. The foundation also states that one in three young people experience threats online, 25 percent have been repeatedly bullied through cell phones and online. And, at least half of young people do not report the bullying to their parents, and only one in five reports to law enforcement.

The numbers are generally not being debated. What is being debated, however, is how serious cyberbullying actually is with regard to long-term impact on the victim. Society has a tendency to minimize threats that come from electronic sources due to the usual lack of physical danger.

Technology can provide tremendous opportunities and conveniences, and most of us would be reluctant to give it up. However, as you read the following selections, consider how technology is changing the face of bullies and the ways that victims are being impacted. Is the psychological, as opposed to physical, damage real and of great concern? Or, is it simply "harmless" and "over blown"?

Stopbullying.Gov

What Is Cyberbullying?

Cyberbullying is *bullying* that takes place using electronic technology. Electronic technology includes devices and equipment such as cell phones, computers, and tablets as well as communication tools including social media sites, text messages, chat, and websites.

Examples of cyberbullying include mean text messages or emails, rumors sent by email or posted on social networking sites, and embarrassing pictures, videos, websites, or fake profiles. . . .

Why Cyberbullying Is Different

Kids who are being cyberbullied are often bullied in person as well. Additionally, kids who are cyberbullied have a harder time getting away from the behavior.

- Cyberbullying can happen 24 hours a day, 7 days a week, and reach a kid even when he or she is alone. It can happen any time of the day or night.
- Cyberbullying messages and images can be posted anonymously and distributed quickly to a very wide audience. It can be difficult and sometimes impossible to trace the source.
- Deleting inappropriate or harassing messages, texts, and pictures is extremely difficult after they have been posted or sent.

Effects of Cyberbullying

Cell phones and computers themselves are not to blame for cyberbullying. Social media sites can be used for positive activities, like connecting kids with friends and family,

helping students with school, and for entertainment. But these tools can also be used to hurt other people. Whether done in person or through technology, the effects of bullying are similar.

Kids who are cyberbullied are more likely to:

- Use alcohol and drugs
- Skip school
- Experience in-person bullying
- Be unwilling to attend school
- Receive poor grades
- Have lower self-esteem
- Have more health problems

Frequency of Cyberbullying

The 2008–2009 *School Crime Supplement* (National Center for Education Statistics and Bureau of Justice Statistics) indicates that 6% of students in grades 6–12 experienced cyberbullying.

The 2011 *Youth Risk Behavior Surveillance Survey* finds that 16% of high school students (grades 9–12) were electronically bullied in the past year.

Research on cyberbullying is growing. However, because kids' technology use changes rapidly, it is difficult to design surveys that accurately capture trends. . . .

STOPBULLYING.gov is a federal government website managed by the U.S. Department of Health & Human Services designed to bring education and awareness, and provide resources to the public about the issue of bullying.

Nick Gillespie

NO

Stop Panicking About Bullies

Childhood is safer than ever before, but today's parents need to worry about something. Nick Gillespie on why busybodies and bureaucrats have zeroed in on bullying.

"When I was younger," a remarkable self-assured, softspoken 15-year-old kid named Aaron tells the camera, "I suffered from bullying because of my lips—as you can see, they're kind of unusually large. So I would kind of get [called] 'Fish Lips'—things like that a lot—and my glasses too, I got those at an early age. That contributed. And the fact that my last name is Cheese didn't really help with the matter either. I would get [called] 'Cheeseburger,' 'Cheese Guy'—things like that, that weren't really very flattering. Just kind of making fun of my name—I'm a pretty sensitive kid, so I would have to fight back the tears when I was being called names.

It's hard not to be impressed with—and not to like—young Aaron Cheese. He is one of the kids featured in the new Cartoon Network special "Stop Bullying: Speak Up," which premiered last week and is available online. I myself am a former geekish, bespectacled child whose lips were a bit too full, and my first name (as other kids quickly discovered) rhymes with two of the most-popular slang terms for male genitalia, so I also identified with Mr. Cheese. My younger years were filled with precisely the sort of schoolyard taunts that he recounts; they led ultimately to at least one fistfight and a lot of sour moods on my part.

As the parent now of two school-age boys, I also worry that my own kids will have to deal with such ugly and destructive behavior. And I welcome the common-sense antibullying strategies relayed in "Stop Bullying": Talk to your friends, your parents and your teachers. Recognize that you're not the problem. Don't be a silent witness to bullying.

But is America really in the midst of a "bullying crisis," as so many now claim? I don't see it. I also suspect that our fears about the ubiquity of bullying are just the latest in a long line of well-intentioned yet hyperbolic alarms about how awful it is to be a kid today.

I have no interest in defending the bullies who dominate sandboxes, extort lunch money and use Twitter to taunt their classmates. But there is no growing crisis. Childhood and adolescence in America have never been less brutal. Even as the country's overprotective parents whip themselves up into a moral panic about kid-on-kid cruelty, the numbers don't point to any explosion of abuse. As for the rising wave of laws and regulations designed to combat meanness among students, they are likely to lump together minor slights with major offenses. The antibullying movement is already conflating serious cases of gay-bashing and vicious harassment with things like . . . a kid named Cheese having a tough time in grade school.

How did we get here? We live in an age of helicopter parents so pushy and overbearing that Colorado Springs banned its annual Easter-egg hunt on account of adults jumping the starter's gun and scooping up treat-filled plastic eggs on behalf of their winsome kids. The Department of Education in New York City—once known as the town too tough for Al Capone—is seeking to ban such words as "dinosaurs," "Halloween" and "dancing" from city-wide tests on the grounds that they could "evoke unpleasant emotions in the students," it was reported this week. (Leave aside for the moment that perhaps the whole point of tests is to "evoke unpleasant emotions.") . . .

Now that schools are peanut-free, latex-free, and soda-free, parents, administrators and teachers have got to worry about something. Since most kids now have access to cable TV, the Internet, unlimited talk and texting, college and a world of opportunities that was unimaginable even 20 years ago, it seems that adults have responded by becoming ever more overprotective and thin-skinned.

Kids might be fatter than they used to be, but by most standards they are safer and better-behaved than they were when I was growing up in the 1970s and '80s. Infant and adolescent mortality, accidents, sex and drug use—all are down from their levels of a few decades ago. Acceptance of homosexuality is up, especially among younger Americans. But given today's rhetoric about bullying, you could be forgiven for thinking that kids today are not simply reading and watching grim, postapocalyptic fantasies like "The Hunger Games" but actually inhabiting such terrifying terrain, a world where "Lord of the Flies" meets "Mad Max 2: The Road Warrior," presided over by Voldemort'. . . .

Which isn't to say that there aren't kids who face terrible cases of bullying. The immensely powerful and highly acclaimed documentary "Bully," whose makers hope to create a nationwide movement against the "bullying crisis," opens in selected theaters this weekend. The film follows the harrowing experiences of a handful of victims of harassment, including two who killed themselves in desperation. It is, above all, a damning indictment of ineffectual and indifferent school officials. No viewer can watch the abuse endured by kids such as Alex, a 13-year-old social misfit in Sioux City, Iowa, or Kelby, a 14-year-old lesbian in small-town Oklahoma, without feeling angry and motivated to change youth culture and the school officials who turn a blind eye.

But is bullying—which the stopbullying.gov website of the Department of Health and Human Services defines as "teasing," "name-calling," "taunting," "leaving someone out on purpose," "telling other children not to be friends with someone," "spreading rumors about someone," "hitting/kicking/pinching," "spitting" and "making mean or rude hand gestures"—really a growing problem in America?

Despite the rare and tragic cases that rightly command our attention and outrage, the data show that things are, in fact, getting better for kids. When it comes to school violence, the numbers are particularly encouraging. According to the National Center for Education Statistics, between 1995 and 2009, the percentage of students who reported "being afraid of attack or harm at school" declined to 4% from 12%. Over the same period, the victimization rate per 1,000 students declined fivefold.

When it comes to bullying numbers, long-term trends are less clear. The makers of "Bully" say that "over 13 million American kids will be bullied this year," and estimates of the percentage of students who are bullied in a given year range from 20% to 70%. NCES changed the way it tabulated bullying incidents in 2005 and cautions against using earlier data. Its biennial reports find that 28% of students ages 12–18 reported being bullied in 2005; that percentage rose to 32% in 2007, before dropping back to 28% in 2009 (the most recent year for which data are available). Such numbers strongly suggest that there is no epidemic afoot (though one wonders if the new anti-bullying laws and media campaigns might lead to more reports going forward). . . .

None of this is to be celebrated, of course, but it hardly paints a picture of contemporary American childhood as an unrestrained Hobbesian nightmare. Before more of our schools' money, time and personnel are diverted away from education in the name of this supposed crisis, we should make an effort to distinguish between the serious abuse suffered by the kids in "Bully" and the sort of lower-level harassment with which the Aaron Cheeses of the world have to deal. . . .

Our problem isn't a world where bullies are allowed to run rampant; it's a world where kids like Aaron are convinced that they are powerless victims.

Nick Gillespie is editor in chief of Reason.com and Reason.tv and the co-author of "The Declaration of Independents: How Libertarian Politics Can Fix What's Wrong with America."

EXPLORING THE ISSUE

Is Cyberbullying Really a Problem?

Critical Thinking and Reflection

1. What does cyberbullying entail and what distinguishes it from more physical acts of bullying?
2. What can parents do to help minimize their child's exposure to cyber bullying?
3. Do you believe that cyberbullying is mostly harmless, or is it a serious threat to teens today? Why?

Is There Common Ground?

No one would stand up and say that bullying, even cyberbullying, is acceptable behavior. Any time that someone is hurt by the words or threats of others, it is important to acknowledge that as unacceptable behavior. What is at issue, however, is how much impact words can actually have on someone. Even adults admit to using the Internet or their text messaging to tease, taunt, or disparage someone else. Plus, the additional anonymity that online sources provide may embolden someone who might otherwise hold their tongue to engage in mistreatment of another. Prevention is obviously important and a major focus of parental and educator efforts. However, what remains to be determined is how much of a focus should be placed on cyberbullying in comparison to more traditional forms of bullying when creating and implementing anti-bullying campaigns.

Create Central

www.mhhe.com/createcentral

Additional Resources

Bullying Statistics. Cyber Bullying Statistics. Retrieved on May 21, 2013, from www.bullyingstatistics.org/content/cyber-bullying-statistics.html

Enough Is Enough. Internet Safety 101. Retrieved on May 21, 2013, from www.internetsafety101.org/cyberbullyingstatistics.htm

Stop Bullying. Reaching Teens Through Social Media. Retrieved on May 21, 2013, from www.stopbullying.gov/blog/2013/04/09/reaching-teens-through-social-media

Internet References . . .

Do Something

www.dosomething.org/tipsandtools/11-facts-about-cyber-bullying

Girl's Health

www.girlshealth.gov/bullying/whatis/cyberbully.cfm